Chapter 16

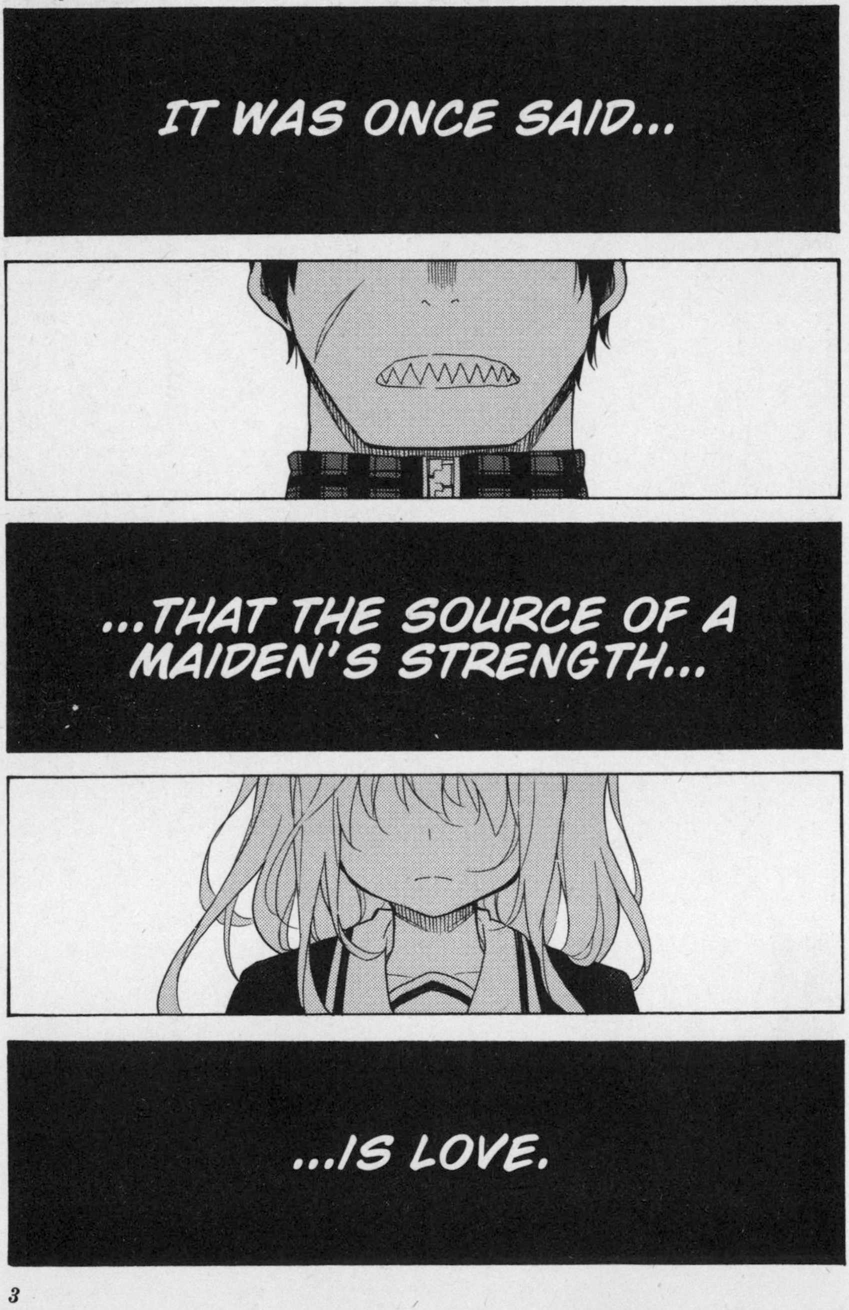
IT WAS ONCE SAID...
...THAT THE SOURCE OF A MAIDEN'S STRENGTH...
...IS LOVE.

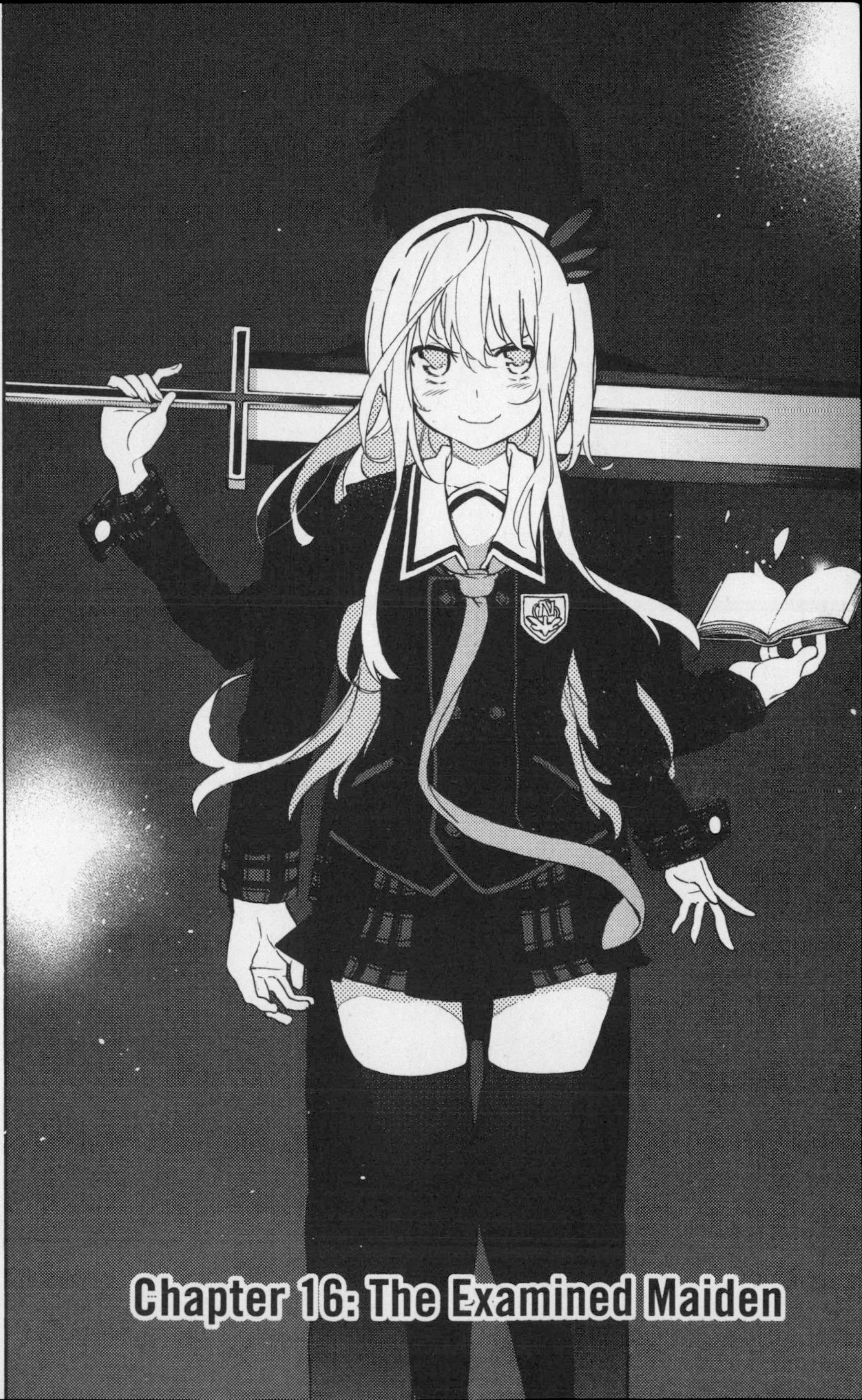

Chapter 16: The Examined Maiden

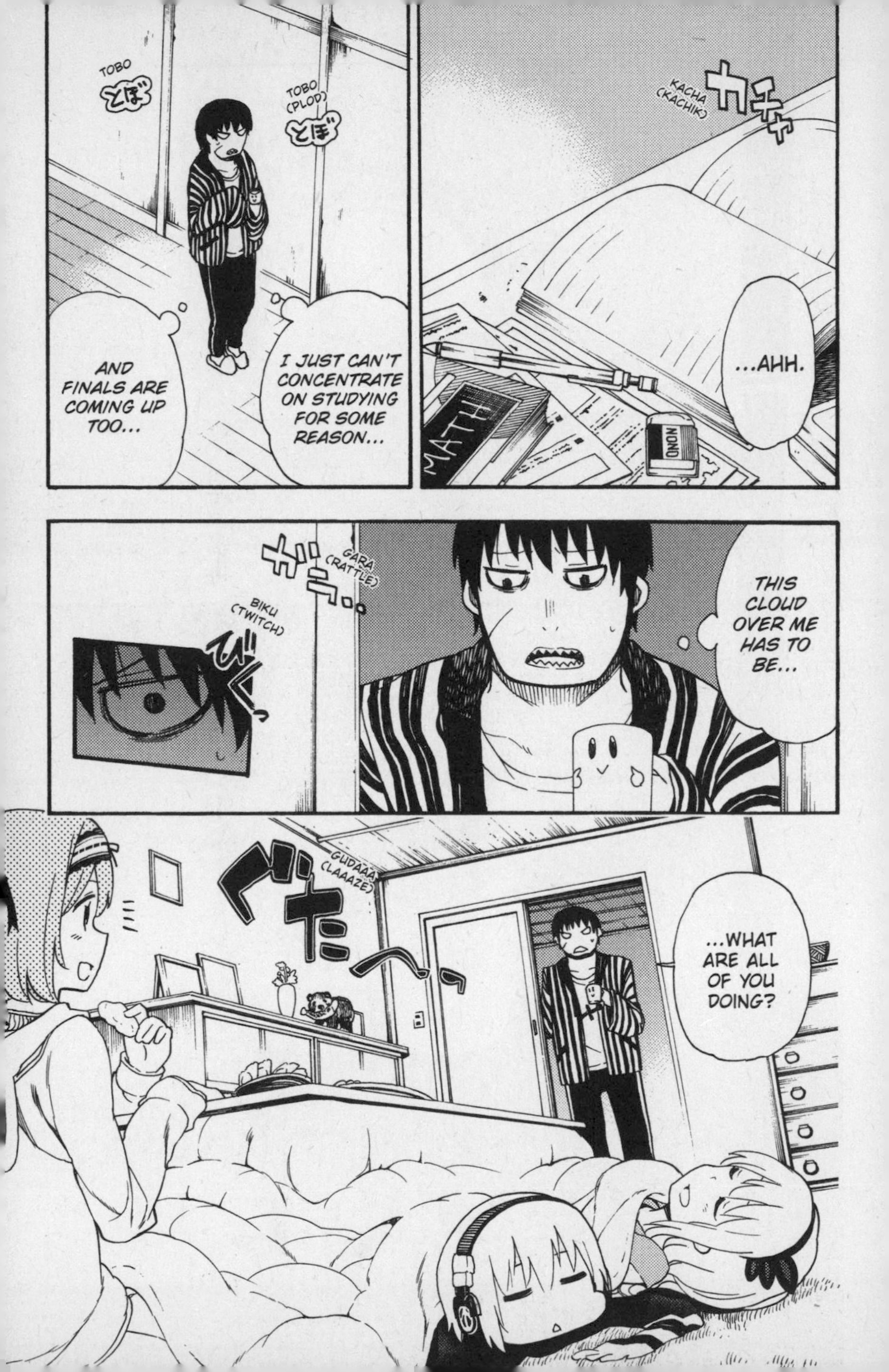

KACHA (KACHIK)
...AHH.
TOBO (PLOD)
TOBO
I JUST CAN'T CONCENTRATE ON STUDYING FOR SOME REASON...
AND FINALS ARE COMING UP TOO...
THIS CLOUD OVER ME HAS TO BE...
GARA (RATTLE)
BIKU (TWITCH)
...WHAT ARE ALL OF YOU DOING?
GUDAAA (LAAAZE)

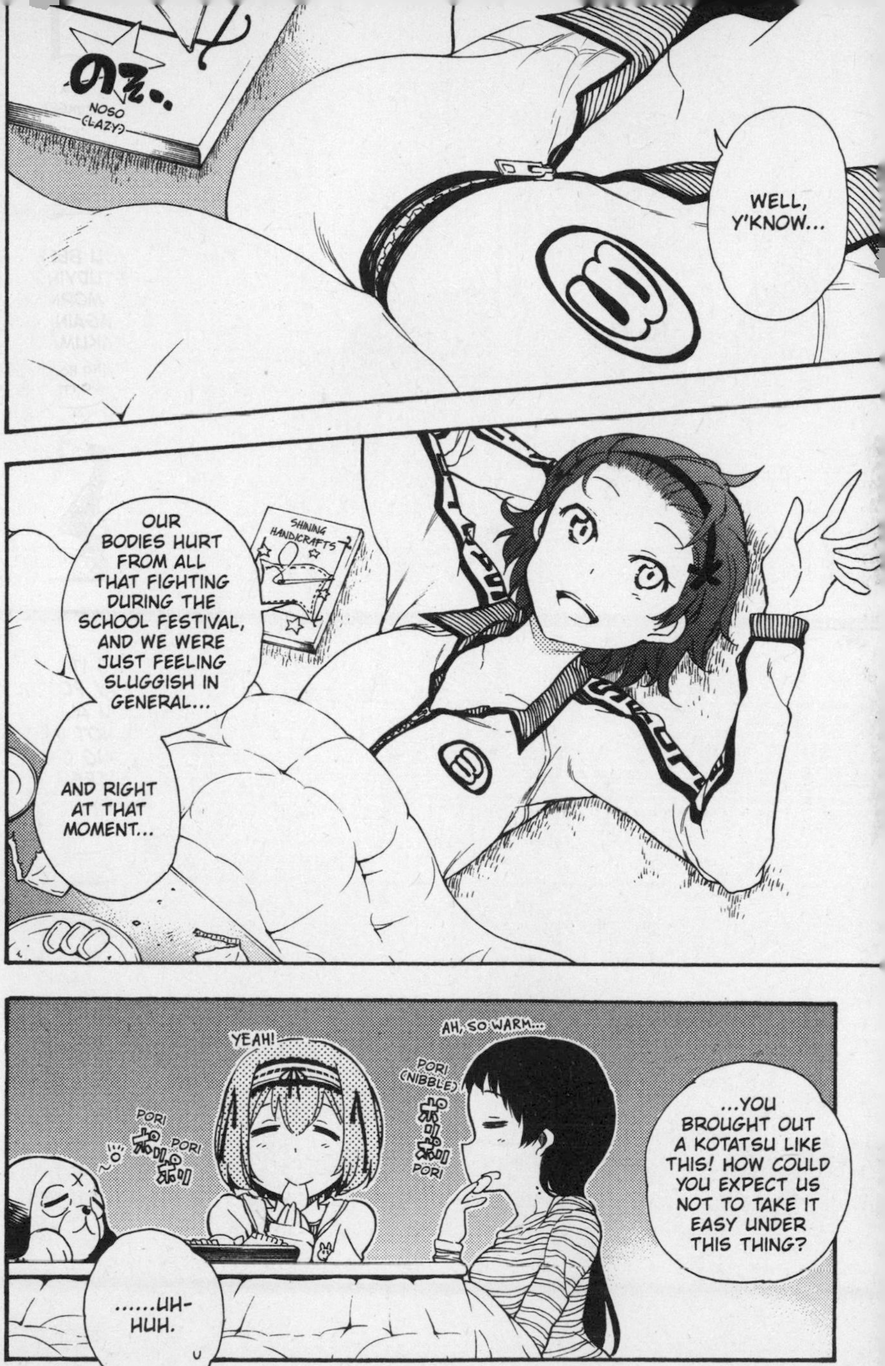
WELL, Y'KNOW...
NOSO (LAZY)
SHINING HANDICRAFTS
OUR BODIES HURT FROM ALL THAT FIGHTING DURING THE SCHOOL FESTIVAL, AND WE WERE JUST FEELING SLUGGISH IN GENERAL...
AND RIGHT AT THAT MOMENT...
...YOU BROUGHT OUT A KOTATSU LIKE THIS! HOW COULD YOU EXPECT US NOT TO TAKE IT EASY UNDER THIS THING?
AH, SO WARM...
PORI (NIBBLE)
PORI
YEAH!
PORI
PORI
......UH-HUH.

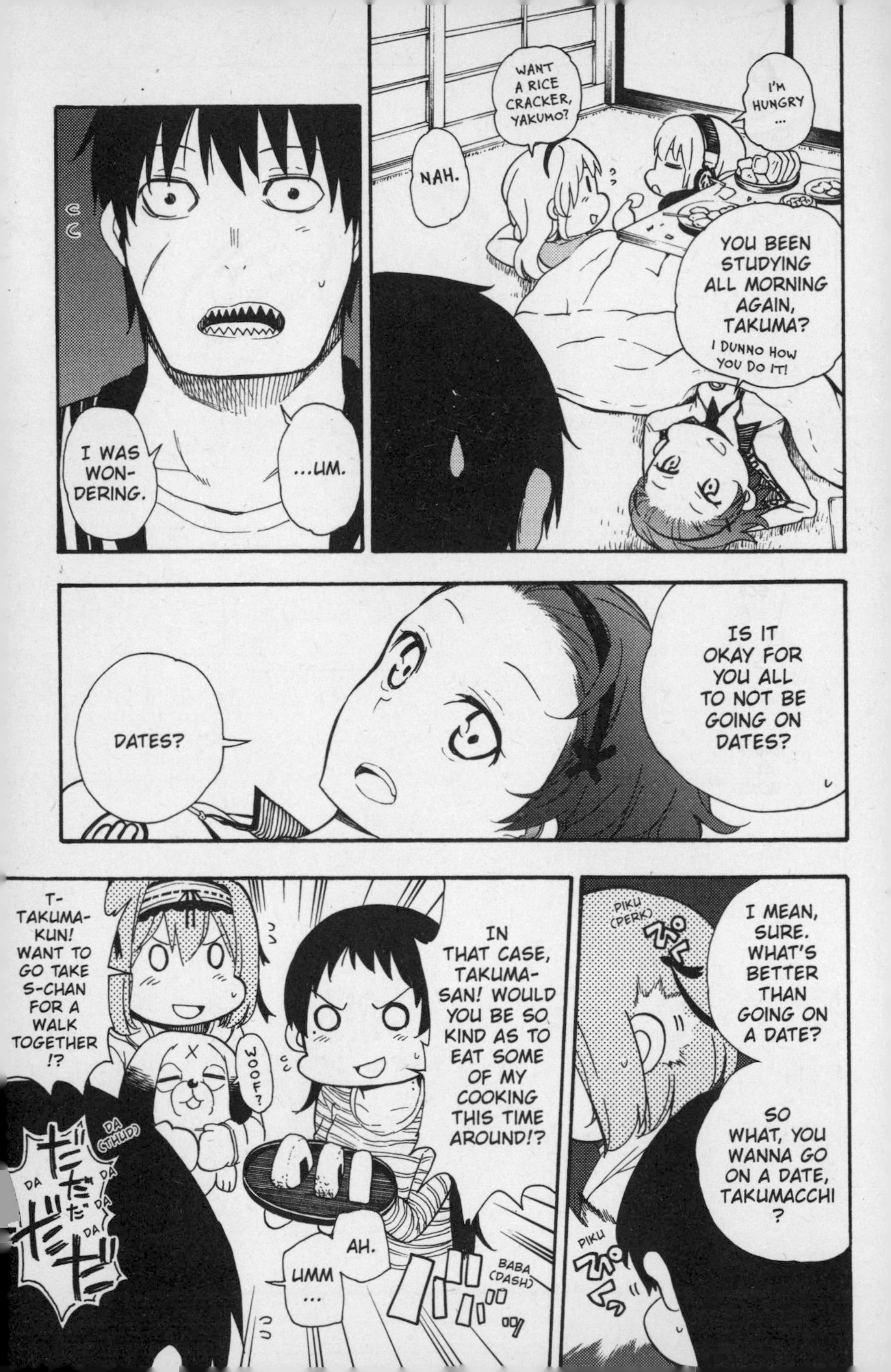
I'M HUNGRY ...
WANT A RICE CRACKER, YAKUMO?
NAH.
YOU BEEN STUDYING ALL MORNING AGAIN, TAKUMA?
I DUNNO HOW YOU DO IT!
...UM.
I WAS WON-DERING.
IS IT OKAY FOR YOU ALL TO NOT BE GOING ON DATES?
DATES?
I MEAN, SURE. WHAT'S BETTER THAN GOING ON A DATE?
PIKU (PERK)
SO WHAT, YOU WANNA GO ON A DATE, TAKUMACCHI?
PIKU
IN THAT CASE, TAKUMA-SAN! WOULD YOU BE SO KIND AS TO EAT SOME OF MY COOKING THIS TIME AROUND!?
AH.
UMM ...
BABA (DASH)
T-TAKUMA-KUN! WANT TO GO TAKE S-CHAN FOR A WALK TOGETHER!?
WOOF?
DA (THUD)
DA
DA
DA
DA

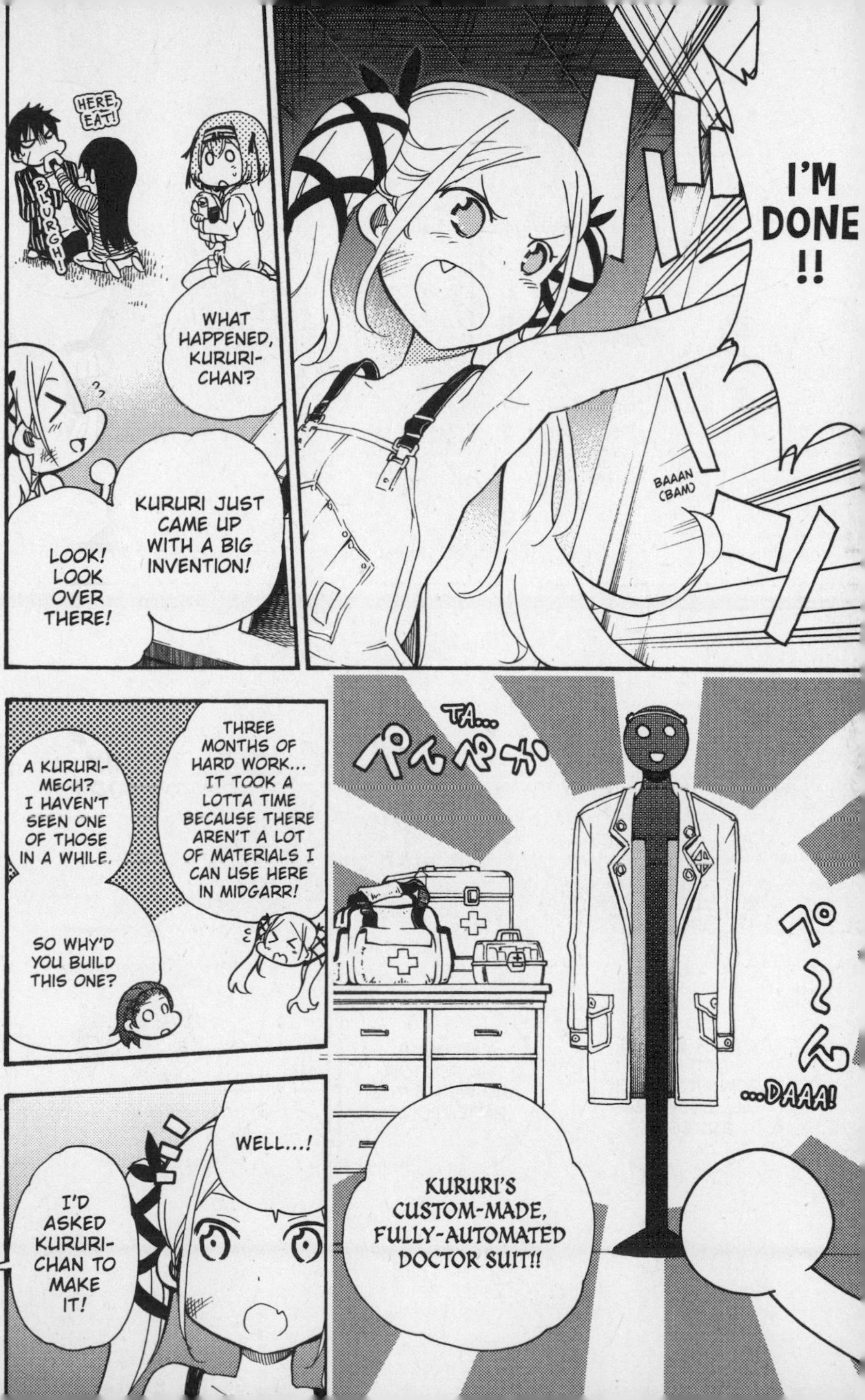
I'M DONE!!
BAAAN (BAM)
HERE, EAT!
BLURGH!
WHAT HAPPENED, KURURI-CHAN?
KURURI JUST CAME UP WITH A BIG INVENTION!
LOOK! LOOK OVER THERE!
TA...
...DAAA!
KURURI'S CUSTOM-MADE, FULLY-AUTOMATED DOCTOR SUIT!!
THREE MONTHS OF HARD WORK... IT TOOK A LOTTA TIME BECAUSE THERE AREN'T A LOT OF MATERIALS I CAN USE HERE IN MIDGARR!
A KURURI-MECH? I HAVEN'T SEEN ONE OF THOSE IN A WHILE.
SO WHY'D YOU BUILD THIS ONE?
WELL...!
I'D ASKED KURURI-CHAN TO MAKE IT!

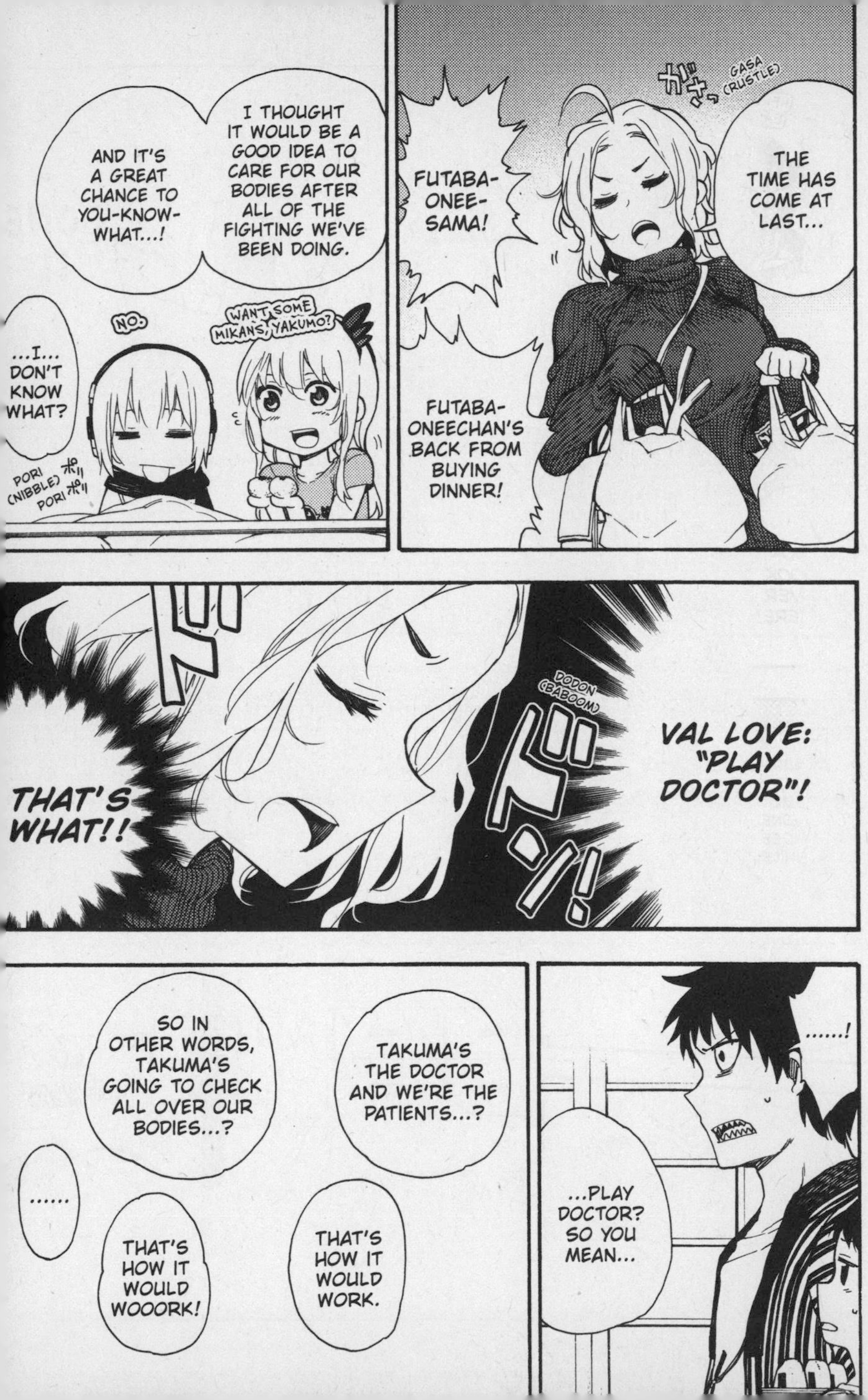
GASA (RUSTLE)
THE TIME HAS COME AT LAST...
FUTABA-ONEE-SAMA!
FUTABA-ONEECHAN'S BACK FROM BUYING DINNER!
I THOUGHT IT WOULD BE A GOOD IDEA TO CARE FOR OUR BODIES AFTER ALL OF THE FIGHTING WE'VE BEEN DOING.
AND IT'S A GREAT CHANCE TO YOU-KNOW-WHAT...!
WANT SOME MIKANS, YAKUMO?
NO.
...I... DON'T KNOW WHAT?
PORI (NIBBLE) PORI
VAL LOVE: "PLAY DOCTOR"!
DODON (BABOOM)
THAT'S WHAT!!
......!
...PLAY DOCTOR? SO YOU MEAN...
TAKUMA'S THE DOCTOR AND WE'RE THE PATIENTS...?
SO IN OTHER WORDS, TAKUMA'S GOING TO CHECK ALL OVER OUR BODIES...?
THAT'S HOW IT WOULD WORK.
THAT'S HOW IT WOULD WOOORK!
......

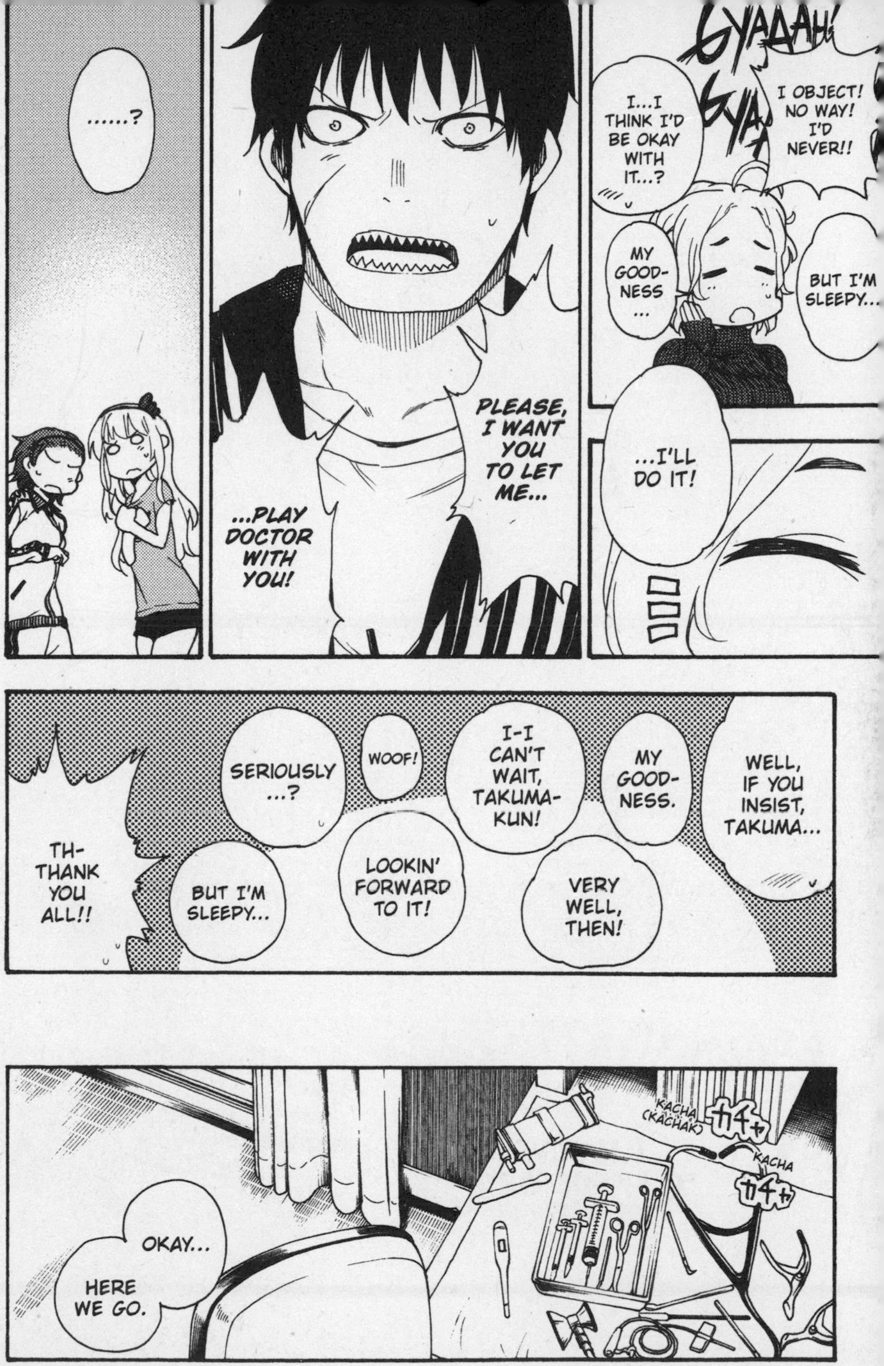
GYAAAH!
GYAA
I OBJECT! NO WAY! I'D NEVER!!
I...I THINK I'D BE OKAY WITH IT...?
BUT I'M SLEEPY...
MY GOODNESS...
...I'LL DO IT!
PLEASE, I WANT YOU TO LET ME...
...PLAY DOCTOR WITH YOU!
......?
WELL, IF YOU INSIST, TAKUMA...
MY GOODNESS.
VERY WELL, THEN!
I-I CAN'T WAIT, TAKUMA-KUN!
LOOKIN' FORWARD TO IT!
WOOF!
SERIOUSLY...?
BUT I'M SLEEPY...
TH-THANK YOU ALL!!
KACHA (KACHAK)
カチャ
KACHA
カチャ
OKAY... HERE WE GO.

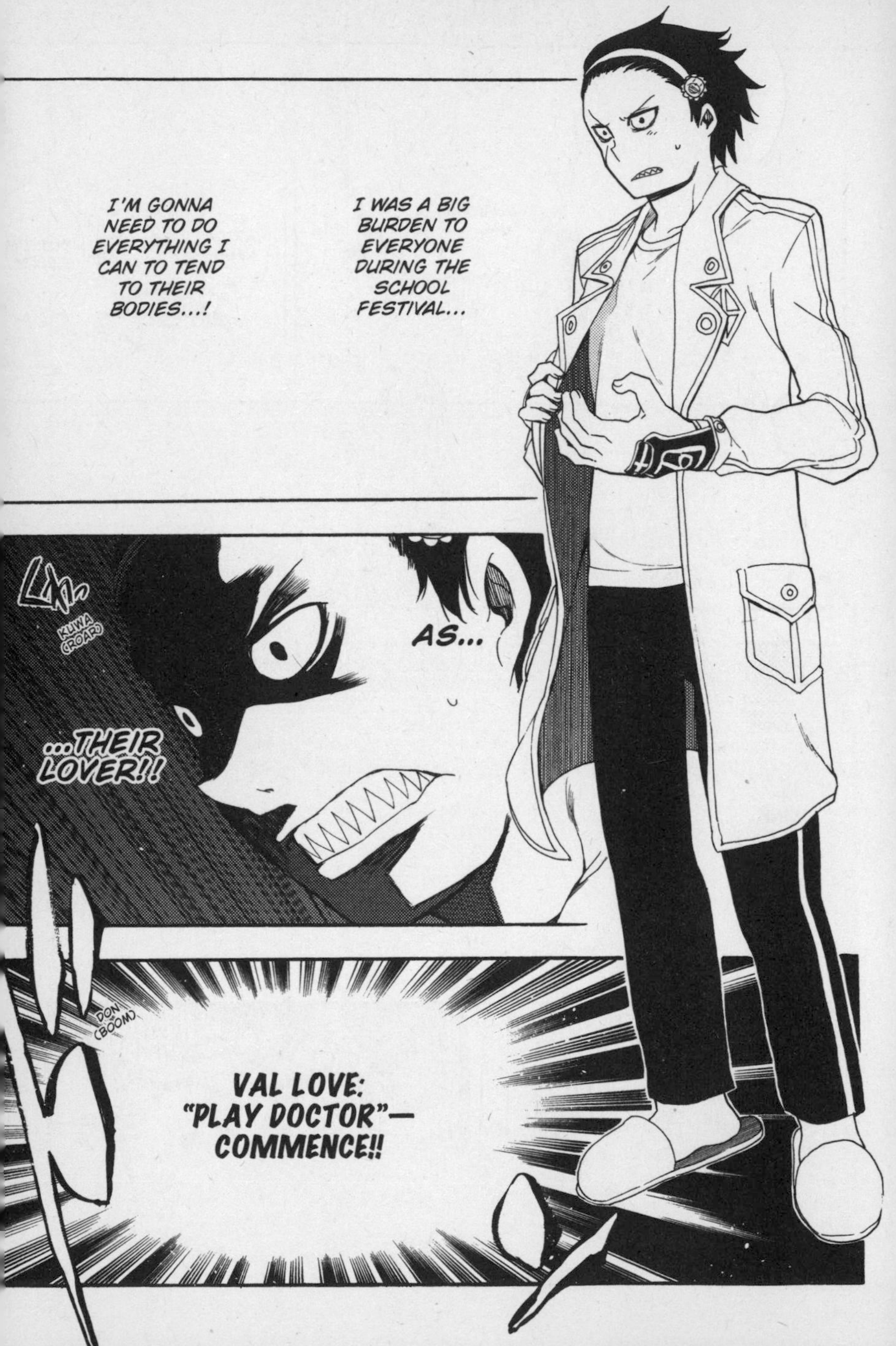
I WAS A BIG BURDEN TO EVERYONE DURING THE SCHOOL FESTIVAL...
I'M GONNA NEED TO DO EVERYTHING I CAN TO TEND TO THEIR BODIES...!
AS...
KUWA (ROAR)
...THEIR LOVER!!
DON (BOOM)
VAL LOVE: "PLAY DOCTOR"—COMMENCE!!

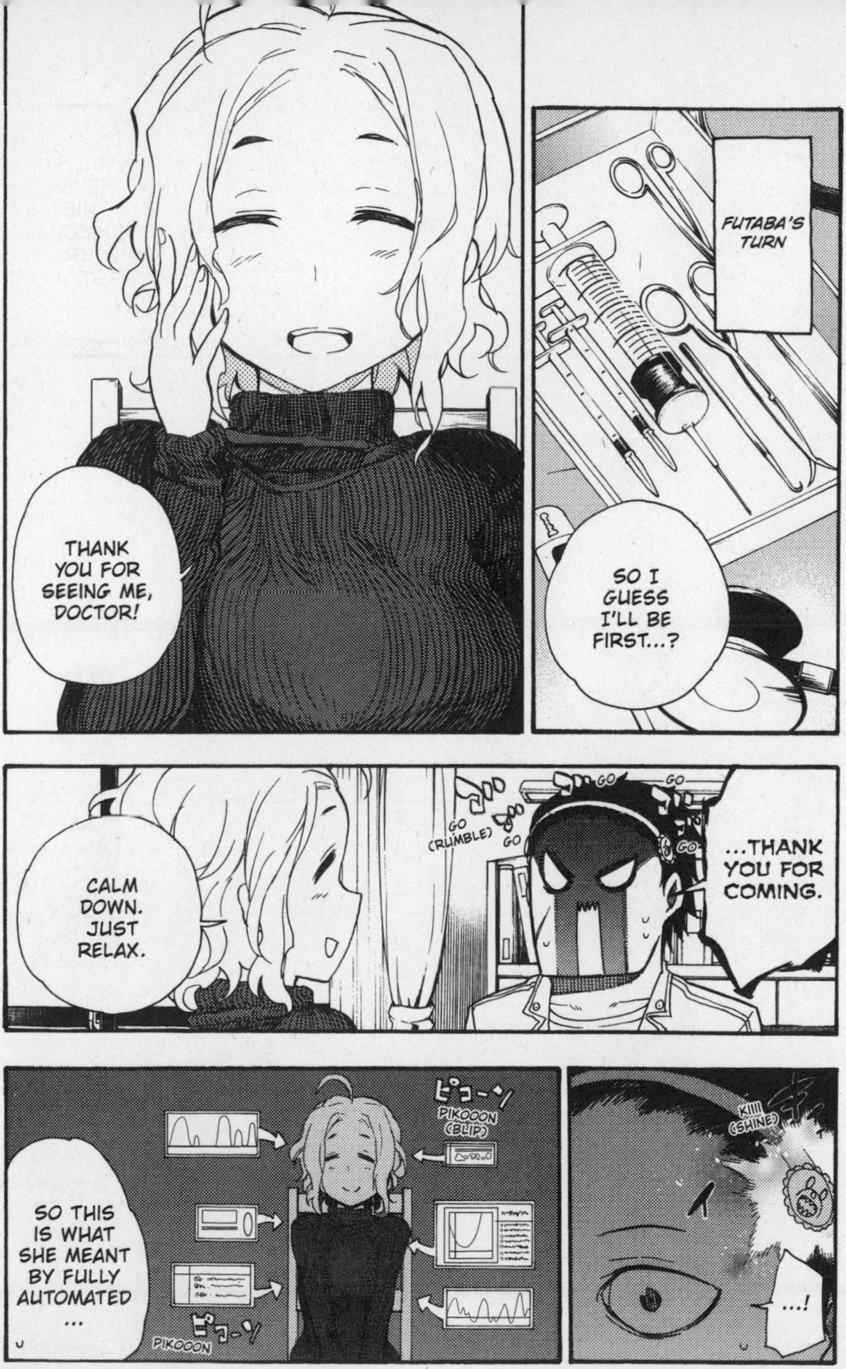

FUTABA'S TURN
SO I GUESS I'LL BE FIRST...?
THANK YOU FOR SEEING ME, DOCTOR!
GO GO
...THANK YOU FOR COMING.
GO (RUMBLE) GO
CALM DOWN. JUST RELAX.
KIIII (SHINE)
...!
PIKOOON (BLIP)
SO THIS IS WHAT SHE MEANT BY FULLY AUTOMATED ...
PIKOOON

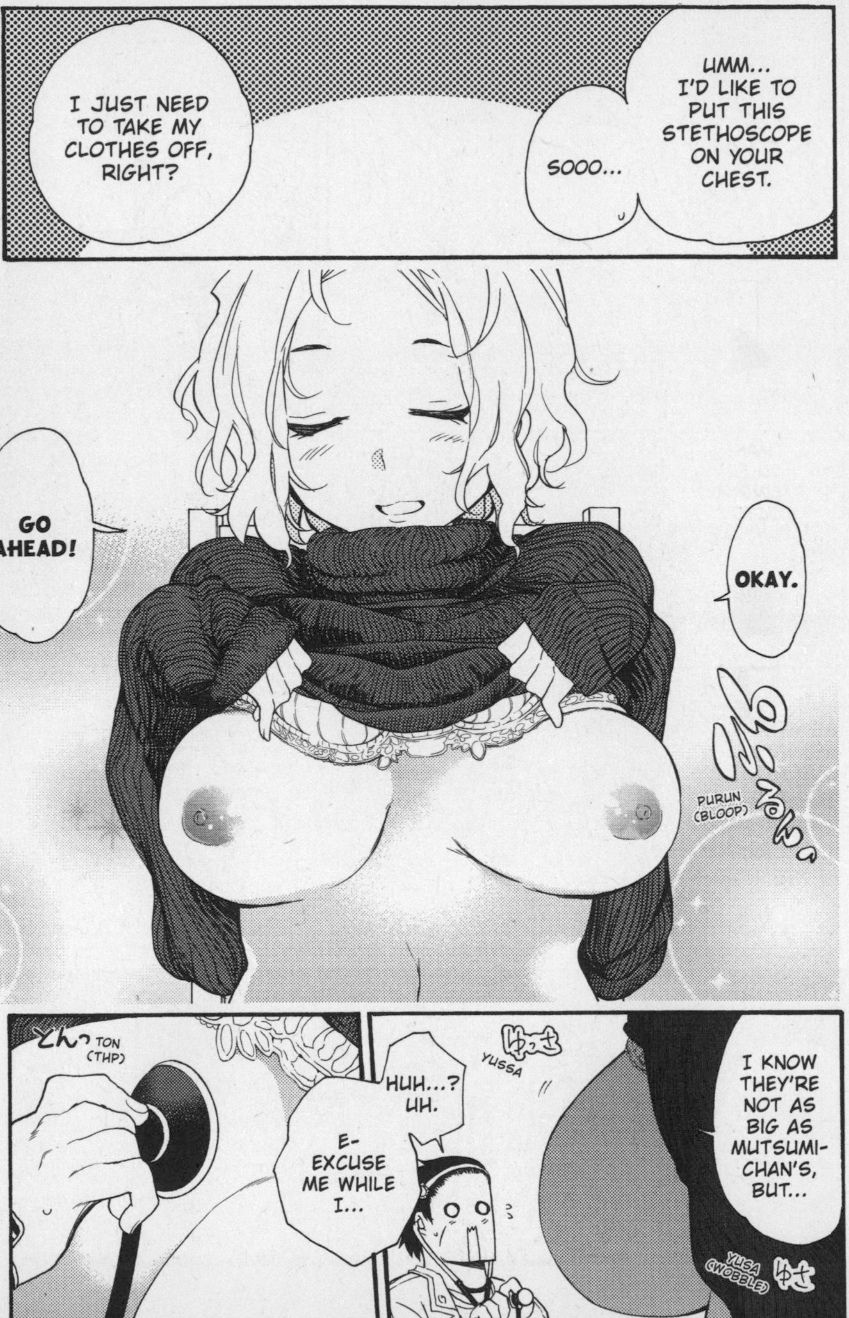
UMM... I'D LIKE TO PUT THIS STETHOSCOPE ON YOUR CHEST.
SOOO...
I JUST NEED TO TAKE MY CLOTHES OFF, RIGHT?
OKAY.
GO AHEAD!
ぷるんっ
PURUN (BLOOP)
I KNOW THEY'RE NOT AS BIG AS MUTSUMI-CHAN'S, BUT...
ゆさ
YUSA (WOBBLE)
ゆっさ
YUSSA
HUH...? UH.
E- EXCUSE ME WHILE I...
とんっ
TON (THP)

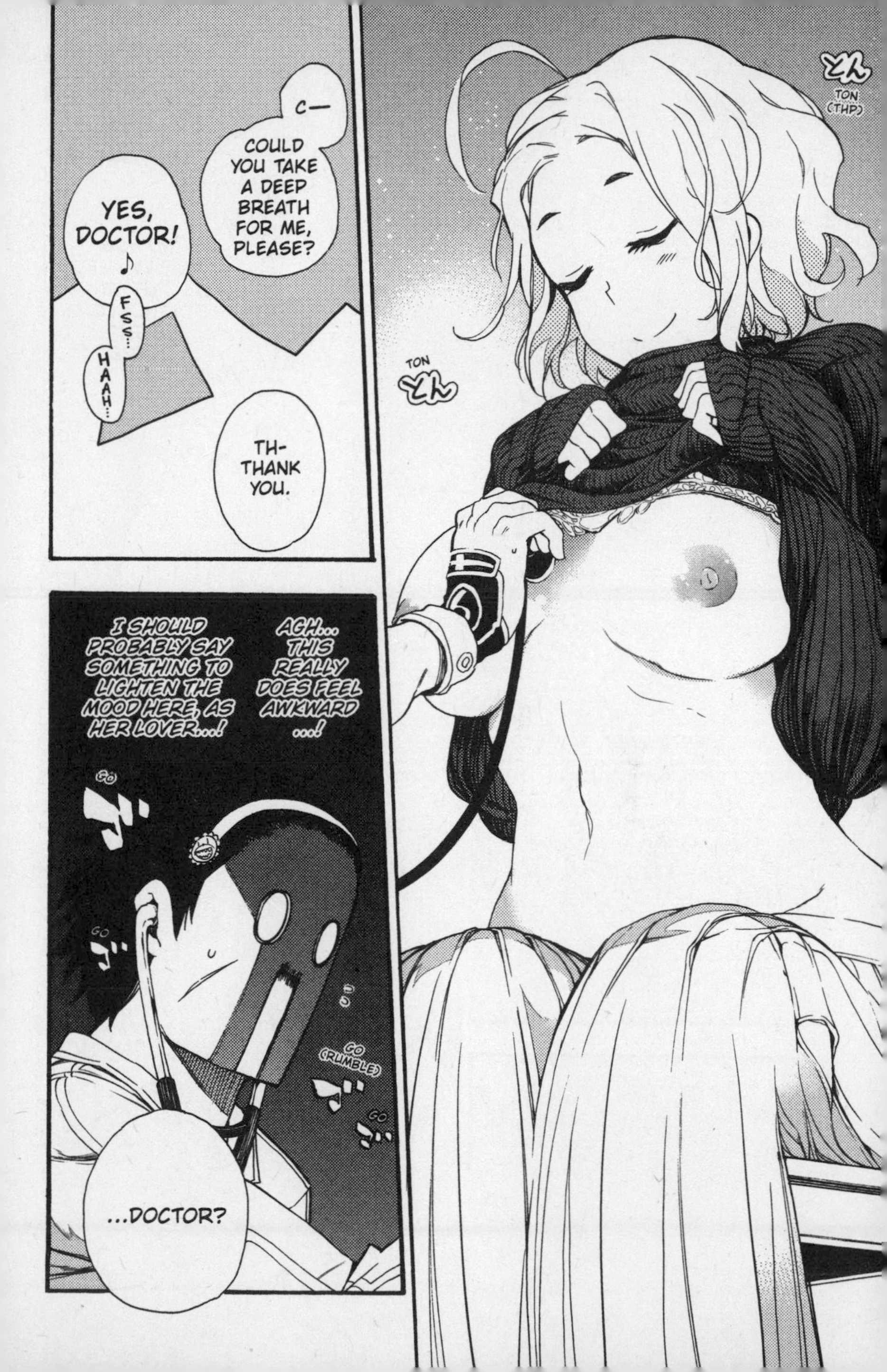
とん
TON (THP)
TON
とん
C—
COULD YOU TAKE A DEEP BREATH FOR ME, PLEASE?
YES, DOCTOR! ♪
FSS... HAAH...
TH-THANK YOU.
AGH... THIS REALLY DOES FEEL AWKWARD...!
I SHOULD PROBABLY SAY SOMETHING TO LIGHTEN THE MOOD HERE, AS HER LOVER...!
GO
ゴ
GO
ゴ
GO (RUMBLE)
GO
...DOCTOR?

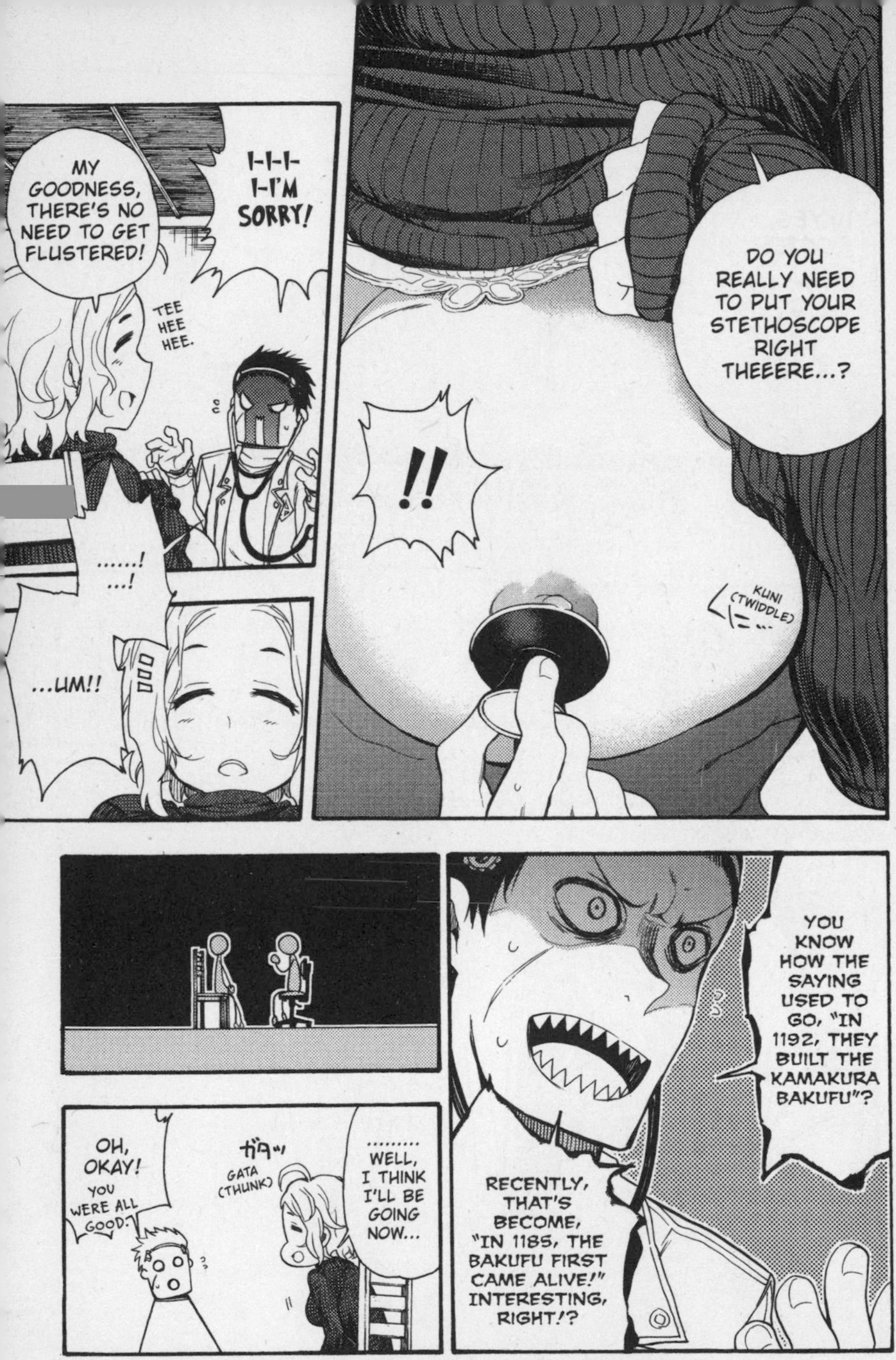
DO YOU REALLY NEED TO PUT YOUR STETHOSCOPE RIGHT THEEERE...?
!!
KUNI (TWIDDLE)
I-I-I- I-I'M SORRY!
MY GOODNESS, THERE'S NO NEED TO GET FLUSTERED!
TEE HEE HEE.
......! ...!
...UM!!
YOU KNOW HOW THE SAYING USED TO GO, "IN 1192, THEY BUILT THE KAMAKURA BAKUFU"?
RECENTLY, THAT'S BECOME, "IN 1185, THE BAKUFU FIRST CAME ALIVE!" INTERESTING, RIGHT!?
.... WELL, I THINK I'LL BE GOING NOW...
ガタッ
GATA (THUNK)
OH, OKAY!
YOU WERE ALL GOOD!

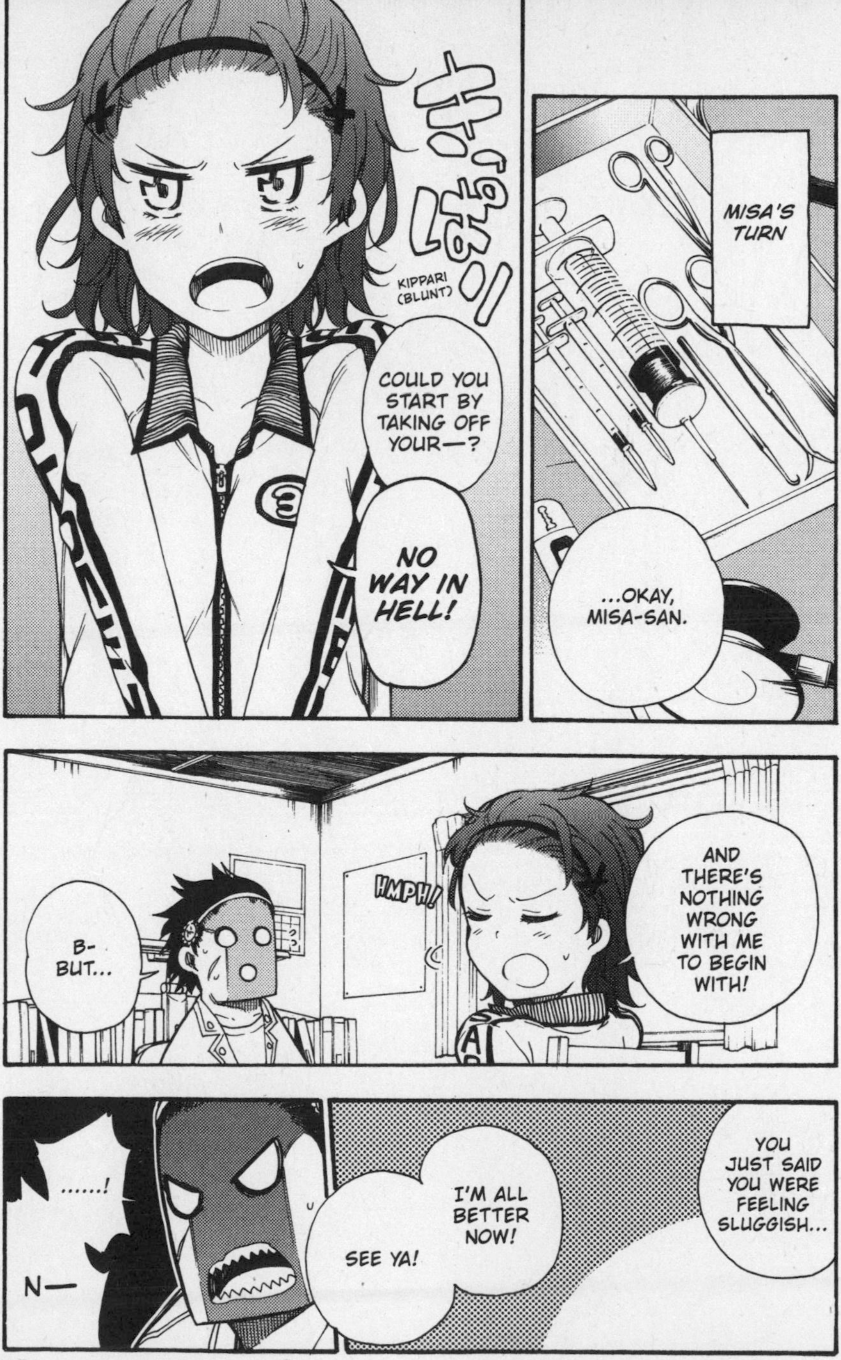

MISA'S TURN
...OKAY, MISA-SAN.
きっぱり!
KIPPARI (BLUNT)
COULD YOU START BY TAKING OFF YOUR—?
NO WAY IN HELL!
AND THERE'S NOTHING WRONG WITH ME TO BEGIN WITH!
HMPH!
B-BUT...
YOU JUST SAID YOU WERE FEELING SLUGGISH...
I'M ALL BETTER NOW!
SEE YA!
......!
N—

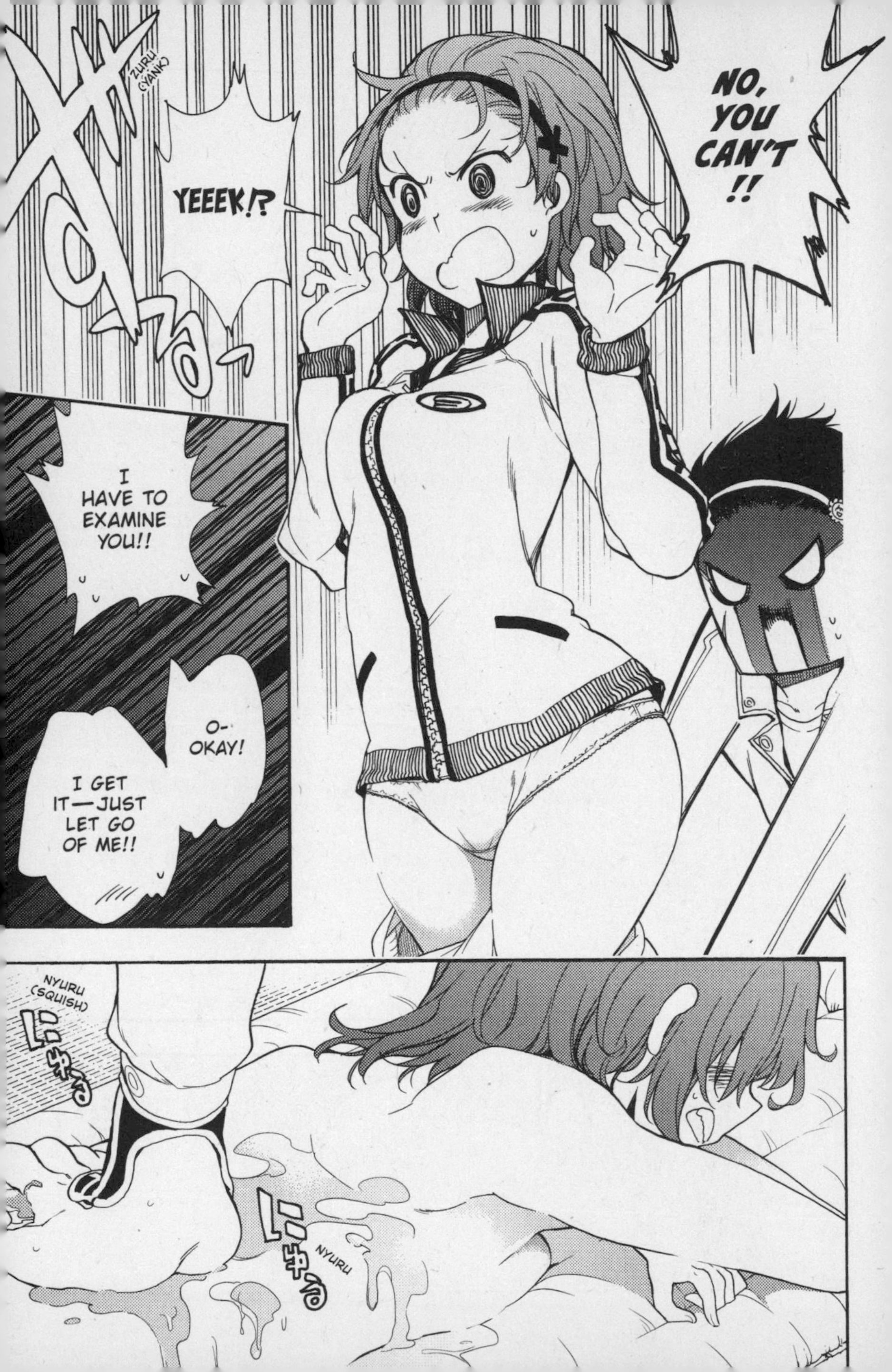

NO, YOU CAN'T!!
ZURU (YANK)
YEEEK!?
I HAVE TO EXAMINE YOU!!
O-OKAY!
I GET IT—JUST LET GO OF ME!!
NYURU (SQUISH)
にゅる
にゅる
NYURU

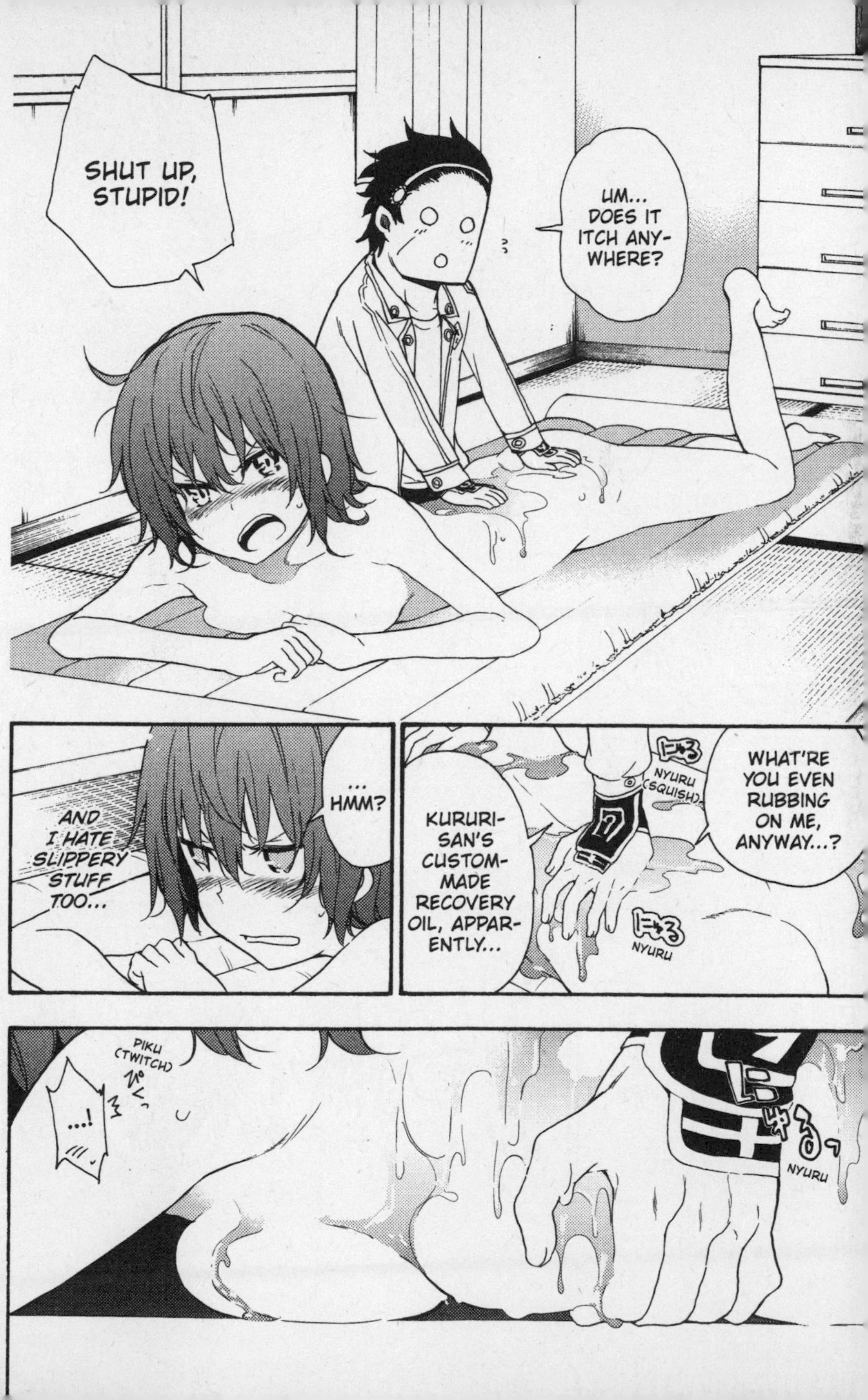
UM... DOES IT ITCH ANYWHERE?
SHUT UP, STUPID!
WHAT'RE YOU EVEN RUBBING ON ME, ANYWAY...?
にゅる
NYURU (SQUISH)
KURURI-SAN'S CUSTOM-MADE RECOVERY OIL, APPARENTLY...
にゅる
NYURU
... HMM?
AND I HATE SLIPPERY STUFF TOO...
NYURU
ぴく
PIKU (TWITCH)
...!

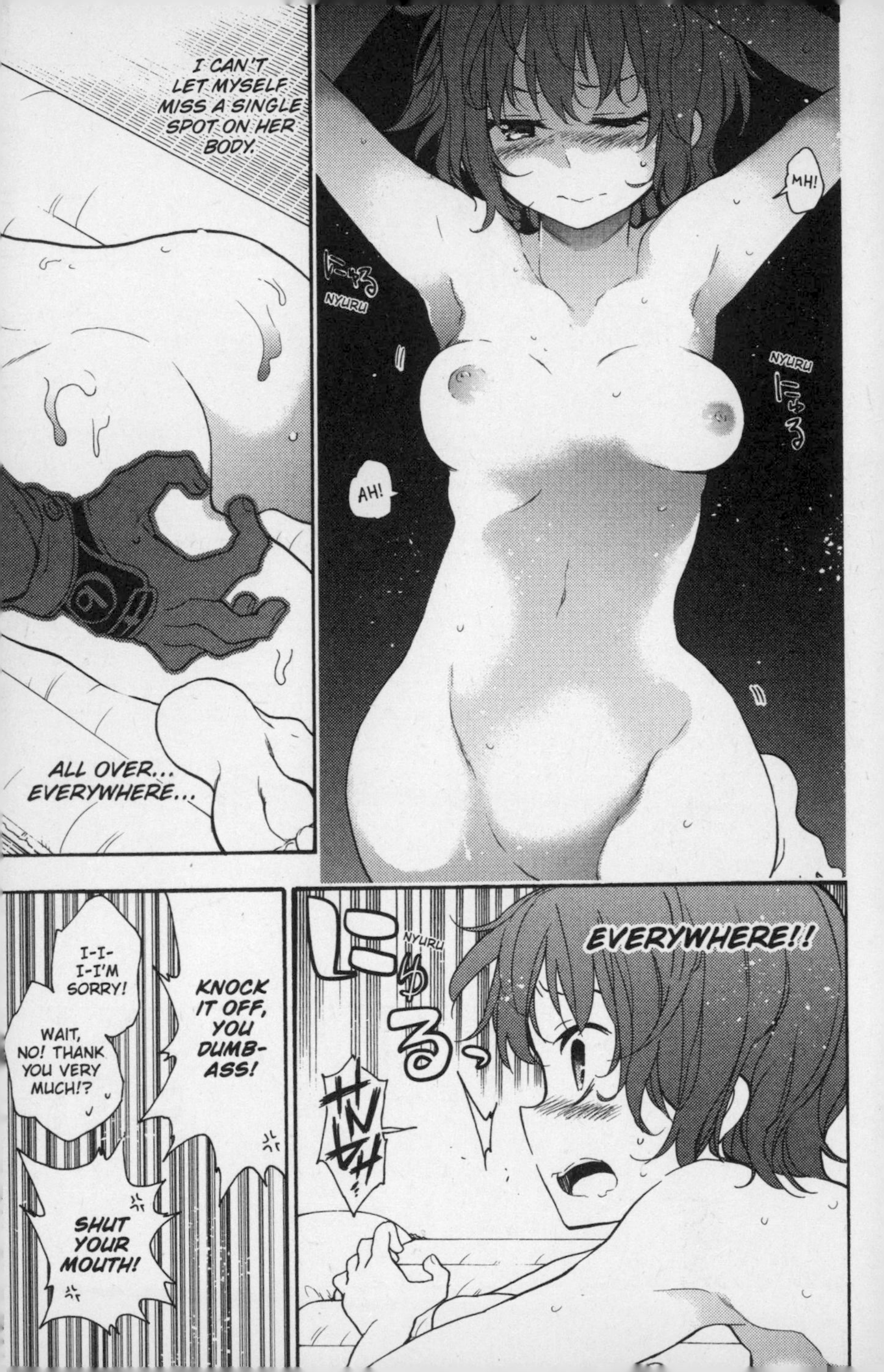
MH!
にゅる
NYURU
にゅる
NYURU
AH!
I CAN'T LET MYSELF MISS A SINGLE SPOT ON HER BODY.
ALL OVER... EVERYWHERE...
EVERYWHERE!!
にゅるっ
NYURU
KNOCK IT OFF, YOU DUMB-ASS!
I-I-I-I'M SORRY!
WAIT, NO! THANK YOU VERY MUCH!?
SHUT YOUR MOUTH!

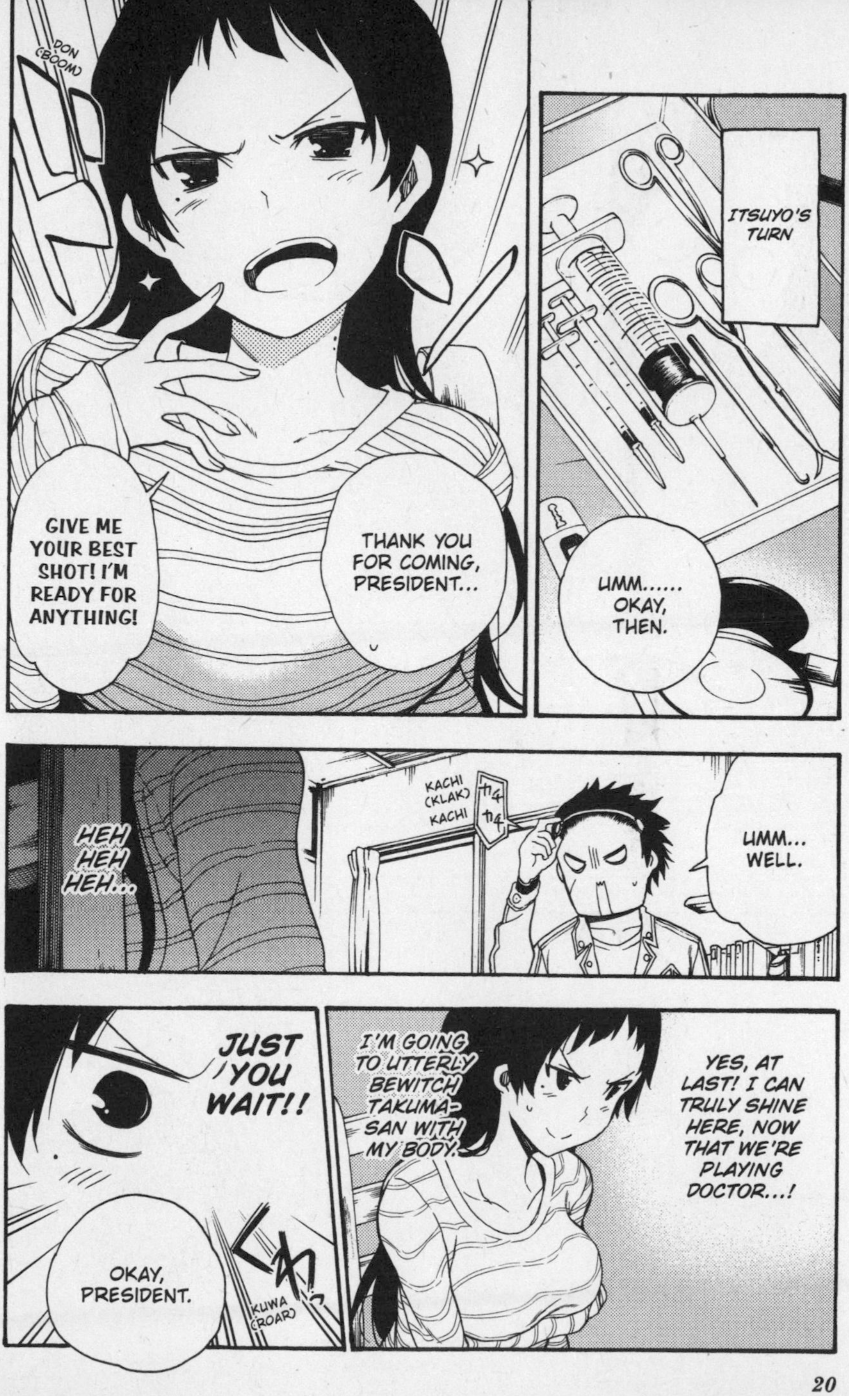
ITSUYO'S TURN
UMM...... OKAY, THEN.
DON (BOOM)
THANK YOU FOR COMING, PRESIDENT...
GIVE ME YOUR BEST SHOT! I'M READY FOR ANYTHING!
UMM... WELL.
KACHI (KLAK) KACHI
HEH HEH HEH...
YES, AT LAST! I CAN TRULY SHINE HERE, NOW THAT WE'RE PLAYING DOCTOR...!
I'M GOING TO UTTERLY BEWITCH TAKUMA-SAN WITH MY BODY.
JUST YOU WAIT!!
OKAY, PRESIDENT.
KUWA (ROAR)

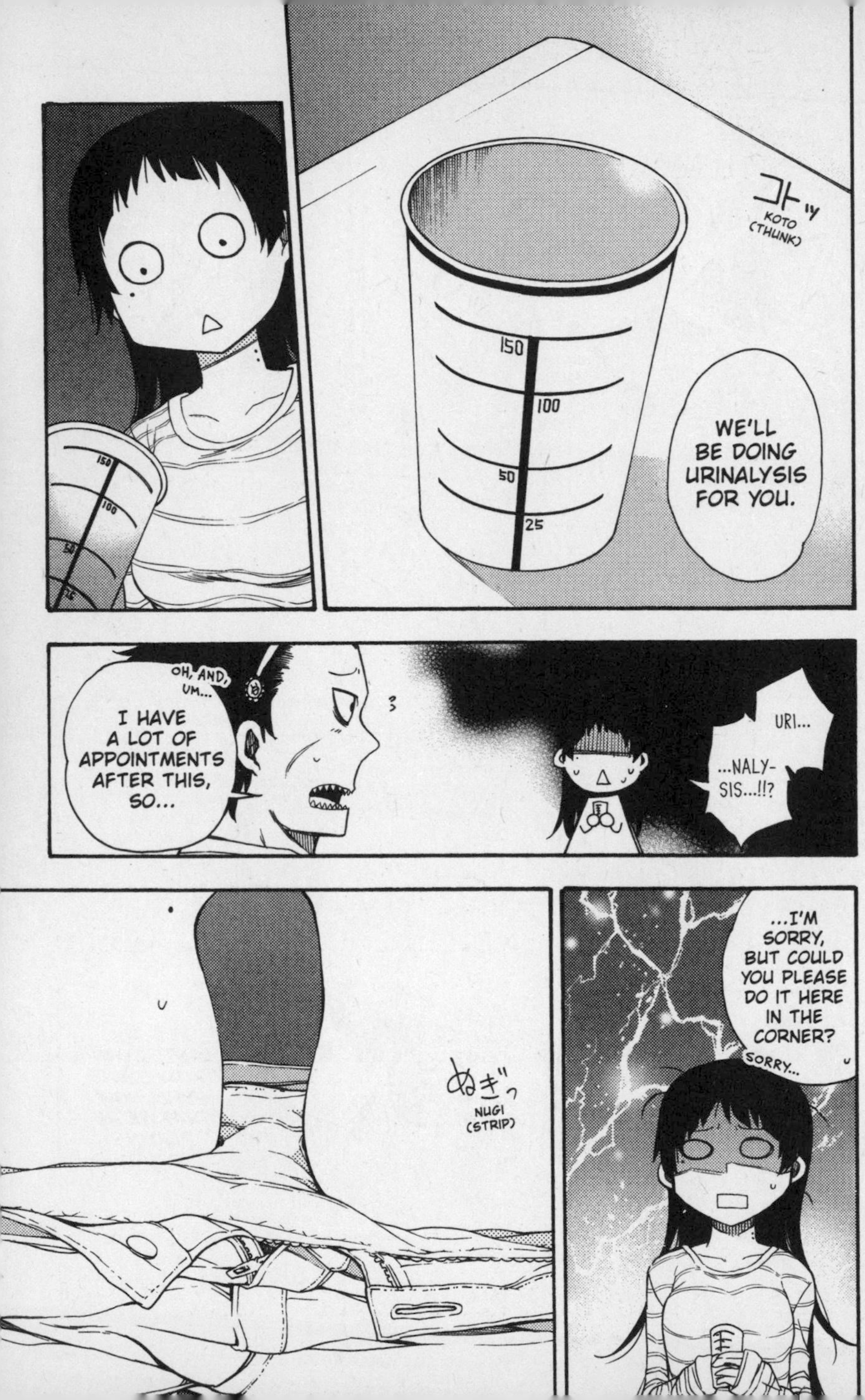
コトッ
KOTO (THUNK)
WE'LL BE DOING URINALYSIS FOR YOU.
URI...
...NALY-SIS...!!?
OH, AND, UM...
I HAVE A LOT OF APPOINTMENTS AFTER THIS, SO...
...I'M SORRY, BUT COULD YOU PLEASE DO IT HERE IN THE CORNER?
SORRY...
ぬぎっ
NUGI (STRIP)

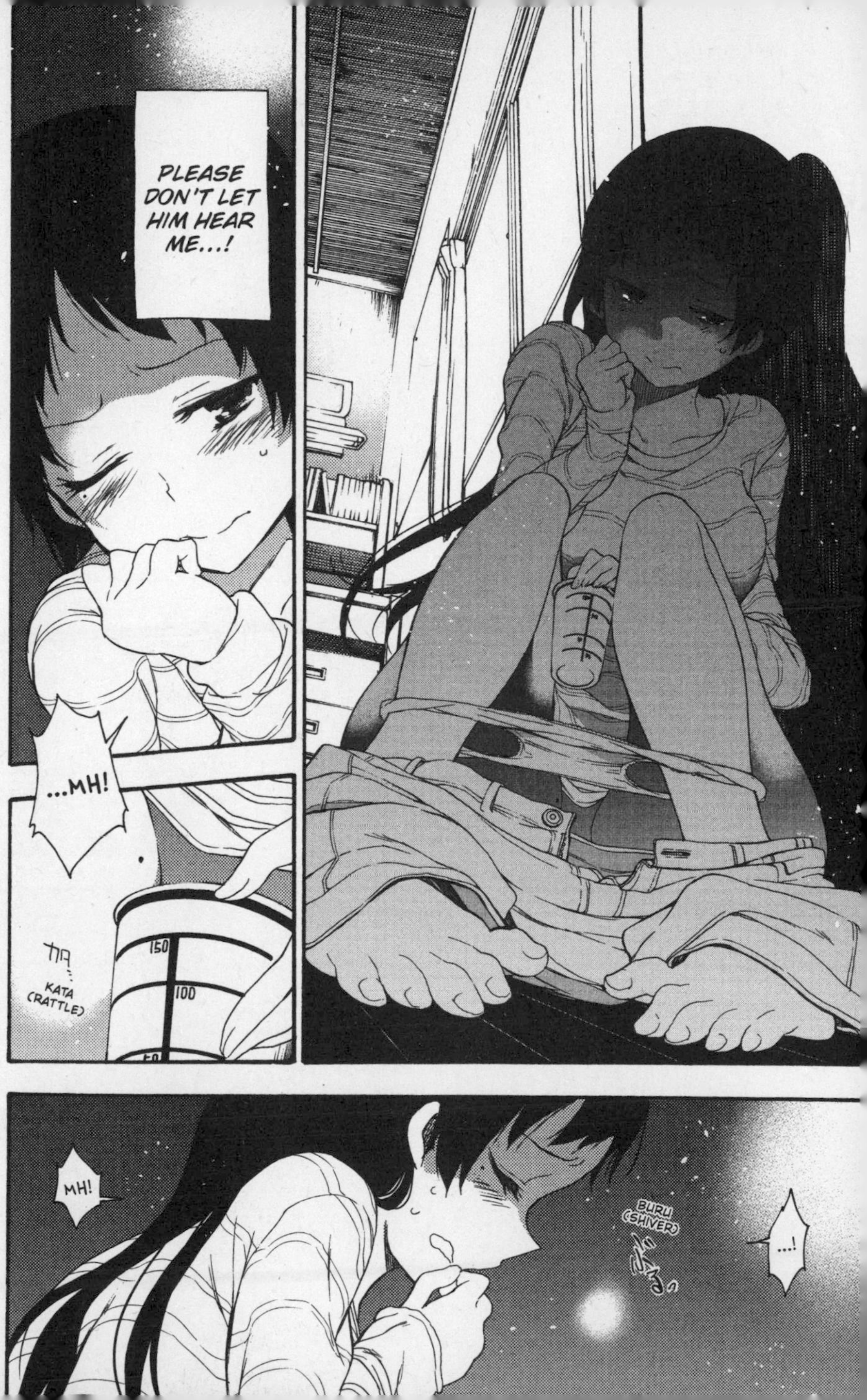
PLEASE DON'T LET HIM HEAR ME...!
...MH!
カタ
KATA (RATTLE)
...!
BURU (SHIVER)
MH!

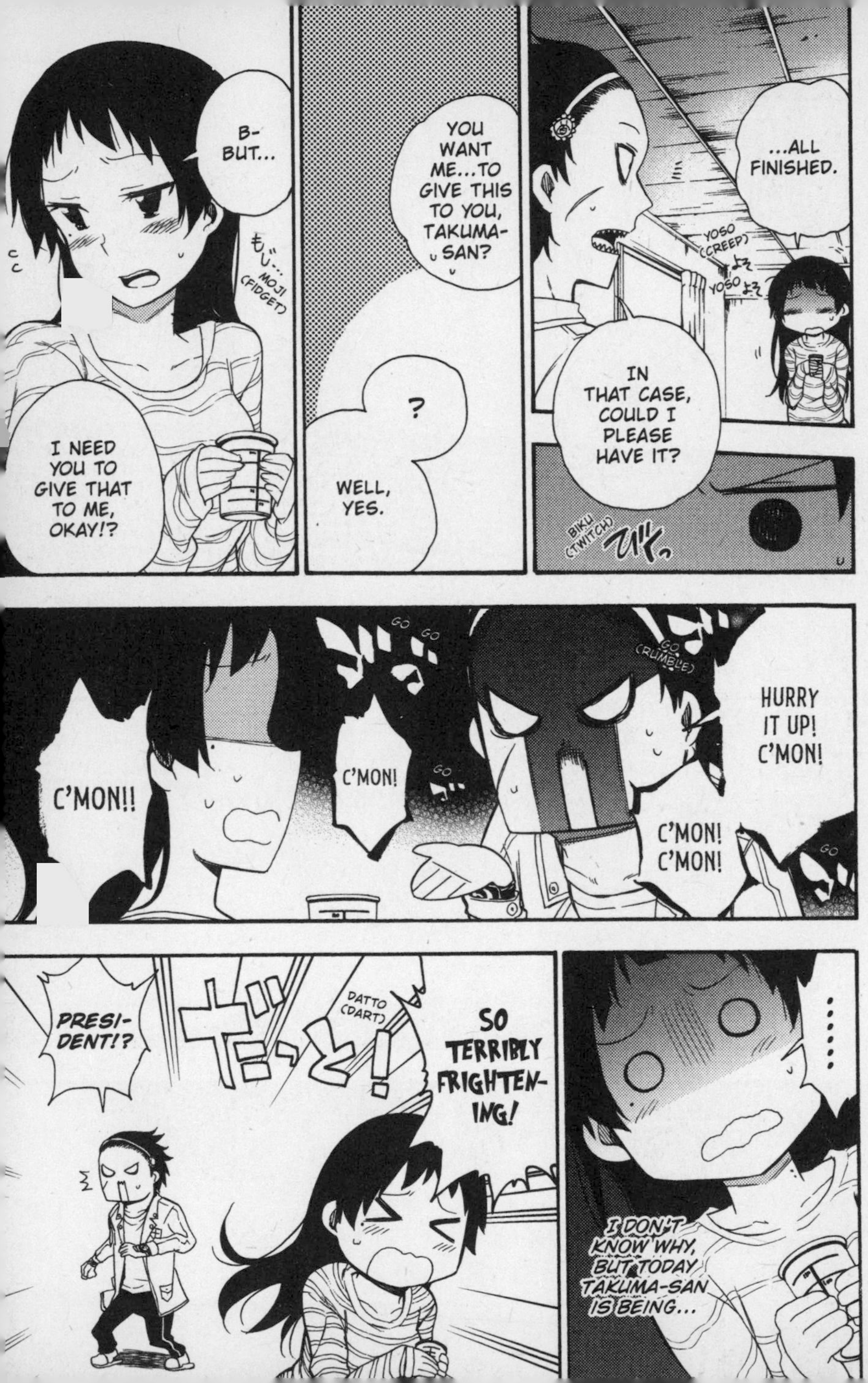
...ALL FINISHED.
YOSO (CREEP) よそ
YOSO よそ
IN THAT CASE, COULD I PLEASE HAVE IT?
BIKU (TWITCH) びくっ
YOU WANT ME...TO GIVE THIS TO YOU, TAKUMA-SAN?
?
WELL, YES.
B-BUT...
もじ… MOJI (FIDGET)
I NEED YOU TO GIVE THAT TO ME, OKAY!?
HURRY IT UP! C'MON!
GO (RUMBLE)
C'MON! C'MON!
GO
GO GO
C'MON!
GO
C'MON!!
......
I DON'T KNOW WHY, BUT TODAY TAKUMA-SAN IS BEING...
SO TERRIBLY FRIGHTENING!
DATTO (DART)
PRESIDENT!?

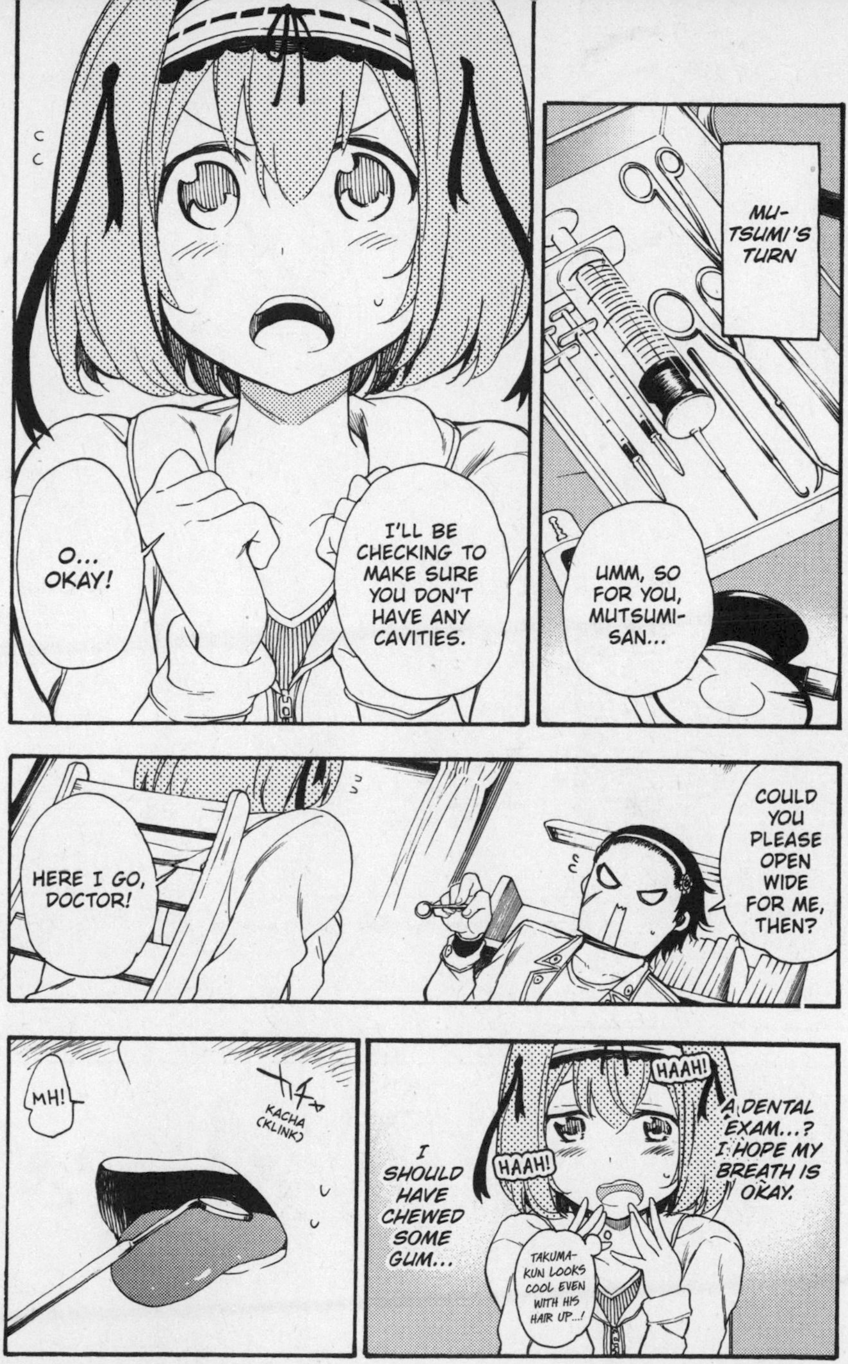
MU-TSUMI'S TURN
UMM, SO FOR YOU, MUTSUMI-SAN...
I'LL BE CHECKING TO MAKE SURE YOU DON'T HAVE ANY CAVITIES.
O... OKAY!
COULD YOU PLEASE OPEN WIDE FOR ME, THEN?
HERE I GO, DOCTOR!
HAAH!
A DENTAL EXAM...? I HOPE MY BREATH IS OKAY.
HAAH!
I SHOULD HAVE CHEWED SOME GUM...
TAKUMA-KUN LOOKS COOL EVEN WITH HIS HAIR UP...!
MH!
KACHA (KLINK)

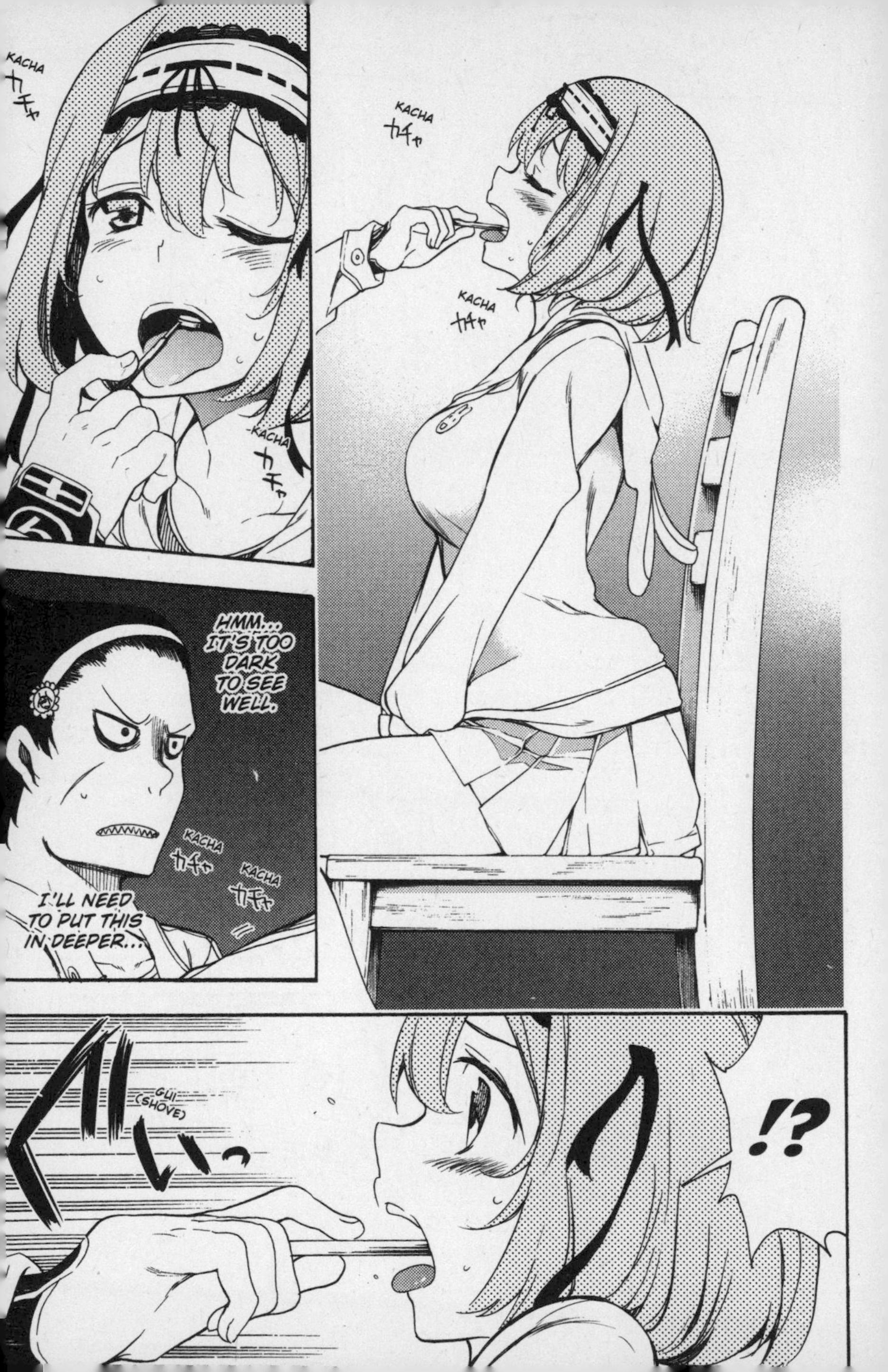
KACHA
カチャ
KACHA
カチャ
KACHA
カチャ
KACHA
カチャ
HMM... IT'S TOO DARK TO SEE WELL.
KACHA
カチャ
KACHA
カチャ
I'LL NEED TO PUT THIS IN DEEPER...
!?
GUI (SHOVE)

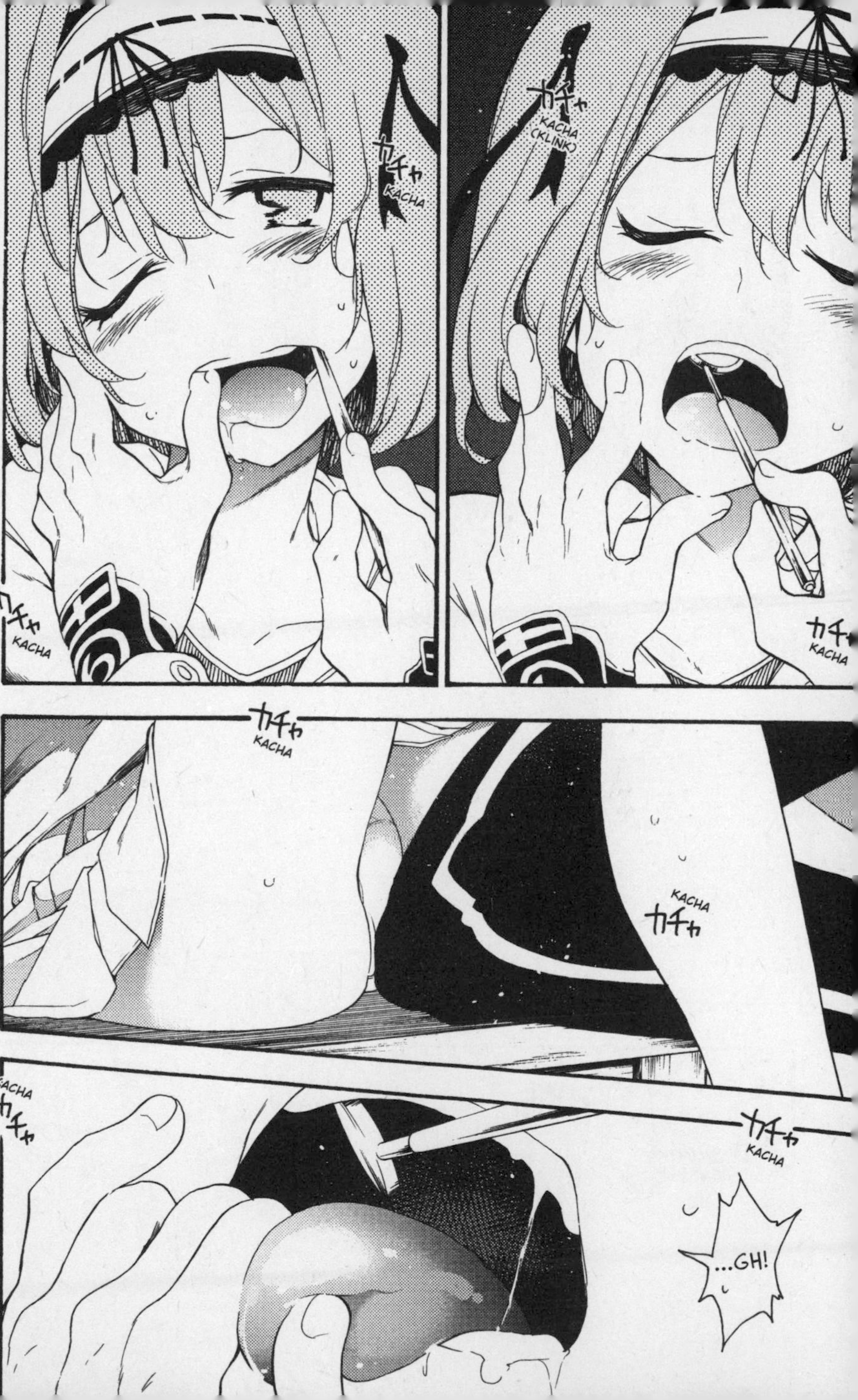

カチャ
KACHA (KLINK)
カチャ
KACHA
カチャ
KACHA
カチャ
KACHA
カチャ
KACHA
KACHA
カチャ
カチャ
KACHA
...GH!
KACHA
カチャ

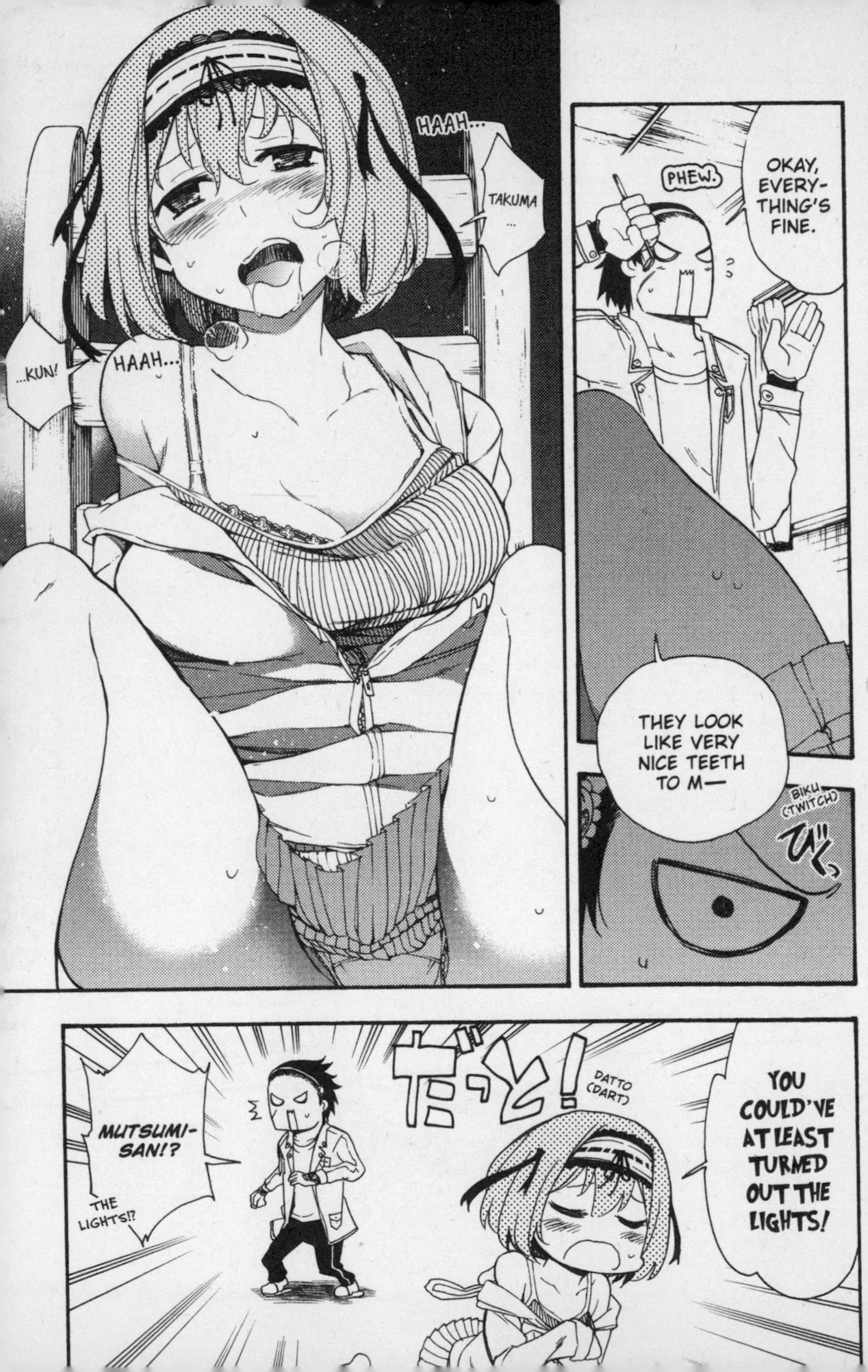
OKAY, EVERYTHING'S FINE.
PHEW.
THEY LOOK LIKE VERY NICE TEETH TO M—
BIKU (TWITCH)
HAAH...
TAKUMA ...
...KUN!
HAAH...
YOU COULD'VE AT LEAST TURNED OUT THE LIGHTS!
DATTO (DART)
MUTSUMI-SAN!?
THE LIGHTS!?

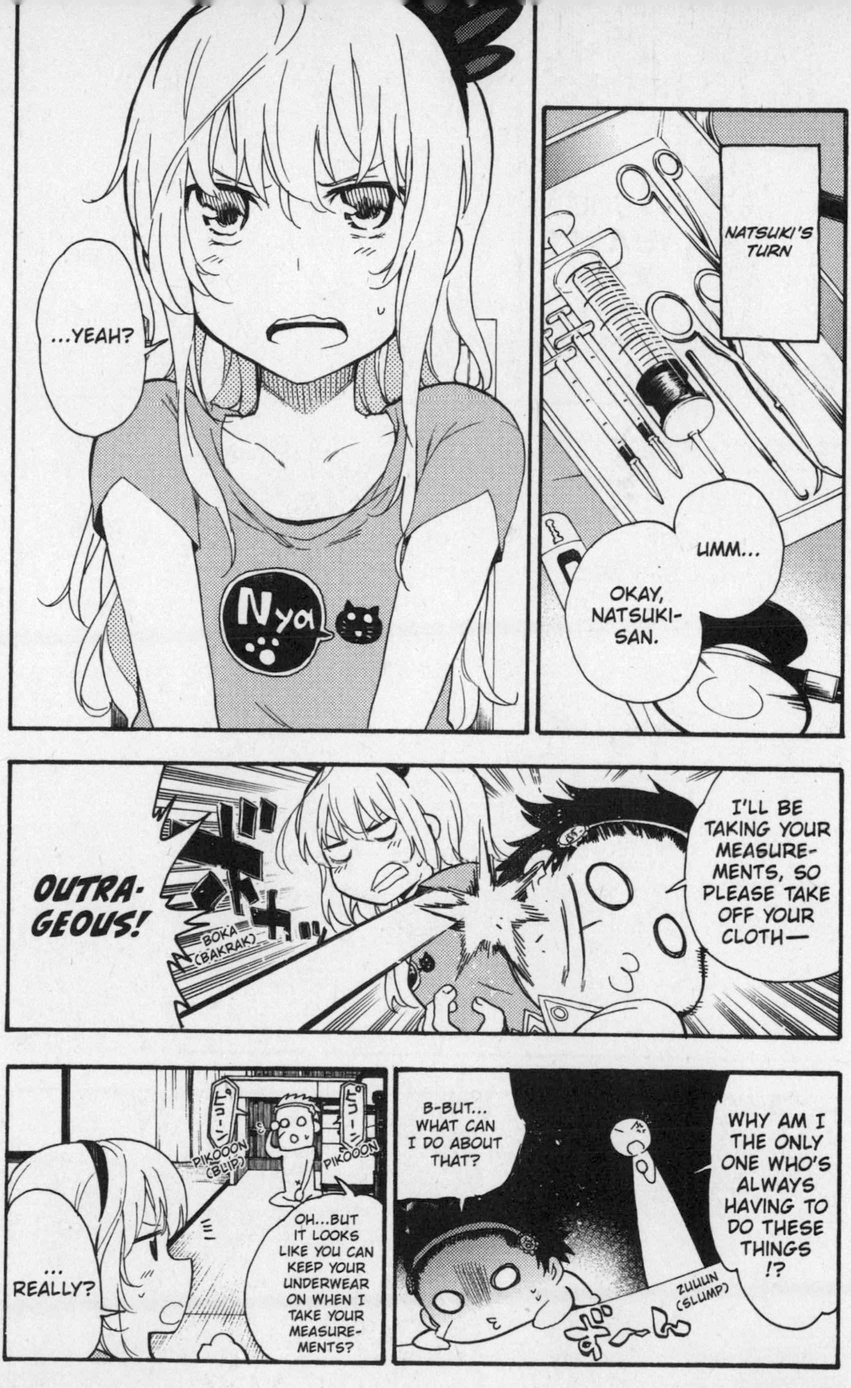
NATSUKI'S TURN
UMM...
OKAY, NATSUKI-SAN.
...YEAH?
I'LL BE TAKING YOUR MEASUREMENTS, SO PLEASE TAKE OFF YOUR CLOTH—
OUTRAGEOUS!
BOKA (BAKRAK)
WHY AM I THE ONLY ONE WHO'S ALWAYS HAVING TO DO THESE THINGS !?
B-BUT... WHAT CAN I DO ABOUT THAT?
ZUUUN (SLUMP)
PIKOOON
PIKOOON (BLIP)
OH...BUT IT LOOKS LIKE YOU CAN KEEP YOUR UNDERWEAR ON WHEN I TAKE YOUR MEASUREMENTS?
... REALLY?

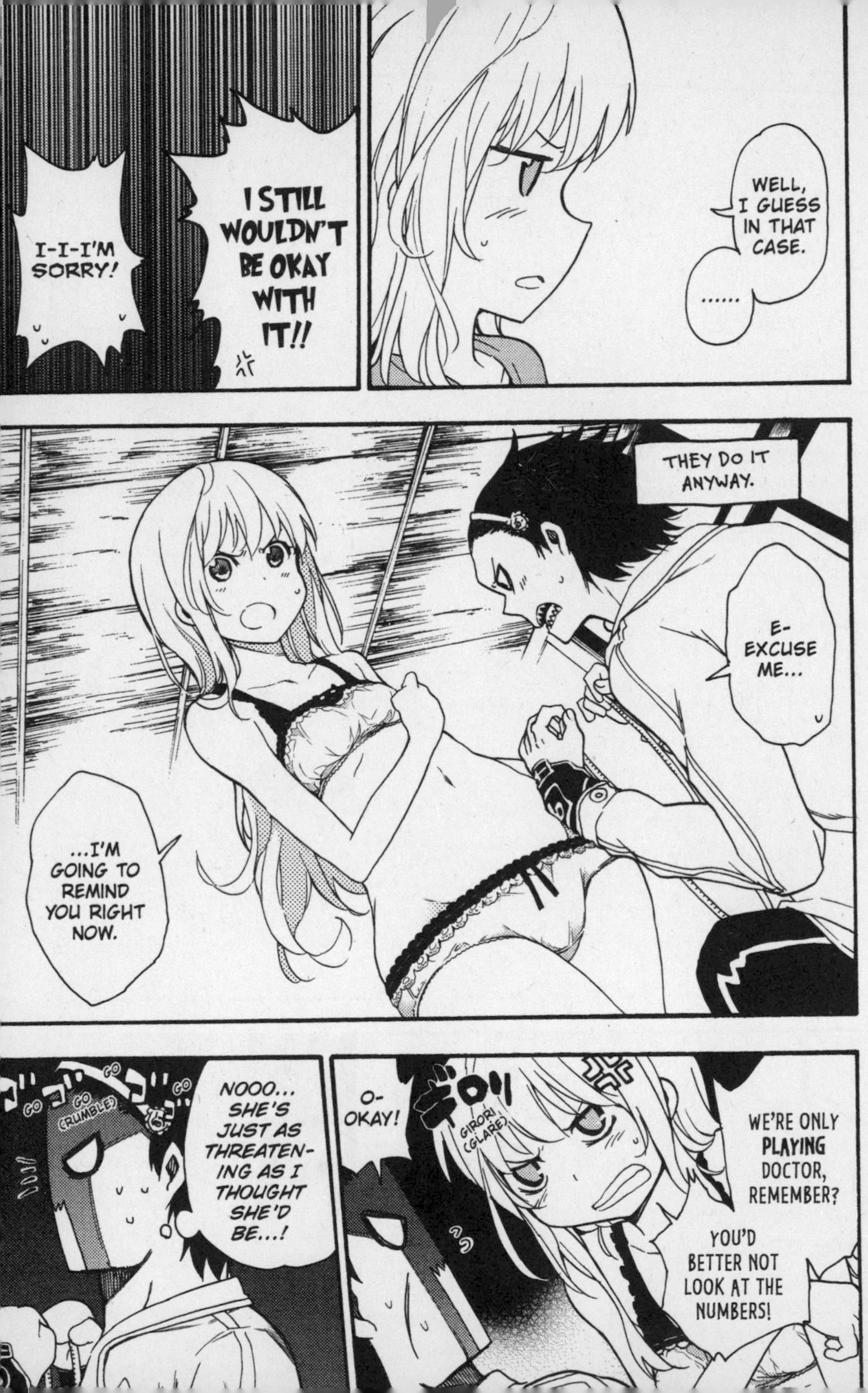
WELL, I GUESS IN THAT CASE.
......
I STILL WOULDN'T BE OKAY WITH IT!!
I-I-I'M SORRY!
THEY DO IT ANYWAY.
E-EXCUSE ME...
...I'M GOING TO REMIND YOU RIGHT NOW.
WE'RE ONLY PLAYING DOCTOR, REMEMBER?
YOU'D BETTER NOT LOOK AT THE NUMBERS!
GIRORI (GLARE)
O-OKAY!
NOOO... SHE'S JUST AS THREATEN-ING AS I THOUGHT SHE'D BE...!
GO GO GO GO (RUMBLE)

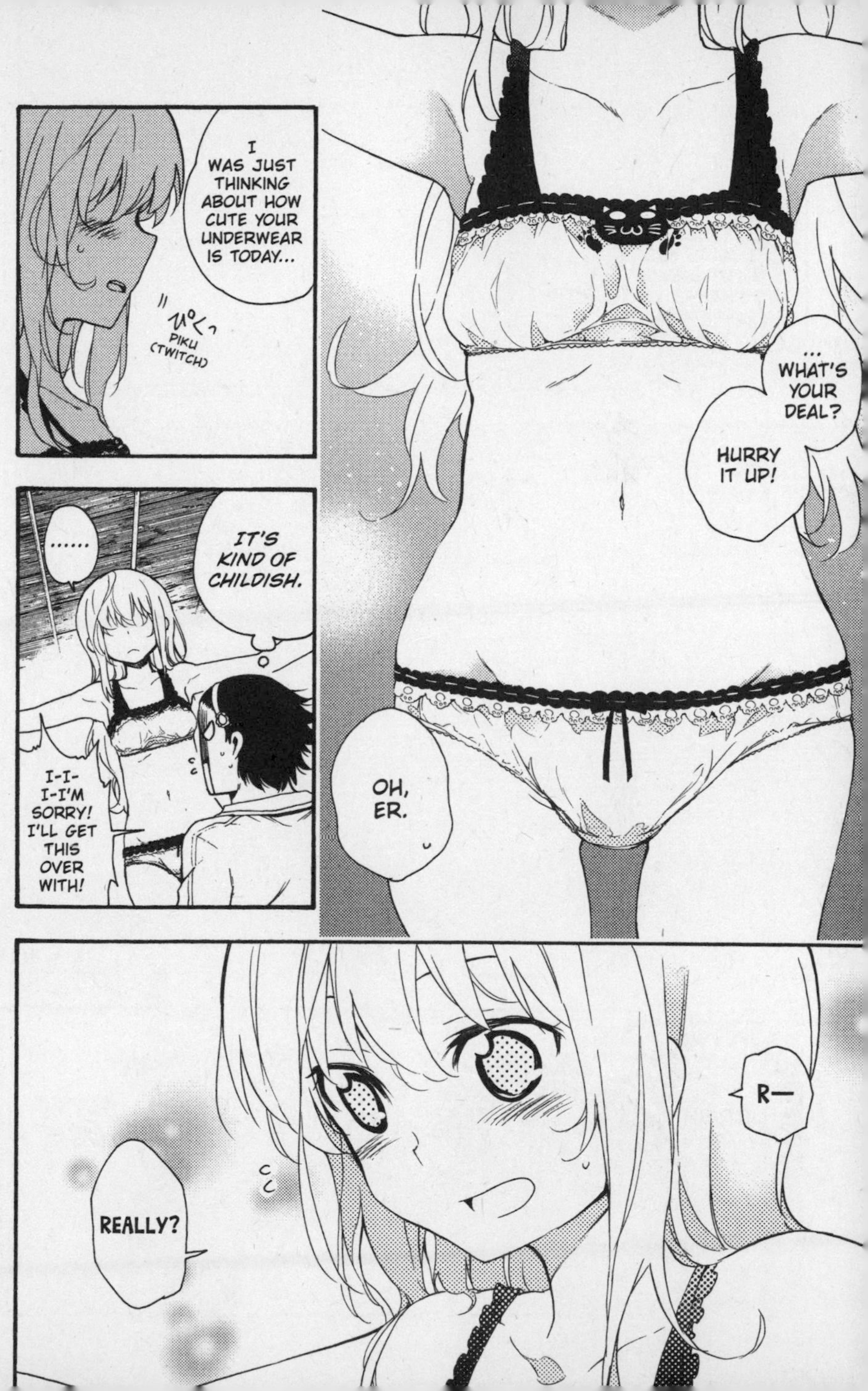
...WHAT'S YOUR DEAL?
HURRY IT UP!
OH, ER.
I WAS JUST THINKING ABOUT HOW CUTE YOUR UNDERWEAR IS TODAY...
ぴくっ
PIKU (TWITCH)
IT'S KIND OF CHILDISH.
......
I-I-I-I'M SORRY! I'LL GET THIS OVER WITH!
R—
REALLY?

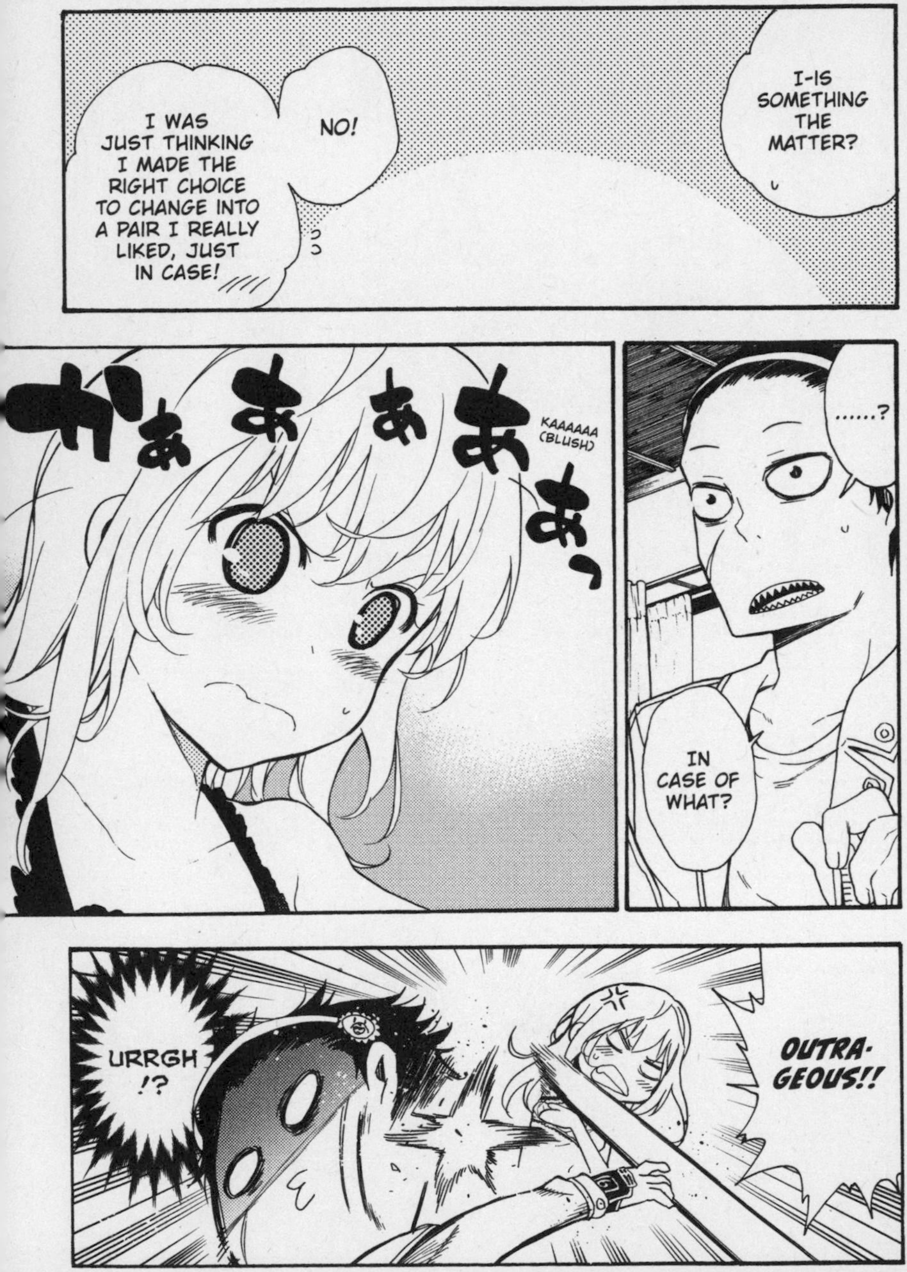
I-IS SOMETHING THE MATTER?
NO!
I WAS JUST THINKING I MADE THE RIGHT CHOICE TO CHANGE INTO A PAIR I REALLY LIKED, JUST IN CASE!
......?
IN CASE OF WHAT?
KAAAAAA (BLUSH)
OUTRA-GEOUS!!
URRGH !?

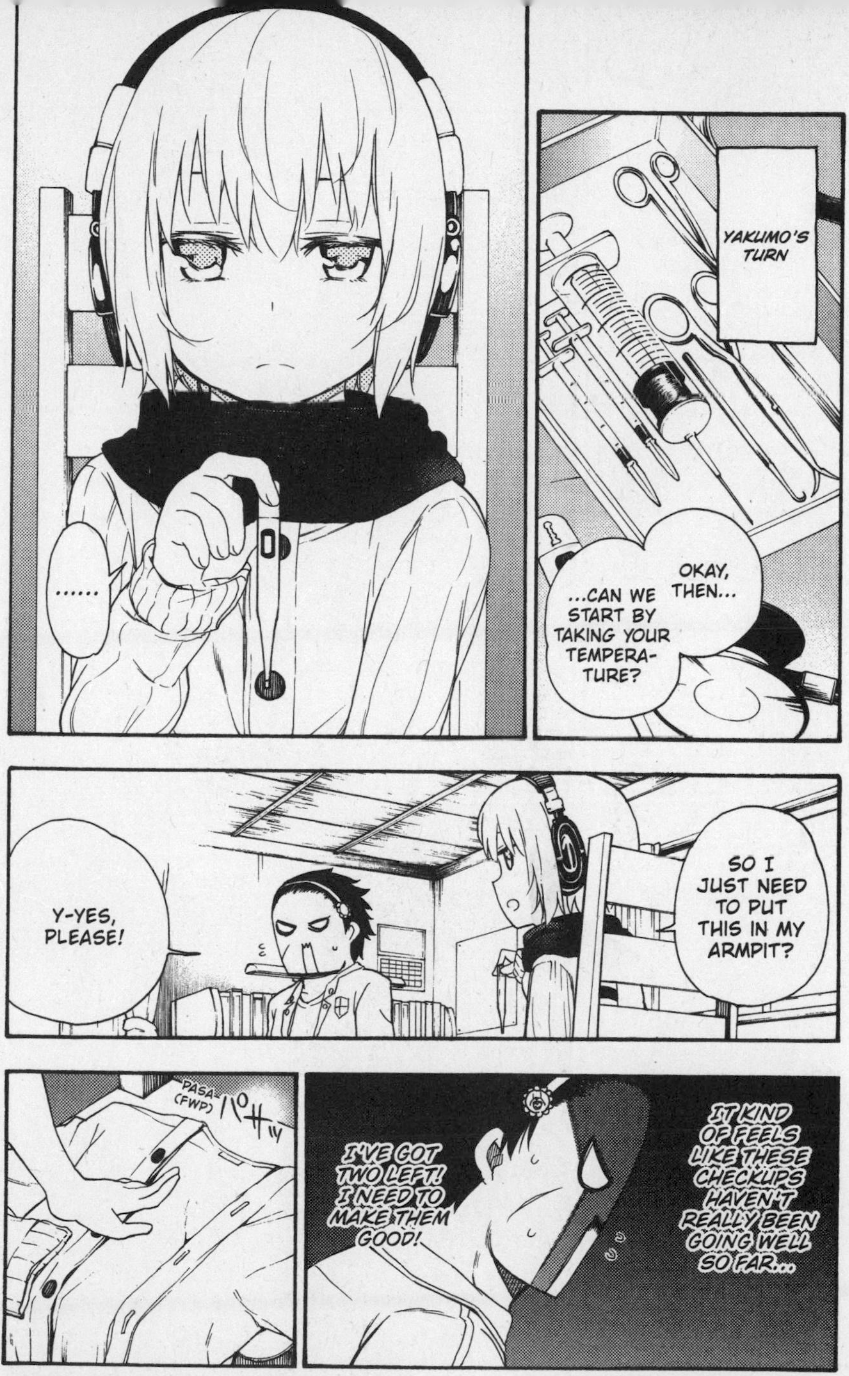
YAKUMO'S TURN
OKAY, THEN...
...CAN WE START BY TAKING YOUR TEMPERATURE?
......
SO I JUST NEED TO PUT THIS IN MY ARMPIT?
Y-YES, PLEASE!
IT KIND OF FEELS LIKE THESE CHECKUPS HAVEN'T REALLY BEEN GOING WELL SO FAR...
I'VE GOT TWO LEFT! I NEED TO MAKE THEM GOOD!
PASA (FWP)

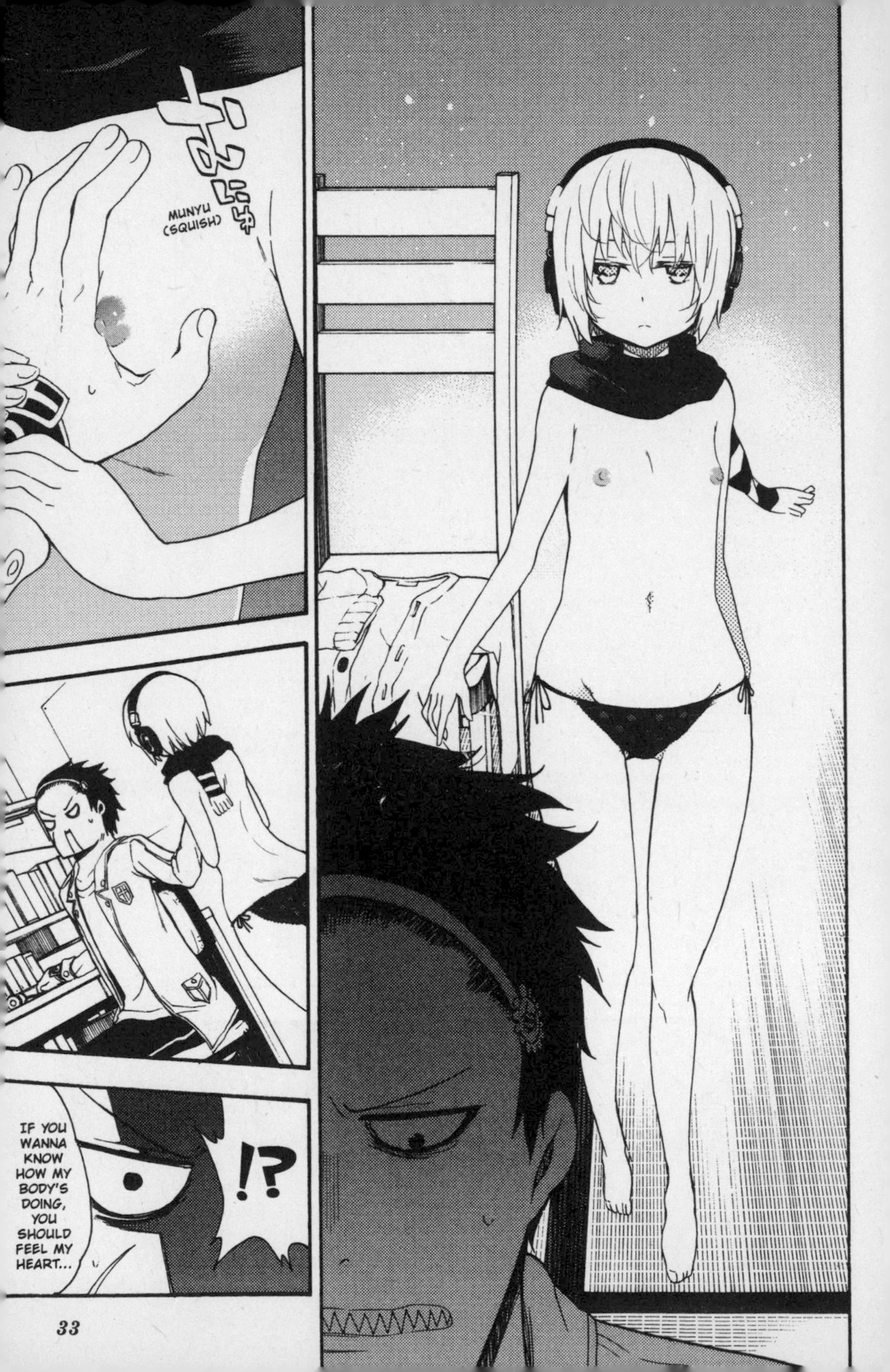
むにゅ
MUNYU (SQUISH)
!?
IF YOU WANNA KNOW HOW MY BODY'S DOING, YOU SHOULD FEEL MY HEART...

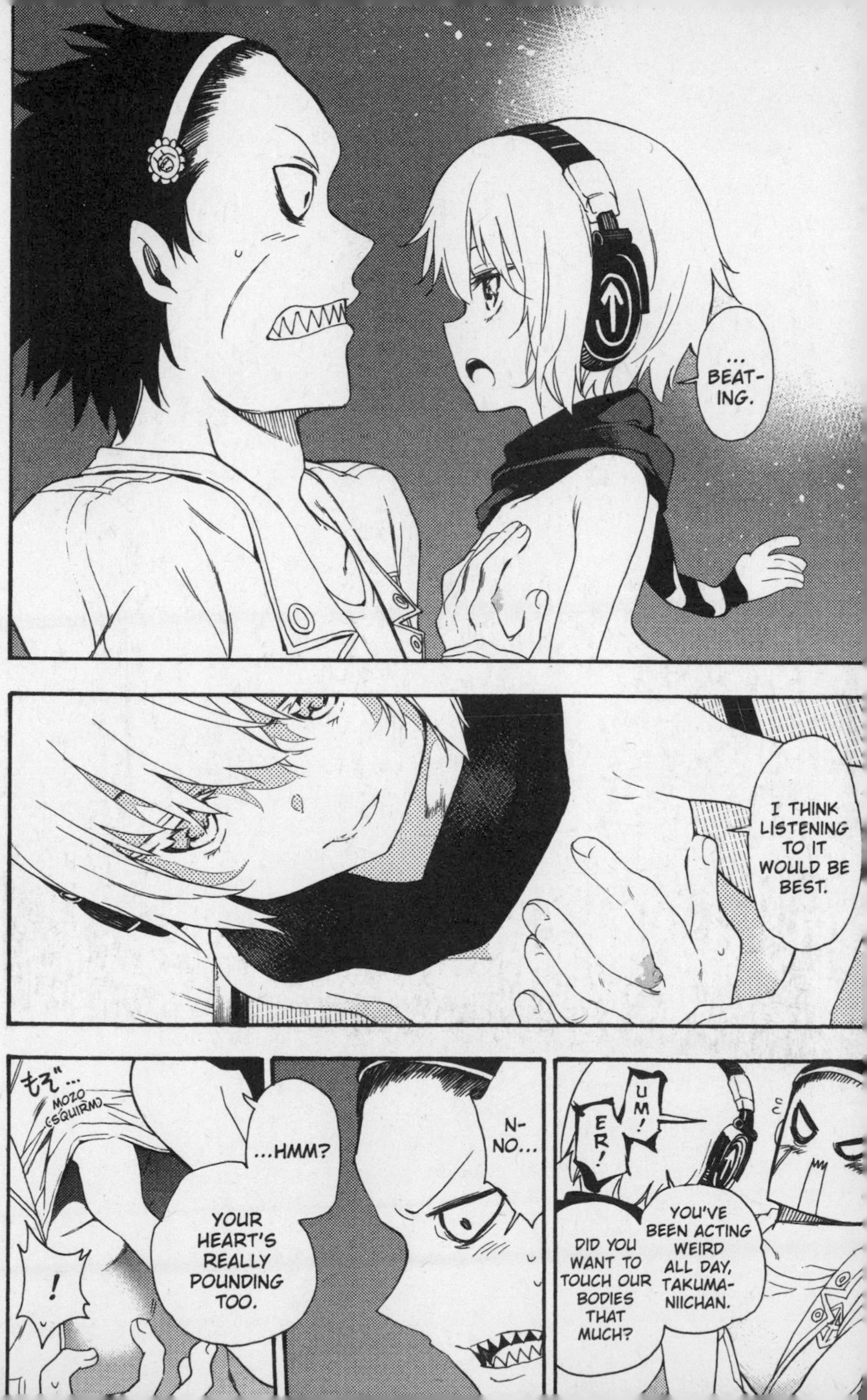
...BEAT-ING.
I THINK LISTENING TO IT WOULD BE BEST.
UM!
ER!
YOU'VE BEEN ACTING WEIRD ALL DAY, TAKUMA-NIICHAN.
DID YOU WANT TO TOUCH OUR BODIES THAT MUCH?
N-NO...
...HMM?
YOUR HEART'S REALLY POUNDING TOO.
もぞ…
MOZO (SQUIRM)
!

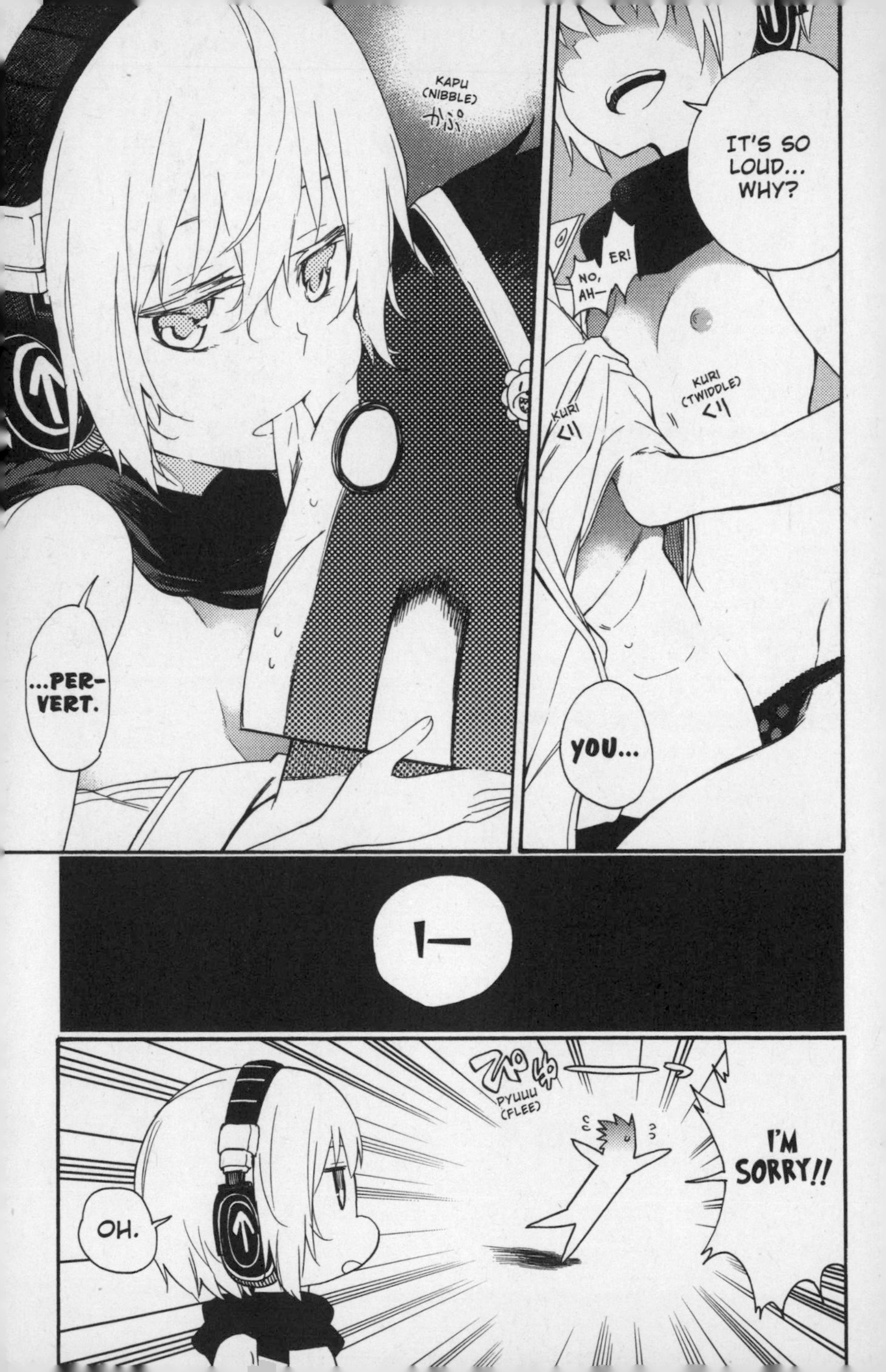
IT'S SO LOUD... WHY?
ER!
NO, AH—
KURI (TWIDDLE)
くり
KURI
くり
YOU...
KAPU (NIBBLE)
かぷ
...PER-VERT.
!—
PYUUU (FLEE)
I'M SORRY!!
OH.

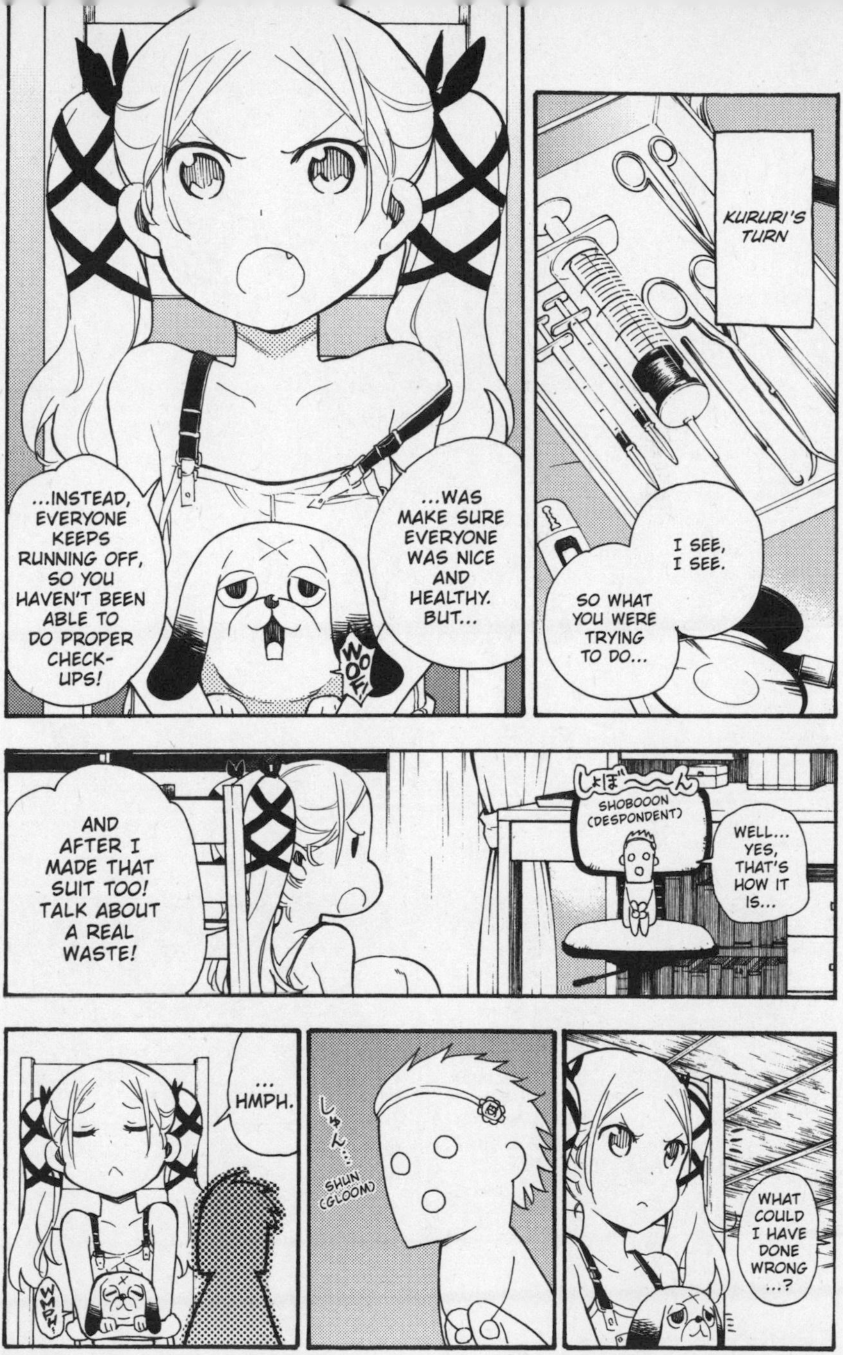
KURURI'S TURN
I SEE, I SEE.
SO WHAT YOU WERE TRYING TO DO...
...WAS MAKE SURE EVERYONE WAS NICE AND HEALTHY. BUT...
...INSTEAD, EVERYONE KEEPS RUNNING OFF, SO YOU HAVEN'T BEEN ABLE TO DO PROPER CHECK-UPS!
WOOF!
しょぼーーん
SHOBOOON (DESPONDENT)
WELL... YES, THAT'S HOW IT IS...
AND AFTER I MADE THAT SUIT TOO! TALK ABOUT A REAL WASTE!
WHAT COULD I HAVE DONE WRONG ...?
しゅん…
SHUN (GLOOM)
... HMPH.
WMPH!

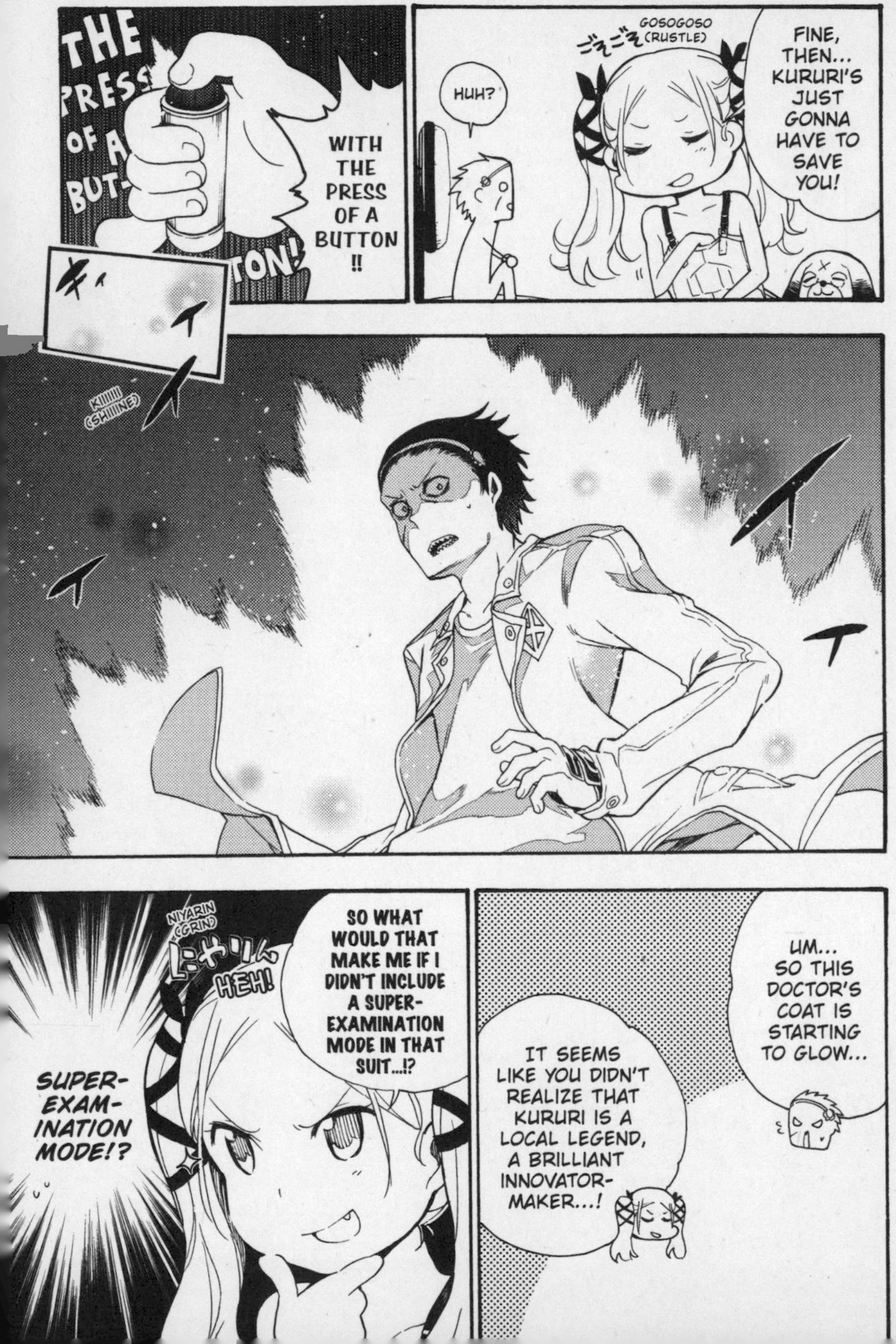
FINE, THEN... KURURI'S JUST GONNA HAVE TO SAVE YOU!
GOSOGOSO (RUSTLE)
HUH?
WITH THE PRESS OF A BUTTON!!
THE PRESS OF A BUT-TON!
KIIIII (SHIIINE)
UM... SO THIS DOCTOR'S COAT IS STARTING TO GLOW...
IT SEEMS LIKE YOU DIDN'T REALIZE THAT KURURI IS A LOCAL LEGEND, A BRILLIANT INNOVATOR-MAKER...!
SO WHAT WOULD THAT MAKE ME IF I DIDN'T INCLUDE A SUPER-EXAMINATION MODE IN THAT SUIT...!?
NIYARIN (GRIN)
HEH!
SUPER-EXAMINATION MODE!?

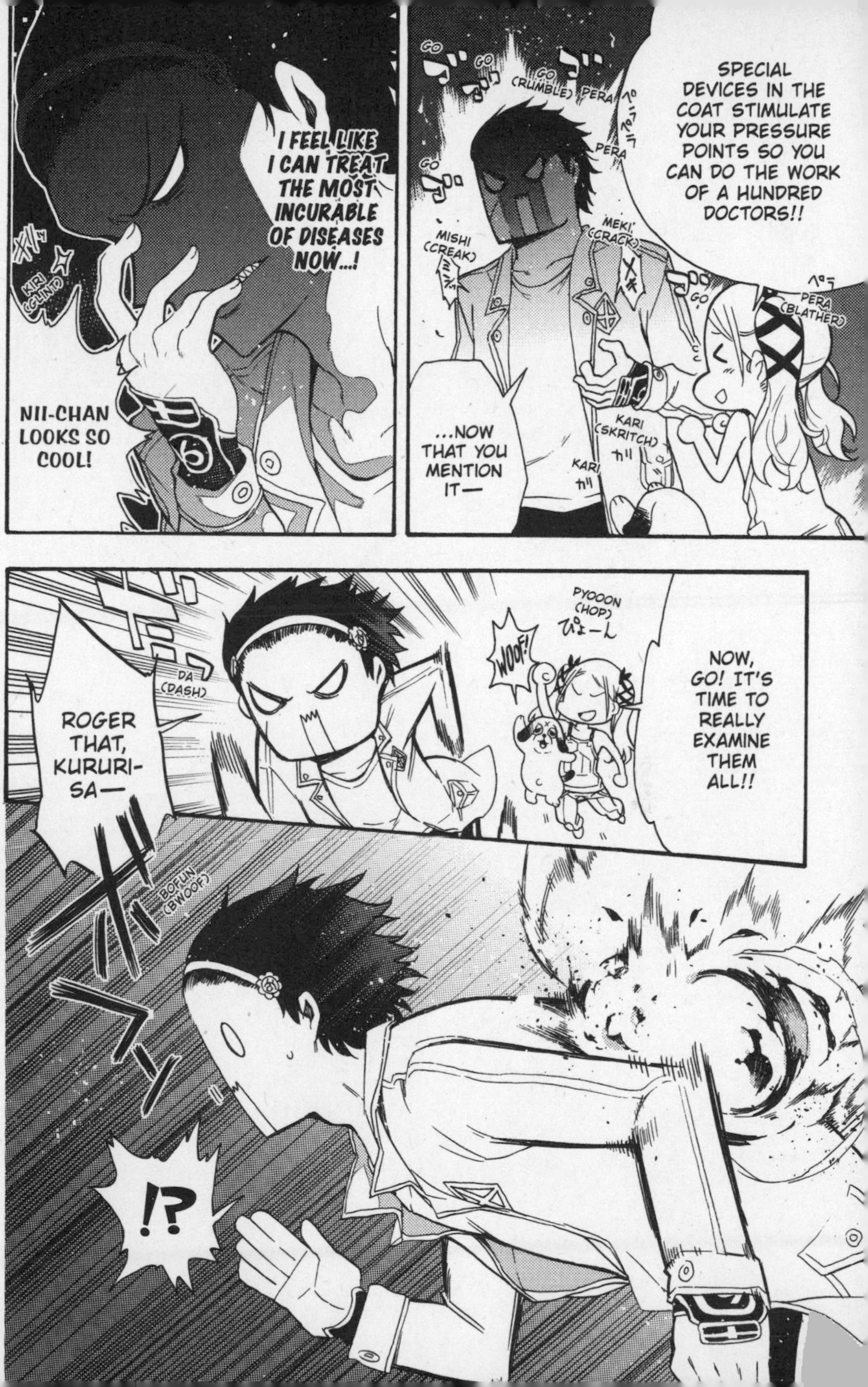
SPECIAL DEVICES IN THE COAT STIMULATE YOUR PRESSURE POINTS SO YOU CAN DO THE WORK OF A HUNDRED DOCTORS!!
GO
GO
GO (RUMBLE)
PERA
PERA
MEKI (CRACK)
MISHI (CREAK)
GO
GO
PERA (BLATHER)
KARI (SKRITCH)
KARI
...NOW THAT YOU MENTION IT—
I FEEL LIKE I CAN TREAT THE MOST INCURABLE OF DISEASES NOW...!
KIRI (GLINT)
NII-CHAN LOOKS SO COOL!
NOW, GO! IT'S TIME TO REALLY EXAMINE THEM ALL!!
PYOOON (HOP)
ぴょーん
WOOF!
DA (DASH)
ROGER THAT, KURURI-SA—
BOFUN (BWOOF)
!?

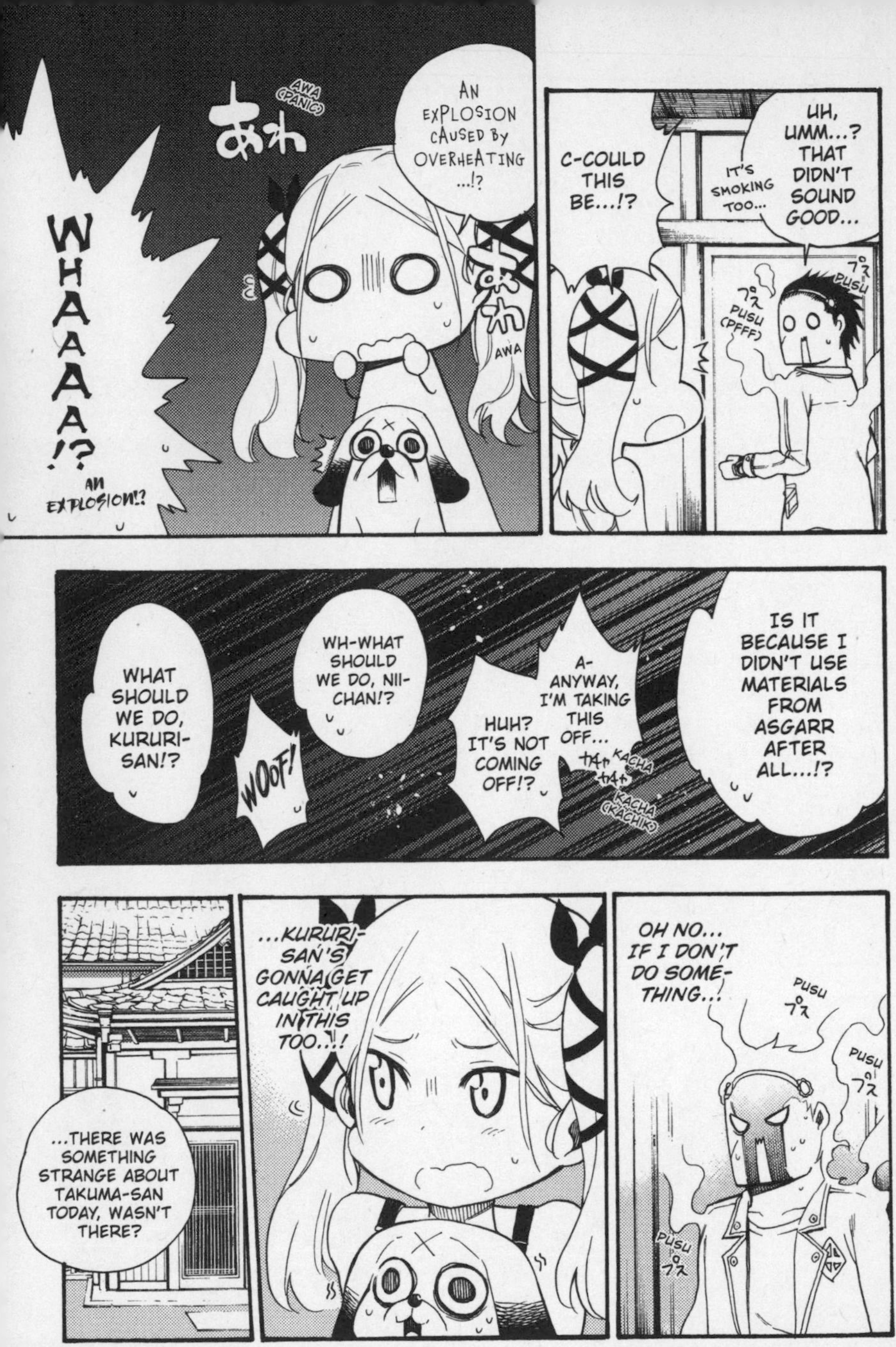
UH, UMM...? THAT DIDN'T SOUND GOOD...
IT'S SMOKING TOO...
C-COULD THIS BE...!?
プス PUSU
プス PUSU (PFFF)
AN EXPLOSION CAUSED BY OVERHEATING ...!?
あわ AWA
あわ AWA (PANIC)
WHAAAAA!?
AN EXPLOSION!?
IS IT BECAUSE I DIDN'T USE MATERIALS FROM ASGARR AFTER ALL...!?
A-ANYWAY, I'M TAKING THIS OFF...
カチャ KACHA
カチャ KACHA (KACHIK)
HUH? IT'S NOT COMING OFF!?
WH-WHAT SHOULD WE DO, NII-CHAN!?
WOOF!
WHAT SHOULD WE DO, KURURI-SAN!?
OH NO... IF I DON'T DO SOME-THING...!
PUSU プス
PUSU プス
PUSU プス
...KURURI-SAN'S GONNA GET CAUGHT UP IN THIS TOO...!
...THERE WAS SOMETHING STRANGE ABOUT TAKUMA-SAN TODAY, WASN'T THERE?

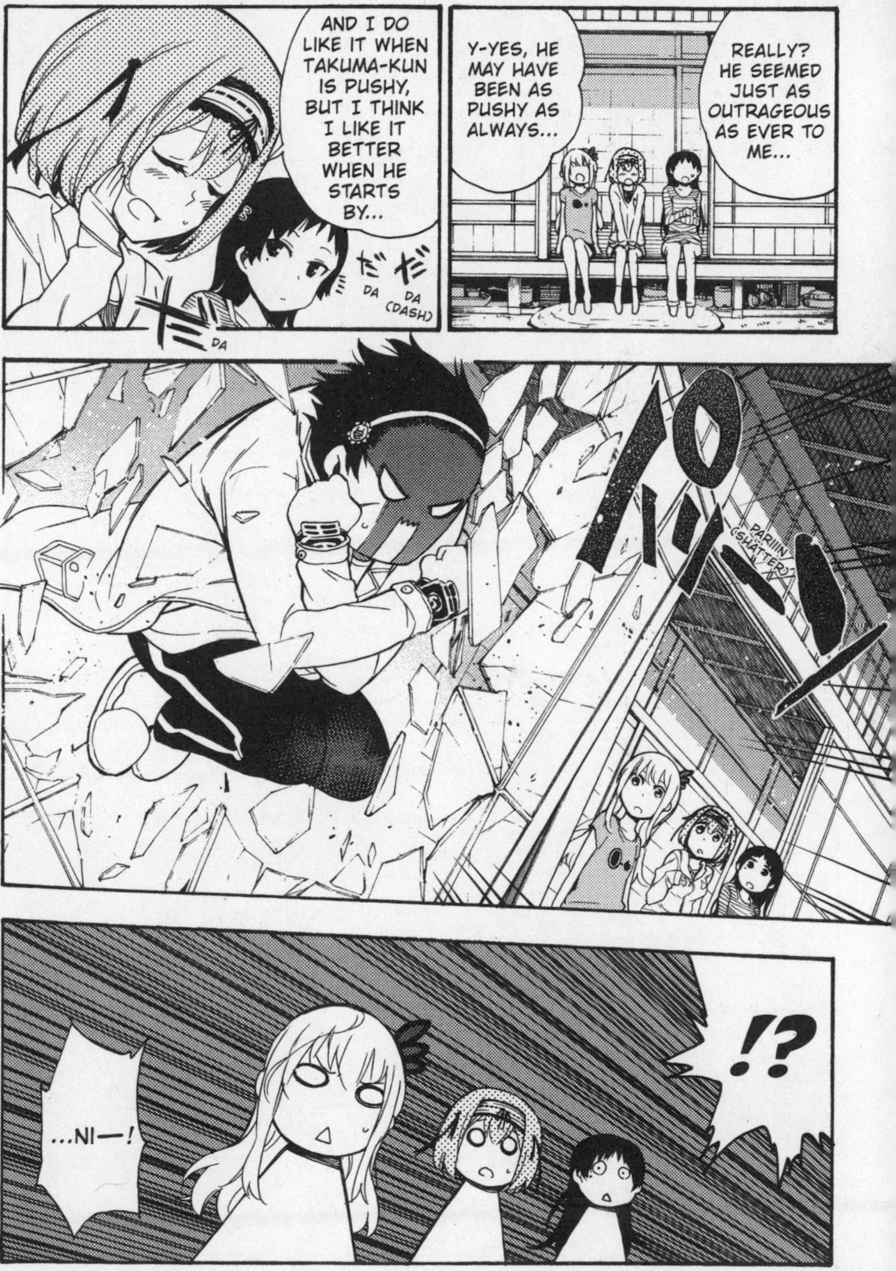
REALLY? HE SEEMED JUST AS OUTRAGEOUS AS EVER TO ME...
Y-YES, HE MAY HAVE BEEN AS PUSHY AS ALWAYS...
AND I DO LIKE IT WHEN TAKUMA-KUN IS PUSHY, BUT I THINK I LIKE IT BETTER WHEN HE STARTS BY...
DA DA (DASH)
DA
PARIIN (SHATTER)
!?
...NI—!

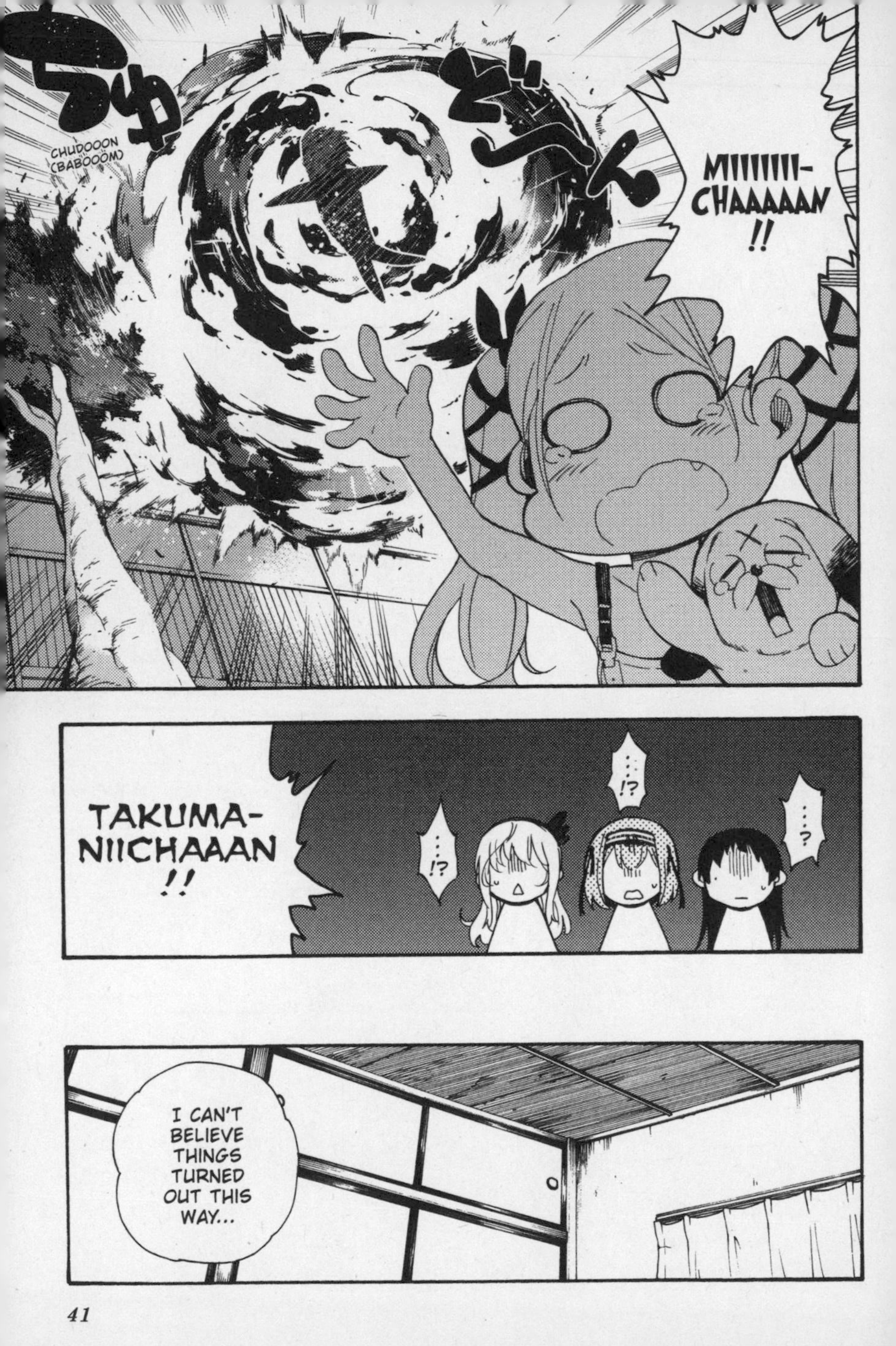
MIIIIIIII-CHAAAAAN!!
CHUDOOON (BABOOOM)
...?
...!?
...!?
TAKUMA-NIICHAAAN!!
I CAN'T BELIEVE THINGS TURNED OUT THIS WAY...

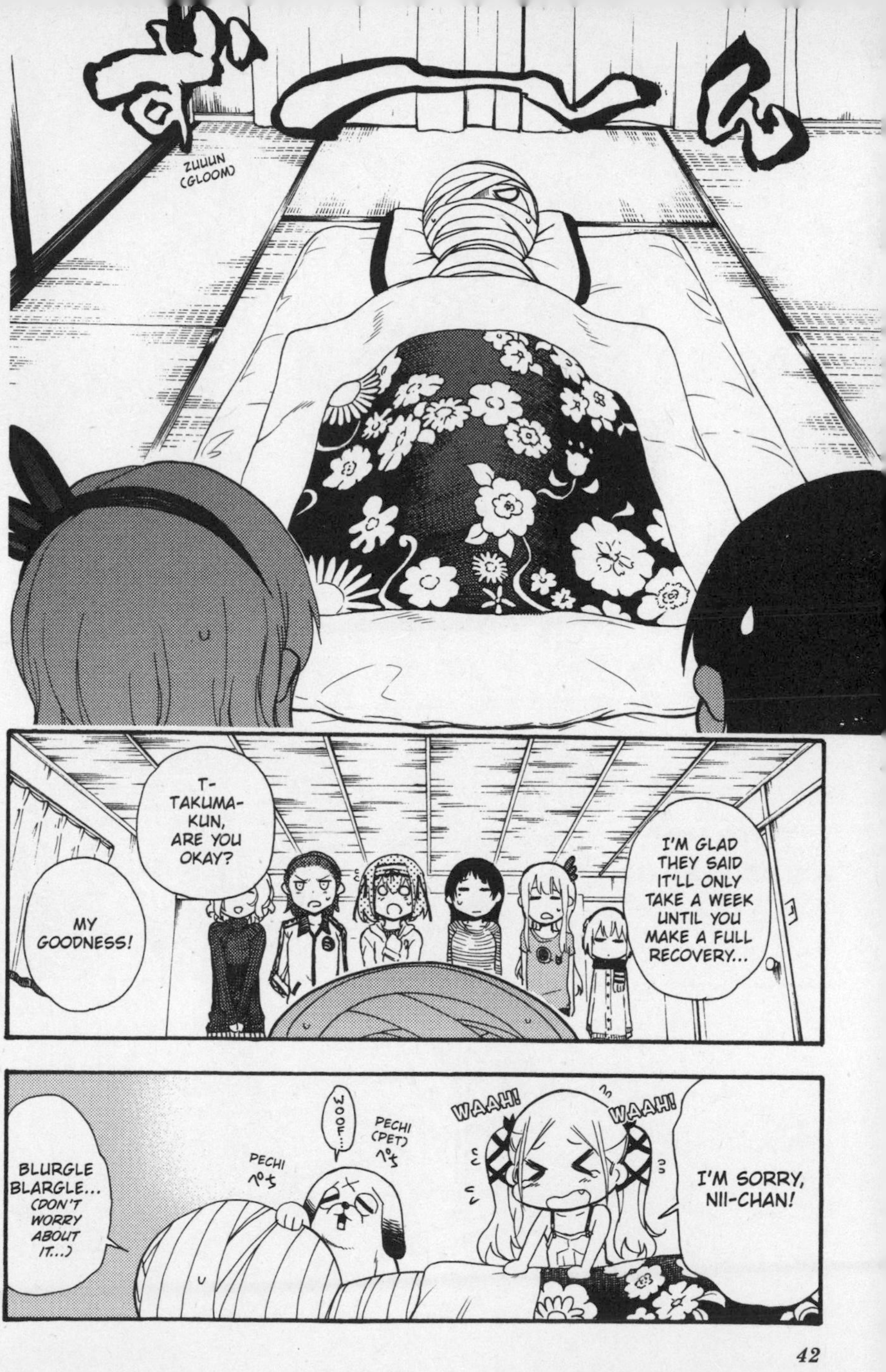
ZUUUN (GLOOM)
I'M GLAD THEY SAID IT'LL ONLY TAKE A WEEK UNTIL YOU MAKE A FULL RECOVERY...
T-TAKUMA-KUN, ARE YOU OKAY?
MY GOODNESS!
I'M SORRY, NII-CHAN!
WAAH!
WAAH!
PECHI (PET) ぺち
WOOF...
PECHI ぺち
BLURGLE BLARGLE... (DON'T WORRY ABOUT IT...)

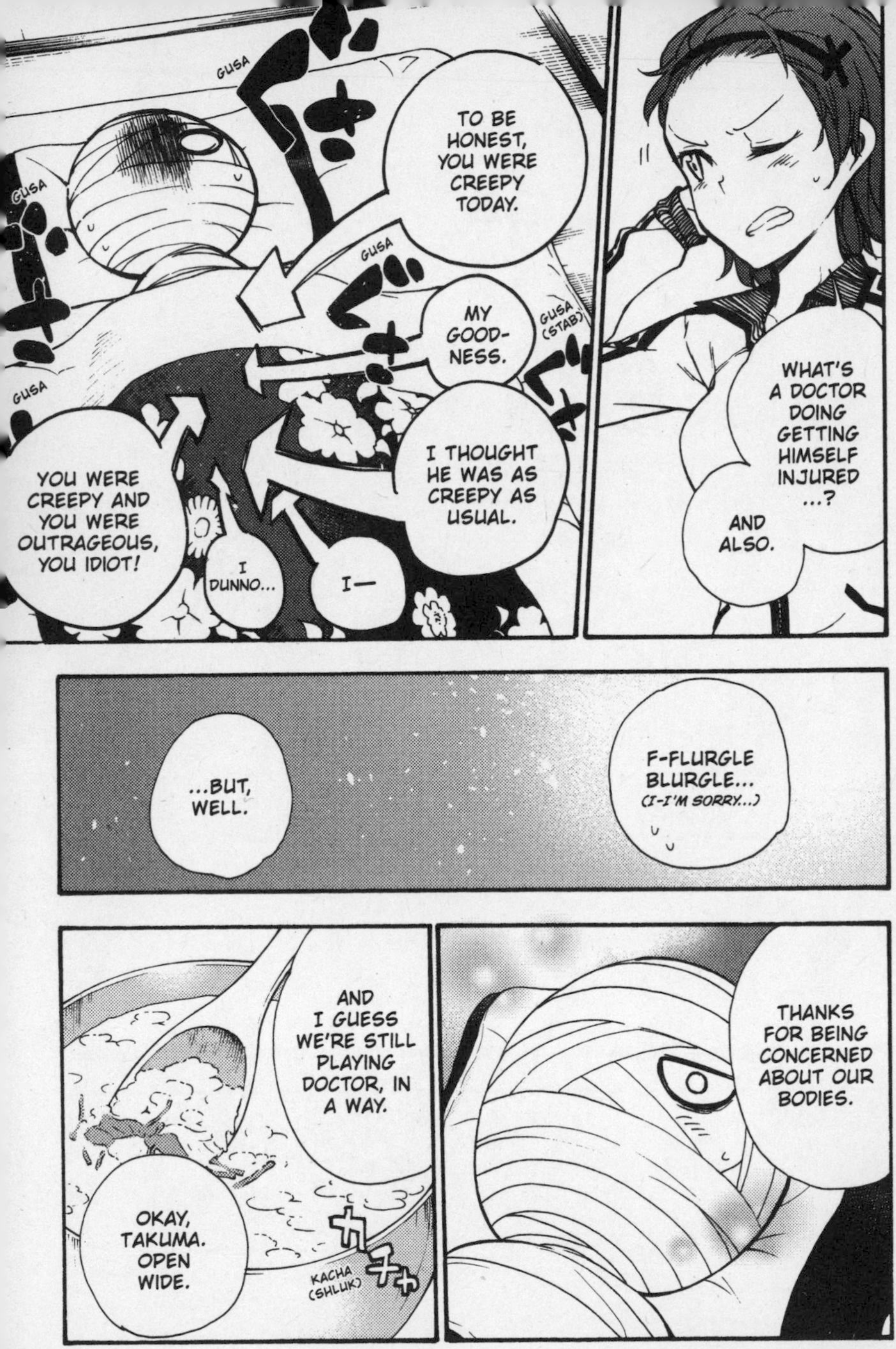
WHAT'S A DOCTOR DOING GETTING HIMSELF INJURED ...?
AND ALSO.
TO BE HONEST, YOU WERE CREEPY TODAY.
GUSA
GUSA
MY GOODNESS.
GUSA (STAB)
I THOUGHT HE WAS AS CREEPY AS USUAL.
GUSA
GUSA
I—
I DUNNO...
YOU WERE CREEPY AND YOU WERE OUTRAGEOUS, YOU IDIOT!
F-FLURGLE BLURGLE... (I-I'M SORRY...)
...BUT, WELL.
THANKS FOR BEING CONCERNED ABOUT OUR BODIES.
AND I GUESS WE'RE STILL PLAYING DOCTOR, IN A WAY.
KACHA (SHLUK)
OKAY, TAKUMA. OPEN WIDE.

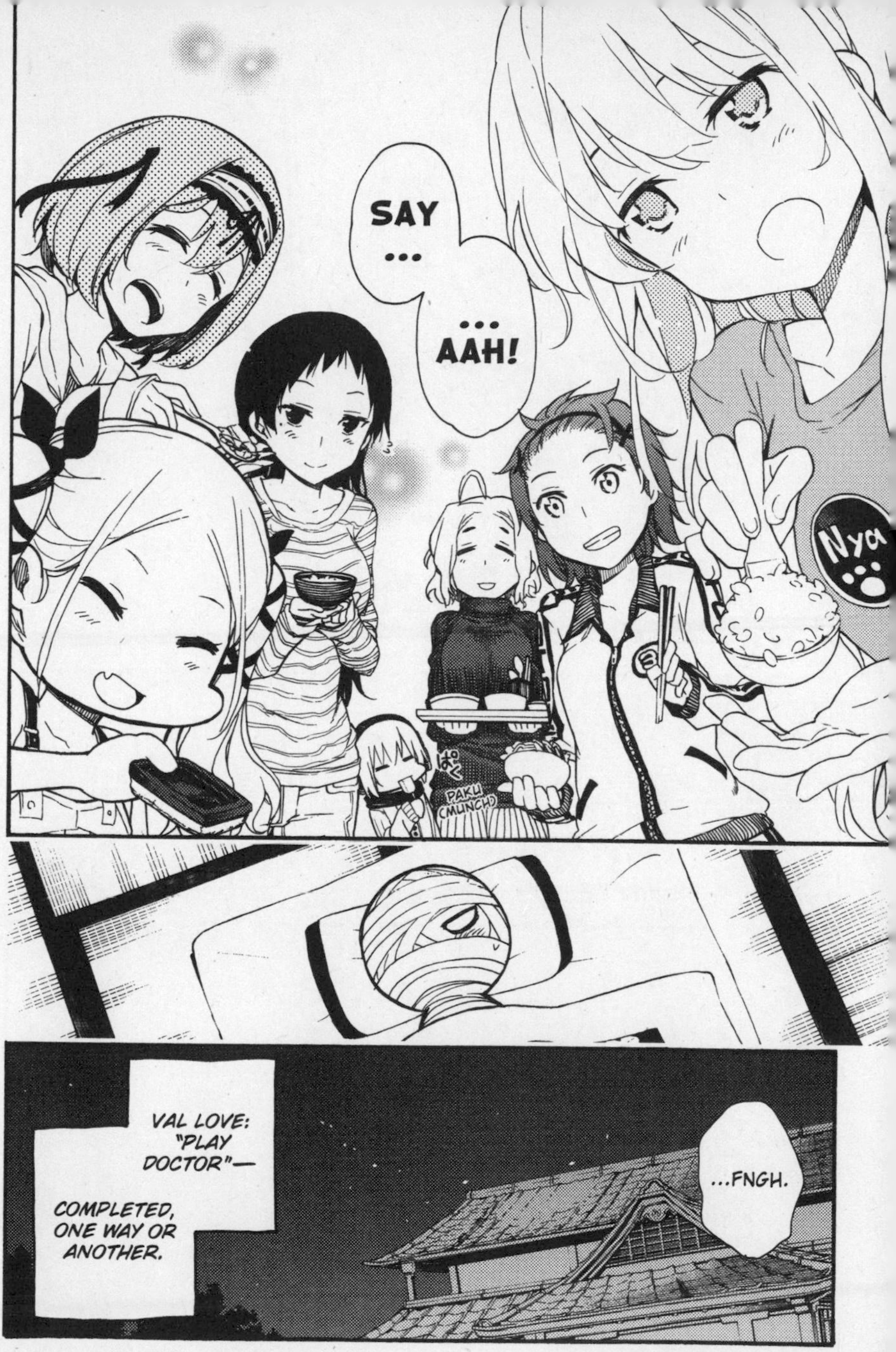
SAY ... ...AAH!
Nya
ぱく
PAKU (MUNCH)
...FNGH.
VAL LOVE: "PLAY DOCTOR"—
COMPLETED, ONE WAY OR ANOTHER.

Val × Love

A MYSTERIOUS LIST

PETA
ペ
た

PETA
(FLAT)
ペ
た

$6 > 2 \geqq 5 > 4 \geqq 1 \geqq 3 \ggg 7 > 8 > 9$

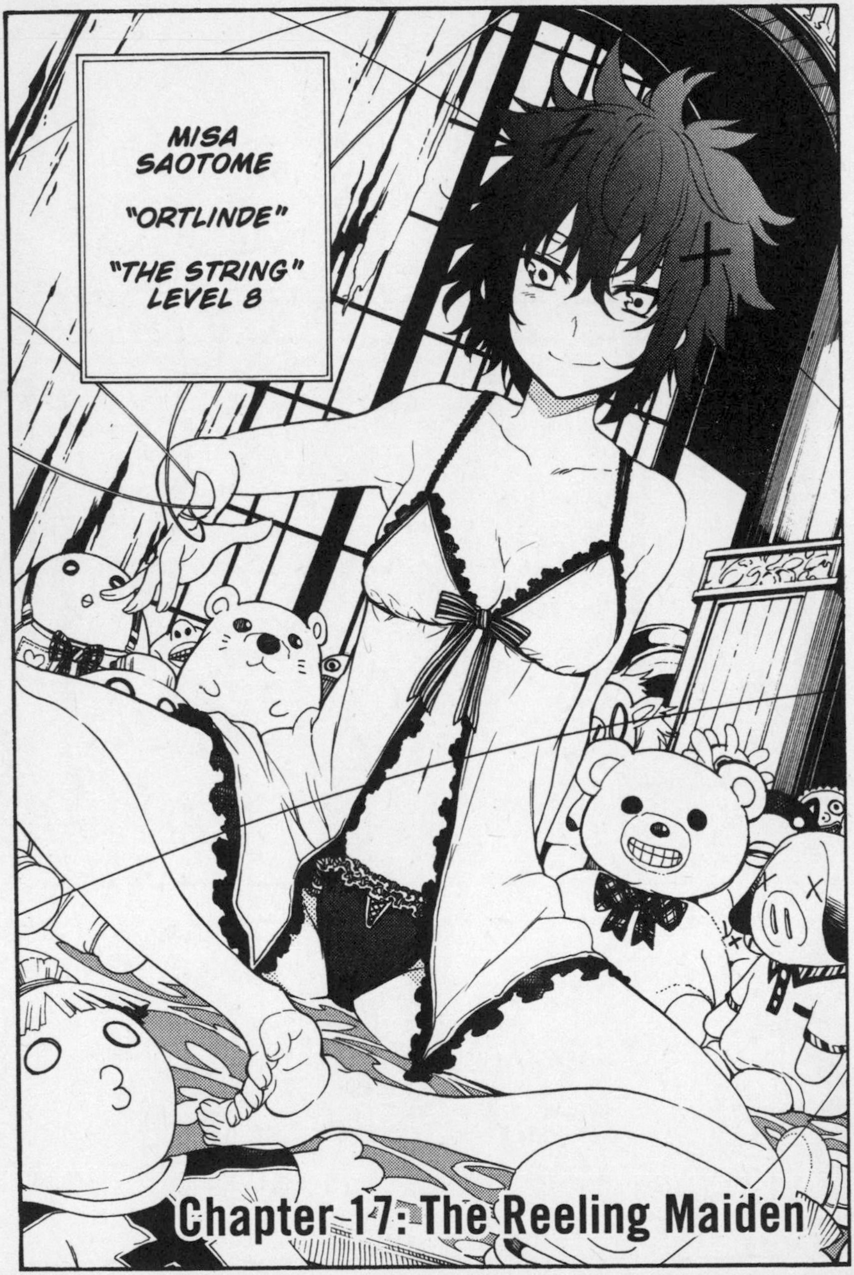
MISA SAOTOME
"ORTLINDE"
"THE STRING" LEVEL 8
Chapter 17: The Reeling Maiden

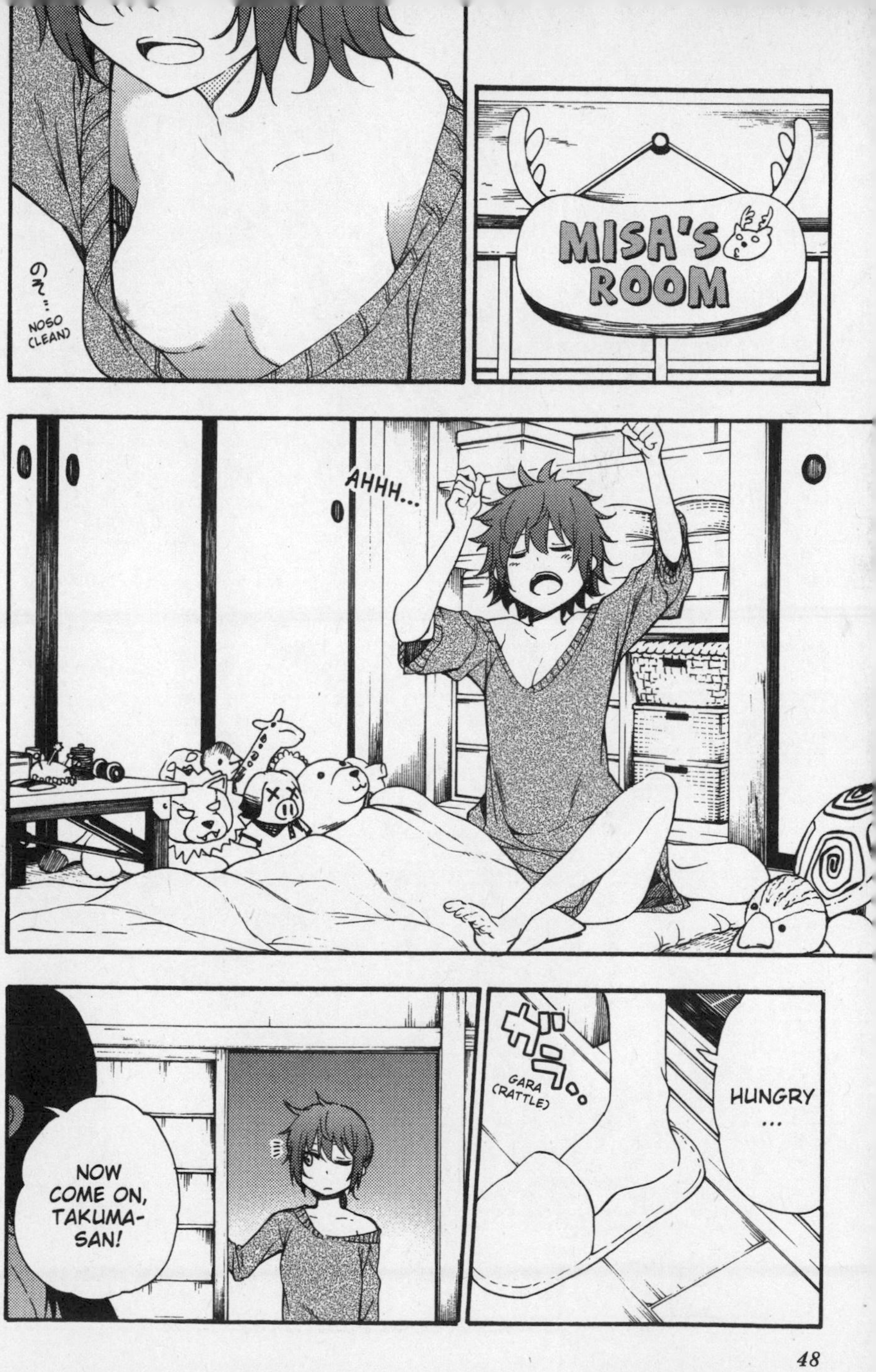
MISA'S ROOM
のそ…
NOSO (LEAN)
AHHH...
HUNGRY ...
ガラ。。
GARA (RATTLE)
NOW COME ON, TAKUMA-SAN!

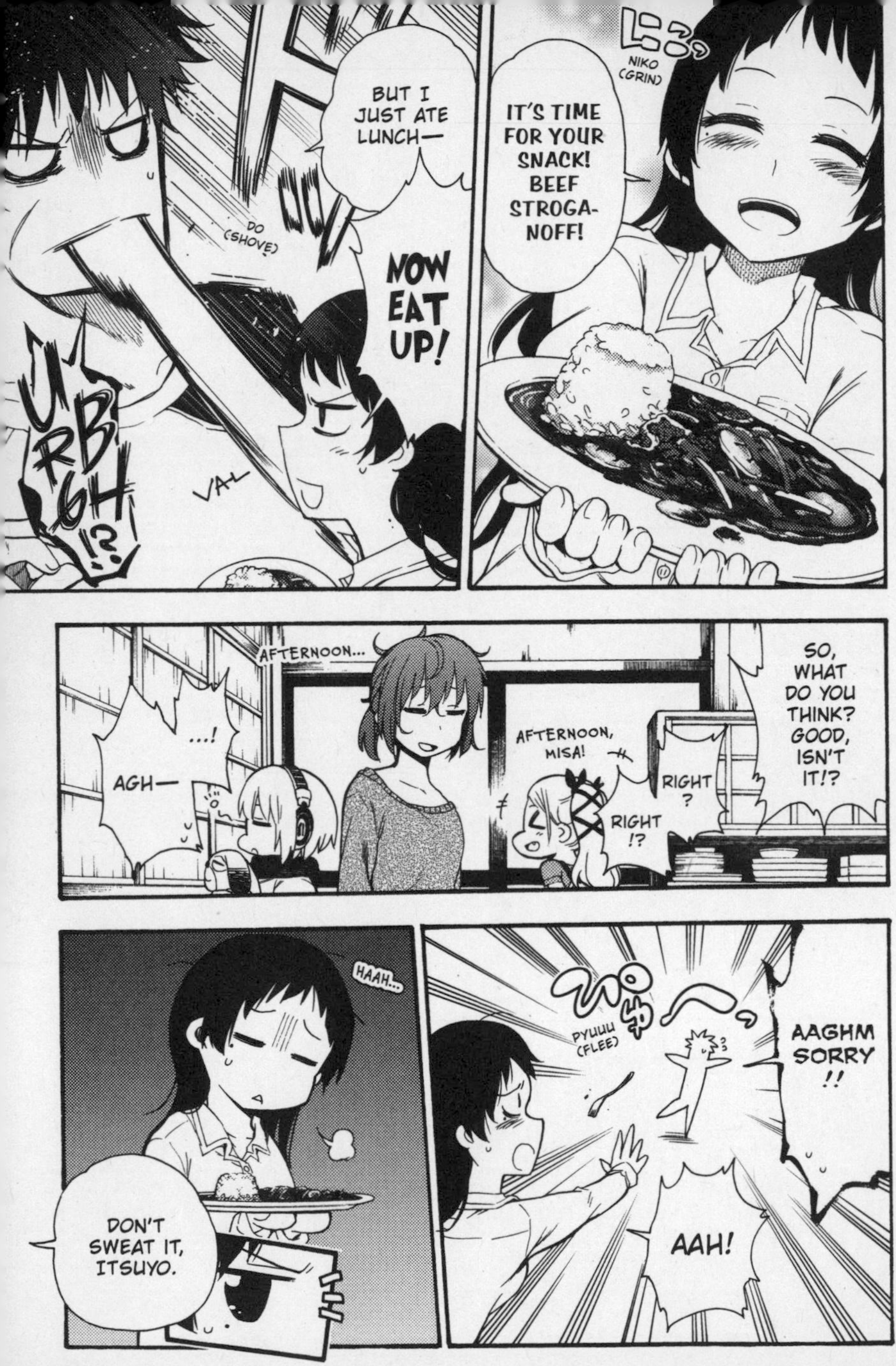
NIKO (GRIN)
IT'S TIME FOR YOUR SNACK! BEEF STROGA-NOFF!
BUT I JUST ATE LUNCH—
DO (SHOVE)
NOW EAT UP!
URBGH!?
SO, WHAT DO YOU THINK? GOOD, ISN'T IT!?
RIGHT?
RIGHT!?
AFTERNOON, MISA!
AFTERNOON...
...!
AGH—
AAGHM SORRY!!
PYUUU (FLEE)
AAH!
HAAH...
DON'T SWEAT IT, ITSUYO.

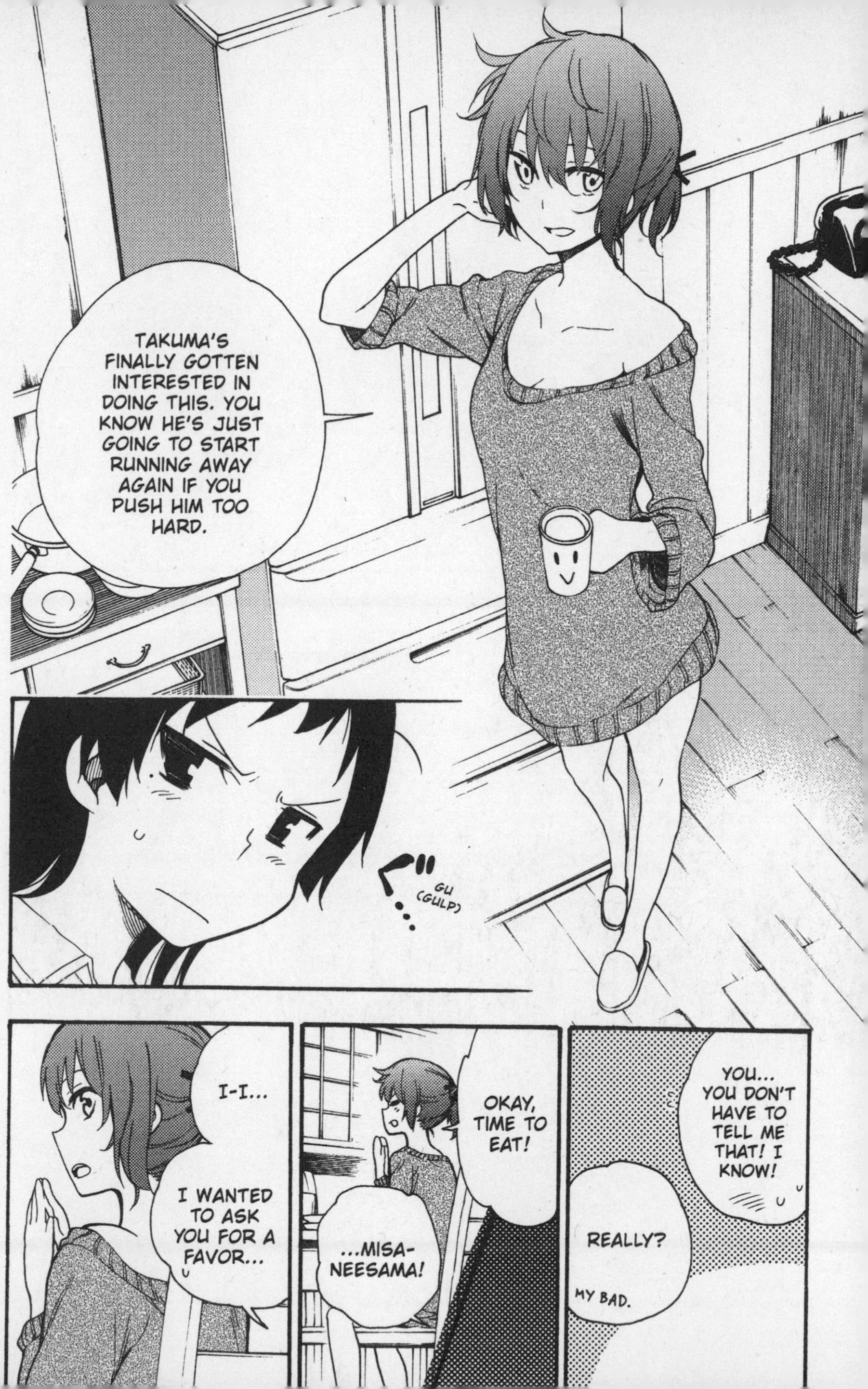
TAKUMA'S FINALLY GOTTEN INTERESTED IN DOING THIS. YOU KNOW HE'S JUST GOING TO START RUNNING AWAY AGAIN IF YOU PUSH HIM TOO HARD.
GU (GULP)
YOU... YOU DON'T HAVE TO TELL ME THAT! I KNOW!
REALLY?
MY BAD.
OKAY, TIME TO EAT!
...MISA-NEESAMA!
I-I...
I WANTED TO ASK YOU FOR A FAVOR...

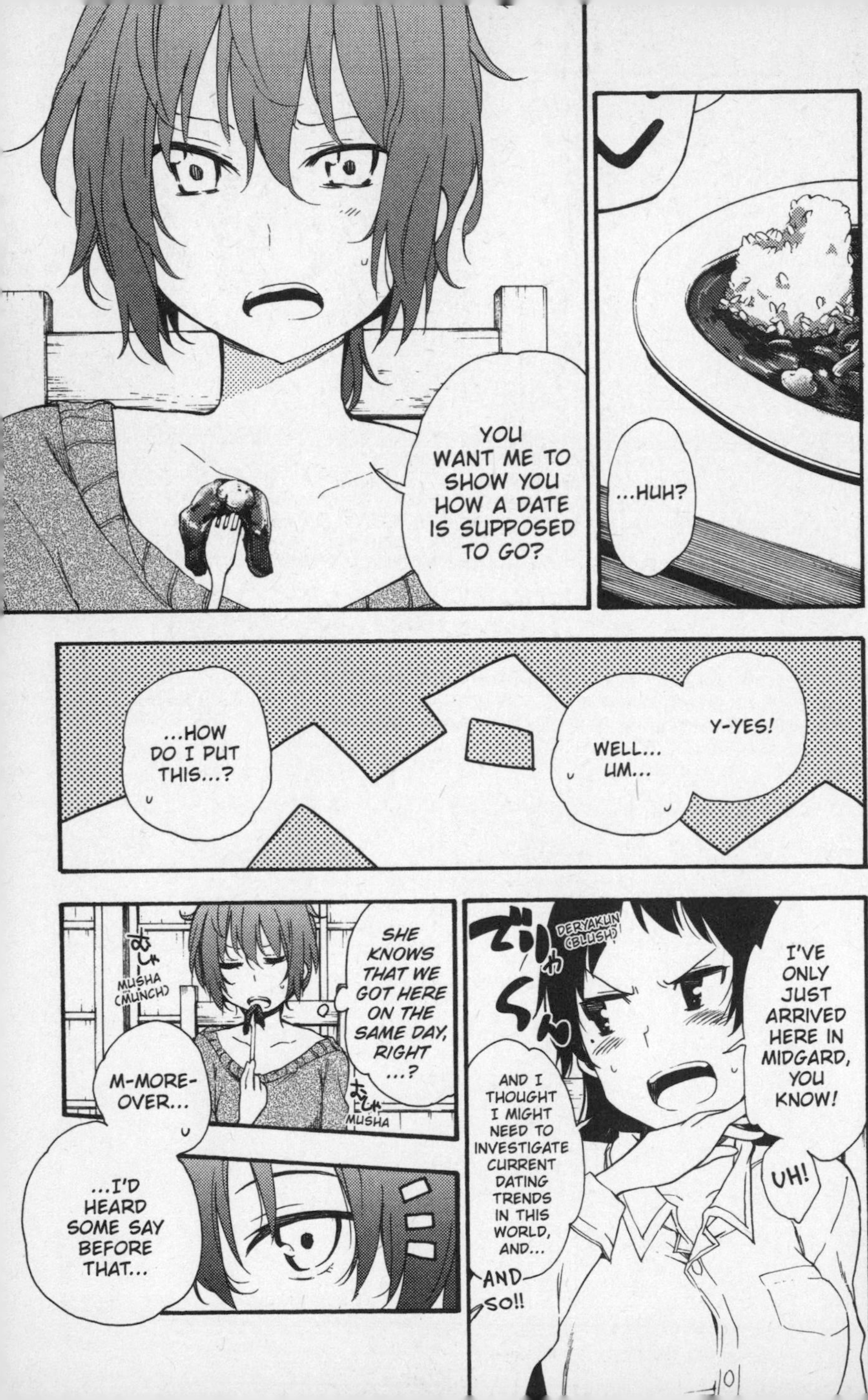
...HUH?
YOU WANT ME TO SHOW YOU HOW A DATE IS SUPPOSED TO GO?
Y-YES!
WELL... UM...
...HOW DO I PUT THIS...?
DERYAKUN (BLUSH)
I'VE ONLY JUST ARRIVED HERE IN MIDGARD, YOU KNOW!
UH!
AND I THOUGHT I MIGHT NEED TO INVESTIGATE CURRENT DATING TRENDS IN THIS WORLD, AND...
AND SO!!
MUSHA (MUNCH)
SHE KNOWS THAT WE GOT HERE ON THE SAME DAY, RIGHT...?
MUSHA
M-MORE-OVER...
...I'D HEARD SOME SAY BEFORE THAT...

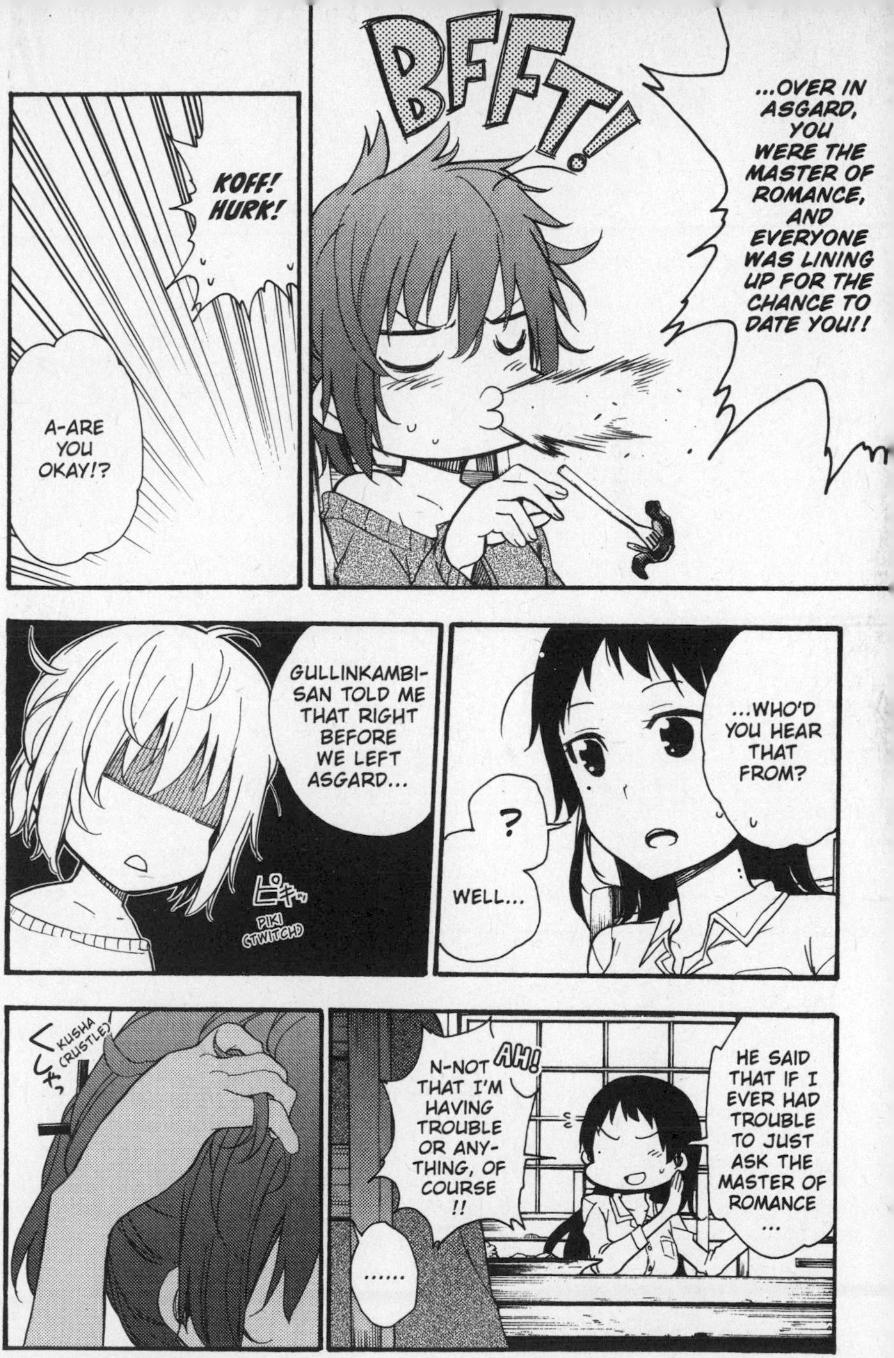

BFFT!!
...OVER IN ASGARD, YOU WERE THE MASTER OF ROMANCE, AND EVERYONE WAS LINING UP FOR THE CHANCE TO DATE YOU!!
KOFF! HURK!
A-ARE YOU OKAY!?
...WHO'D YOU HEAR THAT FROM?
?
WELL...
GULLINKAMBI-SAN TOLD ME THAT RIGHT BEFORE WE LEFT ASGARD...
ピキッ
PIKI (TWITCH)
HE SAID THAT IF I EVER HAD TROUBLE TO JUST ASK THE MASTER OF ROMANCE...
AH!
N-NOT THAT I'M HAVING TROUBLE OR ANYTHING, OF COURSE!!
......
くしゃっ
KUSHA (RUSTLE)

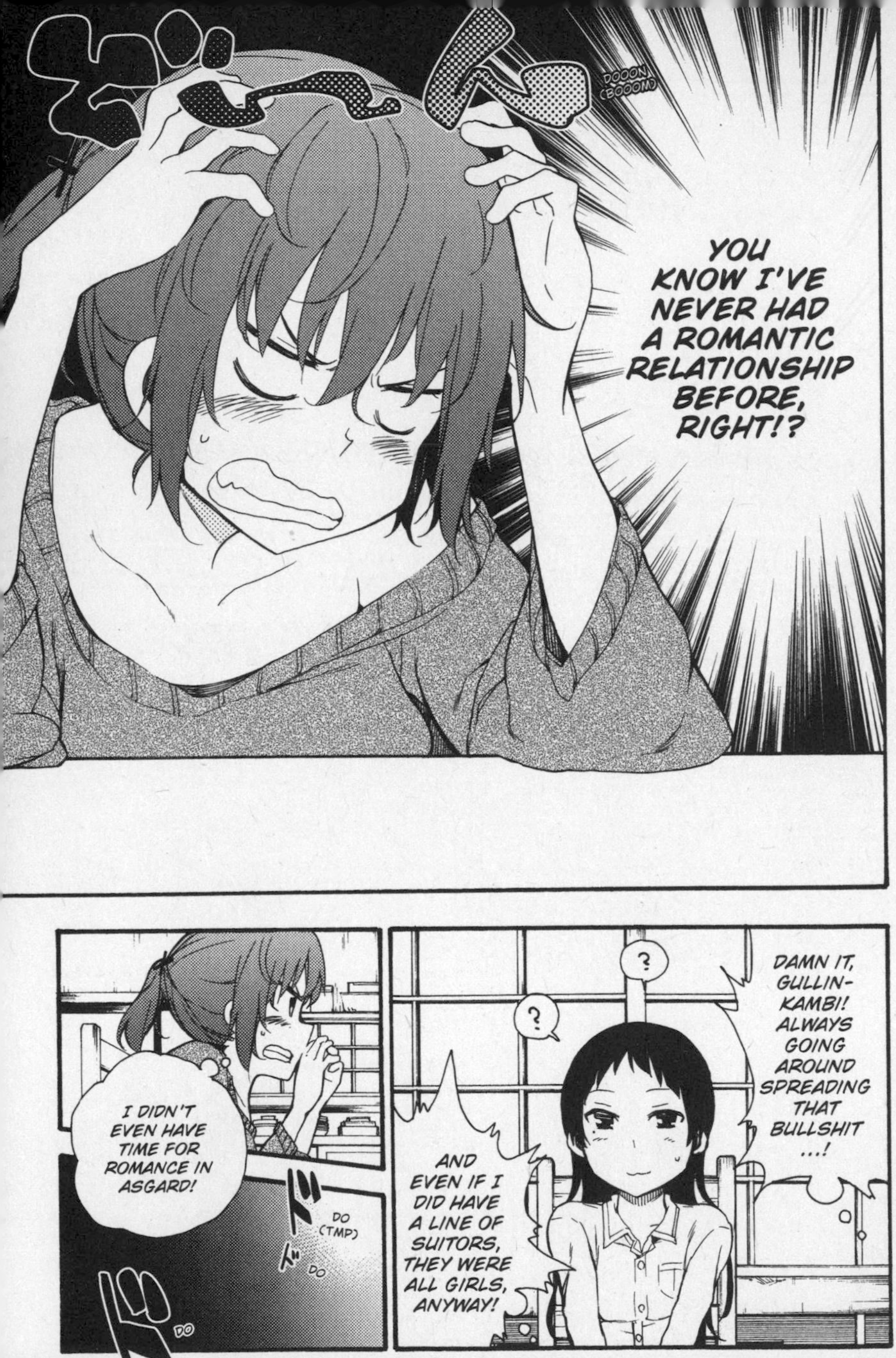
DOOON (BOOOM)
YOU KNOW I'VE NEVER HAD A ROMANTIC RELATIONSHIP BEFORE, RIGHT!?
?
?
DAMN IT, GULLIN-KAMBI! ALWAYS GOING AROUND SPREADING THAT BULLSHIT ...!
AND EVEN IF I DID HAVE A LINE OF SUITORS, THEY WERE ALL GIRLS, ANYWAY!
I DIDN'T EVEN HAVE TIME FOR ROMANCE IN ASGARD!
DO (TMP)
DO
DO

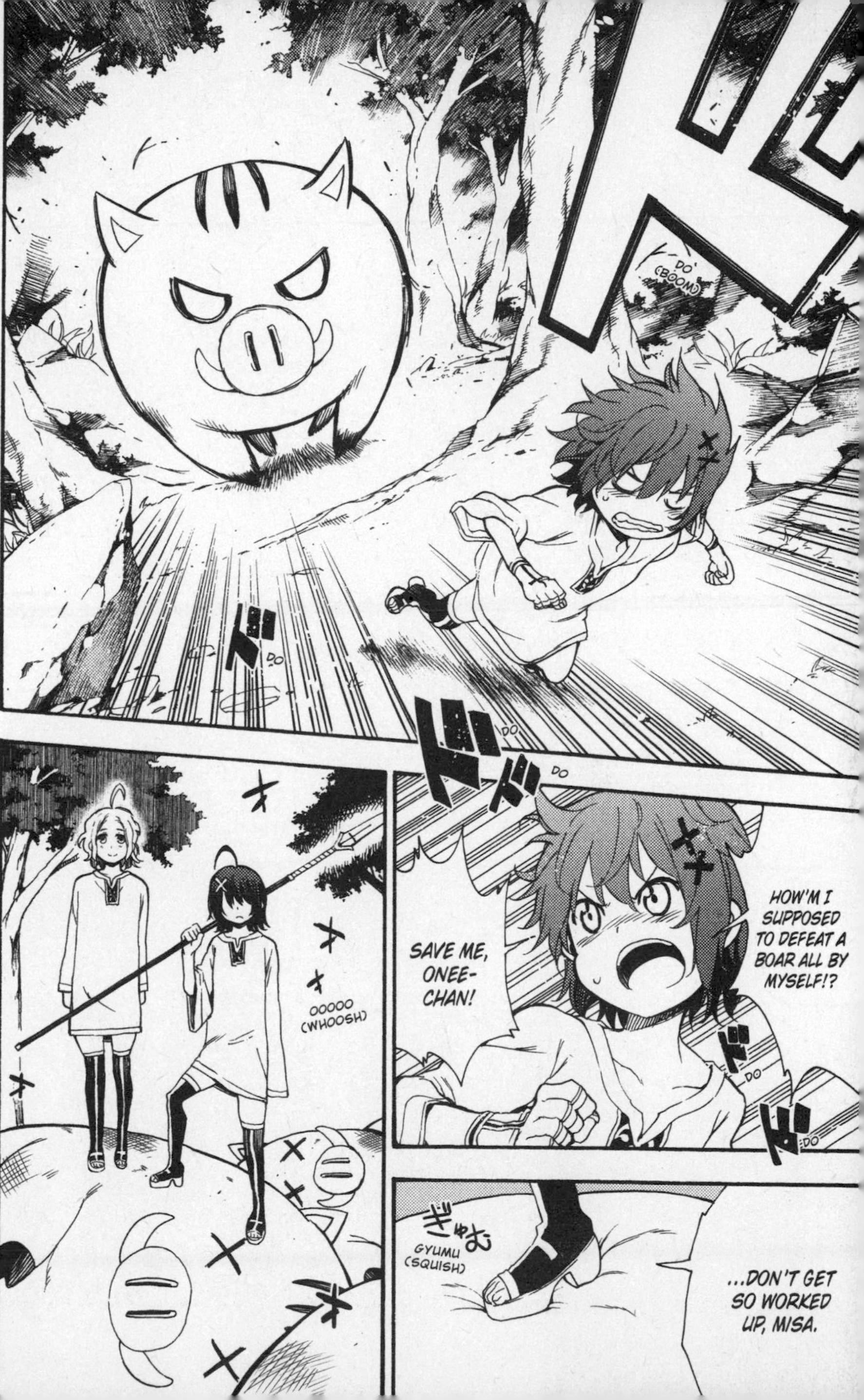
DO (BOOM)
DO
DO
DO
HOW'M I SUPPOSED TO DEFEAT A BOAR ALL BY MYSELF!?
SAVE ME, ONEE-CHAN!
DO
DO
...DON'T GET SO WORKED UP, MISA.
ぎゅむ
GYUMU (SQUISH)
OOOOO (WHOOSH)

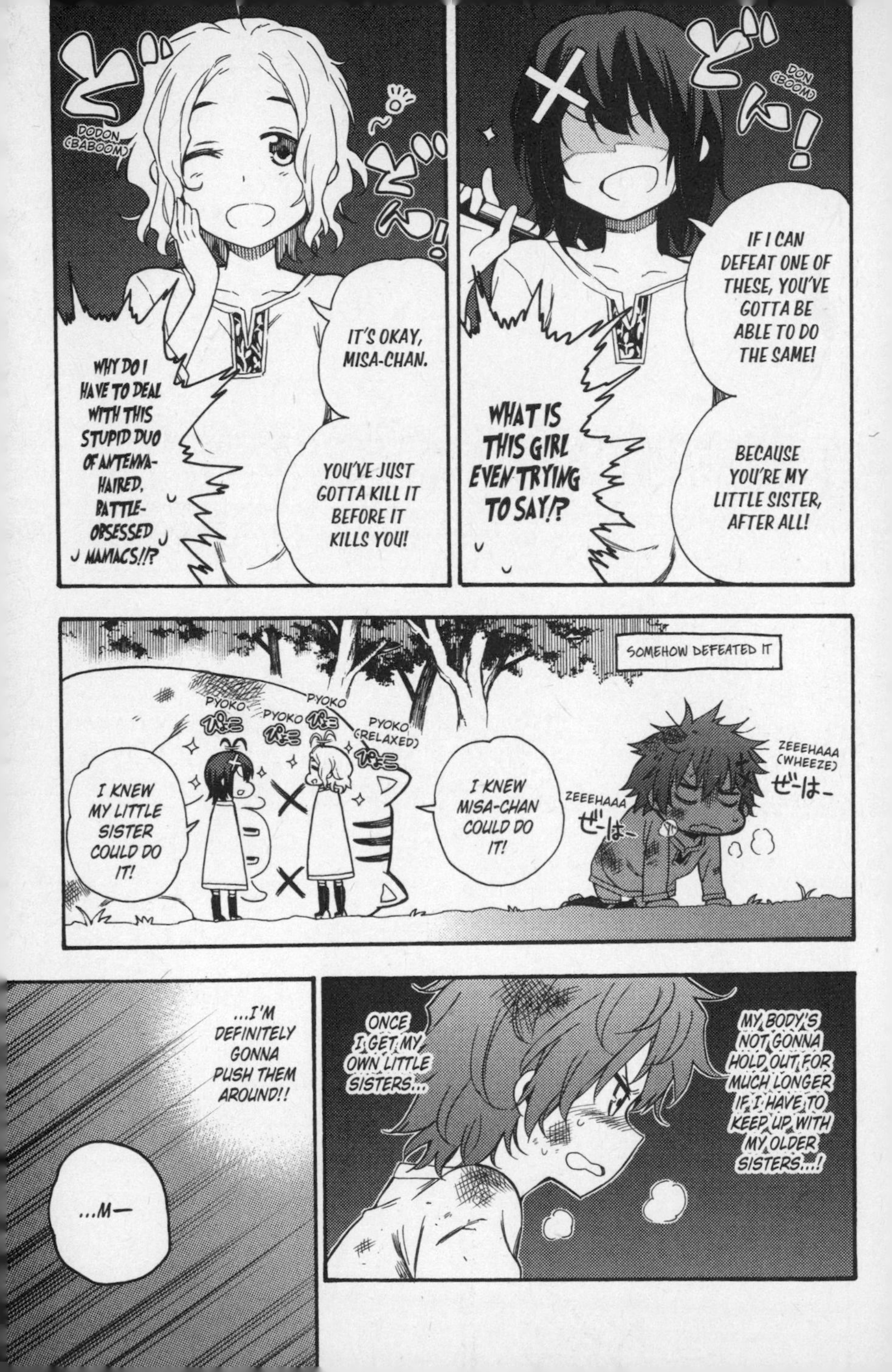
DON (BOOM)
どん！
IF I CAN DEFEAT ONE OF THESE, YOU'VE GOTTA BE ABLE TO DO THE SAME!
BECAUSE YOU'RE MY LITTLE SISTER, AFTER ALL!
WHAT IS THIS GIRL EVEN TRYING TO SAY!?
DODON (BABOOM)
IT'S OKAY, MISA-CHAN.
YOU'VE JUST GOTTA KILL IT BEFORE IT KILLS YOU!
WHY DO I HAVE TO DEAL WITH THIS STUPID DUO OF ANTENNA-HAIRED, BATTLE-OBSESSED MANIACS!!?
SOMEHOW DEFEATED IT
ZEEEHAAA (WHEEZE)
ぜーはー
ZEEEHAAA
ぜーはー
I KNEW MISA-CHAN COULD DO IT!
PYOKO (RELAXED)
PYOKO
PYOKO
I KNEW MY LITTLE SISTER COULD DO IT!
MY BODY'S NOT GONNA HOLD OUT FOR MUCH LONGER IF I HAVE TO KEEP UP WITH MY OLDER SISTERS...!
ONCE I GET MY OWN LITTLE SISTERS...
...I'M DEFINITELY GONNA PUSH THEM AROUND!!
...M—

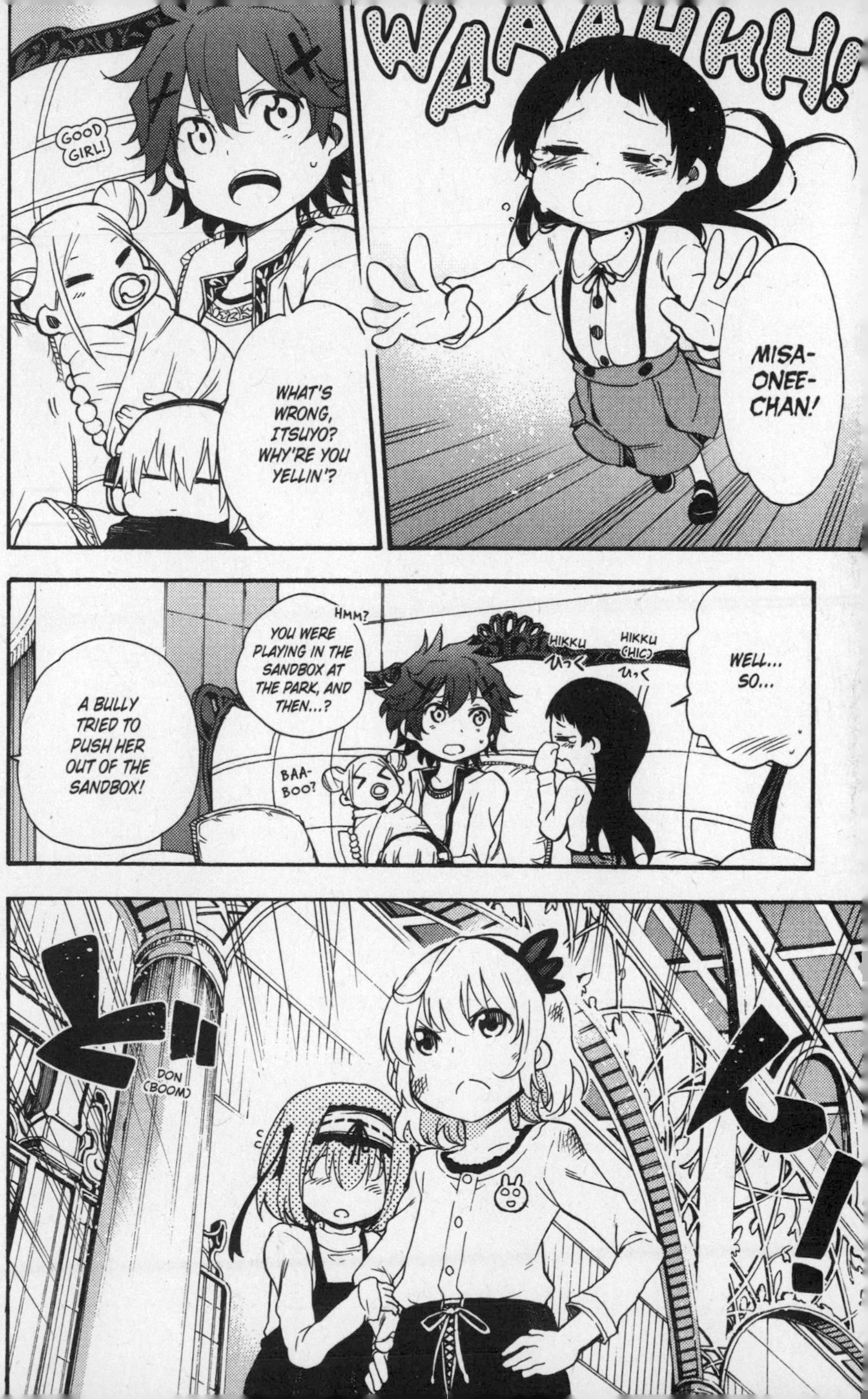
WAAAHHH!
MISA-ONEE-CHAN!
WHAT'S WRONG, ITSUYO? WHY'RE YOU YELLIN'?
GOOD GIRL!
WELL... SO...
HIKKU (HIC)
HIKKU
HMM?
YOU WERE PLAYING IN THE SANDBOX AT THE PARK, AND THEN...?
BAA-BOO?
A BULLY TRIED TO PUSH HER OUT OF THE SANDBOX!
DON (BOOM)

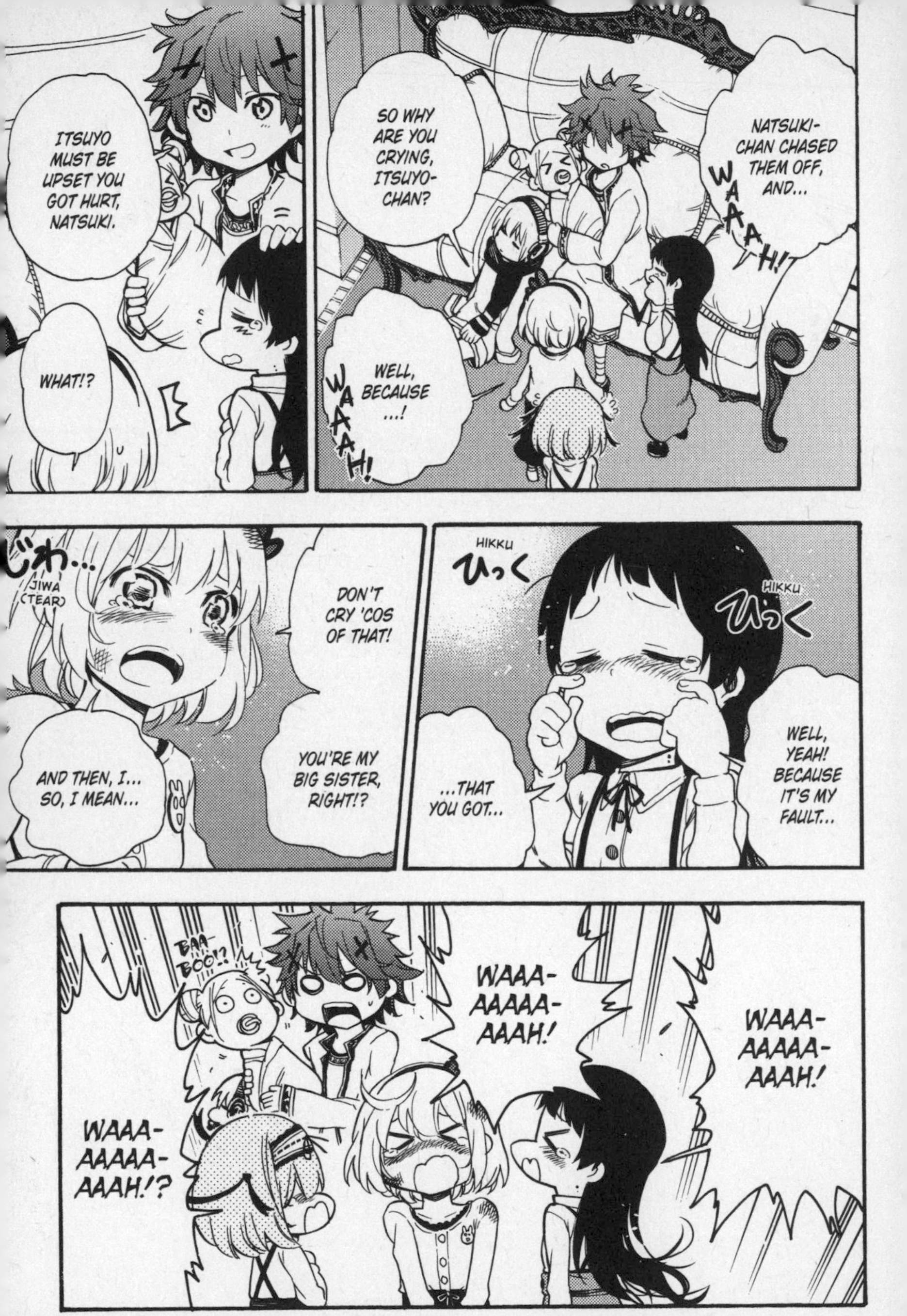
NATSUKI-CHAN CHASED THEM OFF, AND...
WAAAAH!
SO WHY ARE YOU CRYING, ITSUYO-CHAN?
WELL, BECAUSE ...!
WAAAAH!
ITSUYO MUST BE UPSET YOU GOT HURT, NATSUKI.
WHAT!?
HIKKU
ひっく
HIKKU
ひっく
WELL, YEAH! BECAUSE IT'S MY FAULT...
...THAT YOU GOT...
じわ...
JIWA (TEAR)
DON'T CRY 'COS OF THAT!
YOU'RE MY BIG SISTER, RIGHT!?
AND THEN, I... SO, I MEAN...
WAAA-AAAAA-AAAH!
WAAA-AAAAA-AAAH!
BAA-BOO!?
WAAA-AAAAA-AAAH!?

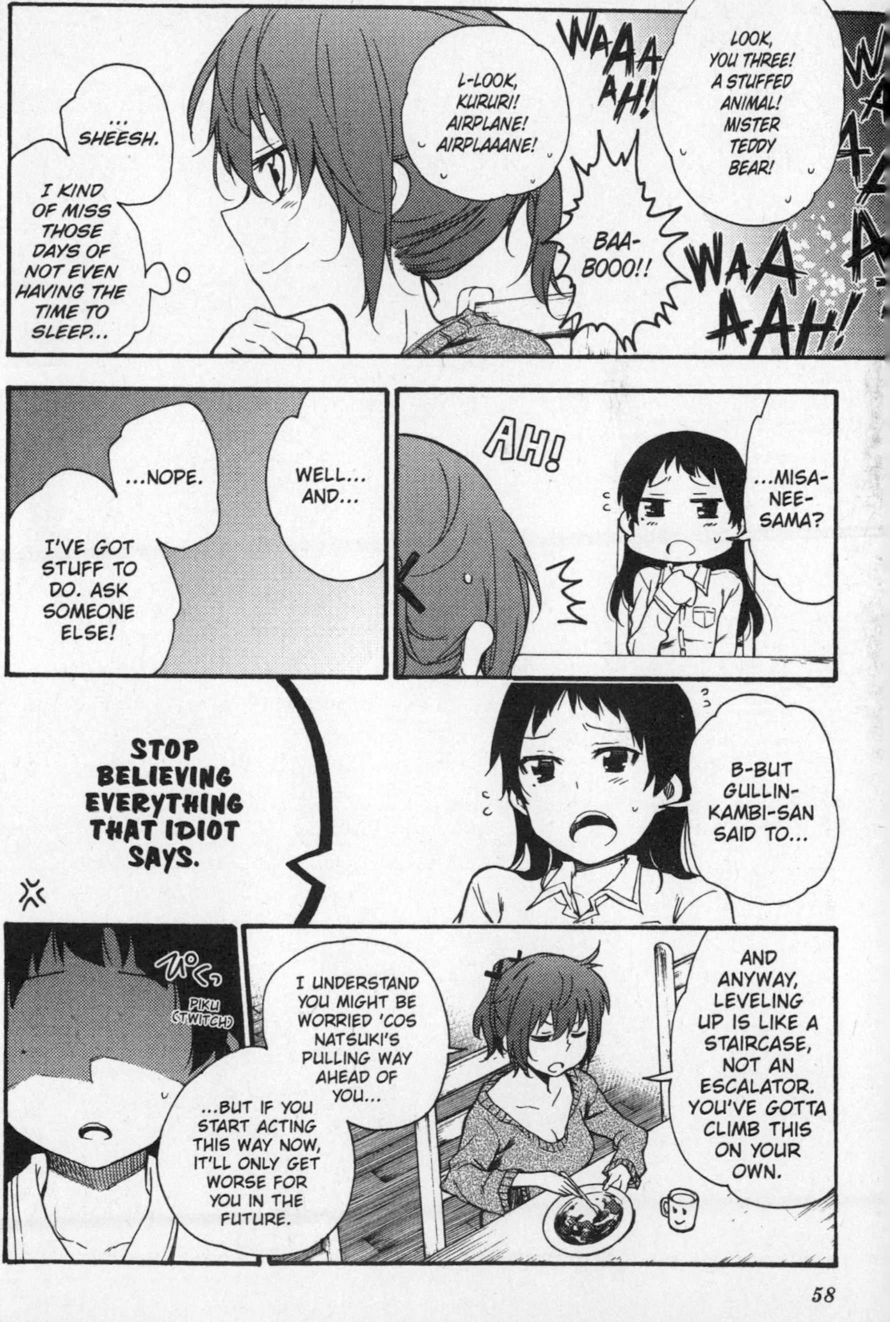
LOOK, YOU THREE! A STUFFED ANIMAL! MISTER TEDDY BEAR!
WAAAAH!
WAAAAH!
L-LOOK, KURURI! AIRPLANE! AIRPLAAANE!
BAA-BOOO!!
...SHEESH.
I KIND OF MISS THOSE DAYS OF NOT EVEN HAVING THE TIME TO SLEEP...
...MISA-NEE-SAMA?
AH!
WELL... AND...
...NOPE.
I'VE GOT STUFF TO DO. ASK SOMEONE ELSE!
B-BUT GULLIN-KAMBI-SAN SAID TO...
STOP BELIEVING EVERYTHING THAT IDIOT SAYS.
AND ANYWAY, LEVELING UP IS LIKE A STAIRCASE, NOT AN ESCALATOR. YOU'VE GOTTA CLIMB THIS ON YOUR OWN.
I UNDERSTAND YOU MIGHT BE WORRIED 'COS NATSUKI'S PULLING WAY AHEAD OF YOU...
...BUT IF YOU START ACTING THIS WAY NOW, IT'LL ONLY GET WORSE FOR YOU IN THE FUTURE.
ぴくっ
PIKU (TWITCH)

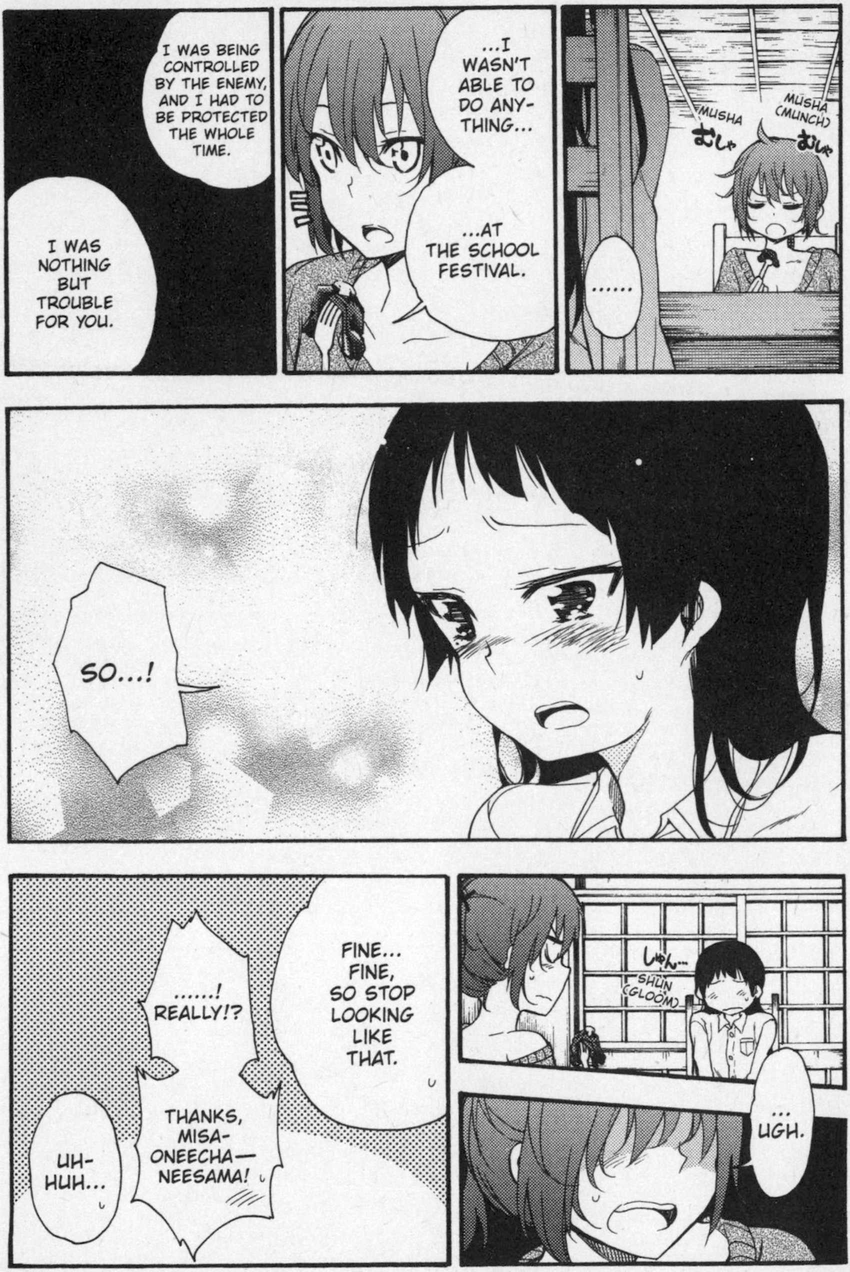

むしゃ
MUSHA (MUNCH)
むしゃ
MUSHA
......
...I WASN'T ABLE TO DO ANY-THING...
...AT THE SCHOOL FESTIVAL.
I WAS BEING CONTROLLED BY THE ENEMY, AND I HAD TO BE PROTECTED THE WHOLE TIME.
I WAS NOTHING BUT TROUBLE FOR YOU.
SO...!
しゅん…
SHUN (GLOOM)
...UGH.
FINE... FINE, SO STOP LOOKING LIKE THAT.
......! REALLY!?
THANKS, MISA-ONEECHA—NEESAMA!
UH-HUH...

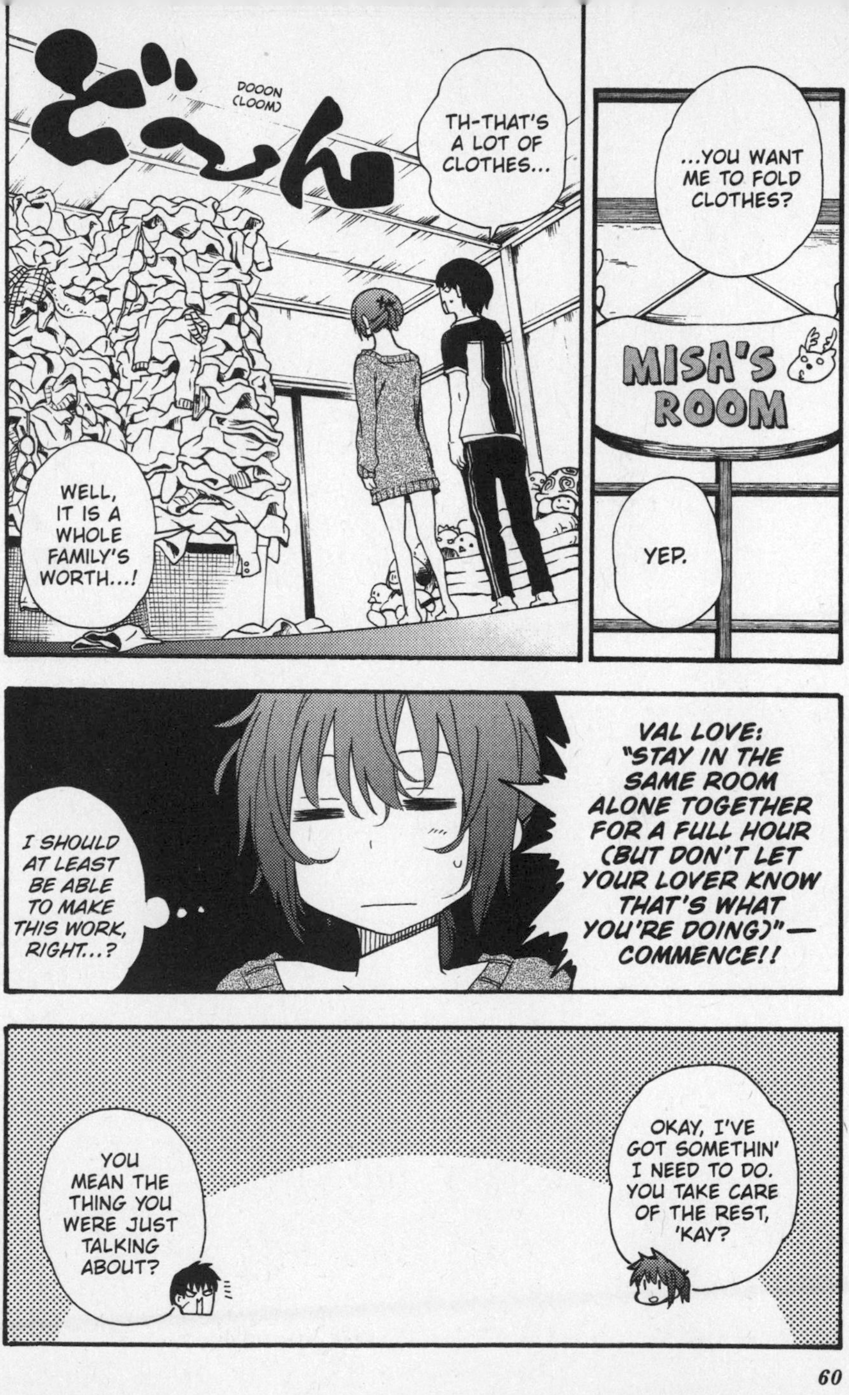
...YOU WANT ME TO FOLD CLOTHES?
MISA'S ROOM
YEP.
どーん
DOOON (LOOM)
TH-THAT'S A LOT OF CLOTHES...
WELL, IT IS A WHOLE FAMILY'S WORTH...!
VAL LOVE: "STAY IN THE SAME ROOM ALONE TOGETHER FOR A FULL HOUR (BUT DON'T LET YOUR LOVER KNOW THAT'S WHAT YOU'RE DOING)"—COMMENCE!!
I SHOULD AT LEAST BE ABLE TO MAKE THIS WORK, RIGHT...?
OKAY, I'VE GOT SOMETHIN' I NEED TO DO. YOU TAKE CARE OF THE REST, 'KAY?
YOU MEAN THE THING YOU WERE JUST TALKING ABOUT?

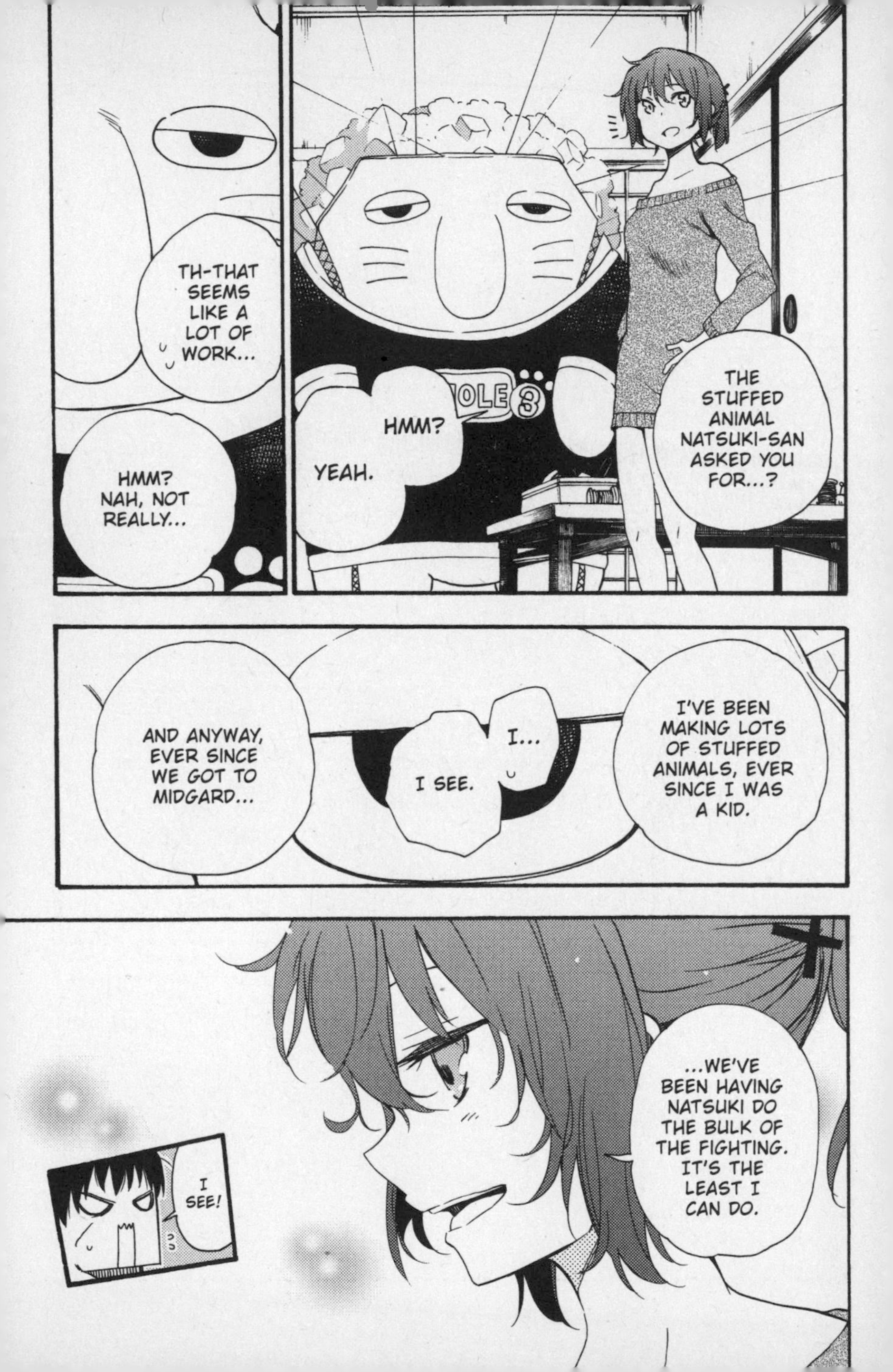
THE STUFFED ANIMAL NATSUKI-SAN ASKED YOU FOR...?
HMM?
YEAH.
TH-THAT SEEMS LIKE A LOT OF WORK...
HMM? NAH, NOT REALLY...
I'VE BEEN MAKING LOTS OF STUFFED ANIMALS, EVER SINCE I WAS A KID.
I... I SEE.
AND ANYWAY, EVER SINCE WE GOT TO MIDGARD...
...WE'VE BEEN HAVING NATSUKI DO THE BULK OF THE FIGHTING. IT'S THE LEAST I CAN DO.
I SEE!

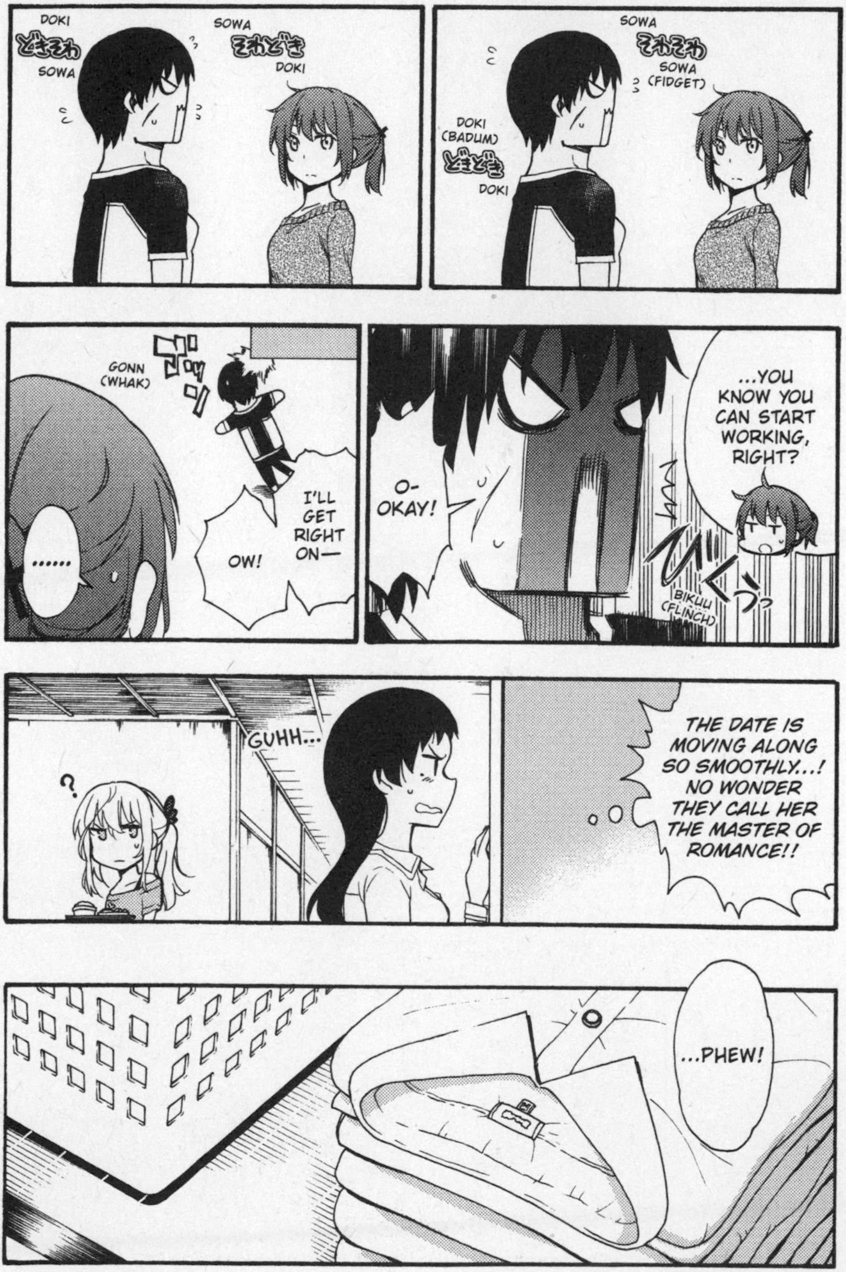
SOWA
そわそわ
SOWA (FIDGET)
DOKI (BADUM)
どきどき
DOKI
DOKI
どきそわ
SOWA
SOWA
そわどき
DOKI
...YOU KNOW YOU CAN START WORKING, RIGHT?
O-OKAY!
BIKUU (FLINCH)
GONN (WHAK)
I'LL GET RIGHT ON—
OW!
......
THE DATE IS MOVING ALONG SO SMOOTHLY...! NO WONDER THEY CALL HER THE MASTER OF ROMANCE!!
GUHH...
?
...PHEW!

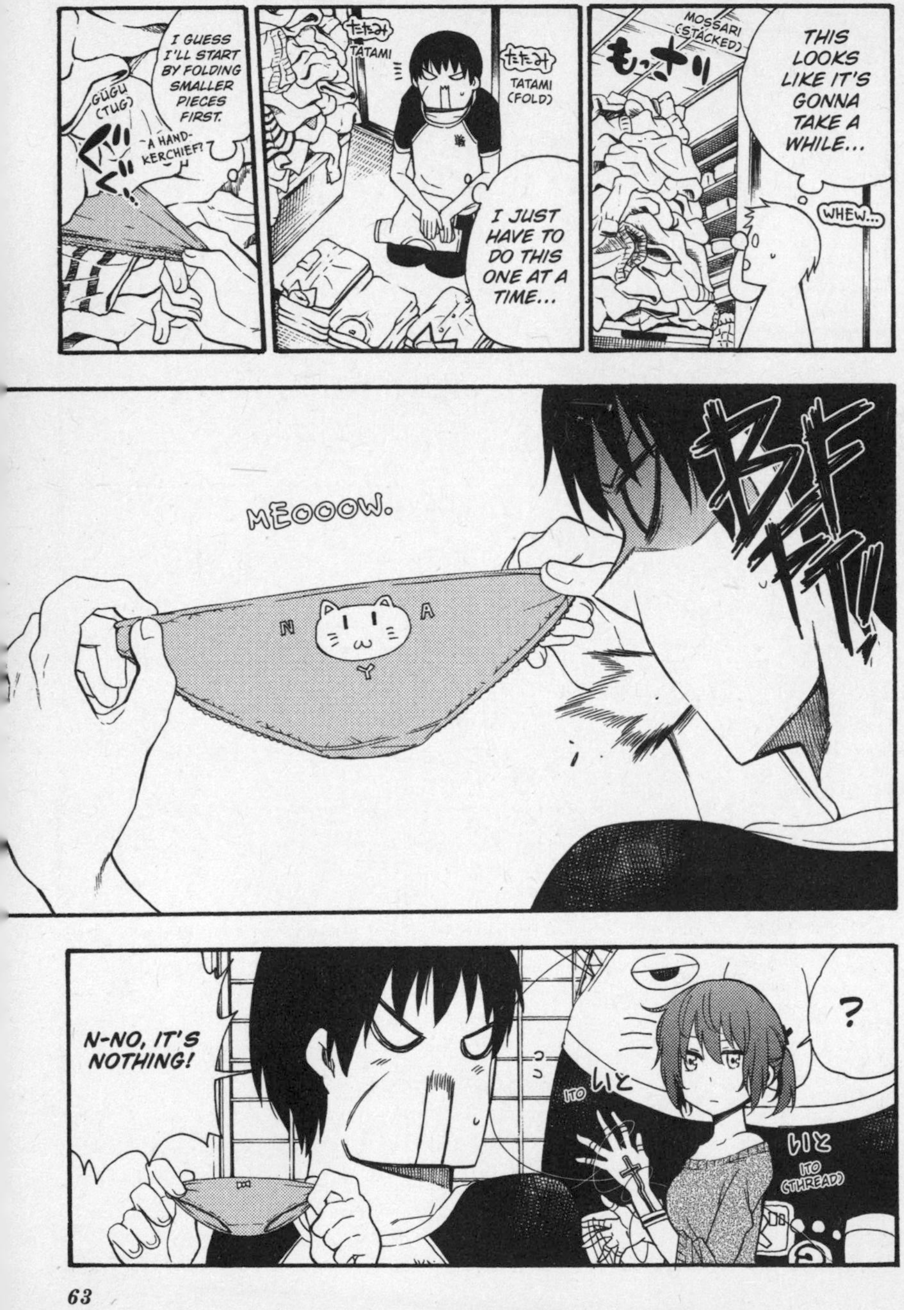
もっさり
MOSSARI (STACKED)
THIS LOOKS LIKE IT'S GONNA TAKE A WHILE...
WHEW...
たたみ
TATAMI
たたみ
TATAMI (FOLD)
I JUST HAVE TO DO THIS ONE AT A TIME...
I GUESS I'LL START BY FOLDING SMALLER PIECES FIRST.
GUGU (TUG)
A HAND-KERCHIEF?
MEOOOW.
N A Y
?
いと
ITO
いと
ITO (THREAD)
N-NO, IT'S NOTHING!

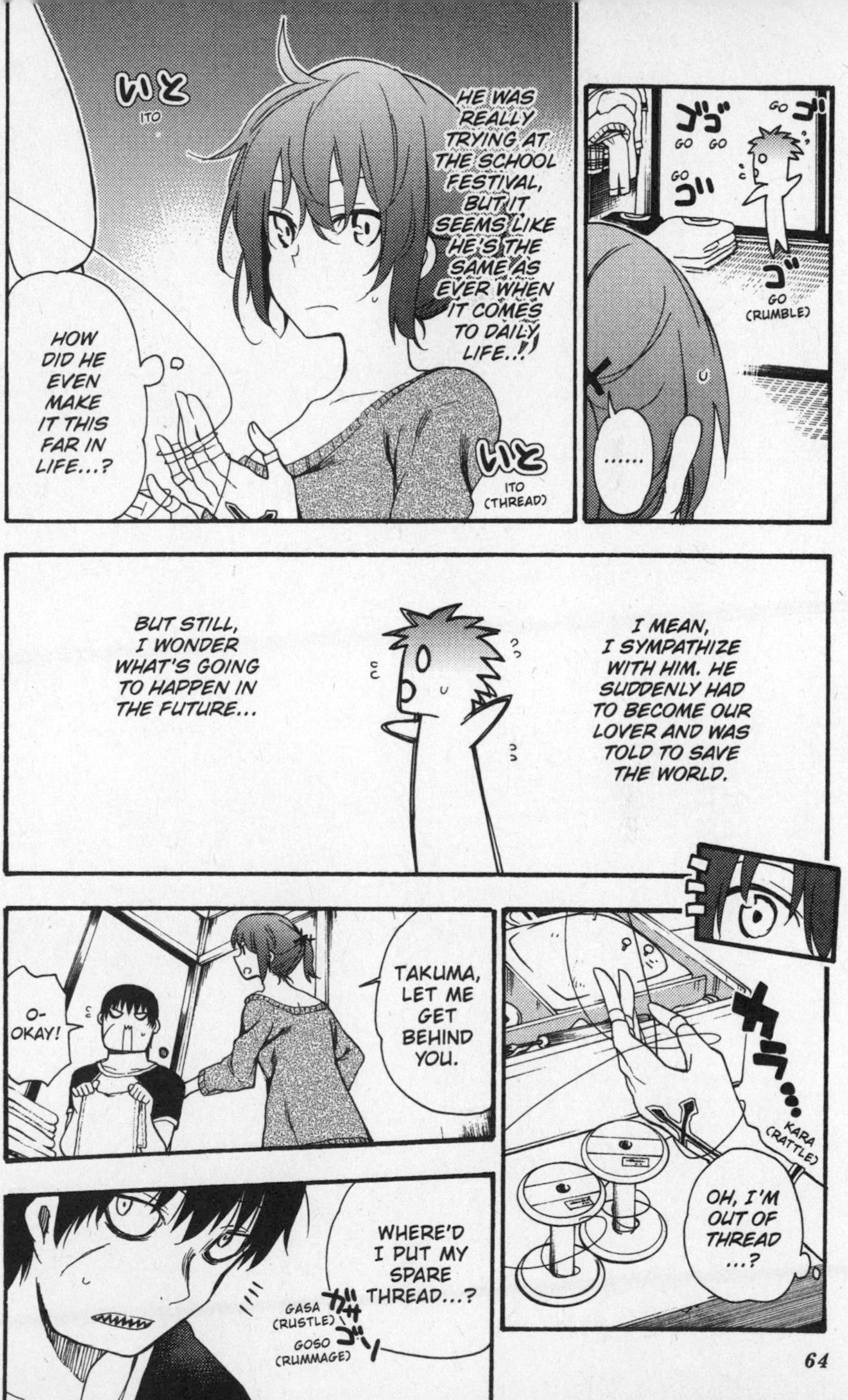
GO GO
GO GO
GO
GO
(RUMBLE)
......
HE WAS REALLY TRYING AT THE SCHOOL FESTIVAL, BUT IT SEEMS LIKE HE'S THE SAME AS EVER WHEN IT COMES TO DAILY LIFE...!
ITO
ITO (THREAD)
HOW DID HE EVEN MAKE IT THIS FAR IN LIFE...?
I MEAN, I SYMPATHIZE WITH HIM. HE SUDDENLY HAD TO BECOME OUR LOVER AND WAS TOLD TO SAVE THE WORLD.
BUT STILL, I WONDER WHAT'S GOING TO HAPPEN IN THE FUTURE...
KARA (RATTLE)
OH, I'M OUT OF THREAD...?
TAKUMA, LET ME GET BEHIND YOU.
O-OKAY!
WHERE'D I PUT MY SPARE THREAD...?
GASA (RUSTLE)
GOSO (RUMMAGE)

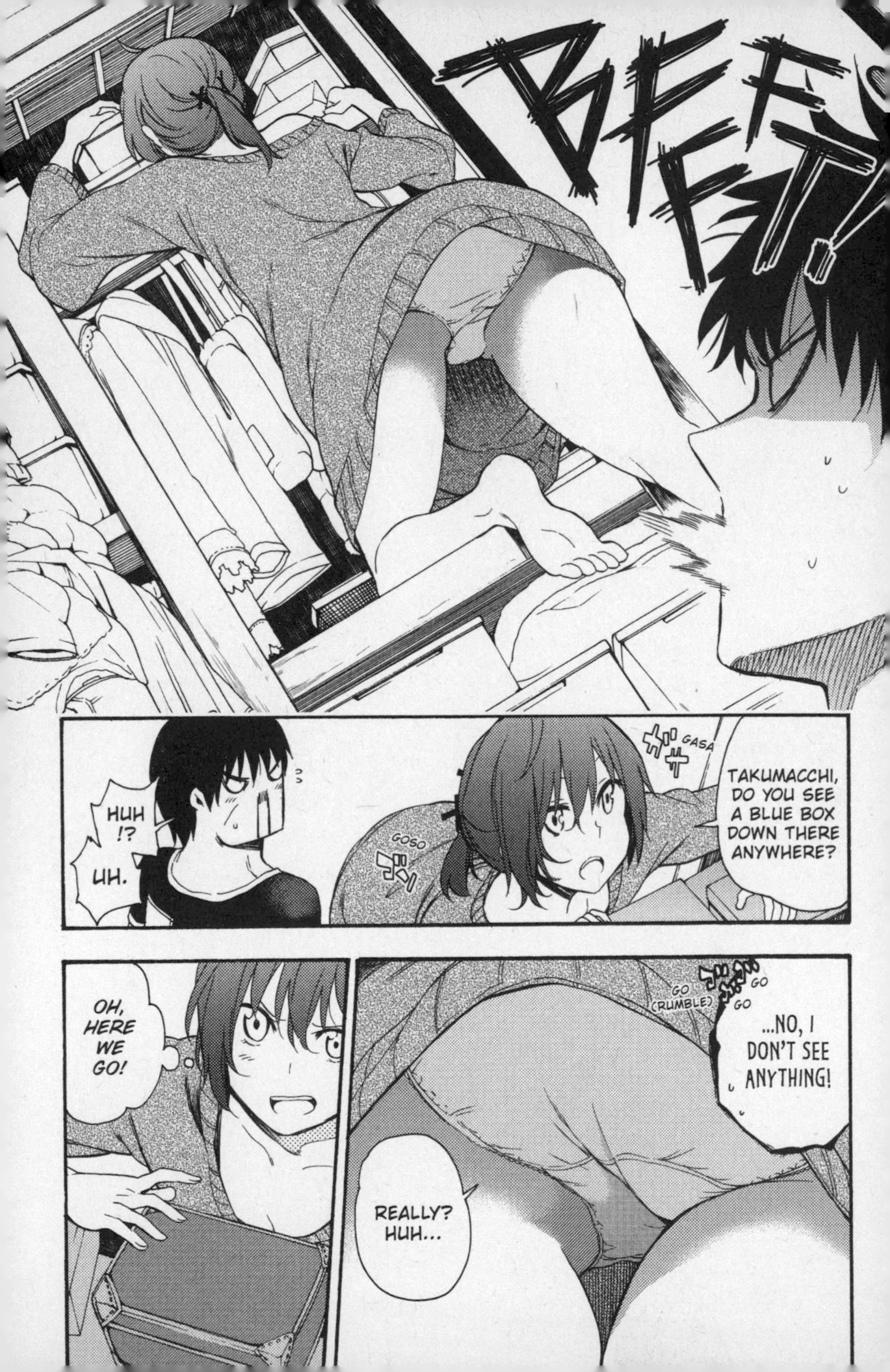
BAFFT!
GASA
TAKUMACCHI, DO YOU SEE A BLUE BOX DOWN THERE ANYWHERE?
GOSO
HUH !?
UH.
GO GO GO (RUMBLE)
...NO, I DON'T SEE ANYTHING!
REALLY? HUH...
OH, HERE WE GO!

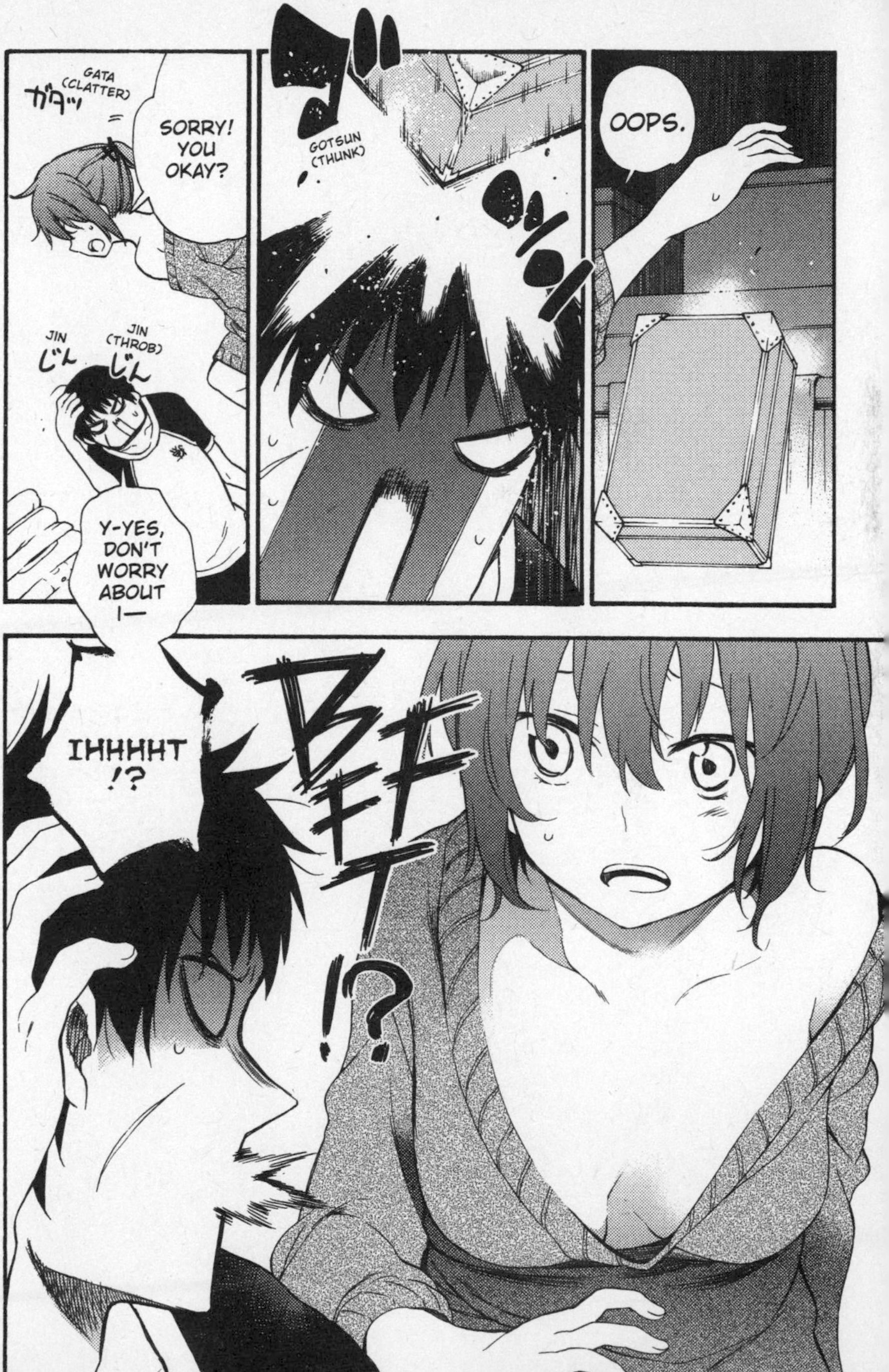
OOPS.
GOTSUN (THUNK)
ゴツン
GATA (CLATTER)
ガタッ
SORRY! YOU OKAY?
JIN じん
JIN (THROB) じん
Y-YES, DON'T WORRY ABOUT I—
IHHHT !?
BFFT!?

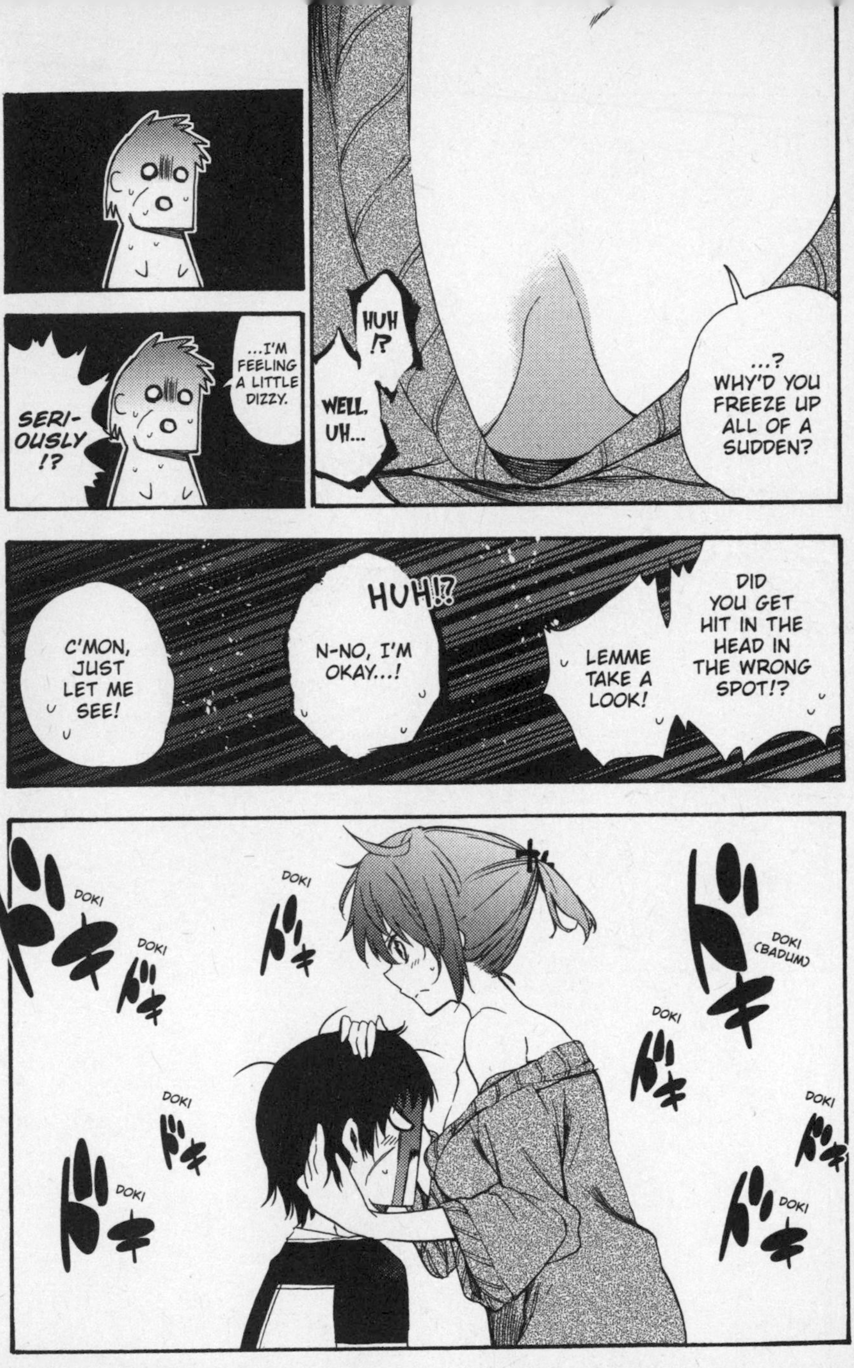
...? WHY'D YOU FREEZE UP ALL OF A SUDDEN?
HUH!?
WELL, UH...
...I'M FEELING A LITTLE DIZZY.
SERI-OUSLY!?
DID YOU GET HIT IN THE HEAD IN THE WRONG SPOT!?
LEMME TAKE A LOOK!
HUH!?
N-NO, I'M OKAY...!
C'MON, JUST LET ME SEE!
DOKI (BADUM)
DOKI
DOKI
DOKI
DOKI
DOKI
DOKI
DOKI
DOKI

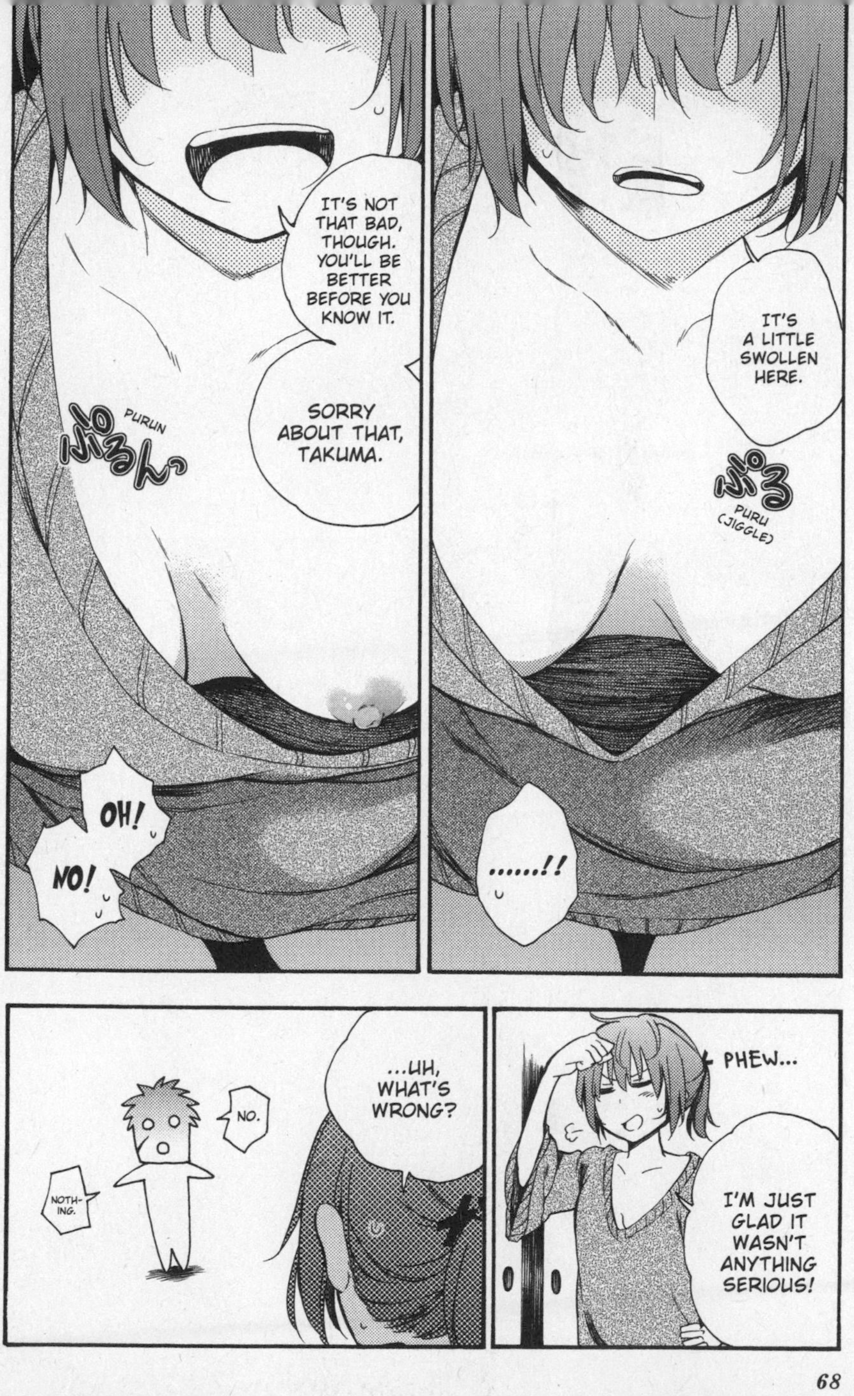
IT'S A LITTLE SWOLLEN HERE.
ぷる
PURU (JIGGLE)
......!!
IT'S NOT THAT BAD, THOUGH. YOU'LL BE BETTER BEFORE YOU KNOW IT.
SORRY ABOUT THAT, TAKUMA.
ぷるん
PURUN
OH!
NO!
PHEW...
I'M JUST GLAD IT WASN'T ANYTHING SERIOUS!
...UH, WHAT'S WRONG?
NO.
NOTH-ING.

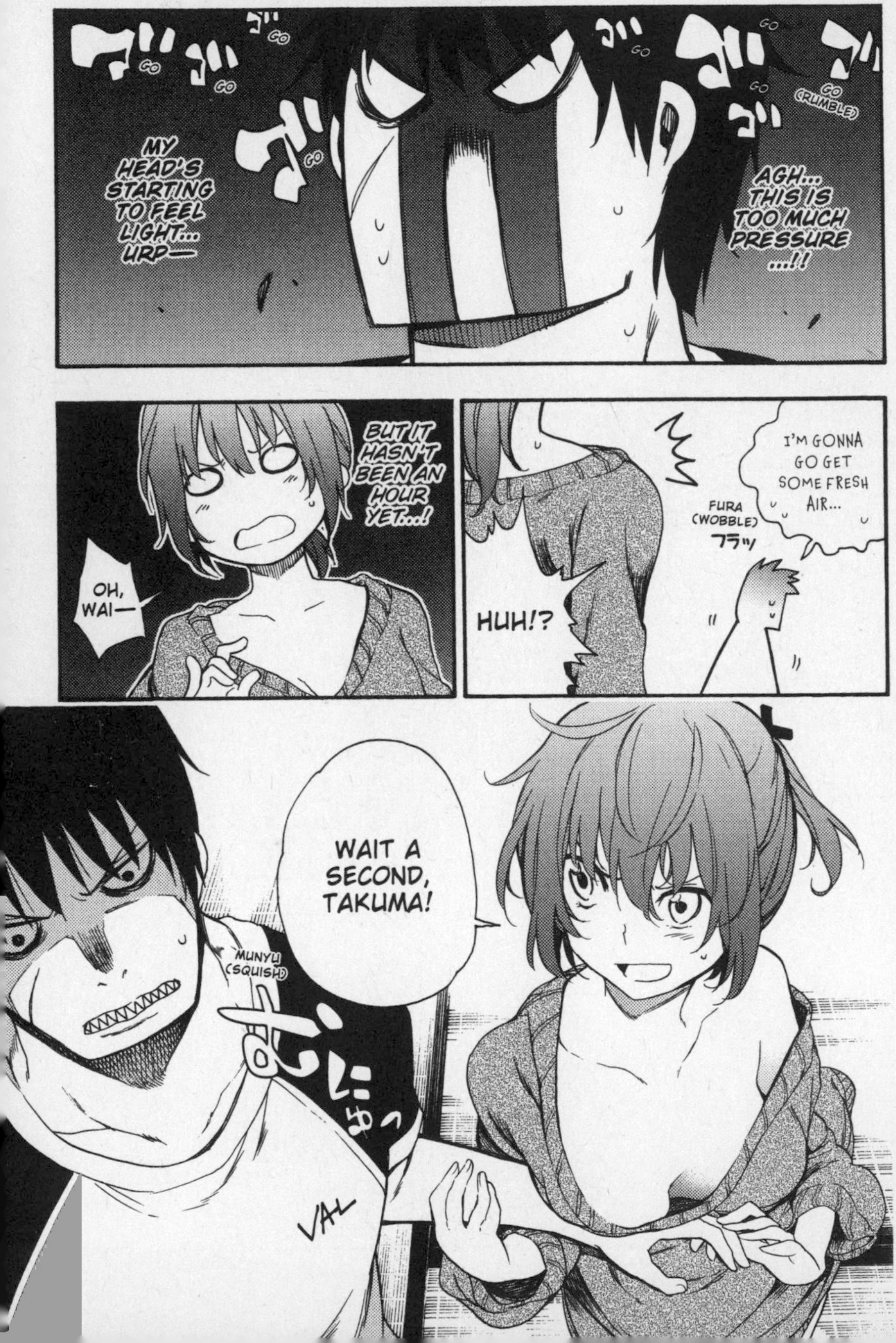
GO (RUMBLE)
GO
GO
GO
AGH... THIS IS TOO MUCH PRESSURE ...!!
GO
GO
GO
GO
MY HEAD'S STARTING TO FEEL LIGHT... URP—
I'M GONNA GO GET SOME FRESH AIR...
FURA (WOBBLE) フラッ
HUH!?
BUT IT HASN'T BEEN AN HOUR YET...!
OH, WAI—
WAIT A SECOND, TAKUMA!
MUNYU (SQUISH)
VAL

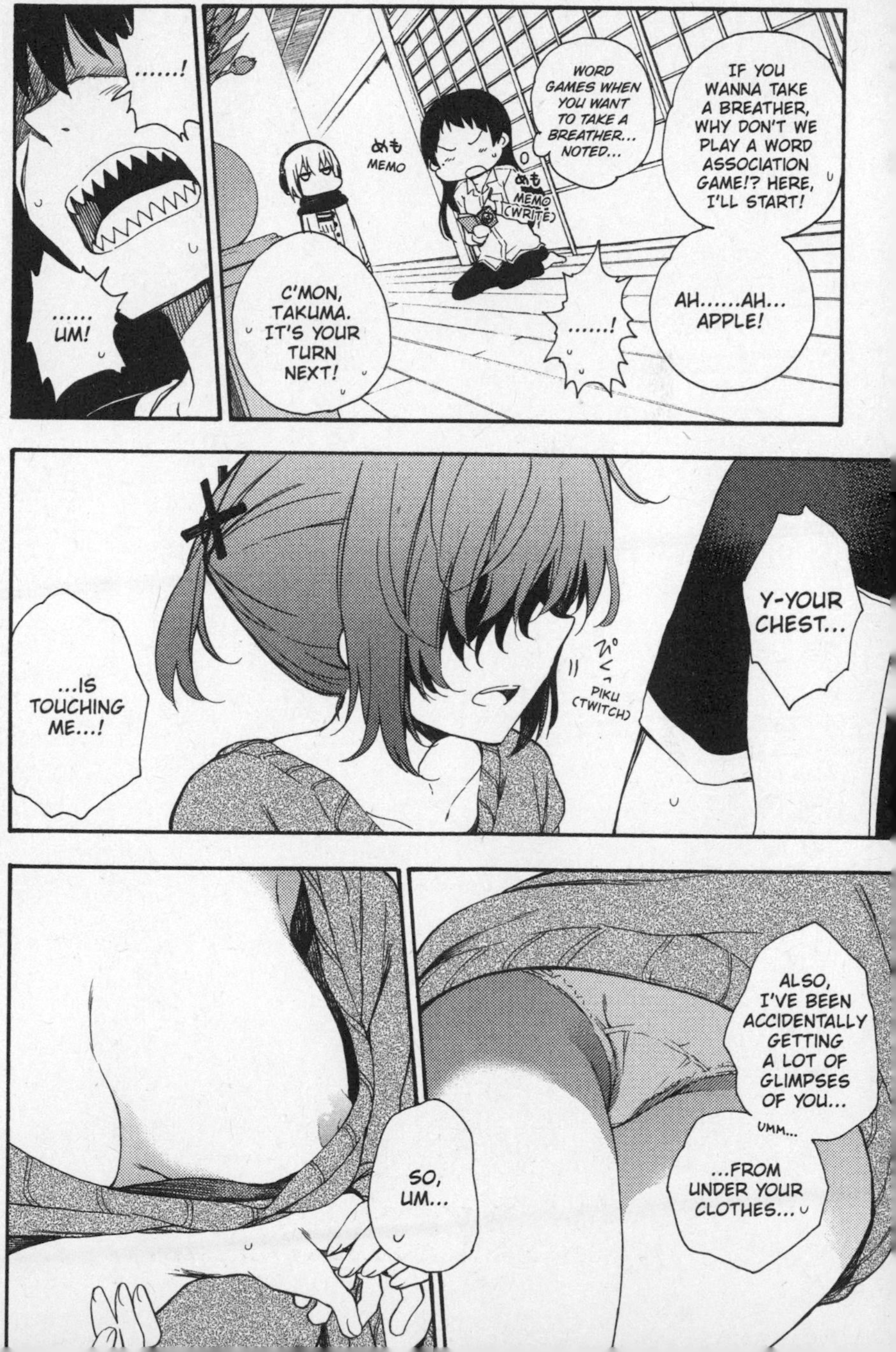
IF YOU WANNA TAKE A BREATHER, WHY DON'T WE PLAY A WORD ASSOCIATION GAME!? HERE, I'LL START!
AH......AH... APPLE!
WORD GAMES WHEN YOU WANT TO TAKE A BREATHER... NOTED...
めも MEMO (WRITE)
......!
めも MEMO
C'MON, TAKUMA. IT'S YOUR TURN NEXT!
......!
...... UM!
Y-YOUR CHEST...
ぴくっ PIKU (TWITCH)
...IS TOUCHING ME...!
ALSO, I'VE BEEN ACCIDENTALLY GETTING A LOT OF GLIMPSES OF YOU...
UMM...
...FROM UNDER YOUR CLOTHES...
SO, UM...

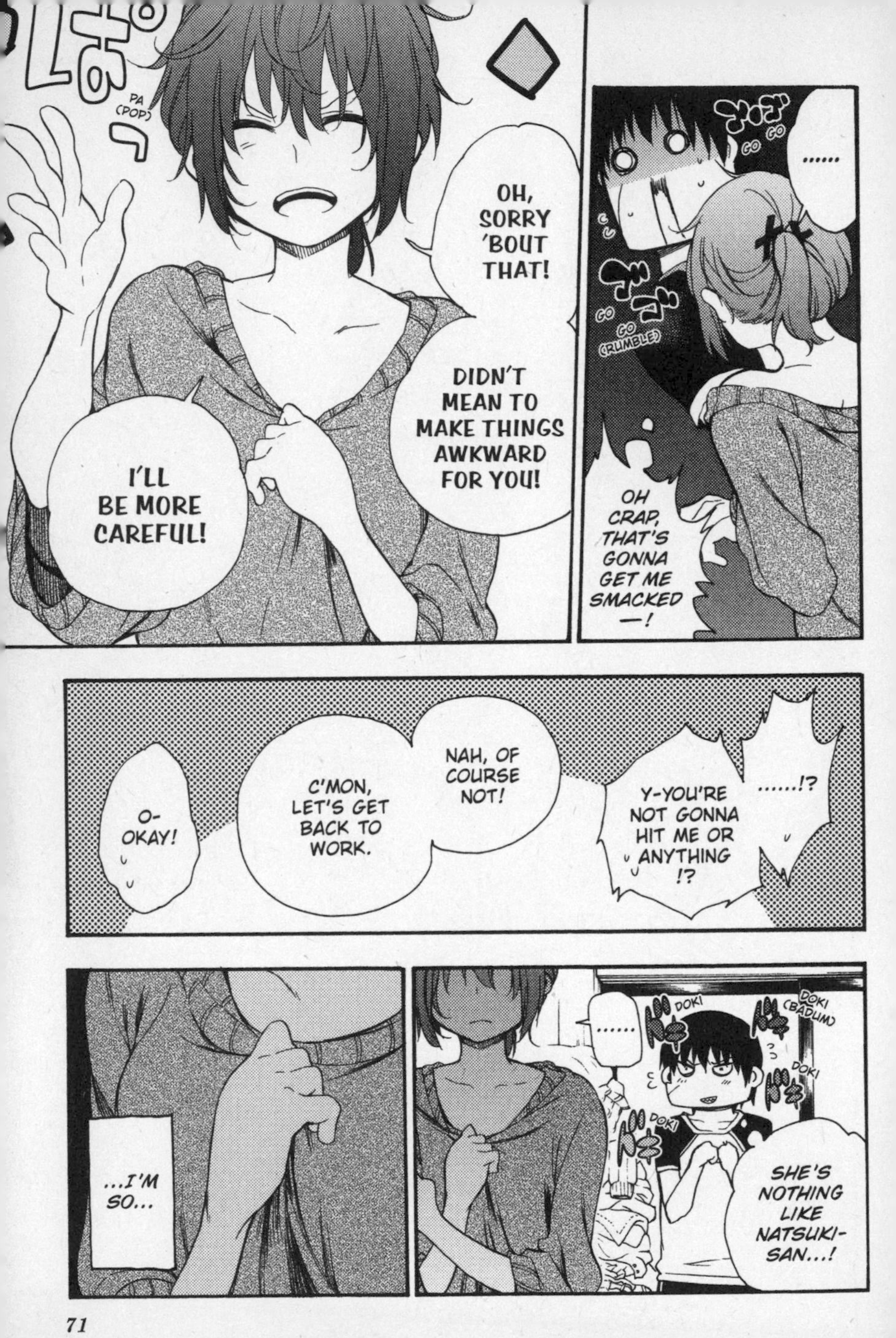
GO GO
......
GO GO (RUMBLE)
OH CRAP, THAT'S GONNA GET ME SMACKED—!
PA (POP)
OH, SORRY 'BOUT THAT!
DIDN'T MEAN TO MAKE THINGS AWKWARD FOR YOU!
I'LL BE MORE CAREFUL!
......!?
Y-YOU'RE NOT GONNA HIT ME OR ANYTHING!?
NAH, OF COURSE NOT!
C'MON, LET'S GET BACK TO WORK.
O-OKAY!
......
DOKI (BADUM)
DOKI
DOKI
DOKI
SHE'S NOTHING LIKE NATSUKI-SAN...!
...I'M SO...

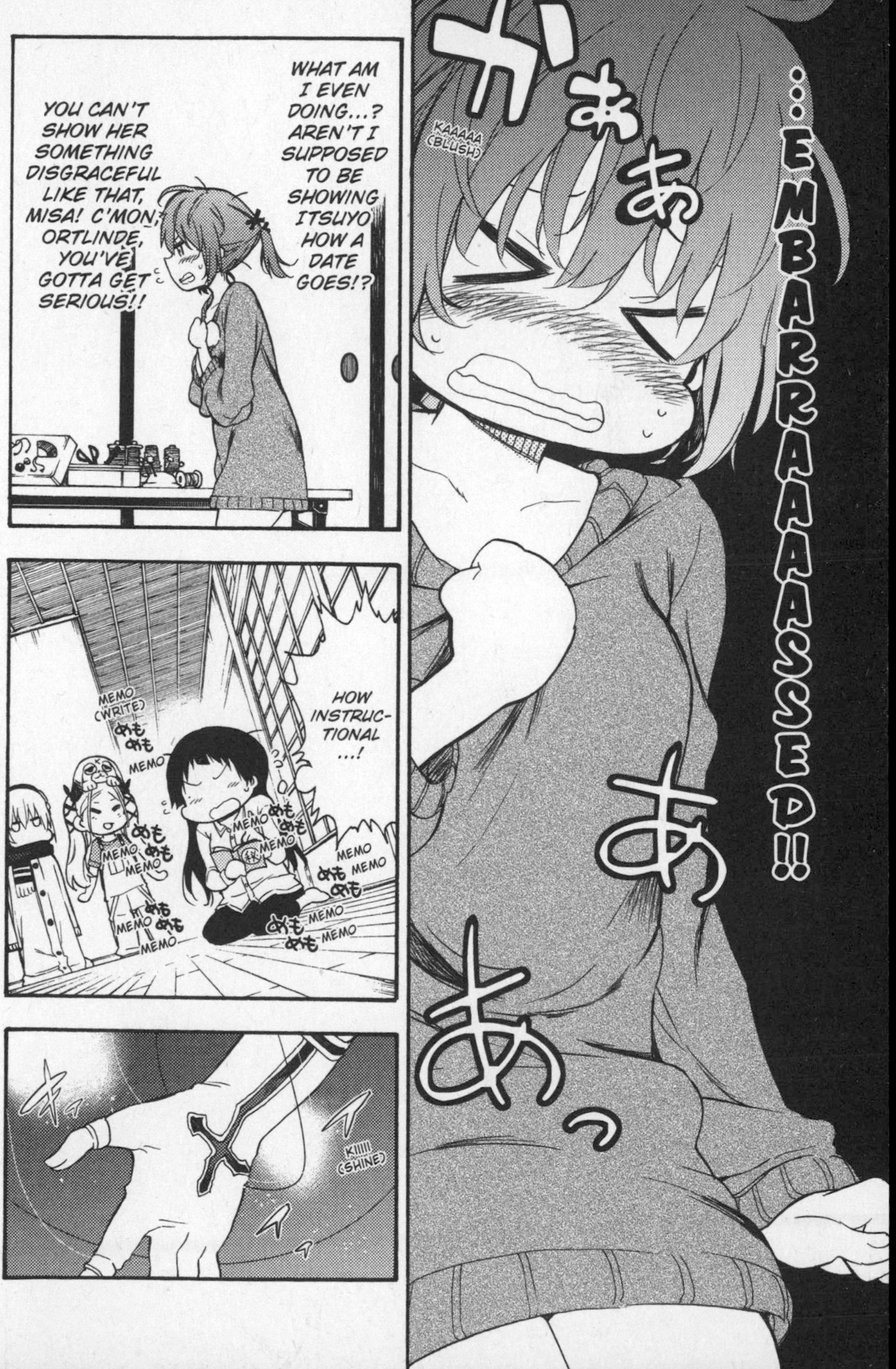

かぁあ
KAAAAA (BLUSH)
...EMBARRAAAAASSED!!
あぁっ
WHAT AM I EVEN DOING...? AREN'T I SUPPOSED TO BE SHOWING ITSUYO HOW A DATE GOES!?
YOU CAN'T SHOW HER SOMETHING DISGRACEFUL LIKE THAT, MISA! C'MON, ORTLINDE, YOU'VE GOTTA GET SERIOUS!!
HOW INSTRUCTIONAL...!
MEMO (WRITE)
めも めも
MEMO
めも めも
MEMO MEMO
めも めも
MEMO MEMO
めも めも
MEMO MEMO
めも めも
MEMO MEMO
めも めも
MEMO MEMO
KIIIII (SHINE)

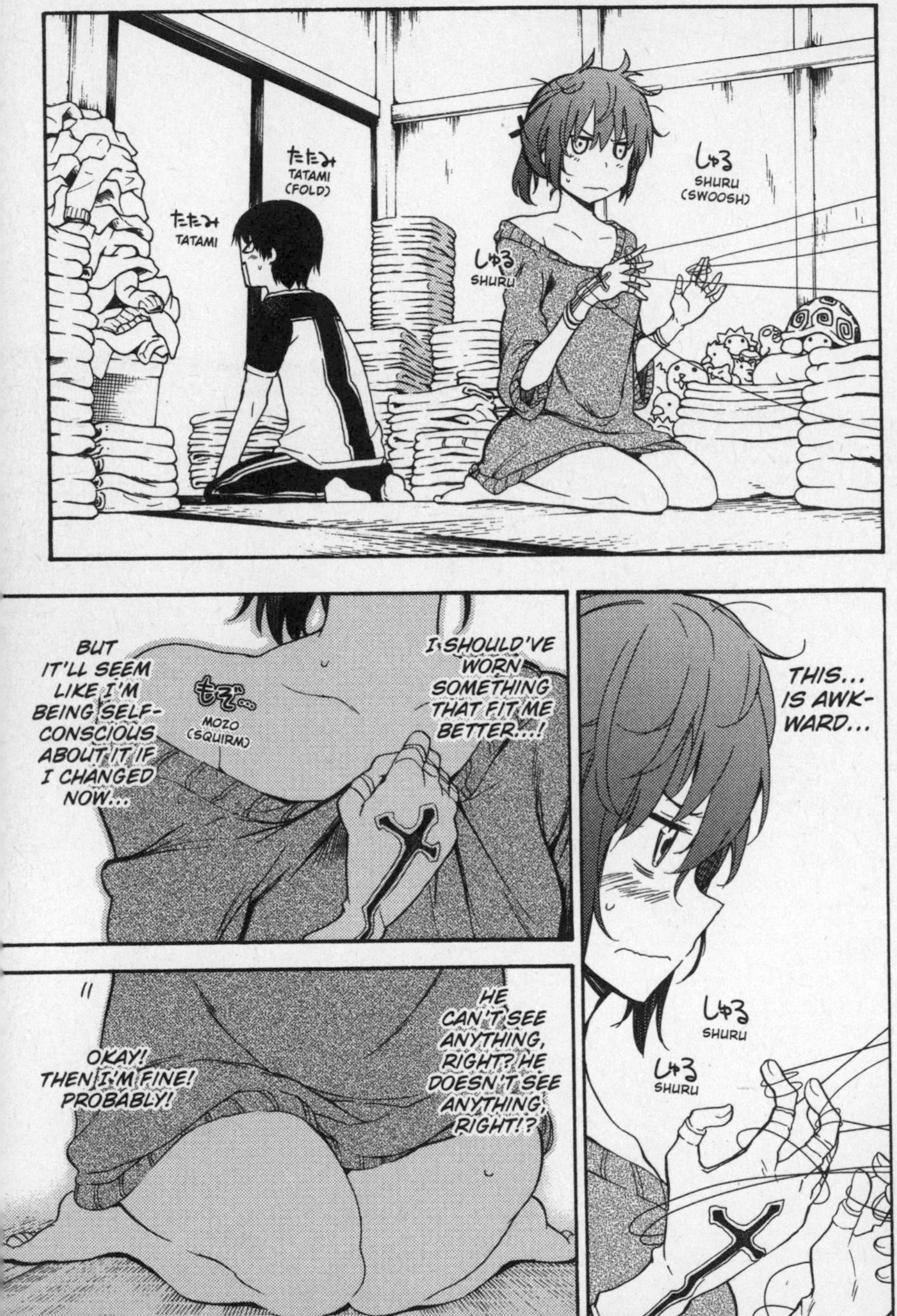

しゅる
SHURU (SWOOSH)
しゅる
SHURU
たたみ
TATAMI (FOLD)
たたみ
TATAMI
THIS... IS AWK-WARD...
しゅる
SHURU
しゅる
SHURU
I SHOULD'VE WORN SOMETHING THAT FIT ME BETTER...!
もぞ...
MOZO (SQUIRM)
BUT IT'LL SEEM LIKE I'M BEING SELF-CONSCIOUS ABOUT IT IF I CHANGED NOW...
HE CAN'T SEE ANYTHING, RIGHT? HE DOESN'T SEE ANYTHING, RIGHT!?
OKAY! THEN I'M FINE! PROBABLY!

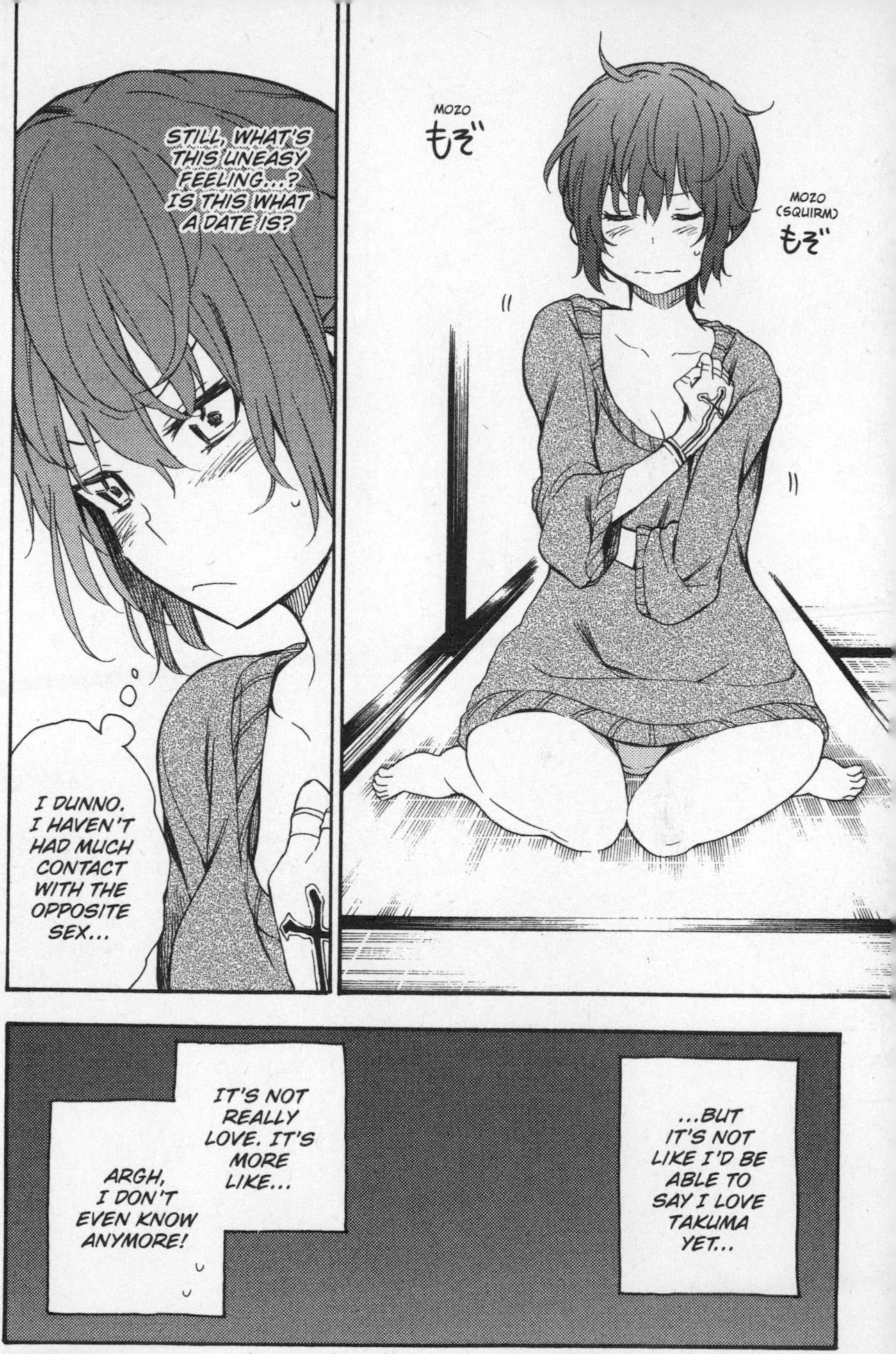
MOZO (SQUIRM)
もぞ
MOZO
もぞ
STILL, WHAT'S THIS UNEASY FEELING...? IS THIS WHAT A DATE IS?
I DUNNO. I HAVEN'T HAD MUCH CONTACT WITH THE OPPOSITE SEX...
...BUT IT'S NOT LIKE I'D BE ABLE TO SAY I LOVE TAKUMA YET...
IT'S NOT REALLY LOVE. IT'S MORE LIKE...
ARGH, I DON'T EVEN KNOW ANYMORE!

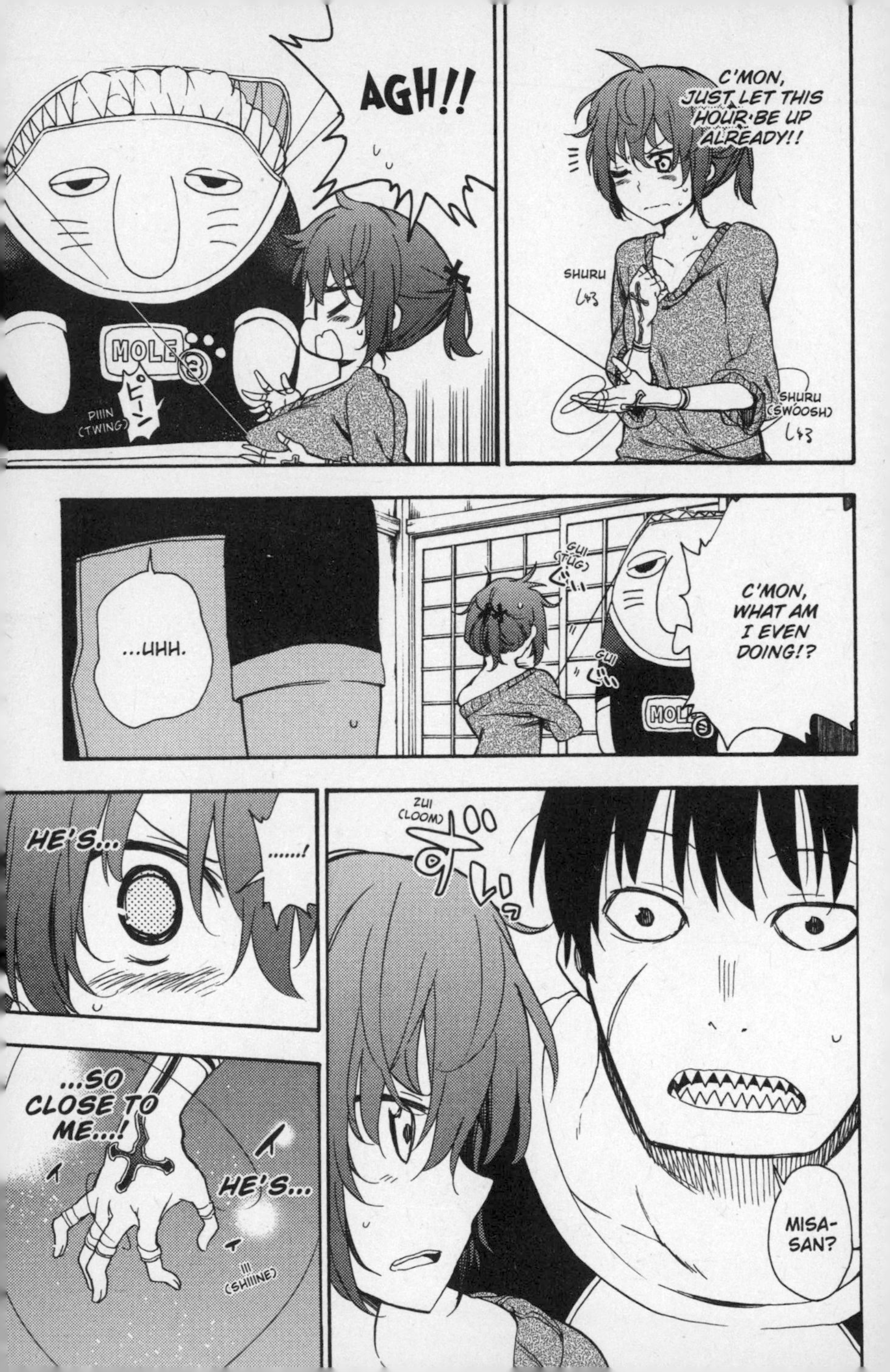
C'MON, JUST LET THIS HOUR BE UP ALREADY!!
SHURU
しゅる
SHURU (SWOOSH)
しゅる
AGH!!
MOLE
PIIIN (TWING)
C'MON, WHAT AM I EVEN DOING!?
GUI (TUG)
GUI
...UHH.
ZUI (LOOM)
MISA-SAN?
HE'S...
......!
...SO CLOSE TO ME...!
HE'S...
III (SHIIINE)

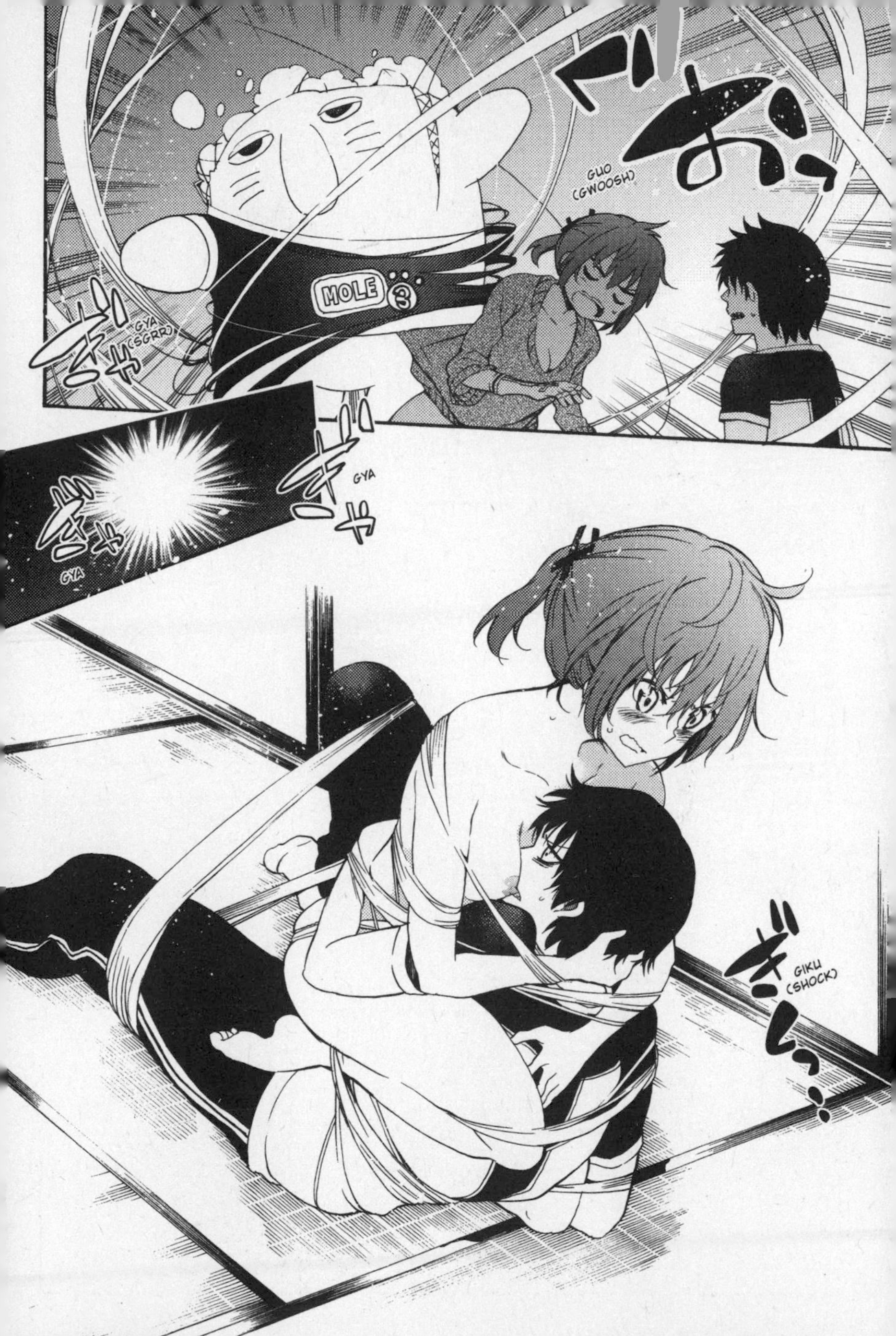
GUO (GWOOSH)
MOLE
GYA (SGRR)
GYA
GYA
GIKU (SHOCK)

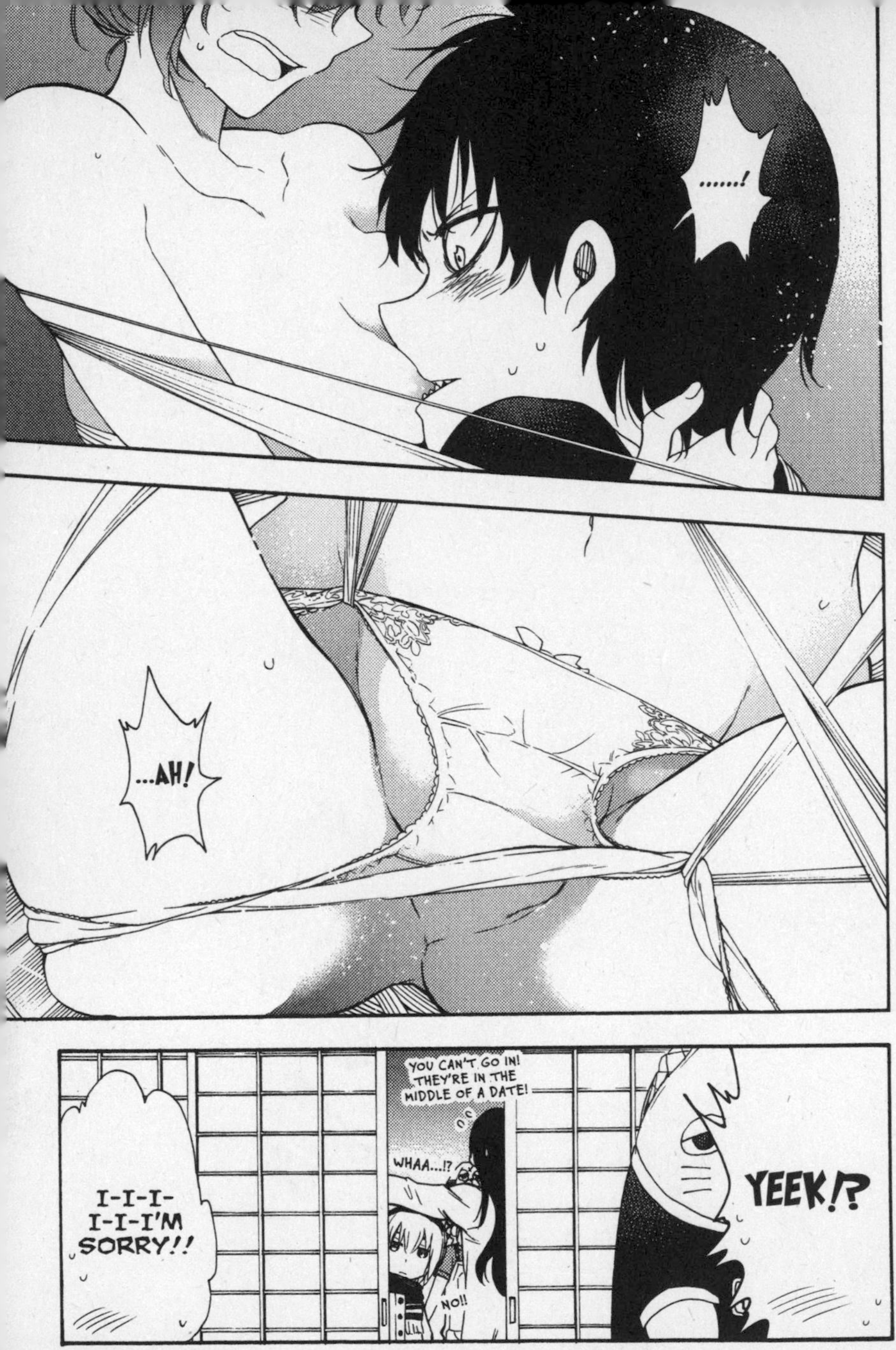
......!
...AH!
YEEK!?
YOU CAN'T GO IN! THEY'RE IN THE MIDDLE OF A DATE!
WHAA...!?
NO!!
I-I-I-
I-I-I'M SORRY!!

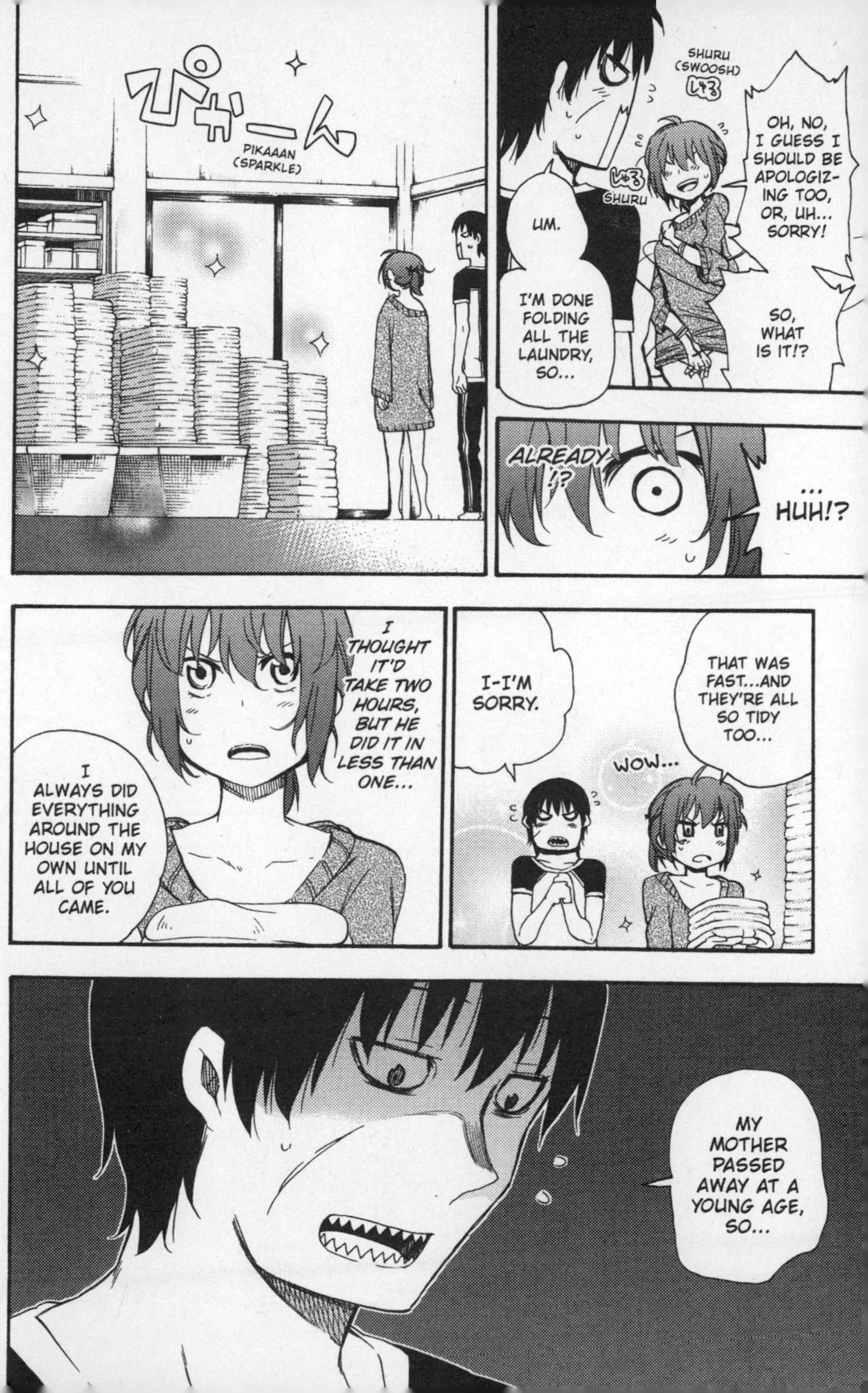
SHURU (SWOOSH)
しゅる
OH, NO, I GUESS I SHOULD BE APOLOGIZING TOO, OR, UH... SORRY!
SO, WHAT IS IT!?
しゅる
SHURU
UM.
I'M DONE FOLDING ALL THE LAUNDRY, SO...
...HUH!?
ALREADY!?
ぴかーん
PIKAAAN (SPARKLE)
THAT WAS FAST...AND THEY'RE ALL SO TIDY TOO...
WOW...
I-I'M SORRY.
I THOUGHT IT'D TAKE TWO HOURS, BUT HE DID IT IN LESS THAN ONE...
I ALWAYS DID EVERYTHING AROUND THE HOUSE ON MY OWN UNTIL ALL OF YOU CAME.
MY MOTHER PASSED AWAY AT A YOUNG AGE, SO...

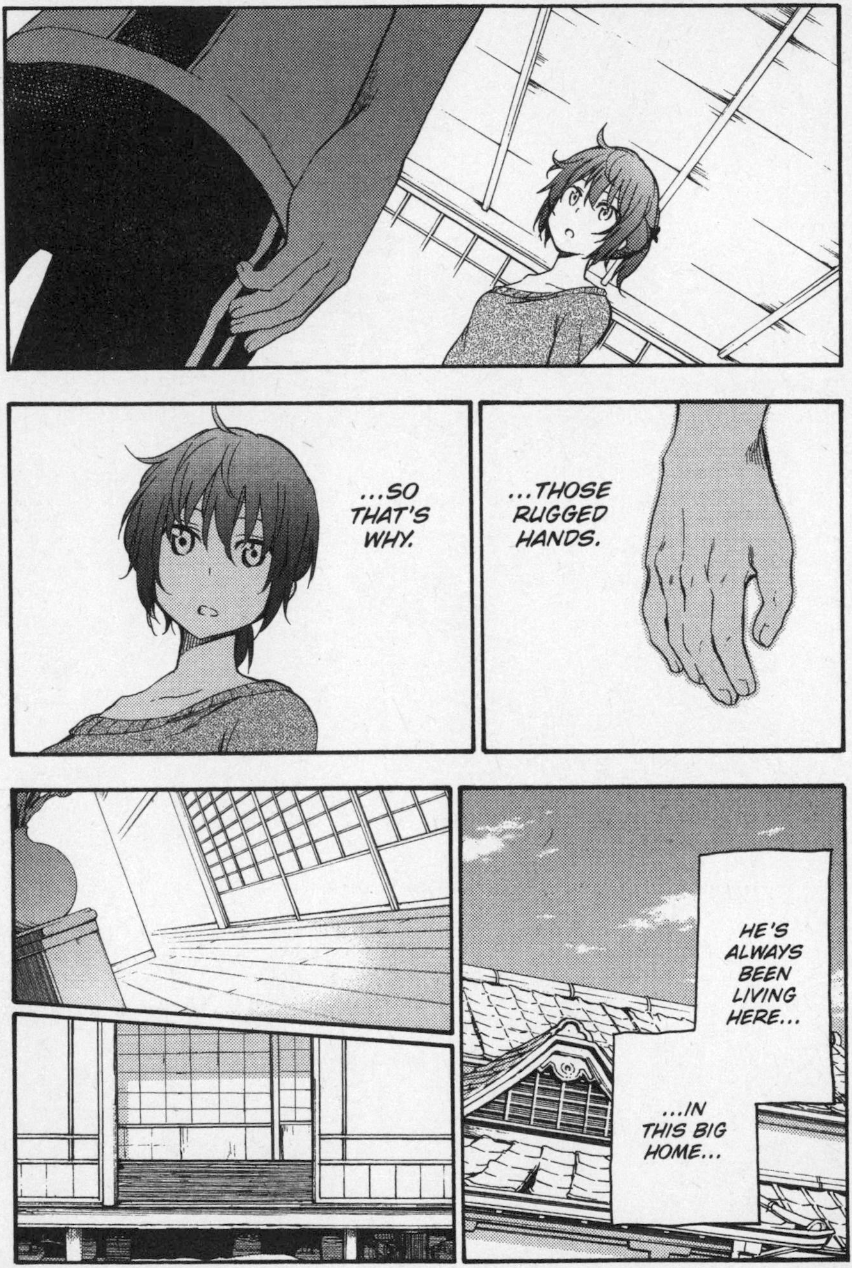
...THOSE RUGGED HANDS.
...SO THAT'S WHY.
HE'S ALWAYS BEEN LIVING HERE...
...IN THIS BIG HOME...

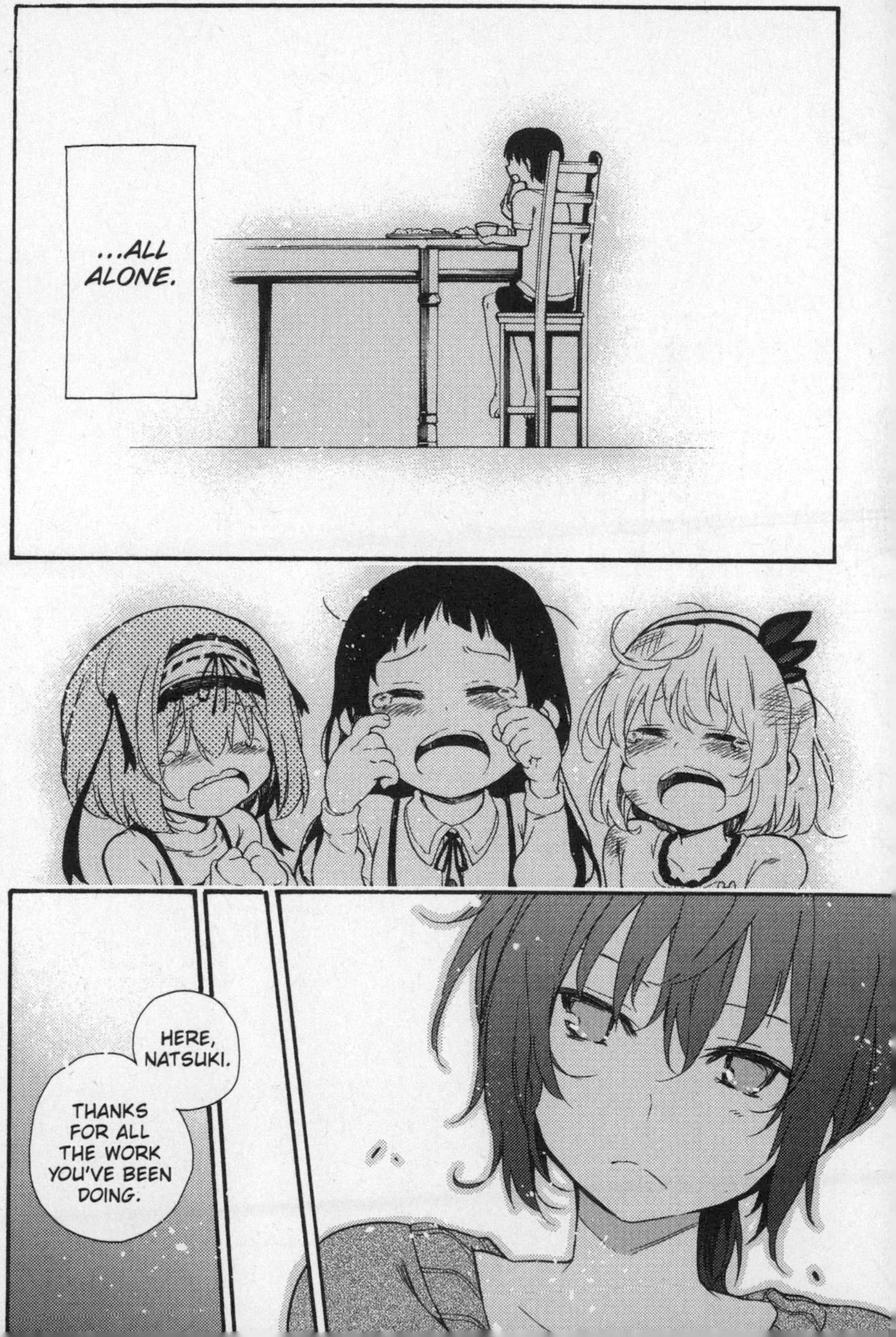
...ALL ALONE.
HERE, NATSUKI.
THANKS FOR ALL THE WORK YOU'VE BEEN DOING.

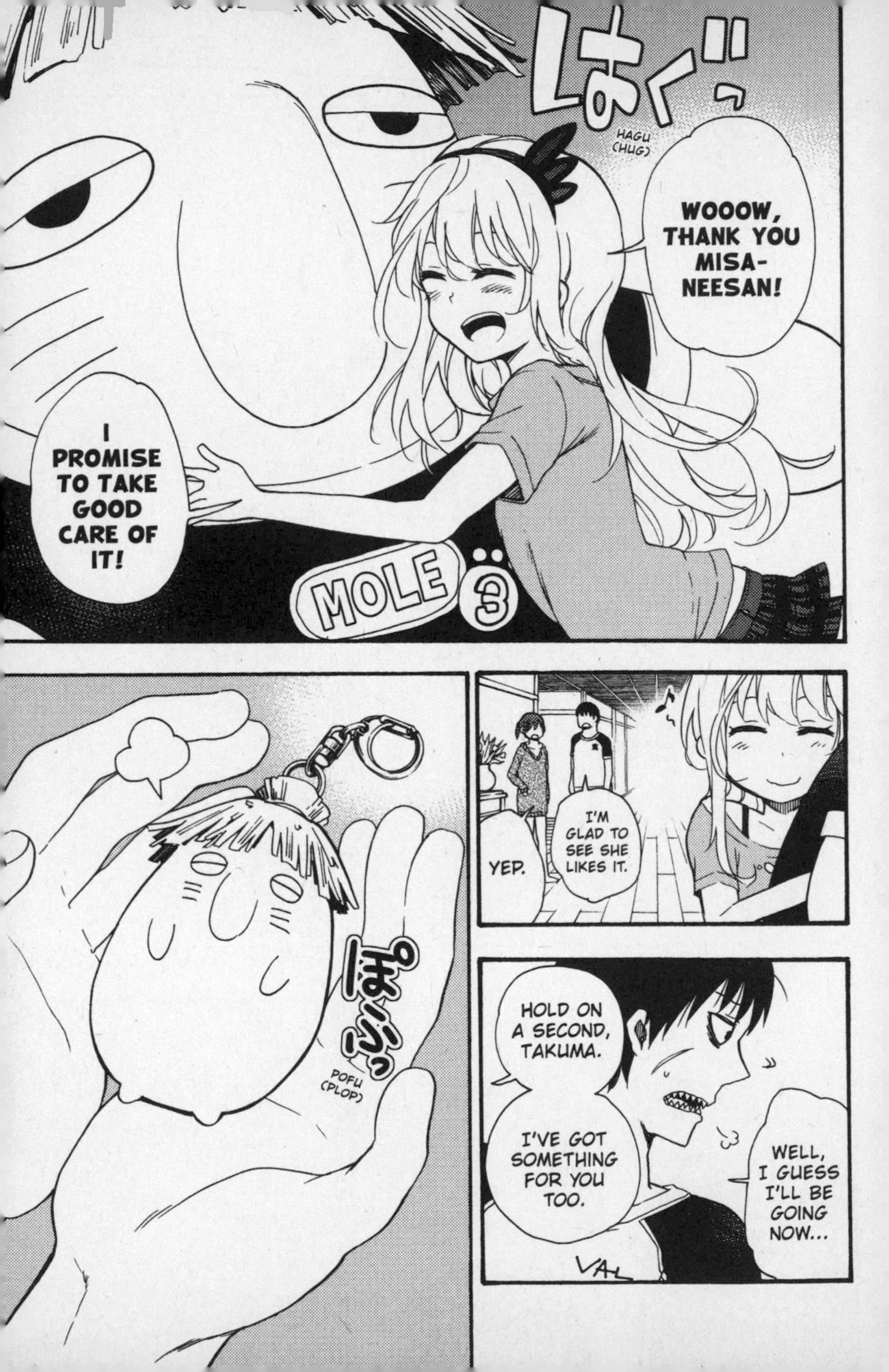

はぐっ
HAGU (HUG)
WOOOW, THANK YOU MISA-NEESAN!
I PROMISE TO TAKE GOOD CARE OF IT!
MOLE 3
I'M GLAD TO SEE SHE LIKES IT.
YEP.
WELL, I GUESS I'LL BE GOING NOW...
HOLD ON A SECOND, TAKUMA.
I'VE GOT SOMETHING FOR YOU TOO.
ぽふっ
POFU (PLOP)

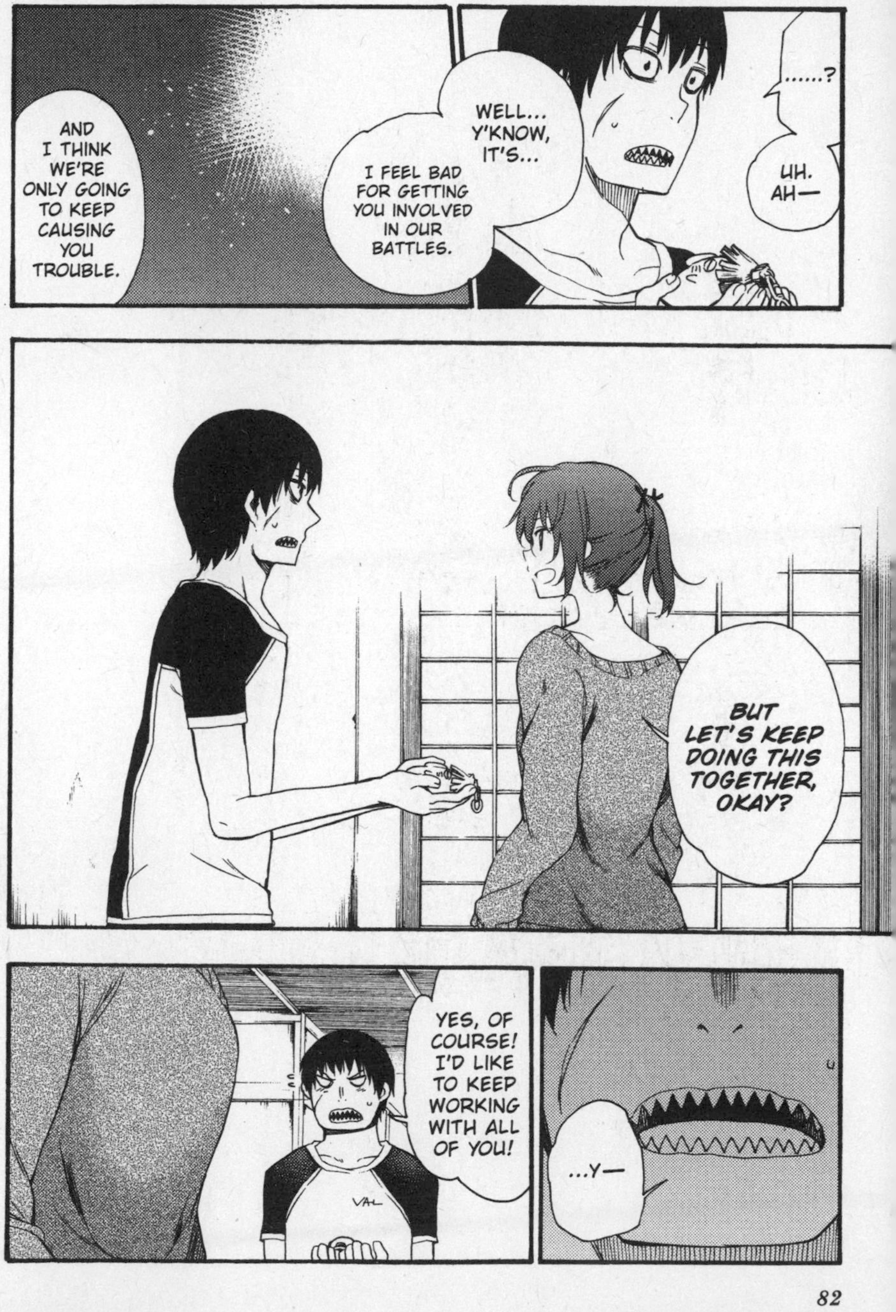
......?
UH. AH—
WELL... Y'KNOW, IT'S...
I FEEL BAD FOR GETTING YOU INVOLVED IN OUR BATTLES.
AND I THINK WE'RE ONLY GOING TO KEEP CAUSING YOU TROUBLE.
BUT LET'S KEEP DOING THIS TOGETHER, OKAY?
...Y—
YES, OF COURSE! I'D LIKE TO KEEP WORKING WITH ALL OF YOU!

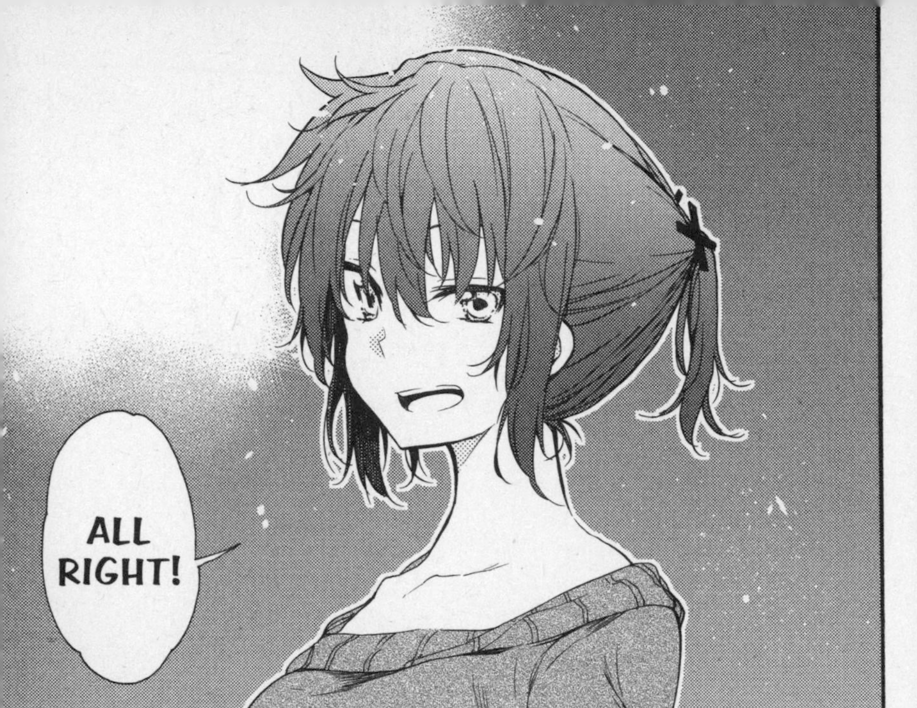
ALL RIGHT!

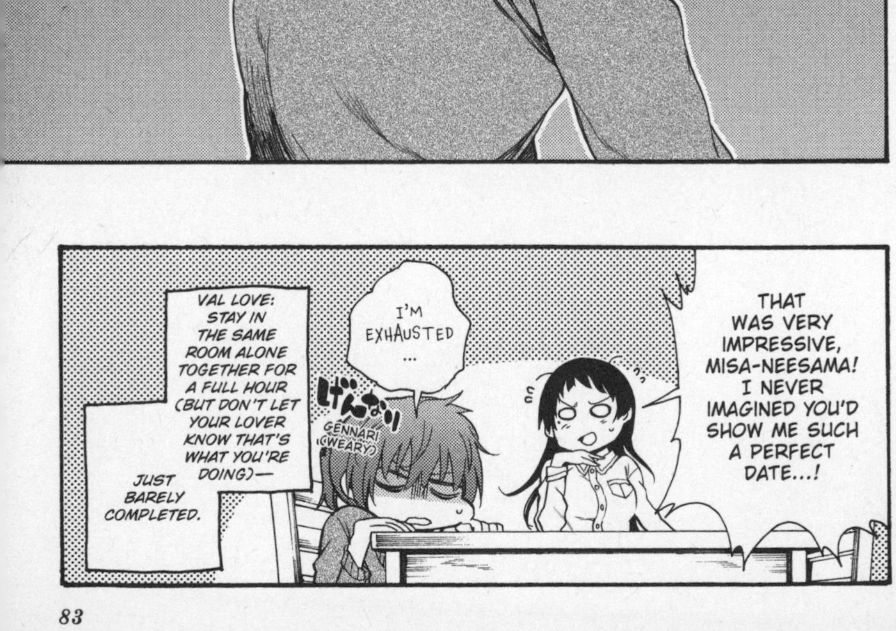
THAT WAS VERY IMPRESSIVE, MISA-NEESAMA! I NEVER IMAGINED YOU'D SHOW ME SUCH A PERFECT DATE...!
I'M EXHAUSTED ...
げんなり
GENNARI (WEARY)
VAL LOVE: STAY IN THE SAME ROOM ALONE TOGETHER FOR A FULL HOUR (BUT DON'T LET YOUR LOVER KNOW THAT'S WHAT YOU'RE DOING)—
JUST BARELY COMPLETED.

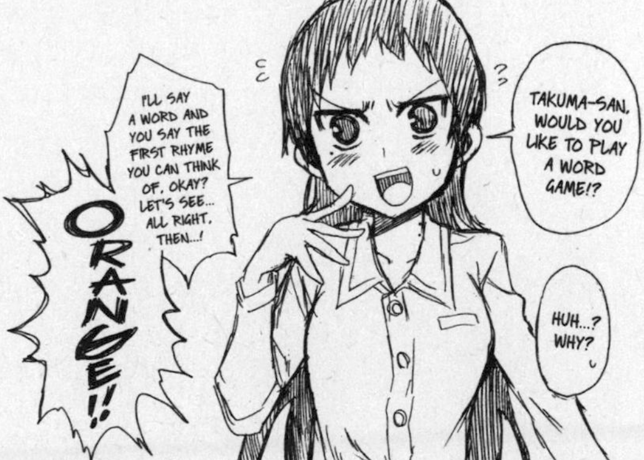
TAKUMA-SAN, WOULD YOU LIKE TO PLAY A WORD GAME!?
HUH...? WHY?
I'LL SAY A WORD AND YOU SAY THE FIRST RHYME YOU CAN THINK OF, OKAY? LET'S SEE... ALL RIGHT, THEN...!
ORANGE!!

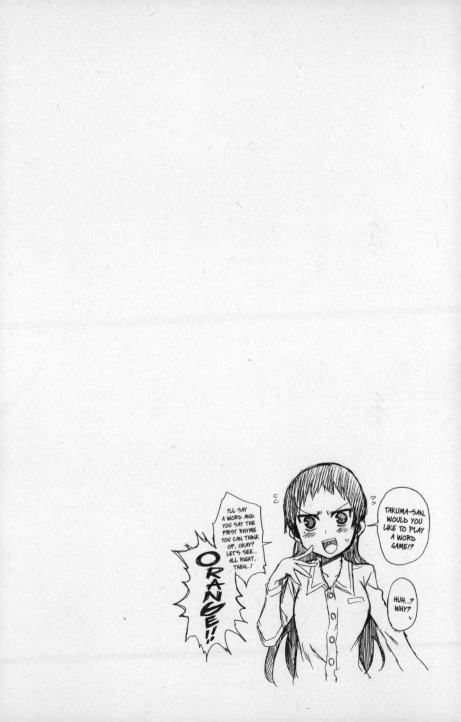

Chapter 18: The Photographed Maiden

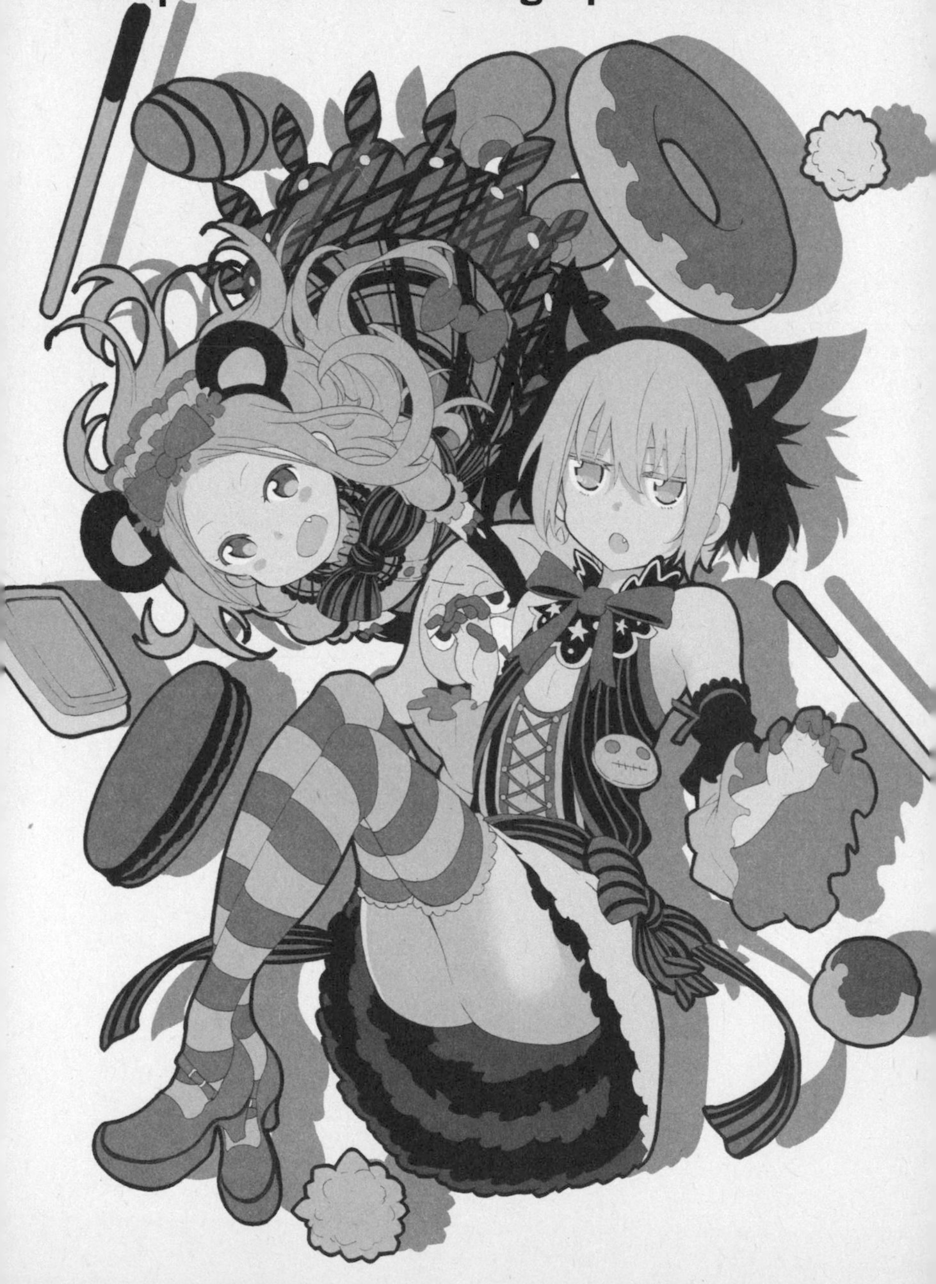

Val × Love

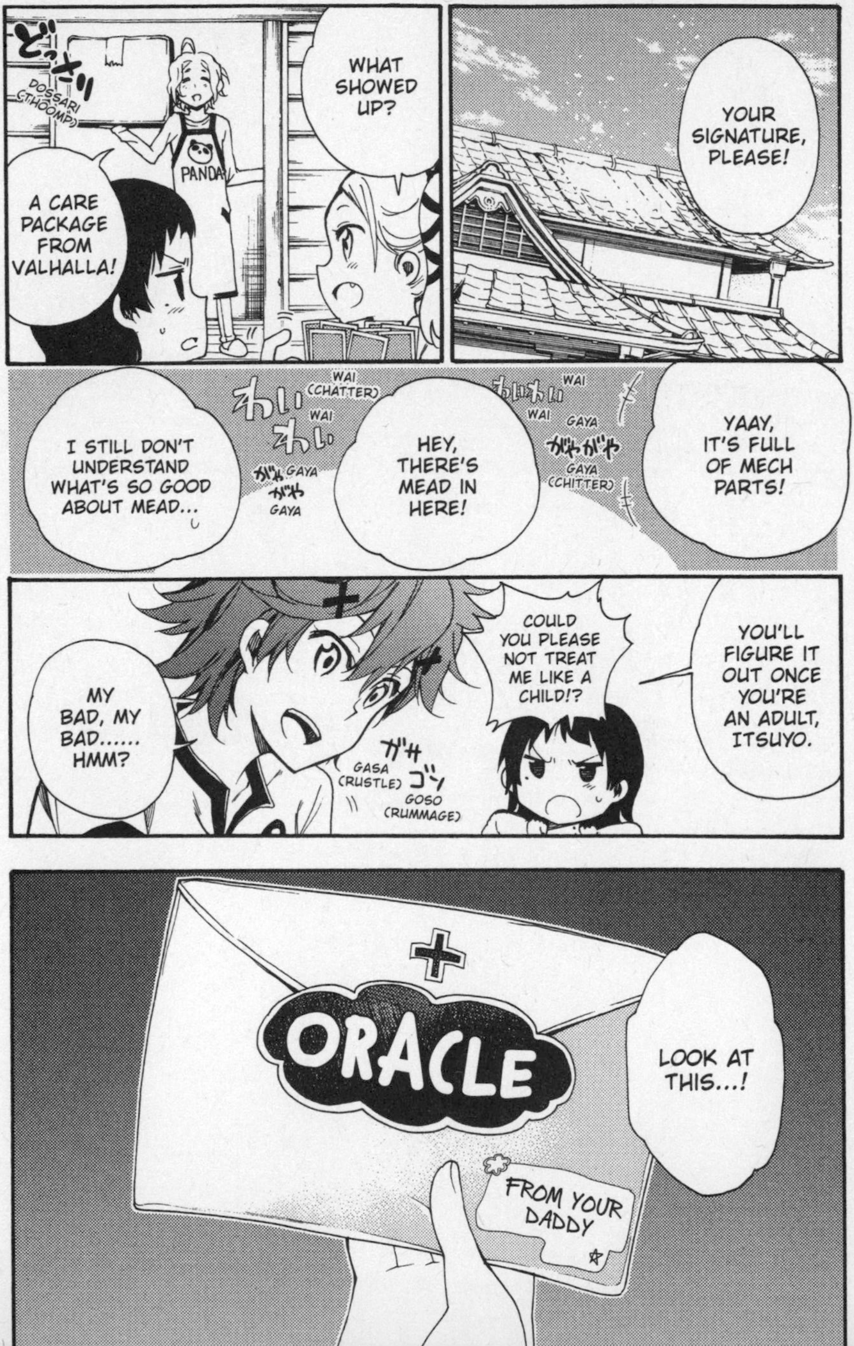
YOUR SIGNATURE, PLEASE!
WHAT SHOWED UP?
どっさり
DOSSARI (THOOMP)
A CARE PACKAGE FROM VALHALLA!
YAAY, IT'S FULL OF MECH PARTS!
わいわい
WAI WAI
がやがや
GAYA GAYA (CHITTER)
HEY, THERE'S MEAD IN HERE!
わいわい
WAI (CHATTER) WAI
がやがや
GAYA GAYA
I STILL DON'T UNDERSTAND WHAT'S SO GOOD ABOUT MEAD...
YOU'LL FIGURE IT OUT ONCE YOU'RE AN ADULT, ITSUYO.
COULD YOU PLEASE NOT TREAT ME LIKE A CHILD!?
ガサ
GASA (RUSTLE)
ゴソ
GOSO (RUMMAGE)
MY BAD, MY BAD...... HMM?
LOOK AT THIS...!
ORACLE
FROM YOUR DADDY

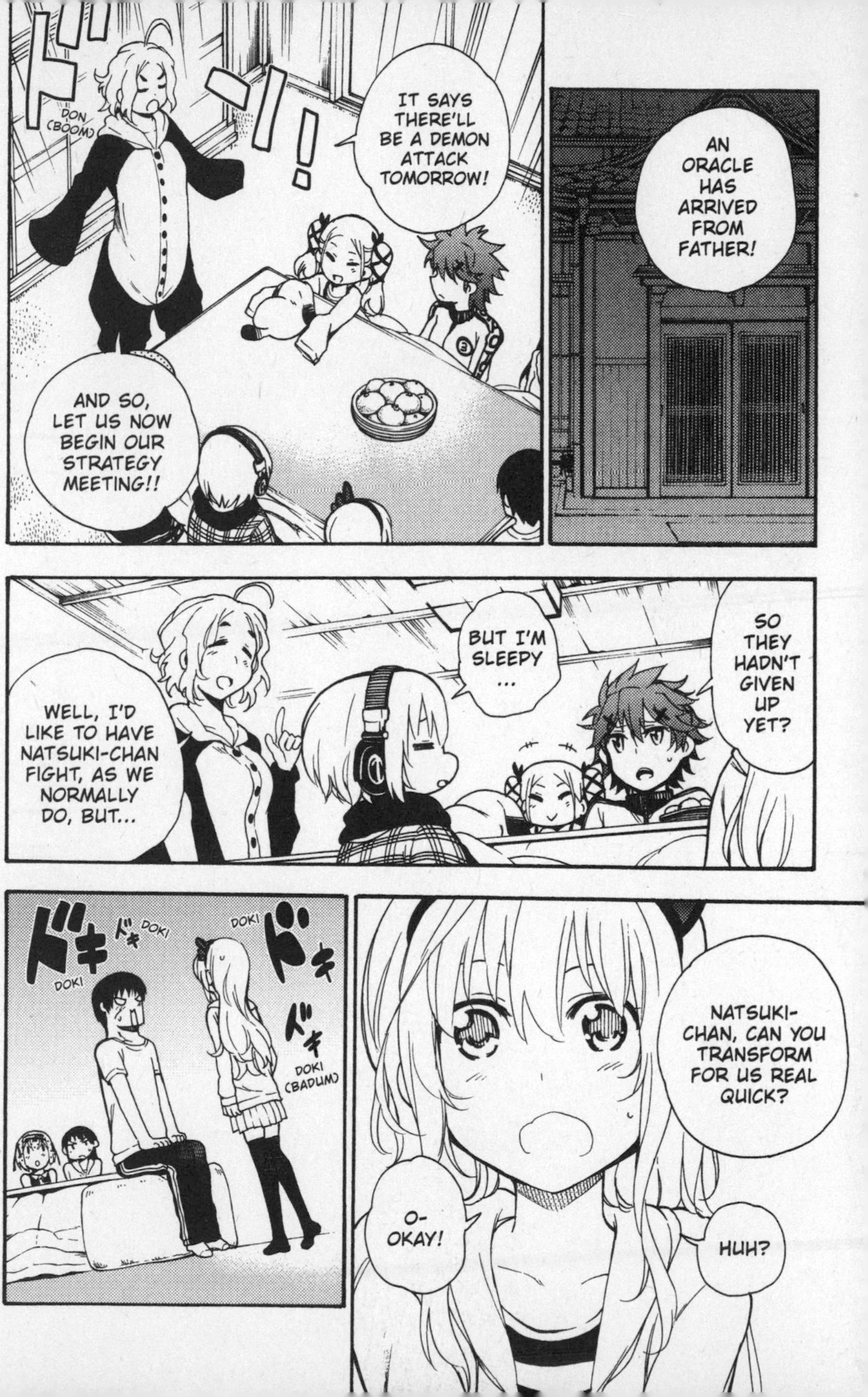
AN ORACLE HAS ARRIVED FROM FATHER!
IT SAYS THERE'LL BE A DEMON ATTACK TOMORROW!
DON (BOOM)
AND SO, LET US NOW BEGIN OUR STRATEGY MEETING!!
SO THEY HADN'T GIVEN UP YET?
BUT I'M SLEEPY ...
WELL, I'D LIKE TO HAVE NATSUKI-CHAN FIGHT, AS WE NORMALLY DO, BUT...
NATSUKI-CHAN, CAN YOU TRANSFORM FOR US REAL QUICK?
HUH?
O-OKAY!
DOKI
DOKI (BADUM)
DOKI
DOKI

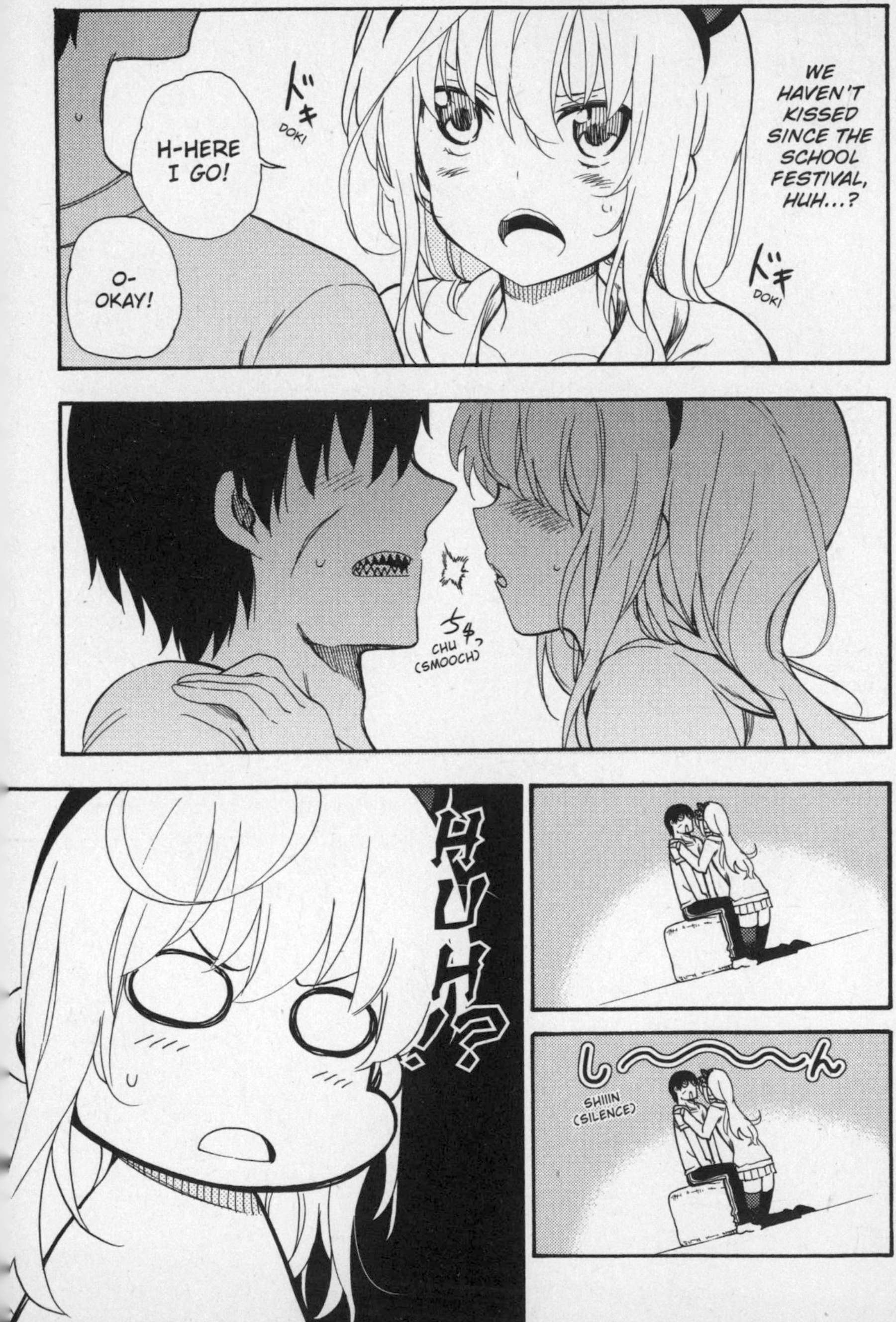
WE HAVEN'T KISSED SINCE THE SCHOOL FESTIVAL, HUH...?
ドキ DOKI
ドキ DOKI
H-HERE I GO!
O-OKAY!
ちゅっ CHU (SMOOCH)
し〜〜〜ん SHIIIN (SILENCE)
HUH!?

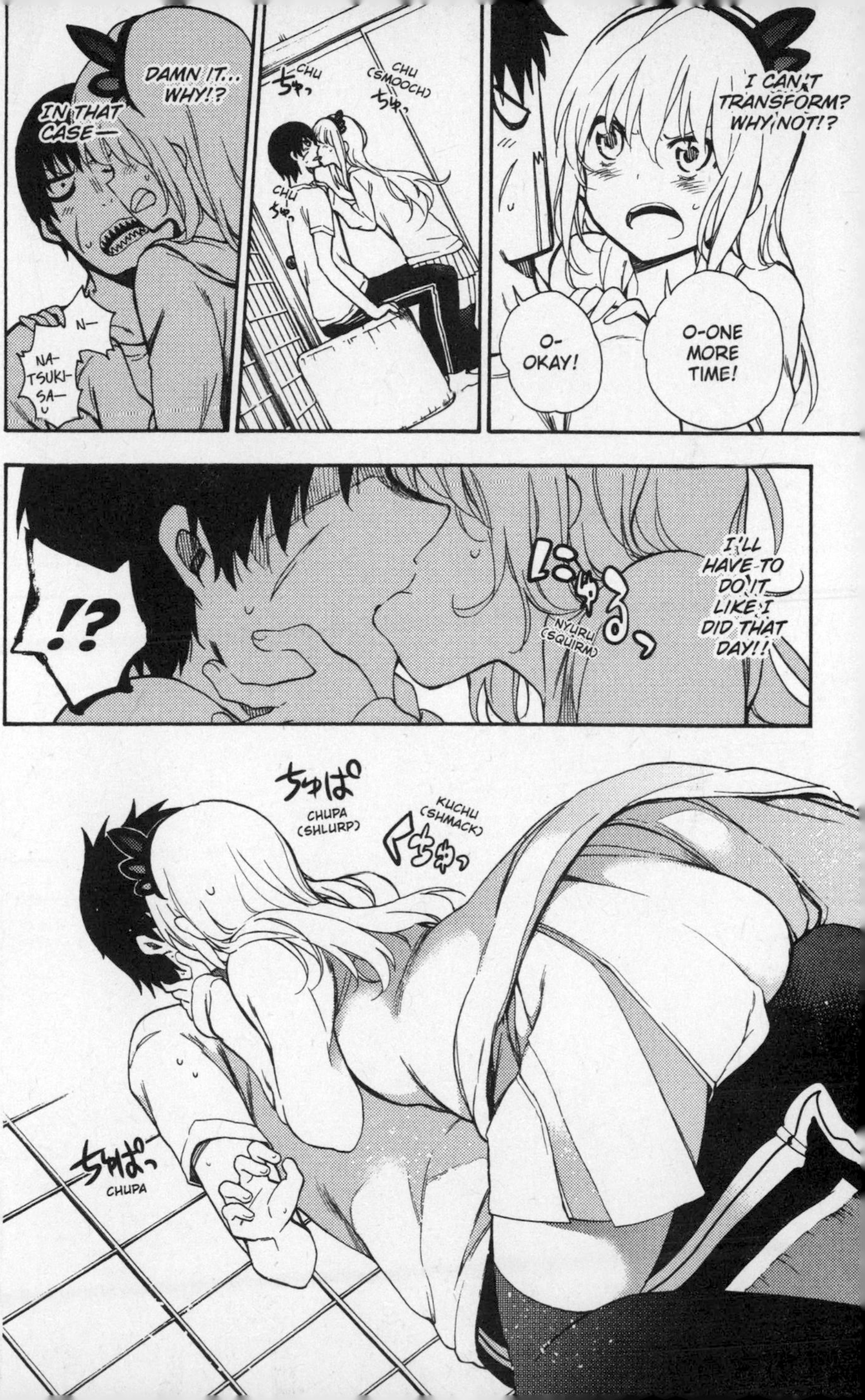
I CAN'T TRANSFORM? WHY NOT!?
O-ONE MORE TIME!
O-OKAY!
ちゅっ
CHU (SMOOCH)
ちゃっ
CHU
ちゅっ
CHU
DAMN IT... WHY!?
IN THAT CASE—
N— NA-TSUKI-SA-U
I'LL HAVE TO DO IT LIKE I DID THAT DAY!!
にゅるっ
NYURU (SQUIRM)
!?
くちゅっ
KUCHU (SHMACK)
ちゅぱ
CHUPA (SHLURP)
ちゅぱっ
CHUPA

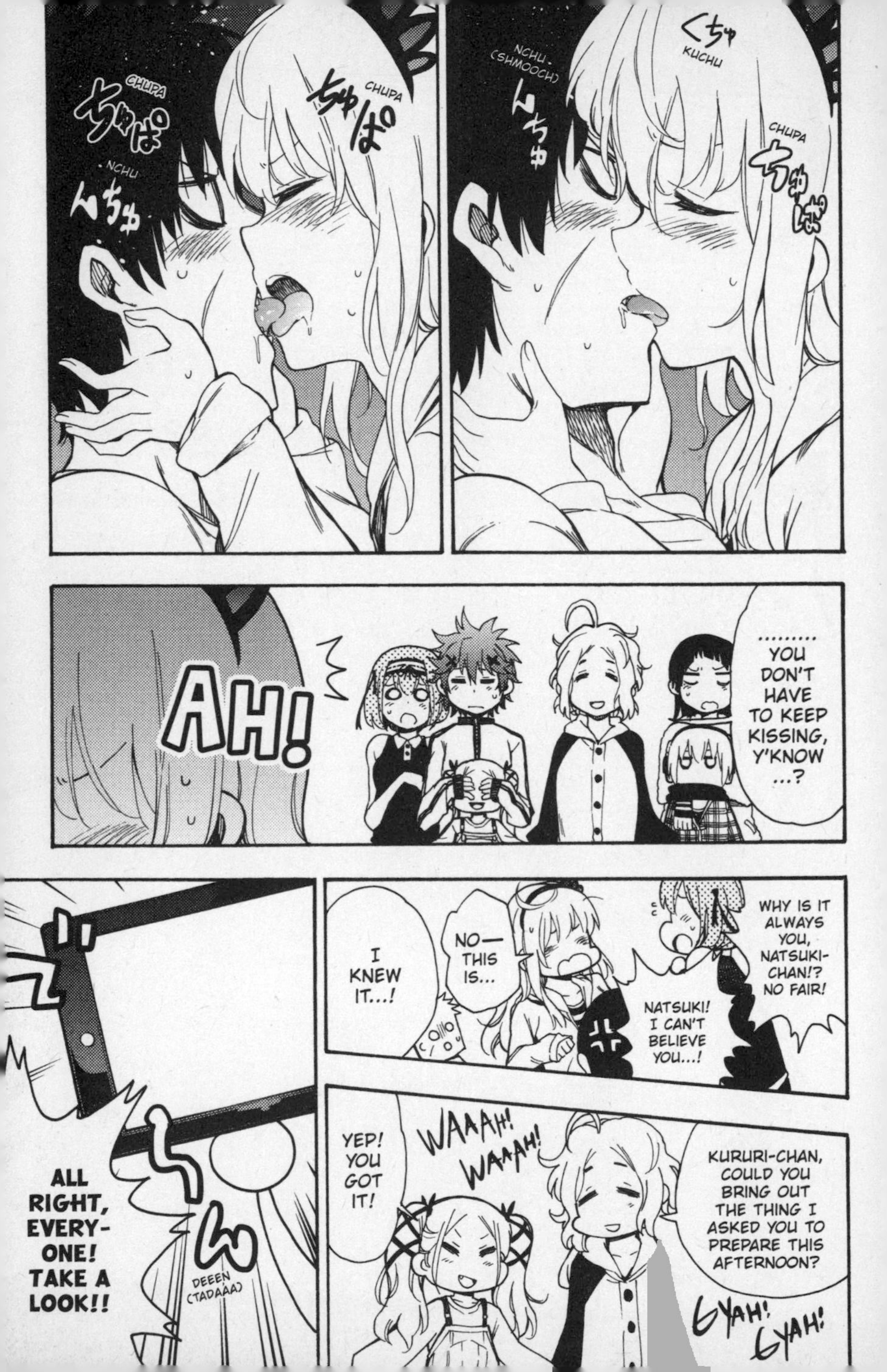
くちゅ
KUCHU
んちゅ
NCHU (SHMOOCH)
ちゅぱ
CHUPA
ちゅぱ
CHUPA
ちゅぱ
CHUPA
んちゅ
NCHU
……… YOU DON'T HAVE TO KEEP KISSING, Y'KNOW …?
AH!
WHY IS IT ALWAYS YOU, NATSUKI-CHAN!? NO FAIR!
NATSUKI! I CAN'T BELIEVE YOU…!
NO— THIS IS…
I KNEW IT…!
KURURI-CHAN, COULD YOU BRING OUT THE THING I ASKED YOU TO PREPARE THIS AFTERNOON?
GYAH! GYAH!
WAAAH! WAAAH!
YEP! YOU GOT IT!
ど～ん
DEEEN (TADAAA)
ALL RIGHT, EVERY-ONE! TAKE A LOOK!!

Itsuyo

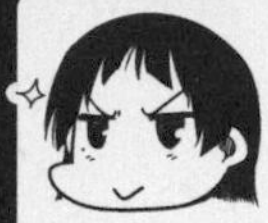

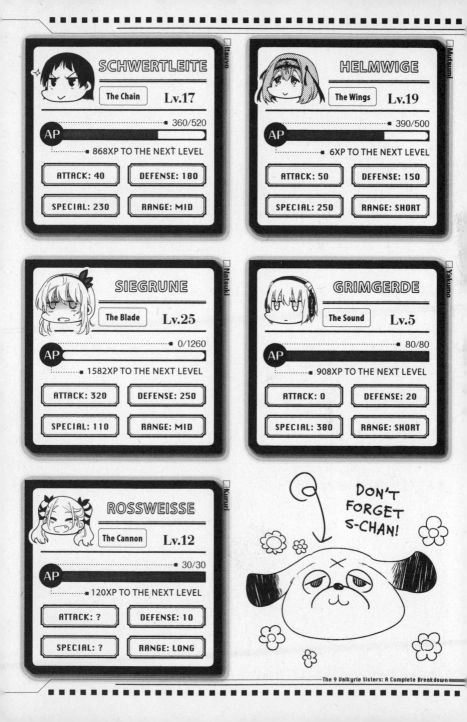

SCHWERTLEITE

The Chain

Lv.17

AP 360/520

868XP TO THE NEXT LEVEL

ATTACK: 40
DEFENSE: 180
SPECIAL: 230
RANGE: MID

Mutsumi

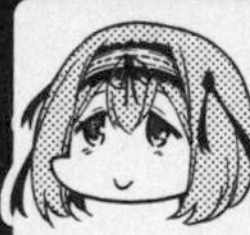

HELMWIGE

The Wings

Lv.19

AP 390/500

6XP TO THE NEXT LEVEL

ATTACK: 50
DEFENSE: 150
SPECIAL: 250
RANGE: SHORT

Natsuki

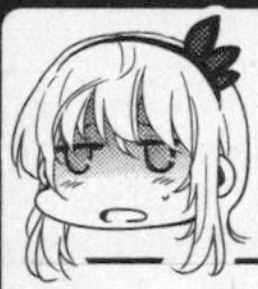

SIEGRUNE

The Blade

Lv.25

AP 0/1260

1582XP TO THE NEXT LEVEL

ATTACK: 320
DEFENSE: 250
SPECIAL: 110
RANGE: MID

Yakumo

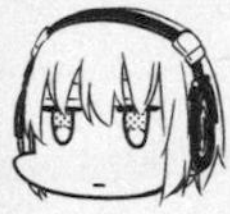

GRIMGERDE

The Sound

Lv.5

AP 80/80

908XP TO THE NEXT LEVEL

ATTACK: 0
DEFENSE: 20
SPECIAL: 380
RANGE: SHORT

Kururi

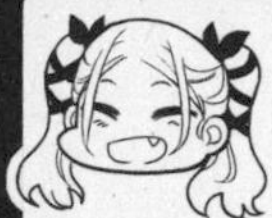

ROSSWEISSE

The Cannon

Lv.12

AP 30/30

120XP TO THE NEXT LEVEL

ATTACK: ?
DEFENSE: 10
SPECIAL: ?
RANGE: LONG

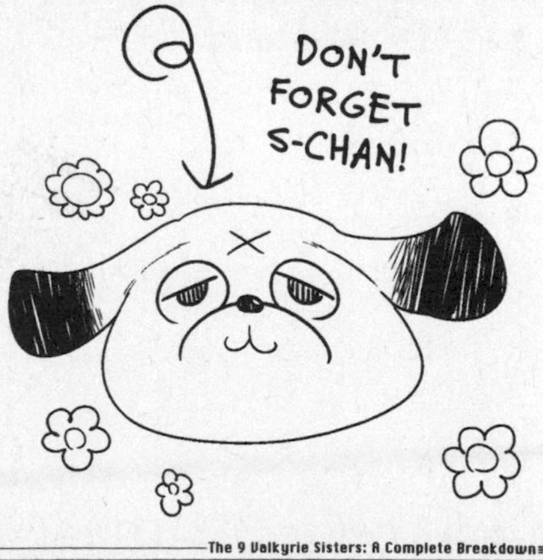
DON'T FORGET S-CHAN!

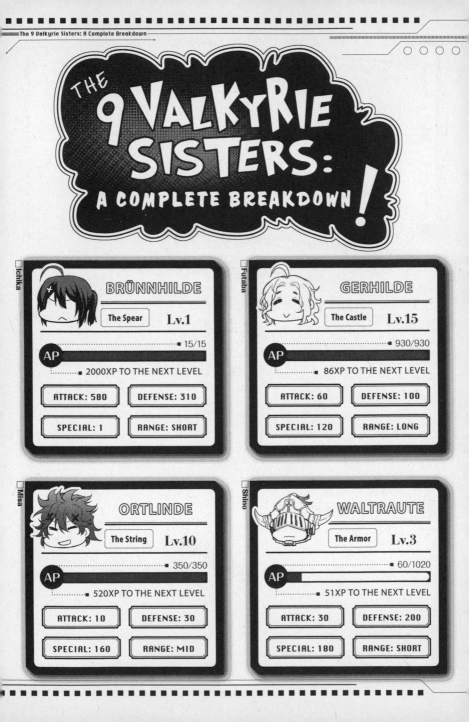

THE 9 VALKYRIE SISTERS: A COMPLETE BREAKDOWN!

Ichika

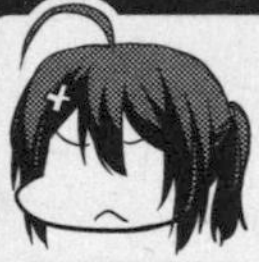

BRÜNNHILDE

The Spear Lv.1

AP 15/15

2000XP TO THE NEXT LEVEL

ATTACK: 580	DEFENSE: 310
SPECIAL: 1	RANGE: SHORT

Futaba

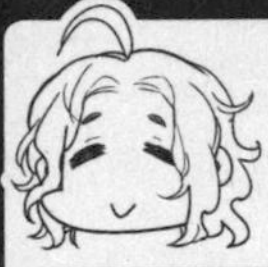

GERHILDE

The Castle Lv.15

AP 930/930

86XP TO THE NEXT LEVEL

ATTACK: 60	DEFENSE: 100
SPECIAL: 120	RANGE: LONG

Misa

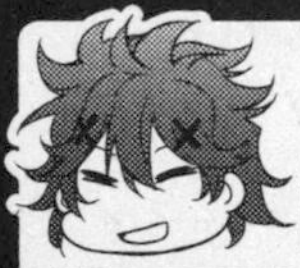

ORTLINDE

The String Lv.10

AP 350/350

520XP TO THE NEXT LEVEL

ATTACK: 10	DEFENSE: 30
SPECIAL: 160	RANGE: MID

Shino

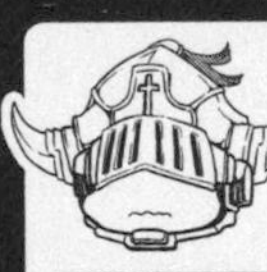

WALTRAUTE

The Armor Lv.3

AP 60/1020

51XP TO THE NEXT LEVEL

ATTACK: 30	DEFENSE: 200
SPECIAL: 180	RANGE: SHORT

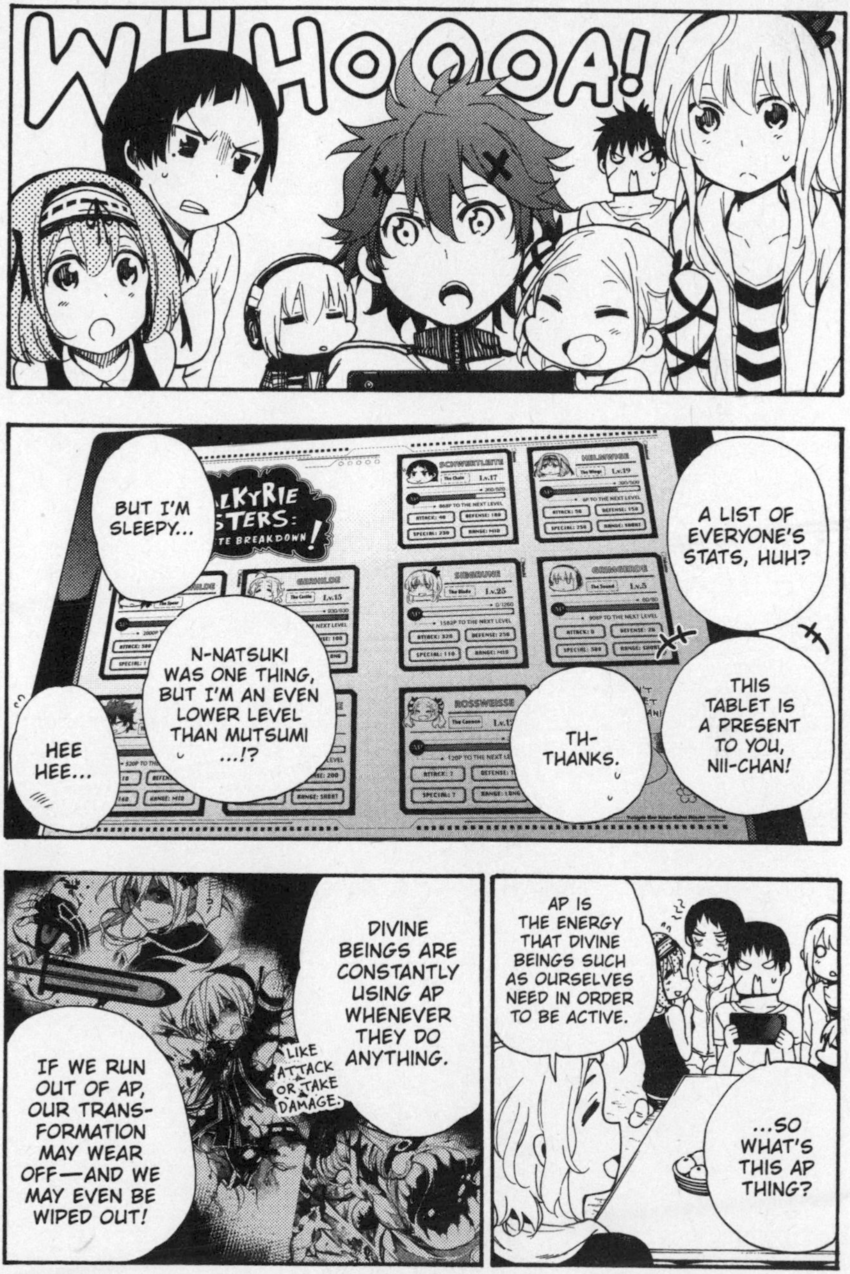
WHHOOOOA!
A LIST OF EVERYONE'S STATS, HUH?
THIS TABLET IS A PRESENT TO YOU, NII-CHAN!
TH- THANKS.
BUT I'M SLEEPY...
N-NATSUKI WAS ONE THING, BUT I'M AN EVEN LOWER LEVEL THAN MUTSUMI ...!?
HEE HEE...
...SO WHAT'S THIS AP THING?
AP IS THE ENERGY THAT DIVINE BEINGS SUCH AS OURSELVES NEED IN ORDER TO BE ACTIVE.
DIVINE BEINGS ARE CONSTANTLY USING AP WHENEVER THEY DO ANYTHING.
LIKE ATTACK OR TAKE DAMAGE.
IF WE RUN OUT OF AP, OUR TRANS-FORMATION MAY WEAR OFF—AND WE MAY EVEN BE WIPED OUT!

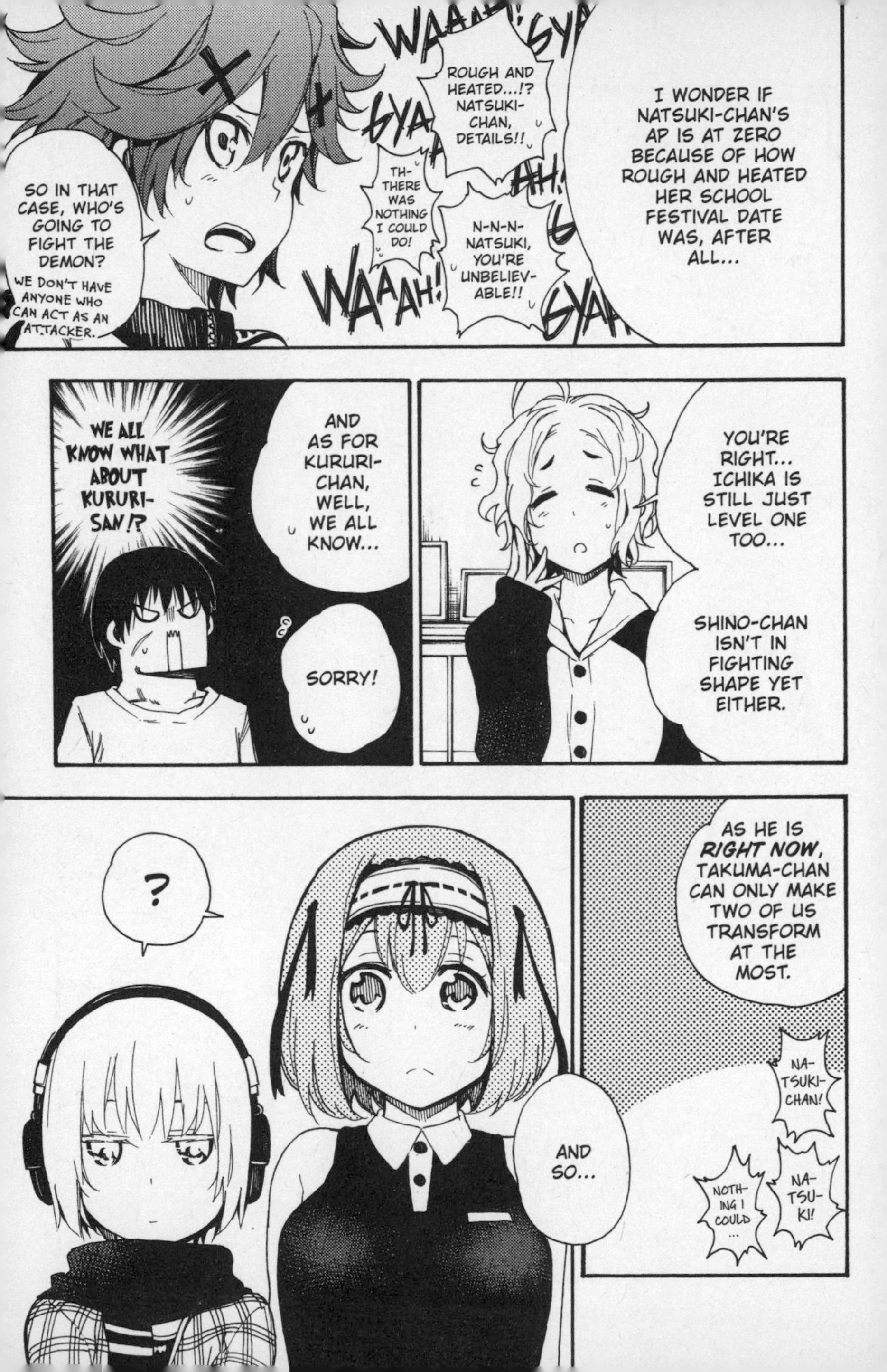
I WONDER IF NATSUKI-CHAN'S AP IS AT ZERO BECAUSE OF HOW ROUGH AND HEATED HER SCHOOL FESTIVAL DATE WAS, AFTER ALL...
ROUGH AND HEATED...!? NATSUKI-CHAN, DETAILS!!
N-N-N-NATSUKI, YOU'RE UNBELIEVABLE!!
TH-THERE WAS NOTHING I COULD DO!
WAAAH!
SO IN THAT CASE, WHO'S GOING TO FIGHT THE DEMON?
WE DON'T HAVE ANYONE WHO CAN ACT AS AN ATTACKER.
YOU'RE RIGHT... ICHIKA IS STILL JUST LEVEL ONE TOO...
SHINO-CHAN ISN'T IN FIGHTING SHAPE YET EITHER.
AND AS FOR KURURI-CHAN, WELL, WE ALL KNOW...
WE ALL KNOW WHAT ABOUT KURURI-SAN!?
SORRY!
AS HE IS RIGHT NOW, TAKUMA-CHAN CAN ONLY MAKE TWO OF US TRANSFORM AT THE MOST.
NATSUKI-CHAN!
NATSUKI!
NOTHING I COULD...
AND SO...
?

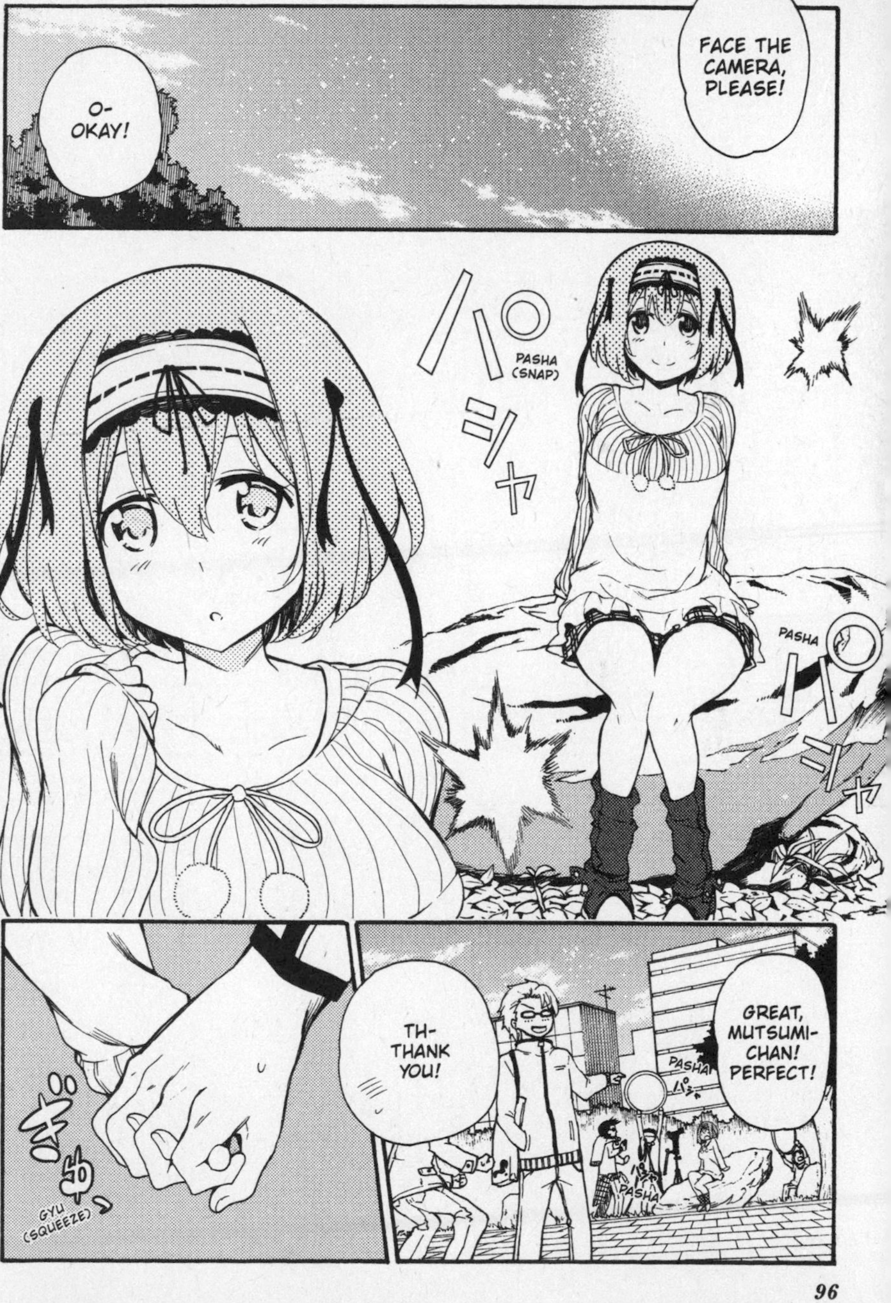
FACE THE CAMERA, PLEASE!
O-OKAY!
PASHA (SNAP)
PASHA
GREAT, MUTSUMI-CHAN! PERFECT!
PASHA
PASHA
TH-THANK YOU!
GYU (SQUEEZE)

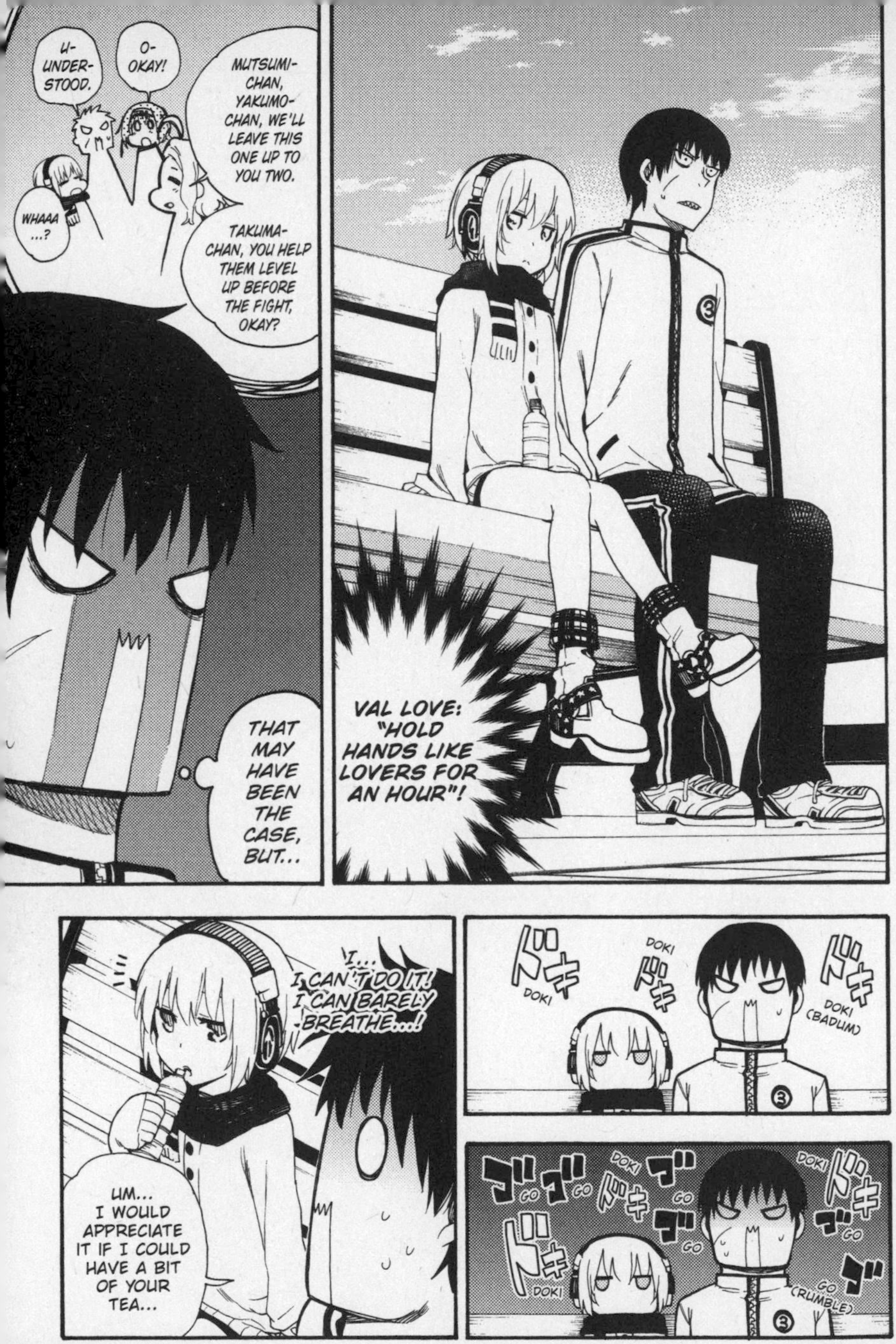
VAL LOVE: "HOLD HANDS LIKE LOVERS FOR AN HOUR"!
MUTSUMI-CHAN, YAKUMO-CHAN, WE'LL LEAVE THIS ONE UP TO YOU TWO.
O-OKAY!
U-UNDERSTOOD.
TAKUMA-CHAN, YOU HELP THEM LEVEL UP BEFORE THE FIGHT, OKAY?
WHAAA ...?
THAT MAY HAVE BEEN THE CASE, BUT...
ドキ DOKI (BADUM)
ドキ DOKI
ドキ DOKI
ドキ DOKI
ゴ GO
ドキ DOKI
ゴ GO
ゴ GO
ドキ DOKI
ゴ GO (RUMBLE)
I... I CAN'T DO IT! I CAN BARELY BREATHE...!
UM... I WOULD APPRECIATE IT IF I COULD HAVE A BIT OF YOUR TEA...

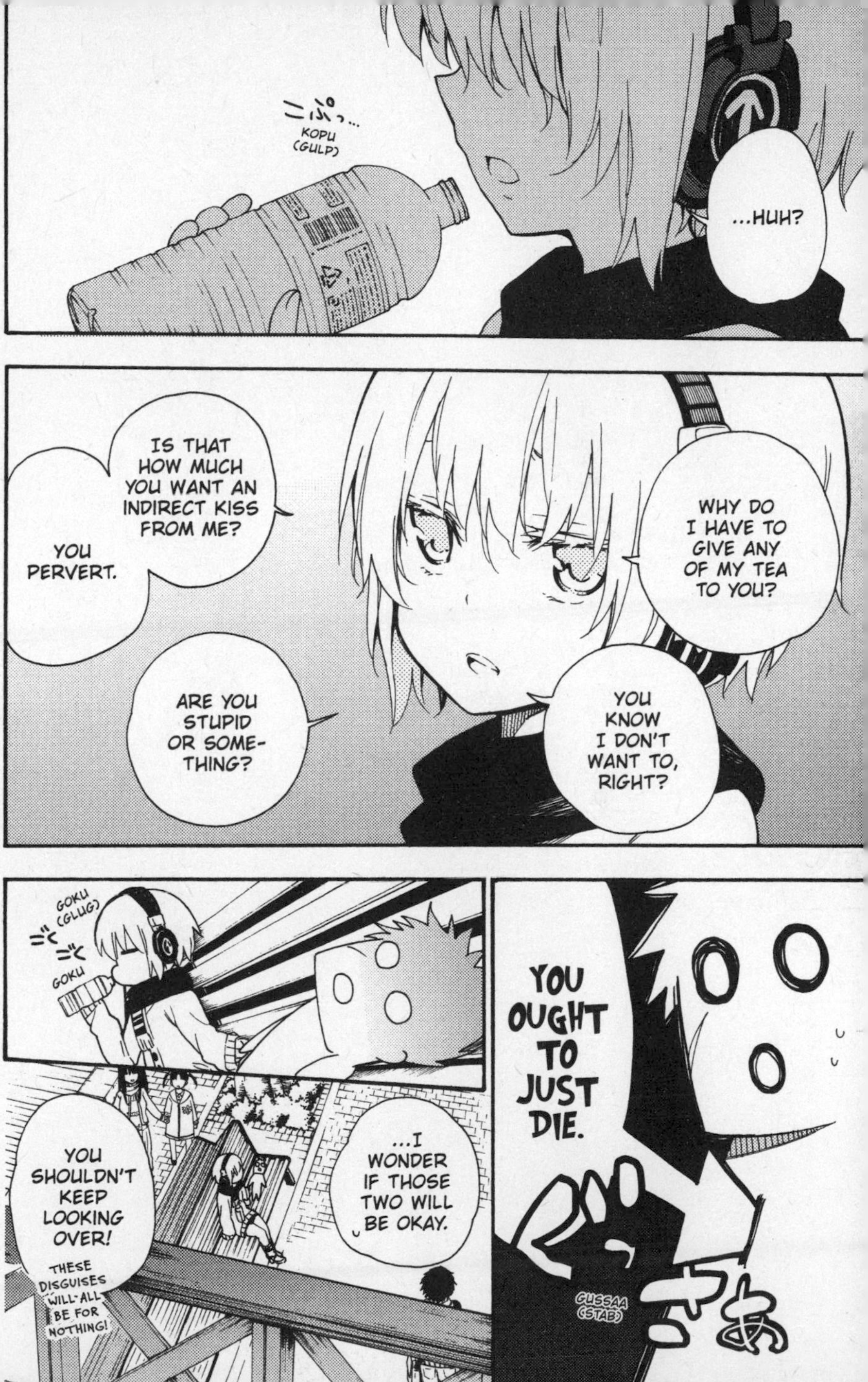
...HUH?
こぷっ...
KOPU (GULP)
WHY DO I HAVE TO GIVE ANY OF MY TEA TO YOU?
YOU KNOW I DON'T WANT TO, RIGHT?
IS THAT HOW MUCH YOU WANT AN INDIRECT KISS FROM ME?
YOU PERVERT.
ARE YOU STUPID OR SOME-THING?
YOU OUGHT TO JUST DIE.
GUSSAA (STAB)
GOKU (GLUG)
ごく
ごく
GOKU
...I WONDER IF THOSE TWO WILL BE OKAY.
YOU SHOULDN'T KEEP LOOKING OVER!
THESE DISGUISES WILL ALL BE FOR NOTHING!

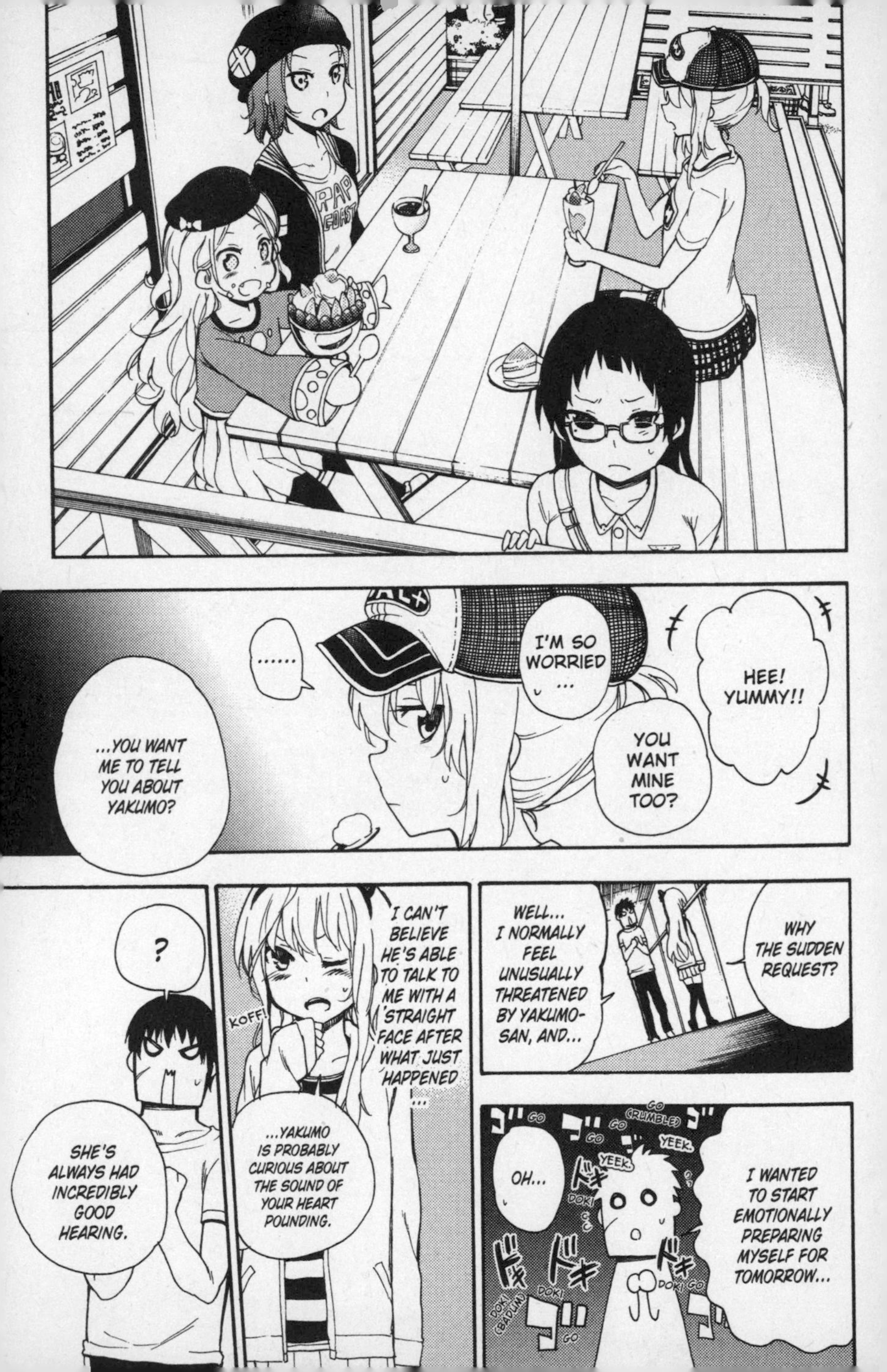
HEE! YUMMY!!
YOU WANT MINE TOO?
I'M SO WORRIED ...
......
...YOU WANT ME TO TELL YOU ABOUT YAKUMO?
WHY THE SUDDEN REQUEST?
WELL... I NORMALLY FEEL UNUSUALLY THREATENED BY YAKUMO-SAN, AND...
I WANTED TO START EMOTIONALLY PREPARING MYSELF FOR TOMORROW...
GO GO GO (RUMBLE)
YEEK. YEEK.
OH...
DOKI DOKI DOKI (BADUM)
GO GO
I CAN'T BELIEVE HE'S ABLE TO TALK TO ME WITH A STRAIGHT FACE AFTER WHAT JUST HAPPENED...
KOFF!
...YAKUMO IS PROBABLY CURIOUS ABOUT THE SOUND OF YOUR HEART POUNDING.
?
SHE'S ALWAYS HAD INCREDIBLY GOOD HEARING.

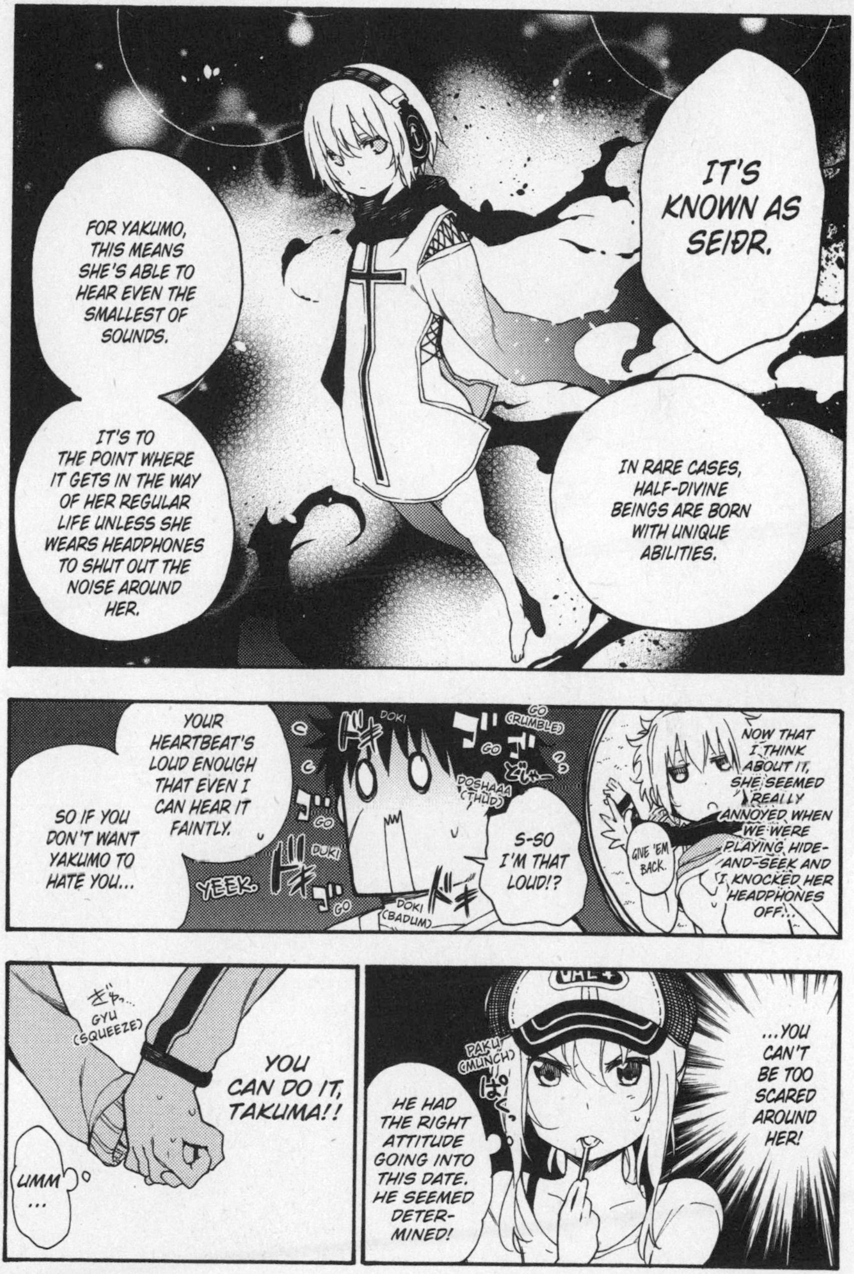
IT'S KNOWN AS SEIÐR.
IN RARE CASES, HALF-DIVINE BEINGS ARE BORN WITH UNIQUE ABILITIES.
FOR YAKUMO, THIS MEANS SHE'S ABLE TO HEAR EVEN THE SMALLEST OF SOUNDS.
IT'S TO THE POINT WHERE IT GETS IN THE WAY OF HER REGULAR LIFE UNLESS SHE WEARS HEADPHONES TO SHUT OUT THE NOISE AROUND HER.
NOW THAT I THINK ABOUT IT, SHE SEEMED REALLY ANNOYED WHEN WE WERE PLAYING HIDE-AND-SEEK AND I KNOCKED HER HEADPHONES OFF...
GIVE 'EM BACK.
GO (RUMBLE)
GO
DOKI
DOSHAAA (THUD)
S-SO I'M THAT LOUD!?
DUKI
GO
DOKI (BADUM)
GO
YEEK.
YOUR HEARTBEAT'S LOUD ENOUGH THAT EVEN I CAN HEAR IT FAINTLY.
SO IF YOU DON'T WANT YAKUMO TO HATE YOU...
...YOU CAN'T BE TOO SCARED AROUND HER!
PAKU (MUNCH)
HE HAD THE RIGHT ATTITUDE GOING INTO THIS DATE. HE SEEMED DETER-MINED!
GYU (SQUEEZE)
YOU CAN DO IT, TAKUMA!!
UMM...

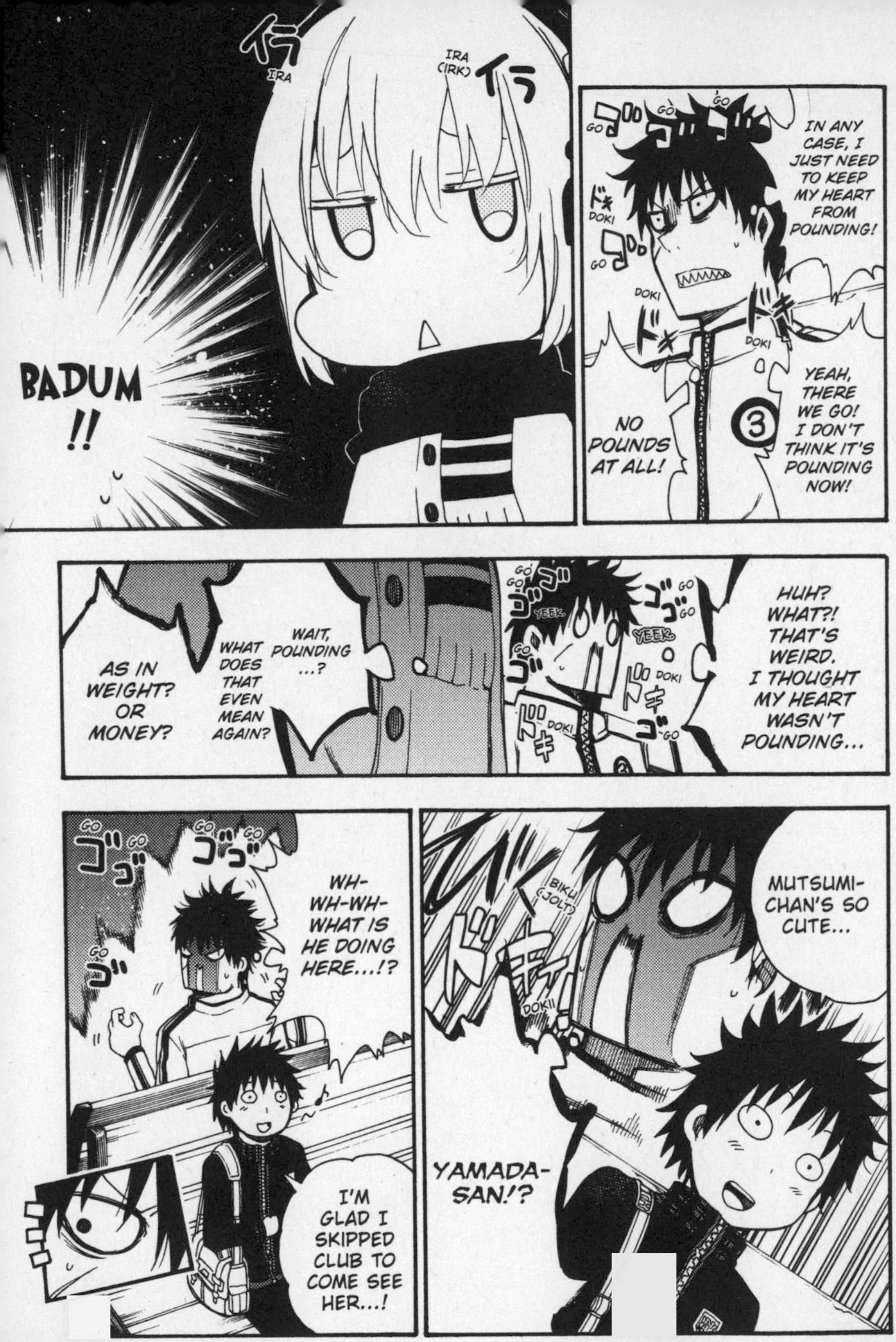
GO GO GO GO
IN ANY CASE, I JUST NEED TO KEEP MY HEART FROM POUNDING!
DOKI
GO
DOKI
DOKI
YEAH, THERE WE GO! I DON'T THINK IT'S POUNDING NOW!
NO POUNDS AT ALL!
IRA
IRA (IRK)
BADUM !!
GO GO GO GO GO
YEEK
YEEK
DOKI
DOKI
GO
HUH? WHAT?! THAT'S WEIRD. I THOUGHT MY HEART WASN'T POUNDING...
WAIT, POUNDING ...?
WHAT DOES THAT EVEN MEAN AGAIN?
AS IN WEIGHT? OR MONEY?
MUTSUMI-CHAN'S SO CUTE...
BIKU (JOLT)
DOKI!
YAMADA-SAN!?
GO GO GO GO
GO
WH-WH-WH-WHAT IS HE DOING HERE...!?
I'M GLAD I SKIPPED CLUB TO COME SEE HER...!

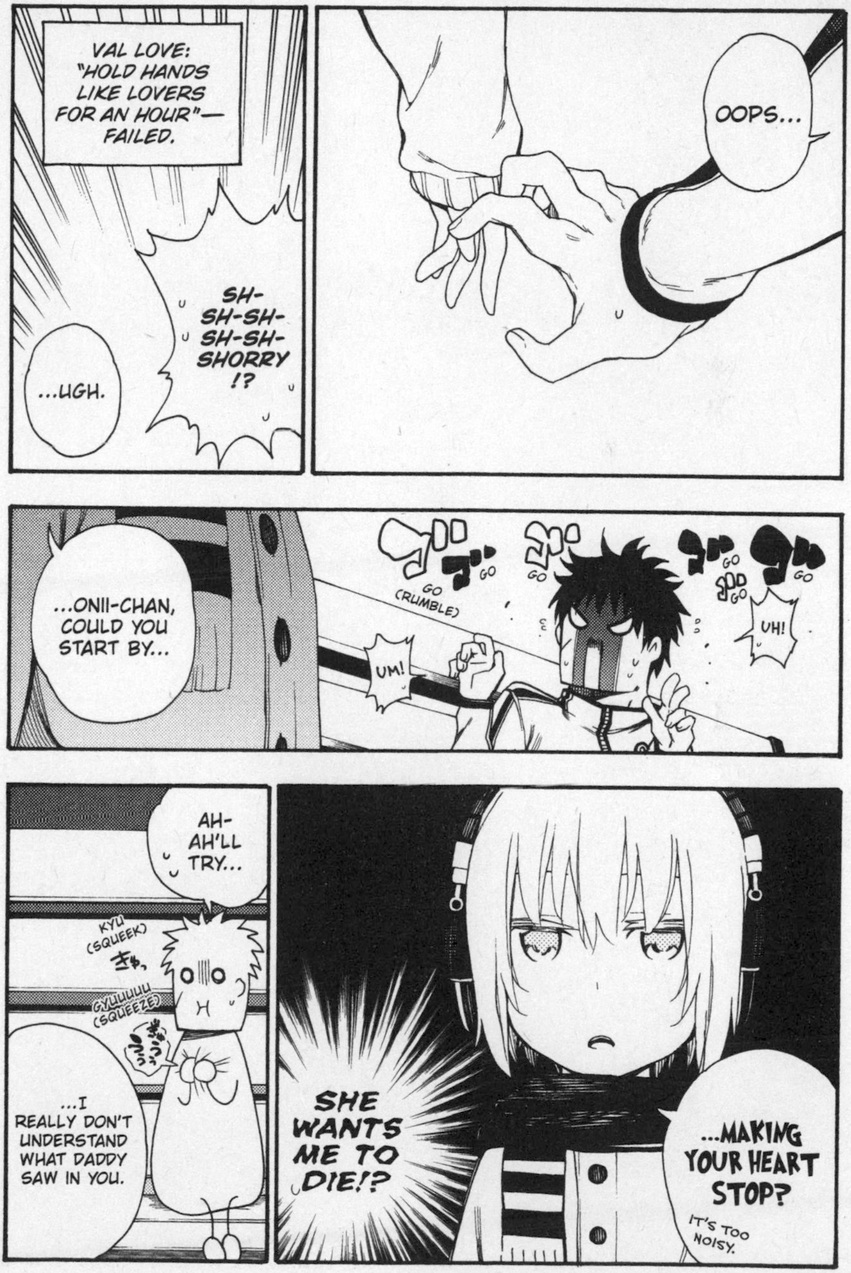
OOPS...
VAL LOVE: "HOLD HANDS LIKE LOVERS FOR AN HOUR"—FAILED.
SH-SH-SH-SH-SH-SHORRY!?
...UGH.
GO GO GO GO GO
UH!
GO (RUMBLE)
UM!
...ONII-CHAN, COULD YOU START BY...
...MAKING YOUR HEART STOP?
IT'S TOO NOISY.
SHE WANTS ME TO DIE!?
AH-AH'LL TRY...
KYU (SQUEEK)
GYUUUUU (SQUEEZE)
...I REALLY DON'T UNDERSTAND WHAT DADDY SAW IN YOU.

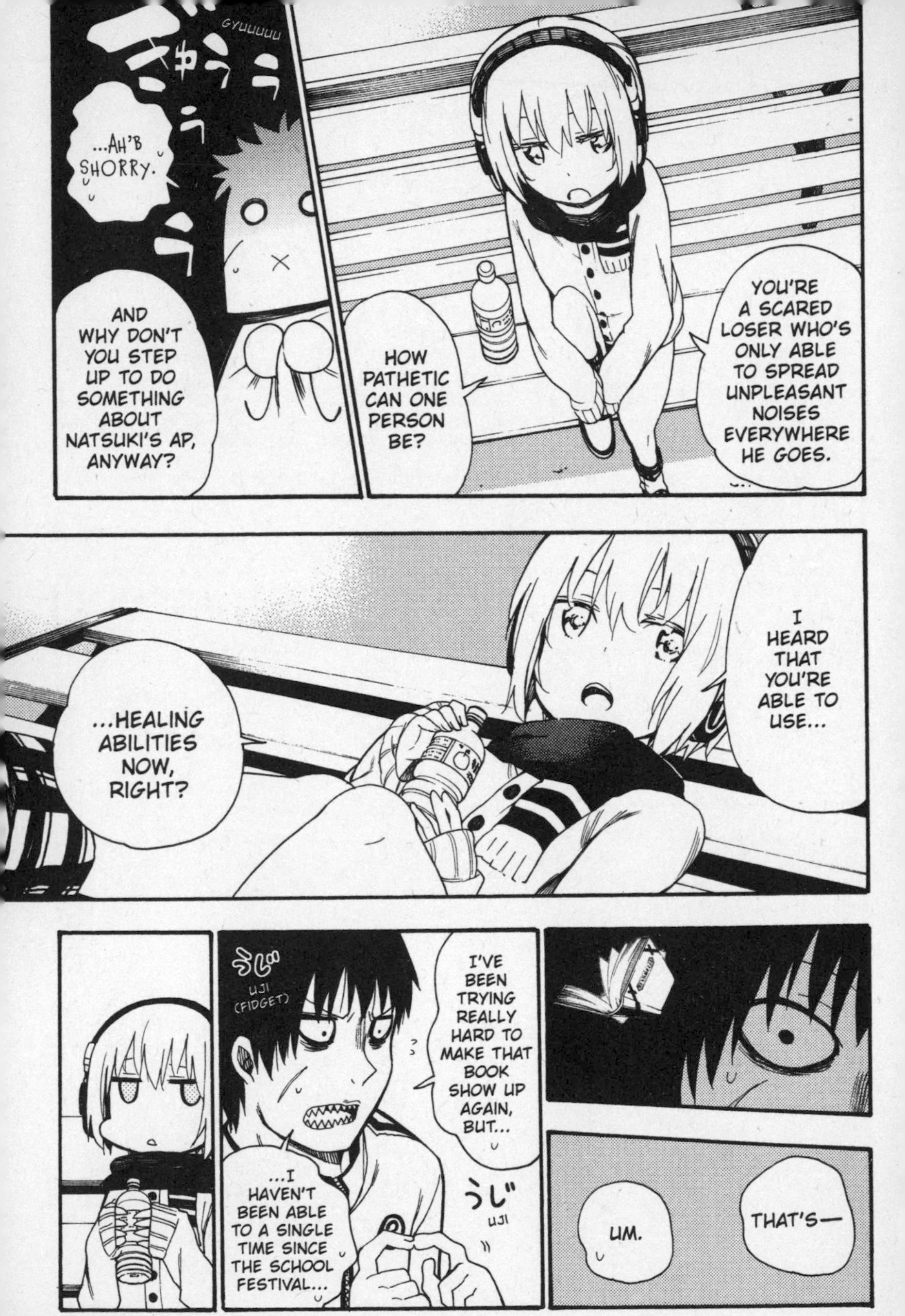
YOU'RE A SCARED LOSER WHO'S ONLY ABLE TO SPREAD UNPLEASANT NOISES EVERYWHERE HE GOES.
HOW PATHETIC CAN ONE PERSON BE?
GYUUUUUU
...AH'B SHORRY.
AND WHY DON'T YOU STEP UP TO DO SOMETHING ABOUT NATSUKI'S AP, ANYWAY?
I HEARD THAT YOU'RE ABLE TO USE...
...HEALING ABILITIES NOW, RIGHT?
THAT'S—
UM.
I'VE BEEN TRYING REALLY HARD TO MAKE THAT BOOK SHOW UP AGAIN, BUT...
うじ
UJI (FIDGET)
...I HAVEN'T BEEN ABLE TO A SINGLE TIME SINCE THE SCHOOL FESTIVAL...
うじ
UJI

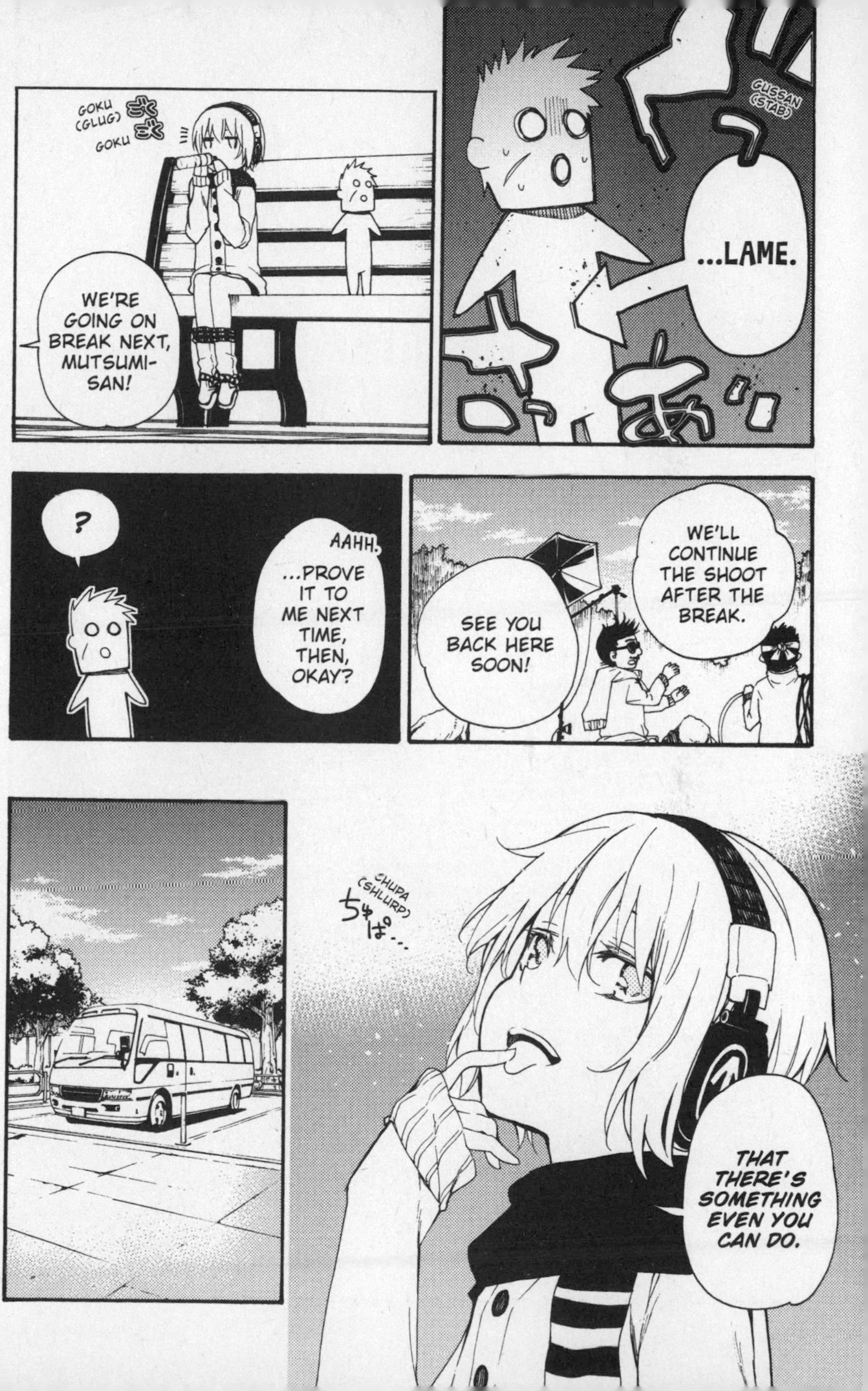
GUSSAN (STAB)
...LAME.
GOKU (GLUG) GOKU
WE'RE GOING ON BREAK NEXT, MUTSUMI-SAN!
WE'LL CONTINUE THE SHOOT AFTER THE BREAK.
SEE YOU BACK HERE SOON!
AAHH.
...PROVE IT TO ME NEXT TIME, THEN, OKAY?
?
CHUPA (SHLURP)
THAT THERE'S SOMETHING EVEN YOU CAN DO.

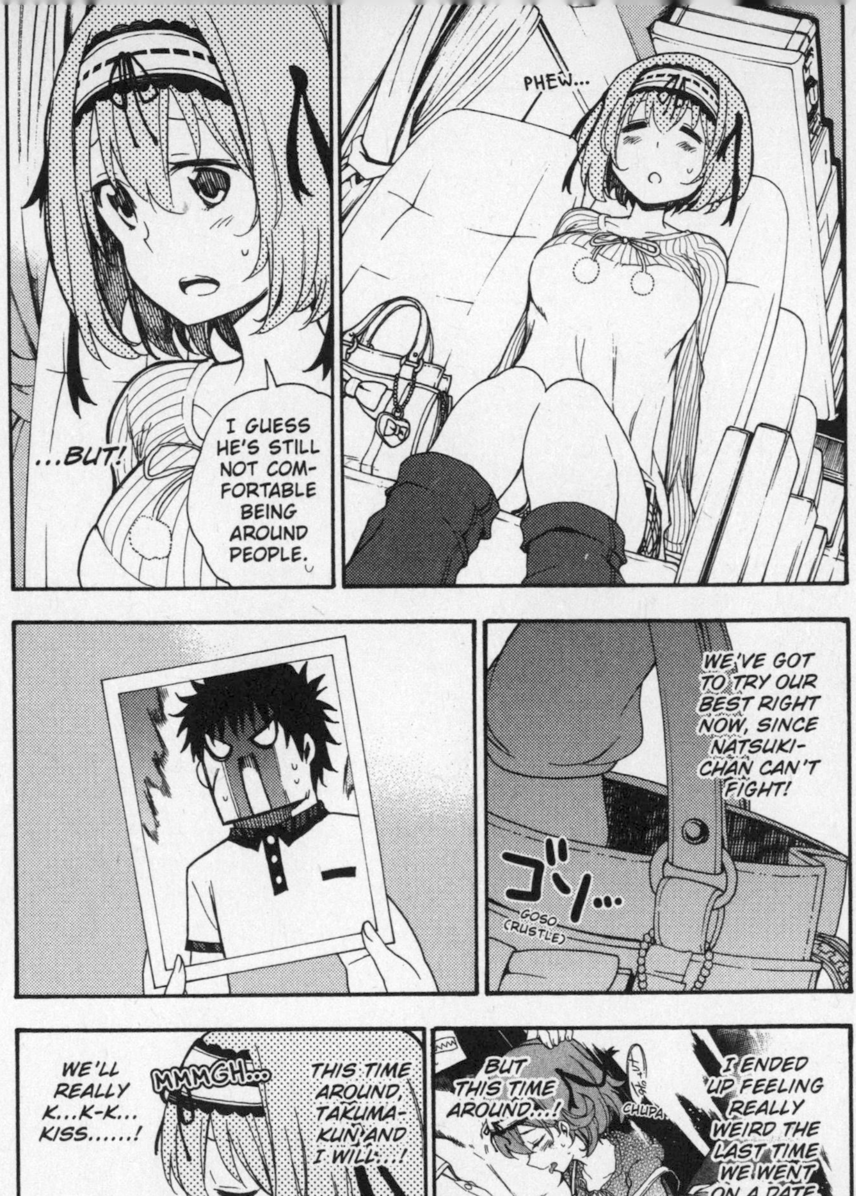
PHEW...
I GUESS HE'S STILL NOT COM-FORTABLE BEING AROUND PEOPLE.
...BUT!
WE'VE GOT TO TRY OUR BEST RIGHT NOW, SINCE NATSUKI-CHAN CAN'T FIGHT!
ゴソ...
GOSO (RUSTLE)
I ENDED UP FEELING REALLY WEIRD THE LAST TIME WE WENT ON A DATE.
BUT THIS TIME AROUND...!
CHUPA
CHUPA
THIS TIME AROUND, TAKUMA-KUN AND I WILL...!
MMMGH...
WE'LL REALLY K...K-K... KISS......!

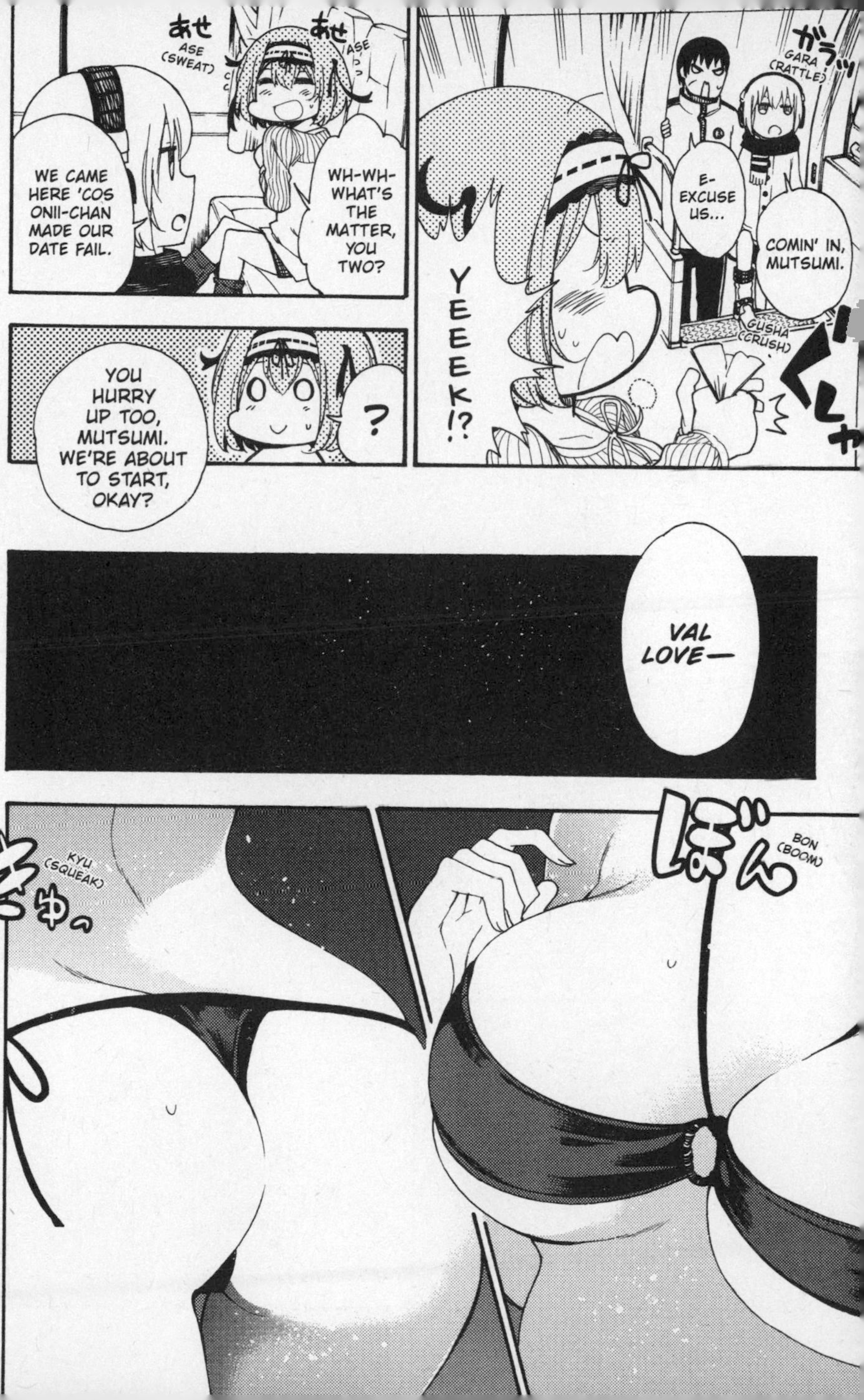
ガラッ
GARA (RATTLE)
COMIN' IN, MUTSUMI.
E-EXCUSE US...
YEEEK!?
ぐしゃ
GUSHA (CRUSH)
あせ
ASE (SWEAT)
あせ
ASE
WH-WH-WHAT'S THE MATTER, YOU TWO?
WE CAME HERE 'COS ONII-CHAN MADE OUR DATE FAIL.
?
YOU HURRY UP TOO, MUTSUMI. WE'RE ABOUT TO START, OKAY?
VAL LOVE—
ぼん
BON (BOOM)
きゅっ
KYU (SQUEAK)

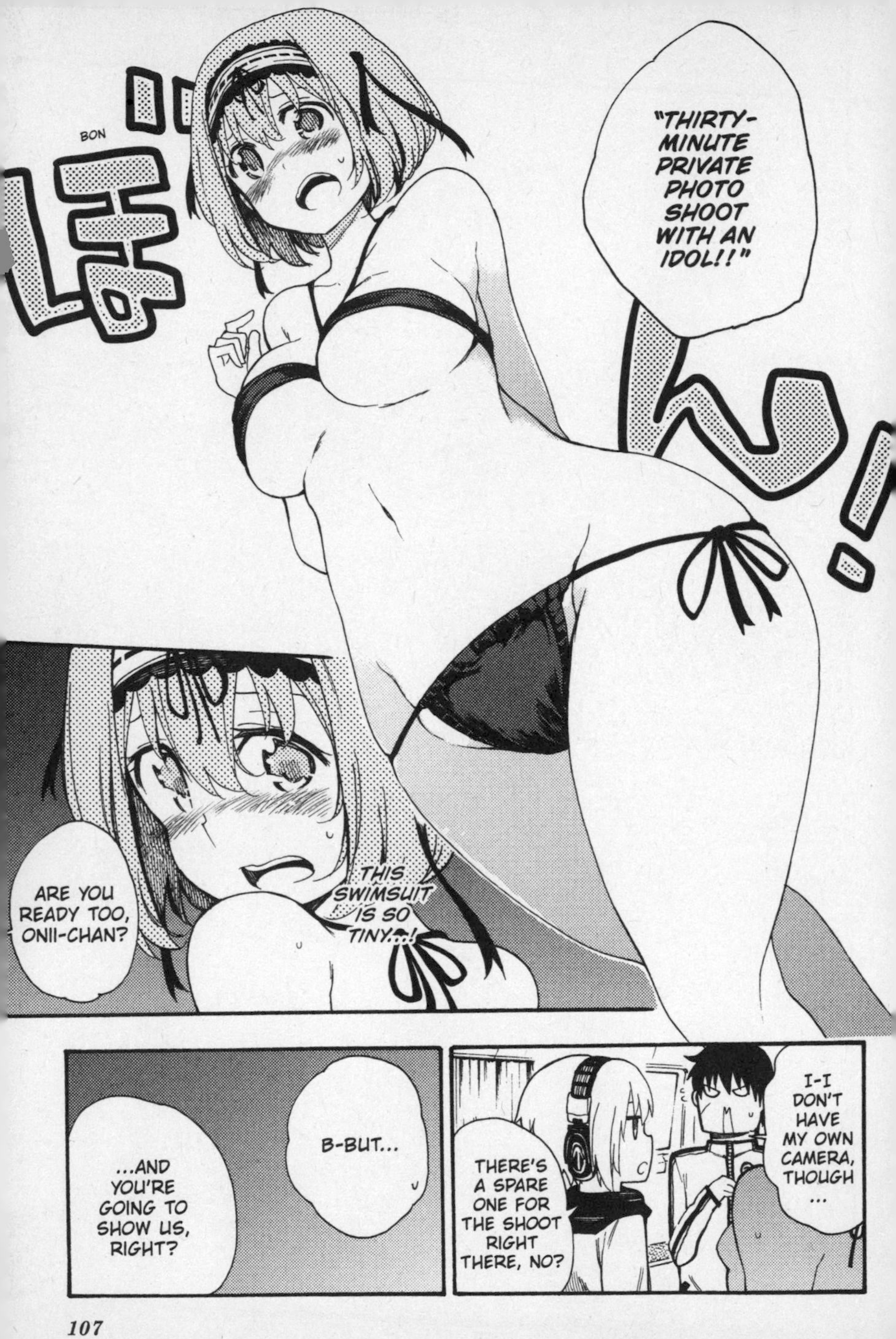
"THIRTY-MINUTE PRIVATE PHOTO SHOOT WITH AN IDOL!!"
BON
ぼん!!
THIS SWIMSUIT IS SO TINY...!
ARE YOU READY TOO, ONII-CHAN?
I-I DON'T HAVE MY OWN CAMERA, THOUGH...
THERE'S A SPARE ONE FOR THE SHOOT RIGHT THERE, NO?
B-BUT...
...AND YOU'RE GOING TO SHOW US, RIGHT?

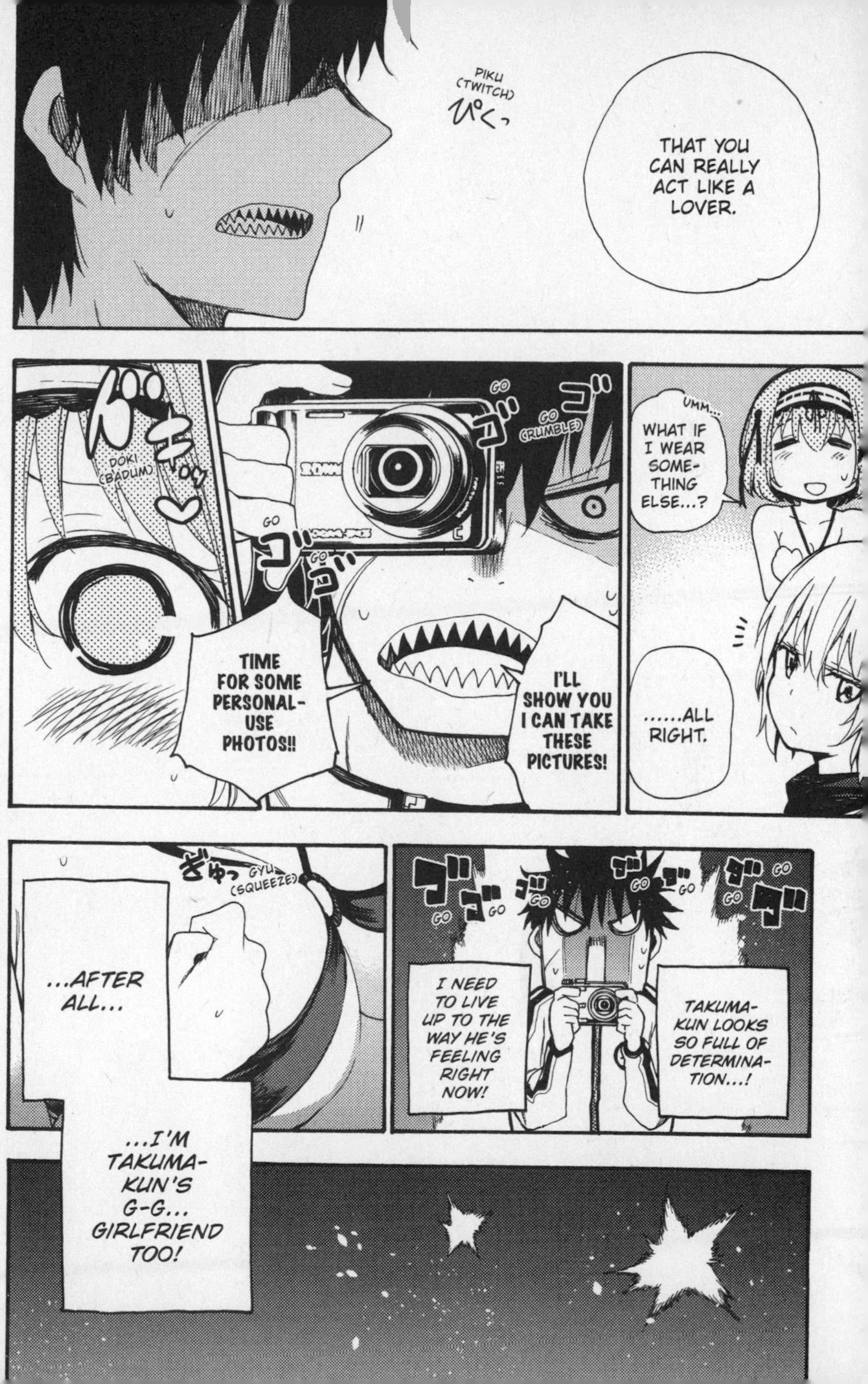
THAT YOU CAN REALLY ACT LIKE A LOVER.
PIKU (TWITCH)
ぴくっ
UMM... WHAT IF I WEAR SOME-THING ELSE...?
......ALL RIGHT.
GO GO (RUMBLE)
I'LL SHOW YOU I CAN TAKE THESE PICTURES!
TIME FOR SOME PERSONAL-USE PHOTOS!!
GO GO
DOKI (BADUM)
GO GO GO GO GO GO GO
TAKUMA-KUN LOOKS SO FULL OF DETERMINA-TION...!
I NEED TO LIVE UP TO THE WAY HE'S FEELING RIGHT NOW!
GYU (SQUEEZE)
...AFTER ALL...
...I'M TAKUMA-KUN'S G-G... GIRLFRIEND TOO!

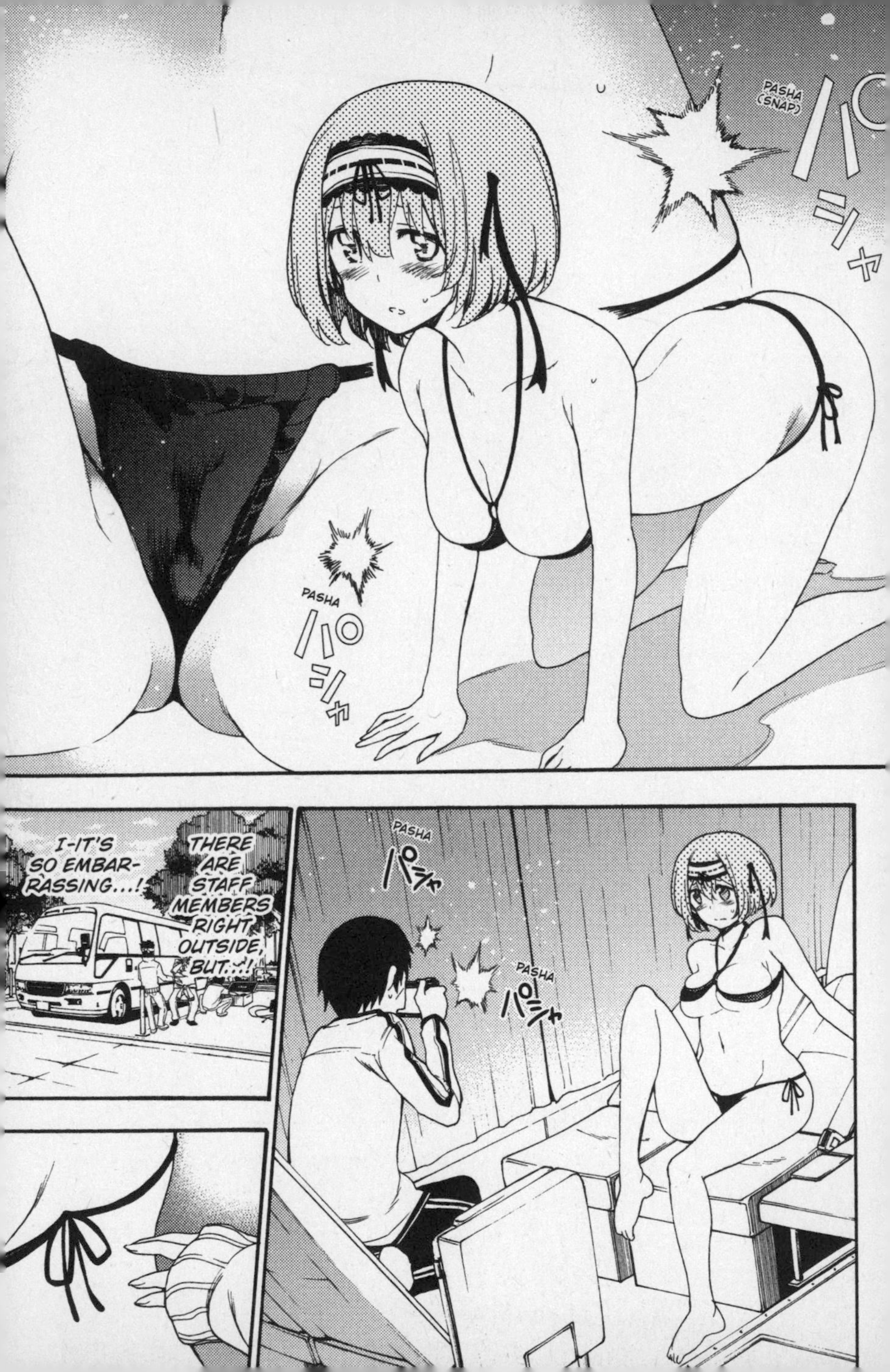
PASHA (SNAP)
パシャ
PASHA
パシャ
PASHA
パシャ
PASHA
パシャ
THERE ARE STAFF MEMBERS RIGHT OUTSIDE, BUT...!
I-IT'S SO EMBARRASSING...!

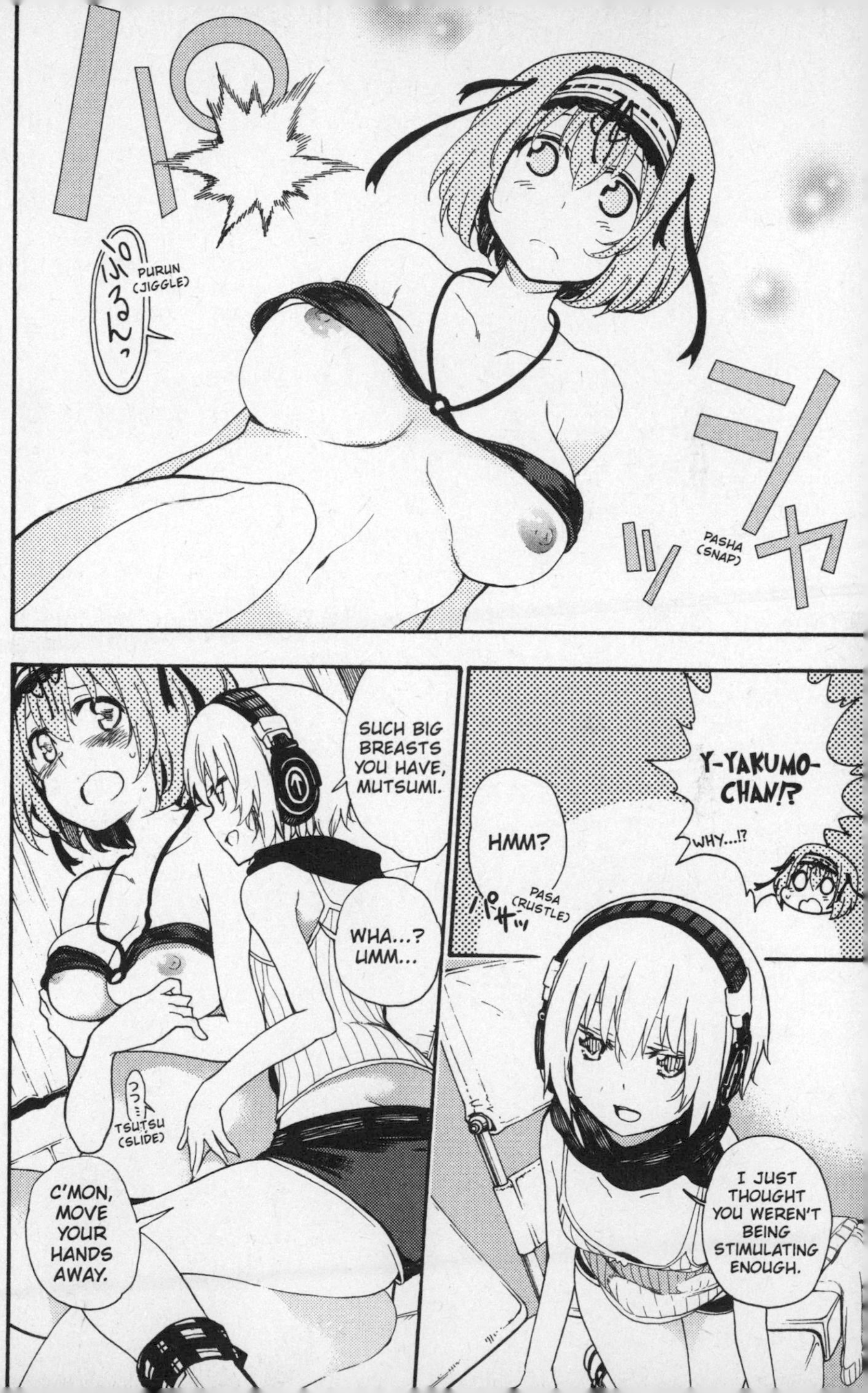
PASHA (SNAP)
ぷるんっ
PURUN (JIGGLE)
Y-YAKUMO-CHAN!?
WHY...!?
HMM?
PASA (RUSTLE)
I JUST THOUGHT YOU WEREN'T BEING STIMULATING ENOUGH.
SUCH BIG BREASTS YOU HAVE, MUTSUMI.
WHA...? UMM...
TSUTSU (SLIDE)
C'MON, MOVE YOUR HANDS AWAY.

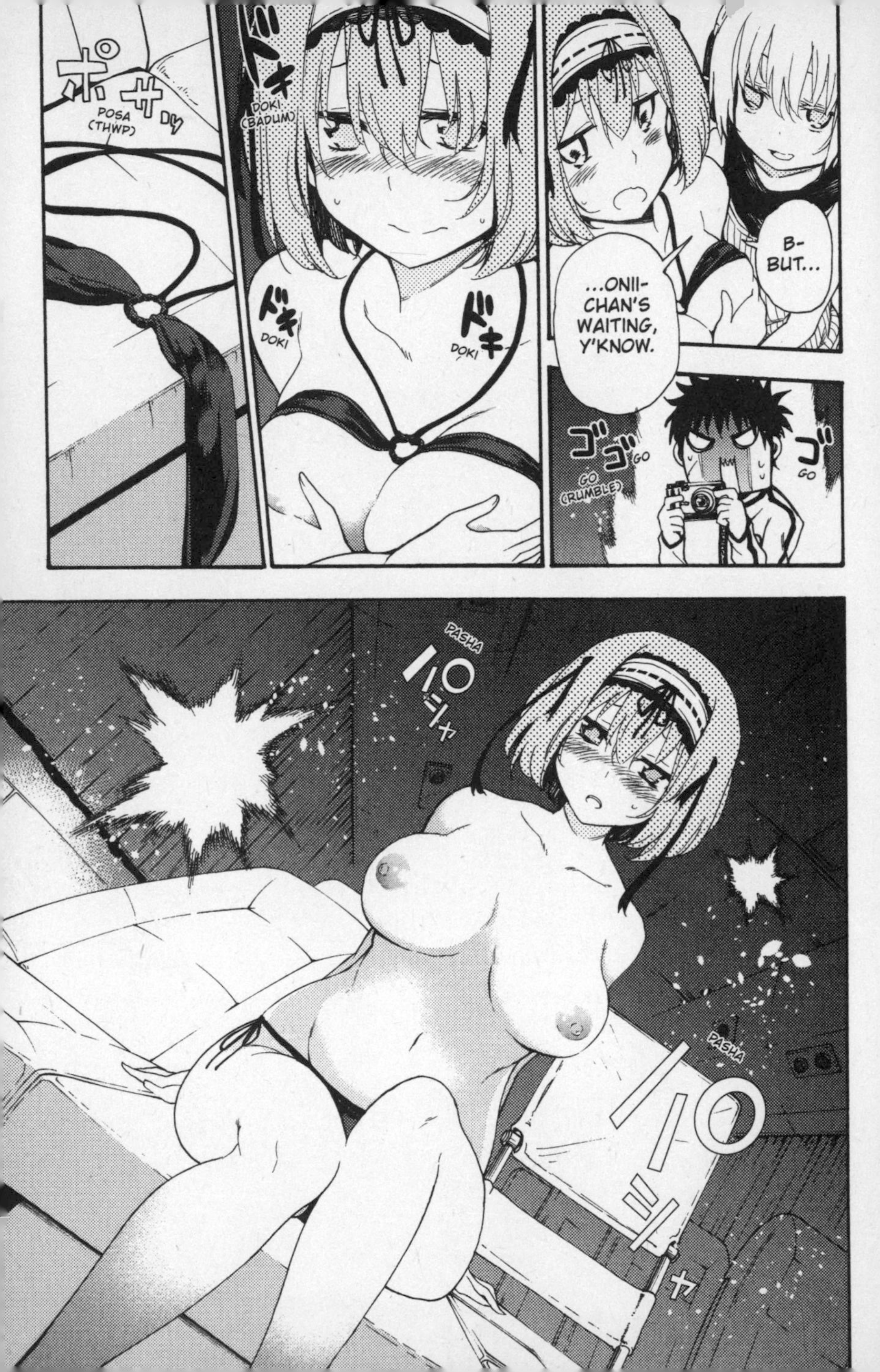
B-BUT...
...ONII-CHAN'S WAITING, Y'KNOW.
ゴゴ
GO GO (RUMBLE)
ゴ
GO
ドキ
DOKI (BADUM)
ドキ
DOKI
ドキ
DOKI
ポサッ
POSA (THWP)
パシャ
PASHA
パシャ
PASHA

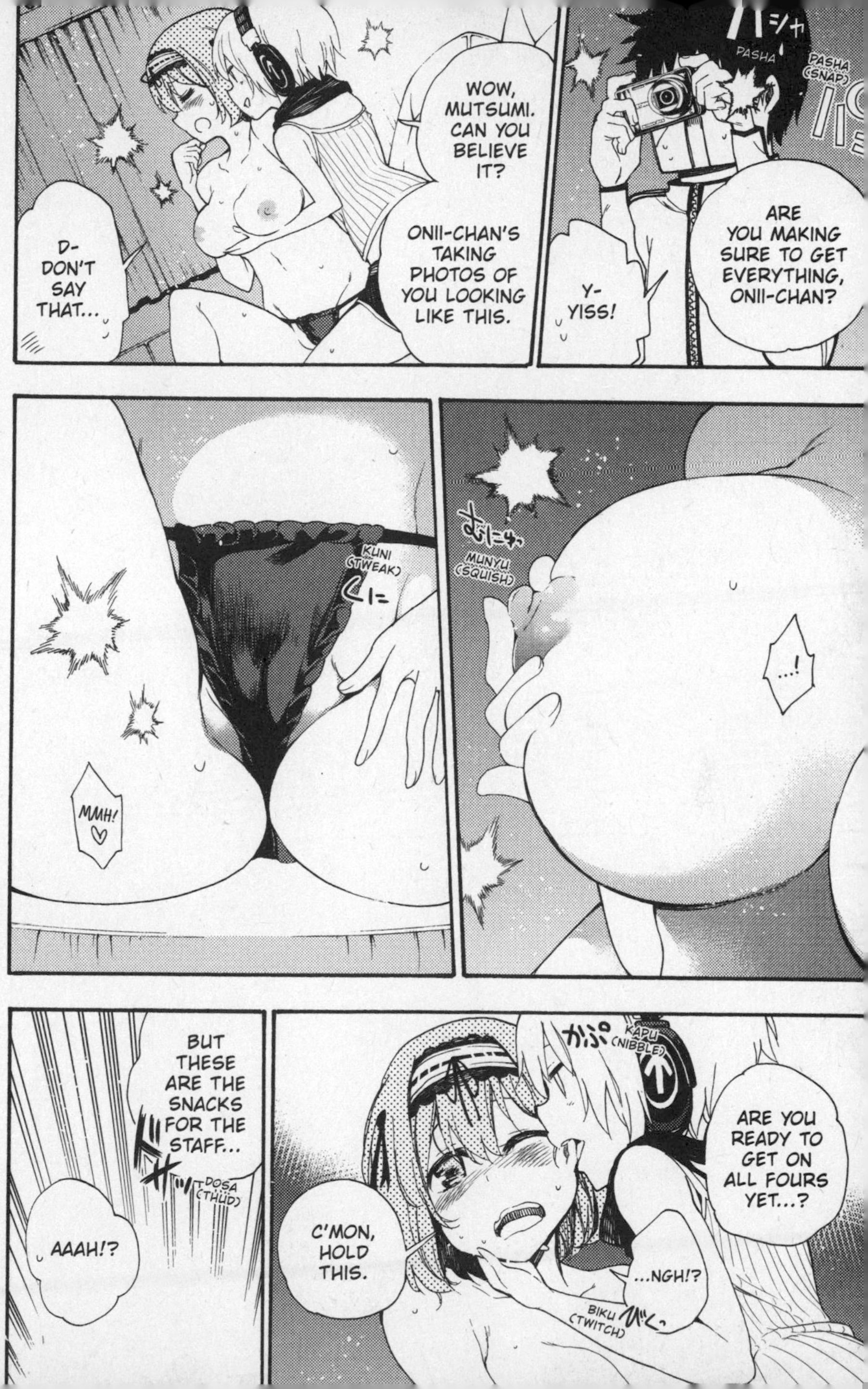
PASHA
PASHA (SNAP)
ARE YOU MAKING SURE TO GET EVERYTHING, ONII-CHAN?
Y-YISS!
WOW, MUTSUMI. CAN YOU BELIEVE IT?
ONII-CHAN'S TAKING PHOTOS OF YOU LOOKING LIKE THIS.
D-DON'T SAY THAT...
MUNYU (SQUISH)
...!
KUNI (TWEAK)
MMH! ♥
KAPU (NIBBLE)
ARE YOU READY TO GET ON ALL FOURS YET...?
...NGH!?
BIKU (TWITCH)
C'MON, HOLD THIS.
BUT THESE ARE THE SNACKS FOR THE STAFF...
DOSA (THUD)
AAAH!?

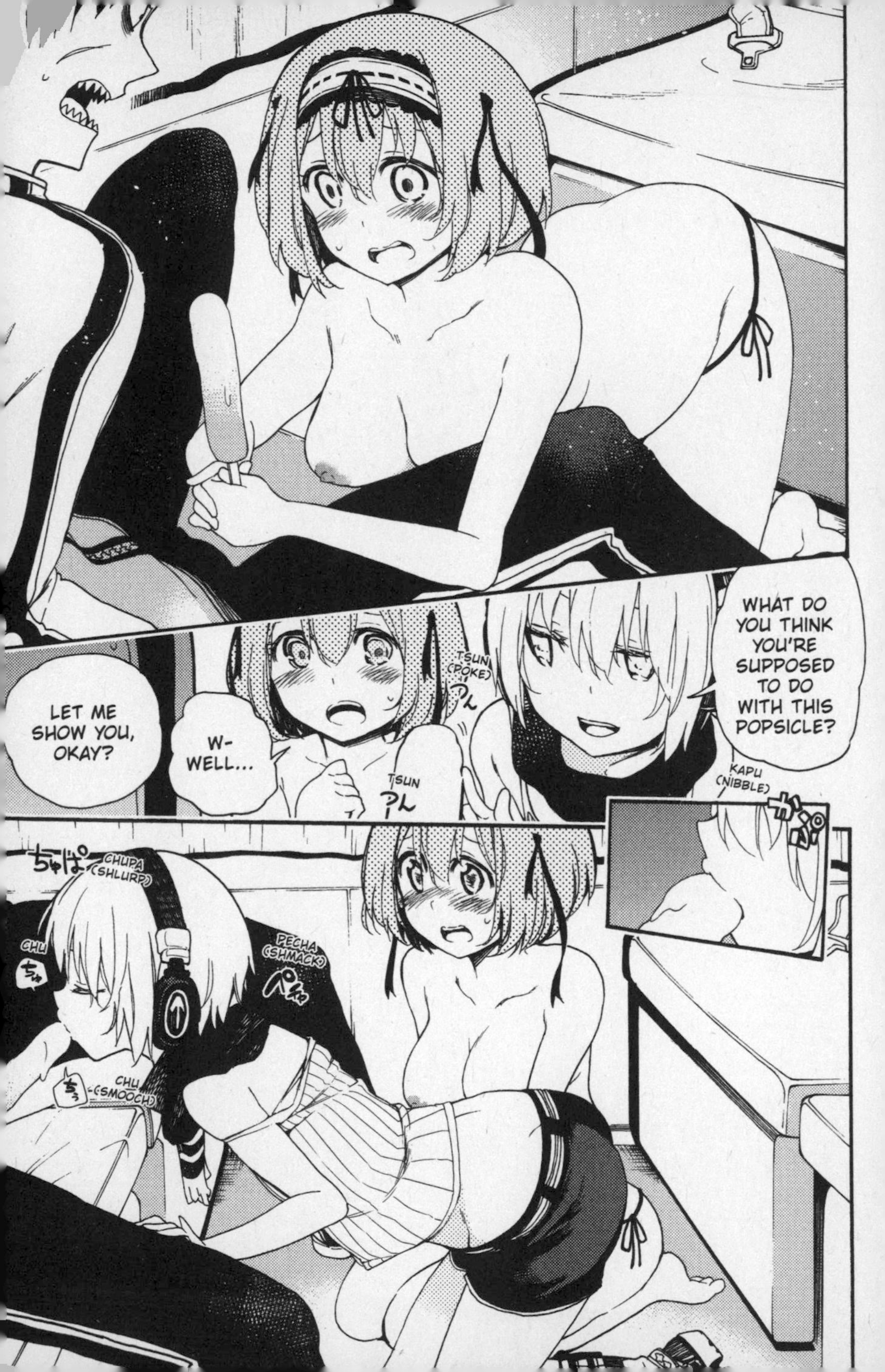
WHAT DO YOU THINK YOU'RE SUPPOSED TO DO WITH THIS POPSICLE?
TSUN (POKE)
つん
W-WELL...
TSUN
つん
LET ME SHOW YOU, OKAY?
KAPU (NIBBLE)
PECHA (SHMACK)
ぺちゃ
ちゅぱ
CHUPA (SHLURP)
CHU
ちゅ
CHU (SMOOCH)

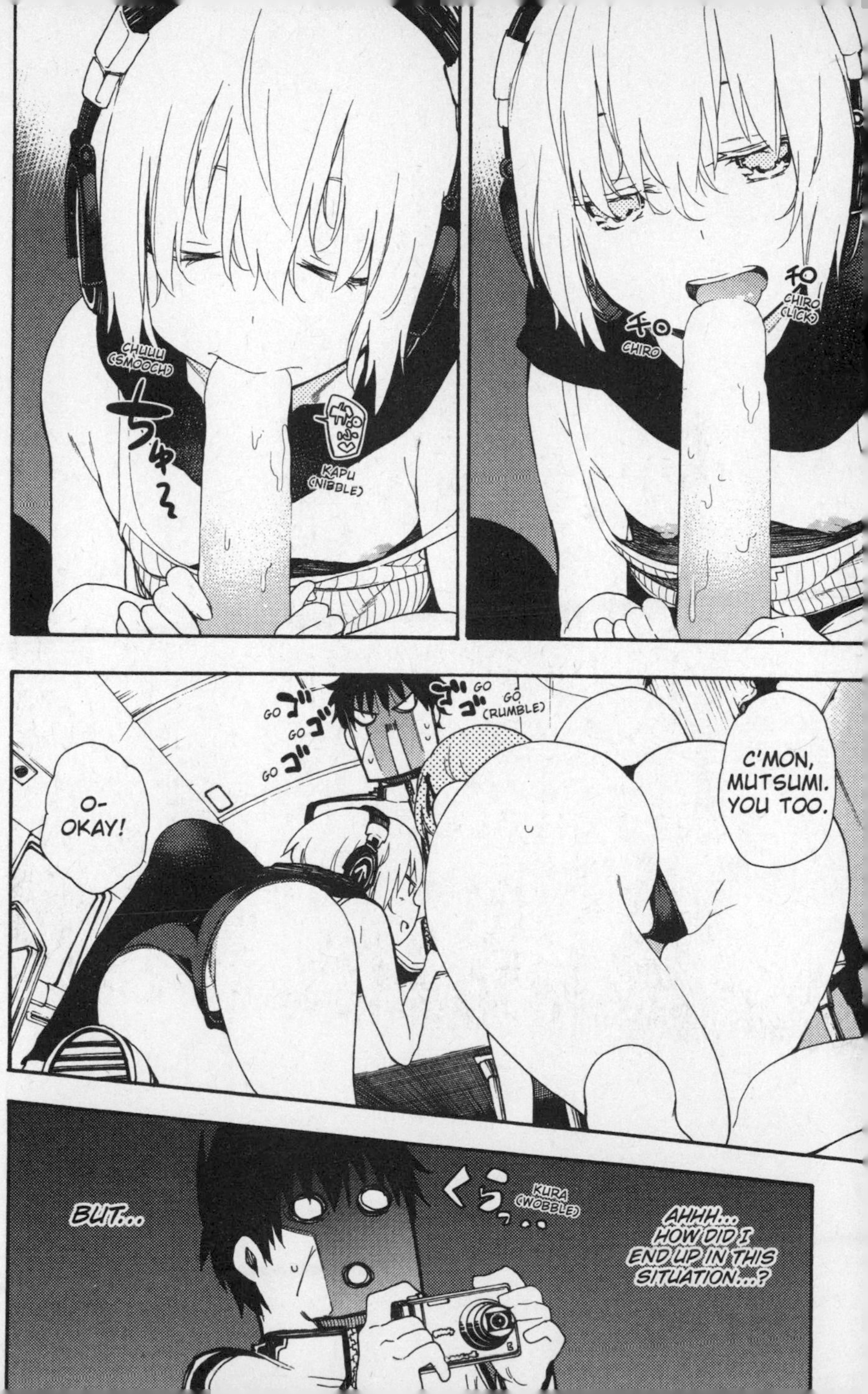

チロ
CHIRO (LICK)
チロ
CHIRO
CHUUU (SMOOCH)
KAPU (NIBBLE)
C'MON, MUTSUMI. YOU TOO.
GO GO (RUMBLE)
GO GO GO
O-OKAY!
AHHH... HOW DID I END UP IN THIS SITUATION...?
KURA (WOBBLE)
BUT...

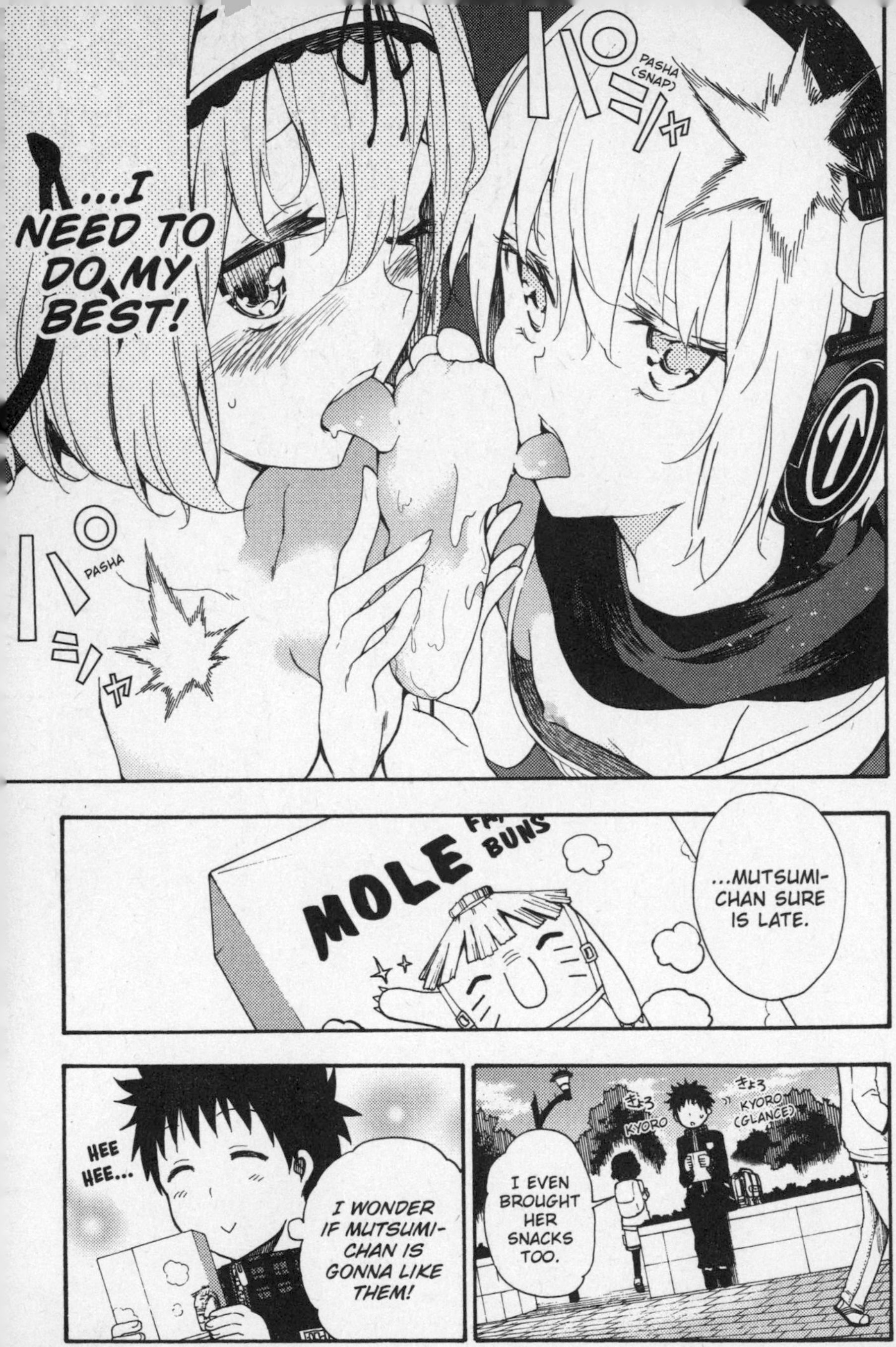
パシャ
PASHA (SNAP)
...I NEED TO DO MY BEST!
パシャ
PASHA
MOLE
BUNS
...MUTSUMI-CHAN SURE IS LATE.
きょろ
KYORO (GLANCE)
きょろ
KYORO
I EVEN BROUGHT HER SNACKS TOO.
I WONDER IF MUTSUMI-CHAN IS GONNA LIKE THEM!
HEE HEE...

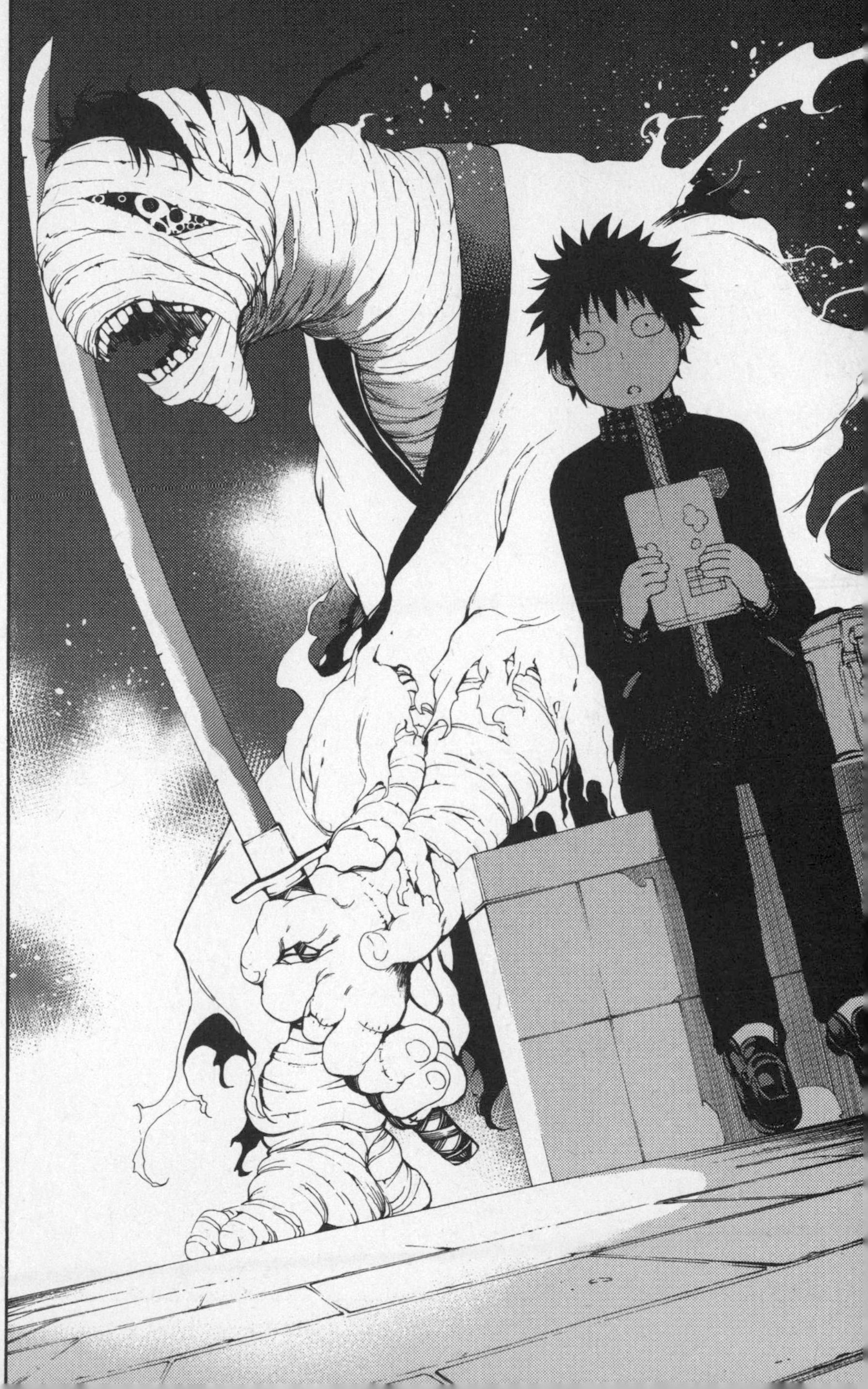

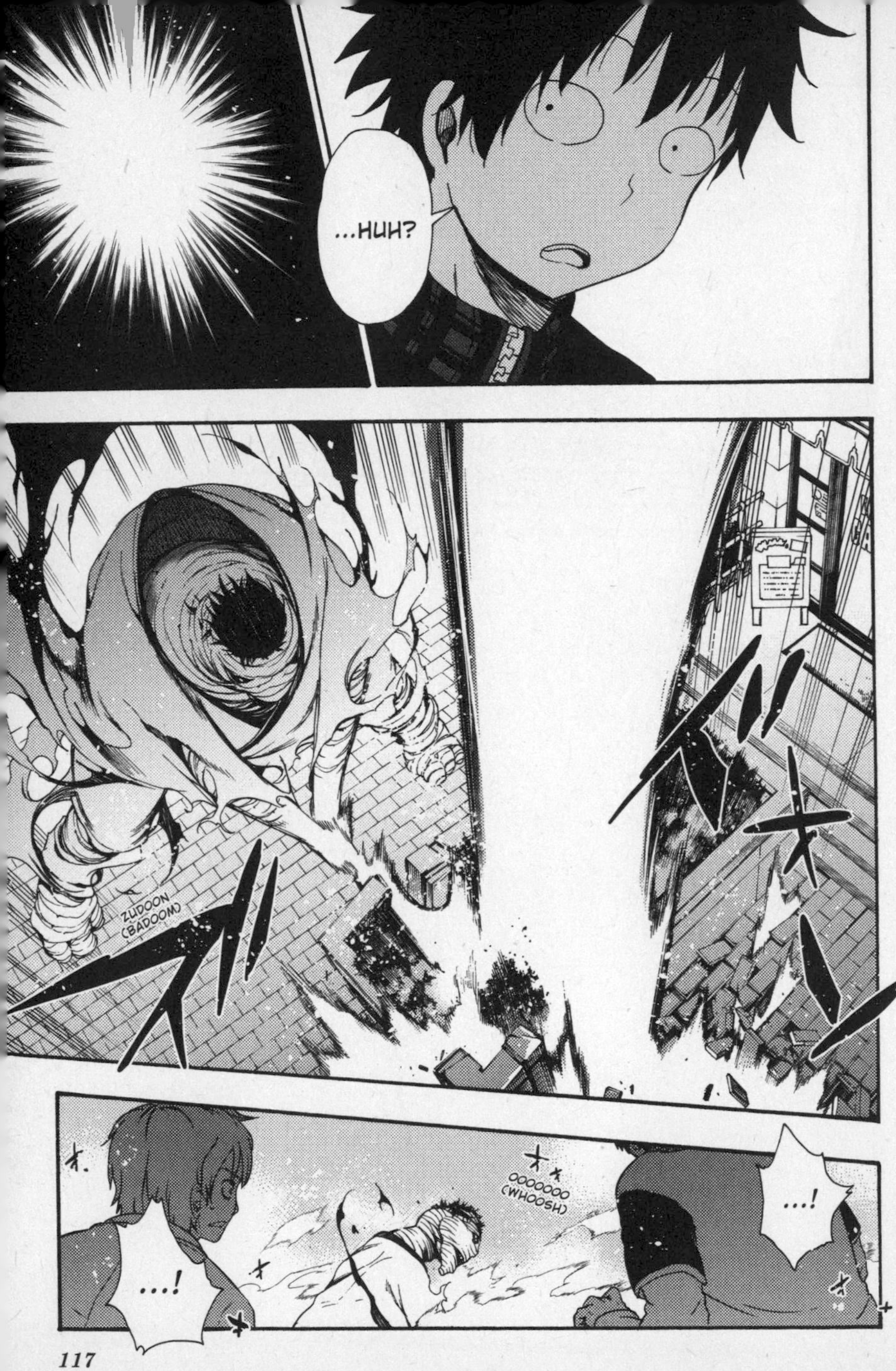
...HUH?
ZUDOON
(BADOOM)
...!
OOOOOOO
(WHOOSH)
...!

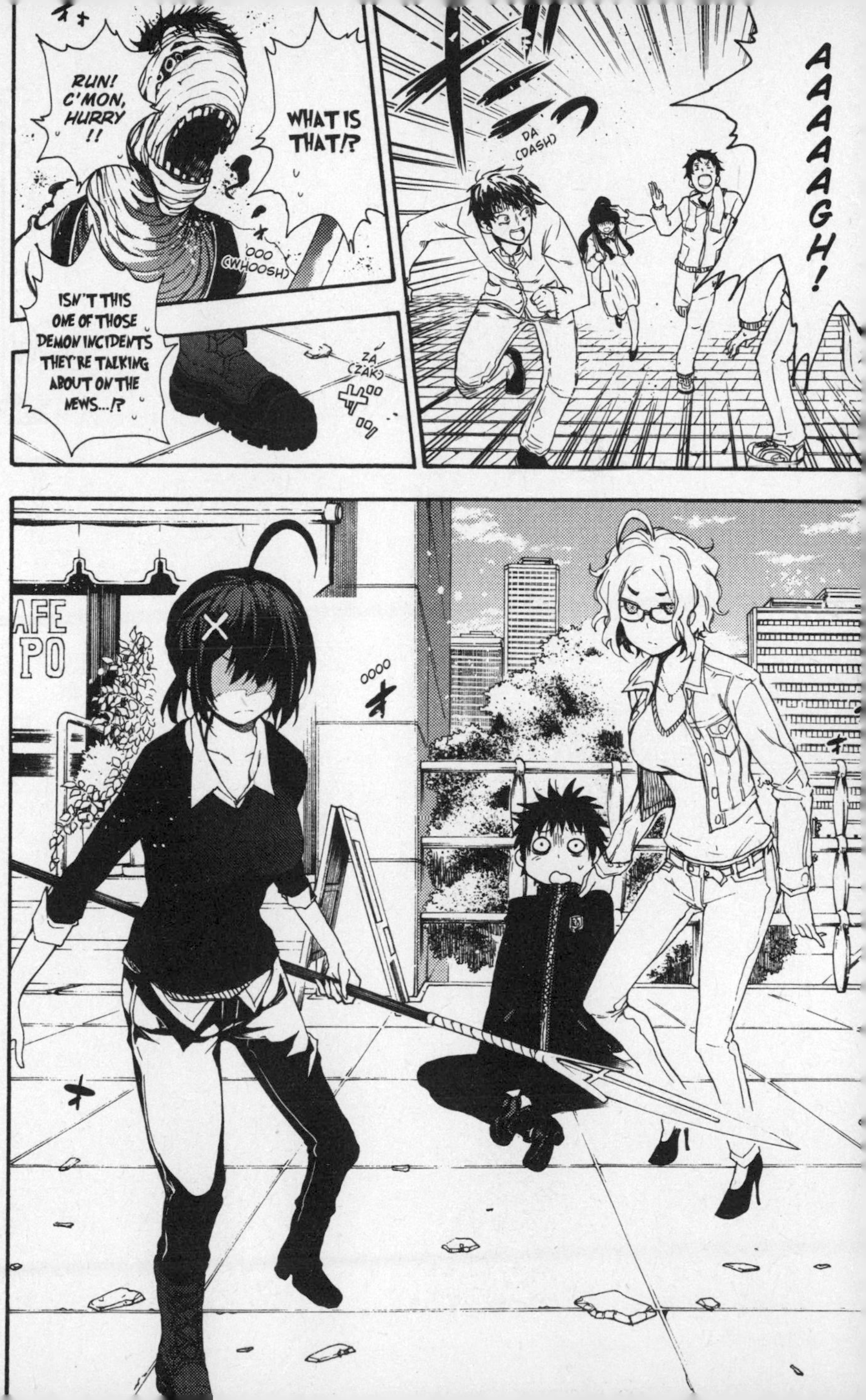
AAAAAGH!
DA (DASH)
RUN! C'MON, HURRY!!
WHAT IS THAT!?
OOO (WHOOSH)
ISN'T THIS ONE OF THOSE DEMON INCIDENTS THEY'RE TALKING ABOUT ON THE NEWS...!?
ZA (ZAK)
AFE
PO

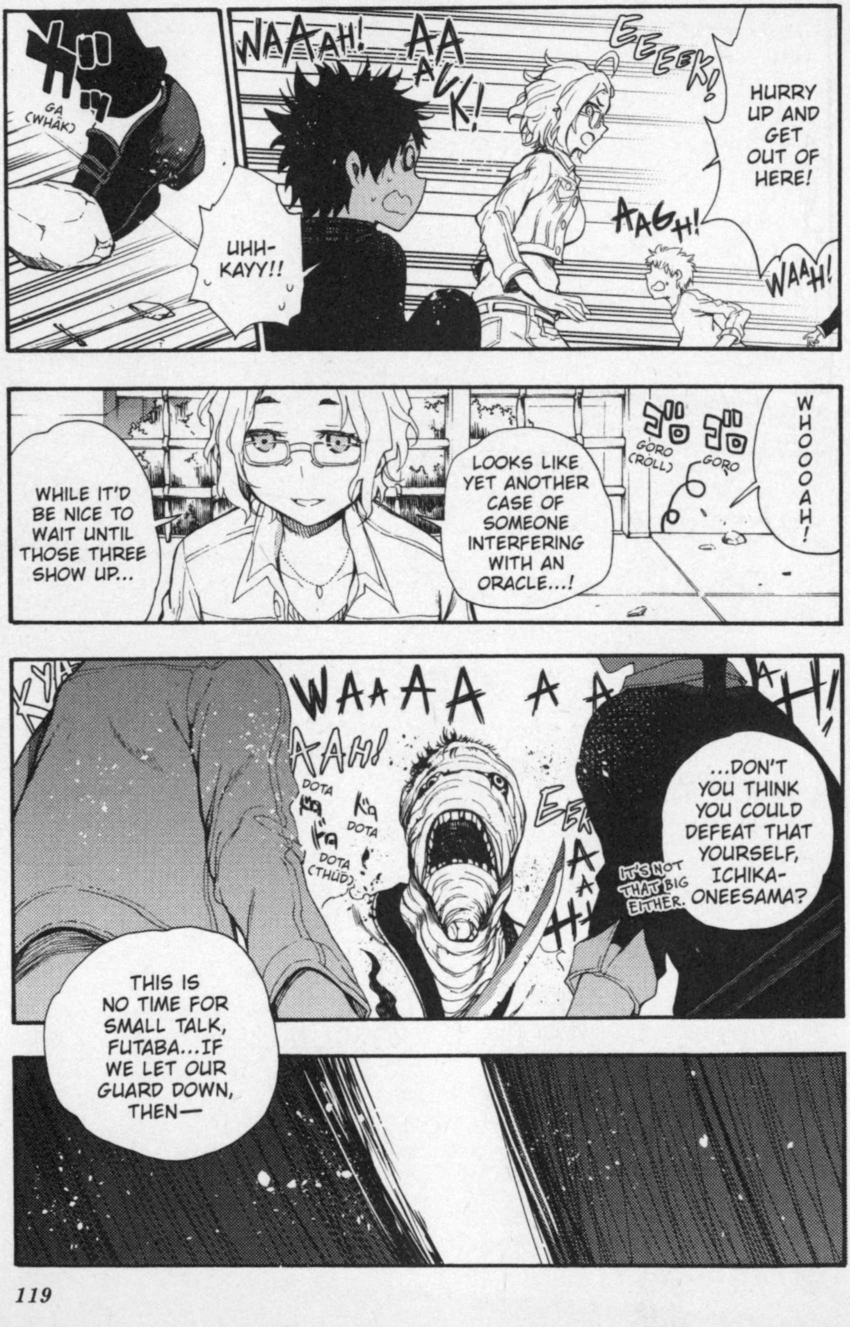
HURRY UP AND GET OUT OF HERE!
EEEEK!
WAAH!
AAGH!
AAAUK!
WAAAH!
UHH-KAYY!!
GA (WHAK)
WHOOOOAH!
GORO (ROLL) GORO
LOOKS LIKE YET ANOTHER CASE OF SOMEONE INTERFERING WITH AN ORACLE...!
WHILE IT'D BE NICE TO WAIT UNTIL THOSE THREE SHOW UP...
...DON'T YOU THINK YOU COULD DEFEAT THAT YOURSELF, ICHIKA-ONEESAMA?
IT'S NOT THAT BIG EITHER.
WAAAA A A AAH!
EEEAAAAH
AAH!
DOTA DOTA DOTA (THUD)
THIS IS NO TIME FOR SMALL TALK, FUTABA...IF WE LET OUR GUARD DOWN, THEN—

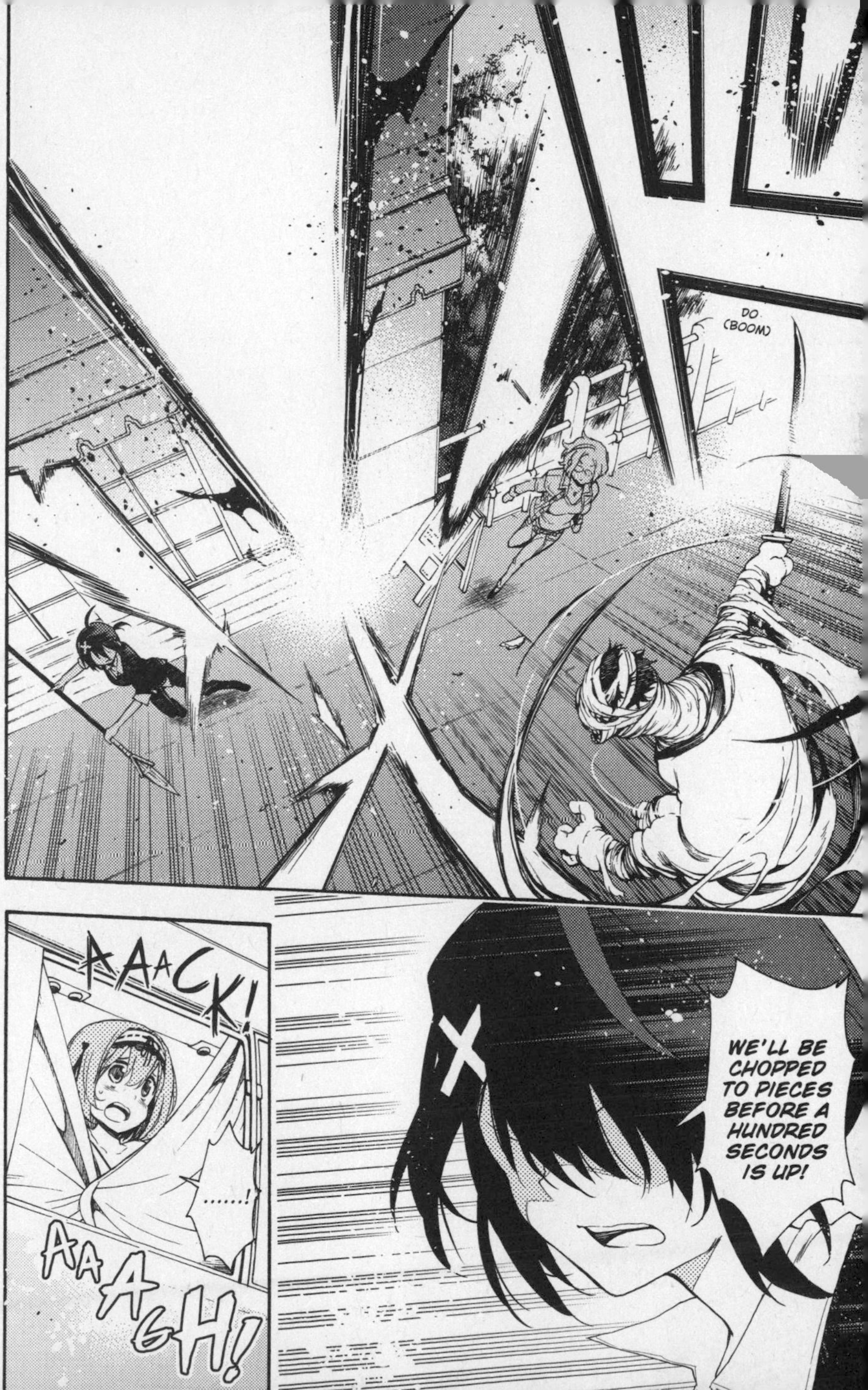
DO.
(BOOM)
WE'LL BE CHOPPED TO PIECES BEFORE A HUNDRED SECONDS IS UP!
AACK!
......!
AAAGH!

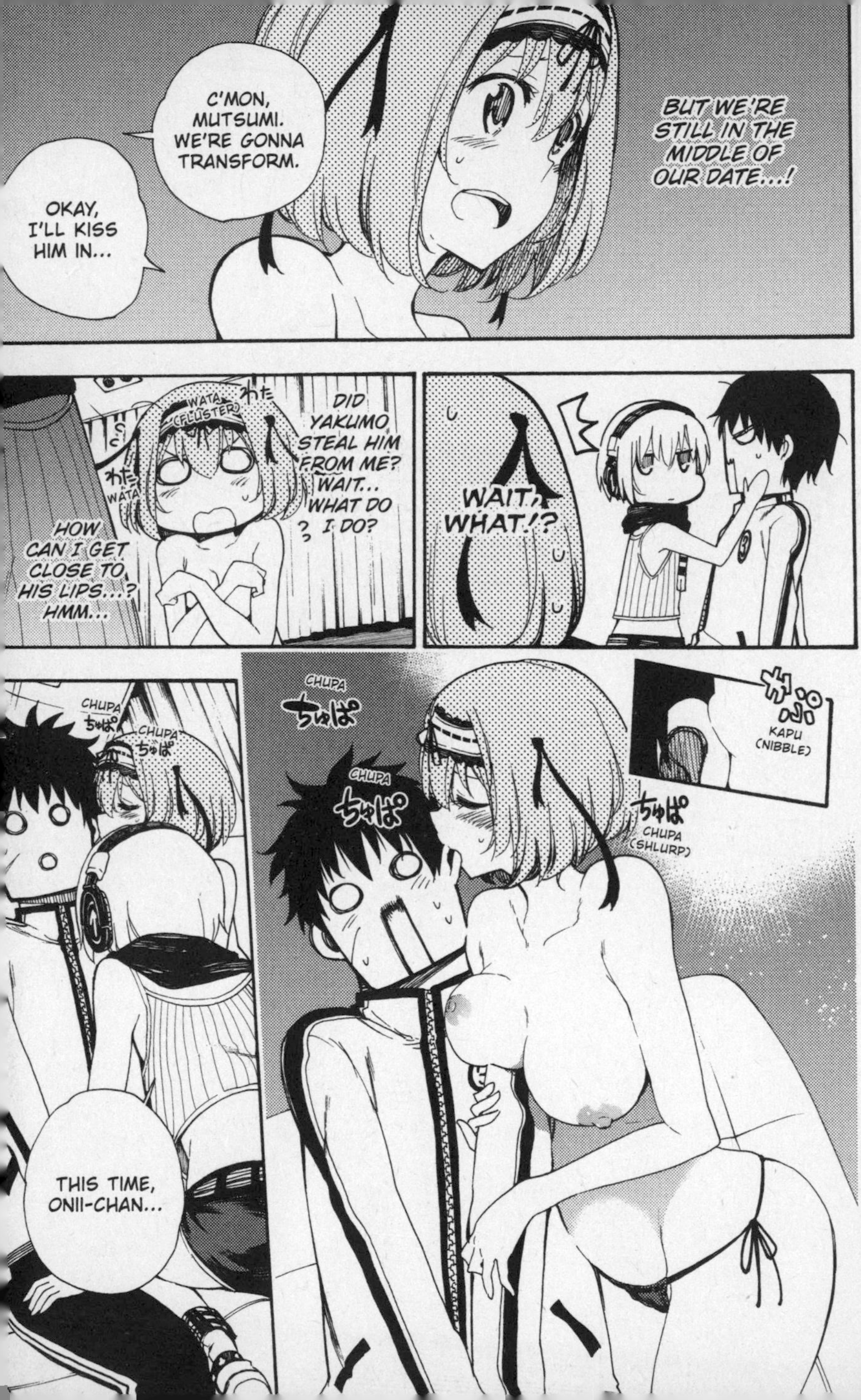

BUT WE'RE STILL IN THE MIDDLE OF OUR DATE...!
C'MON, MUTSUMI. WE'RE GONNA TRANSFORM.
OKAY, I'LL KISS HIM IN...
WAIT, WHAT!?
わた
WATA (FLUSTER)
DID YAKUMO STEAL HIM FROM ME? WAIT... WHAT DO I DO?
わた
WATA
HOW CAN I GET CLOSE TO HIS LIPS...? HMM...
かぷ
KAPU (NIBBLE)
ちゅぱ
CHUPA
ちゅぱ
CHUPA
ちゅぱ
CHUPA (SHLURP)
ちゅぱ
CHUPA
ちゅぱ
CHUPA
THIS TIME, ONII-CHAN...

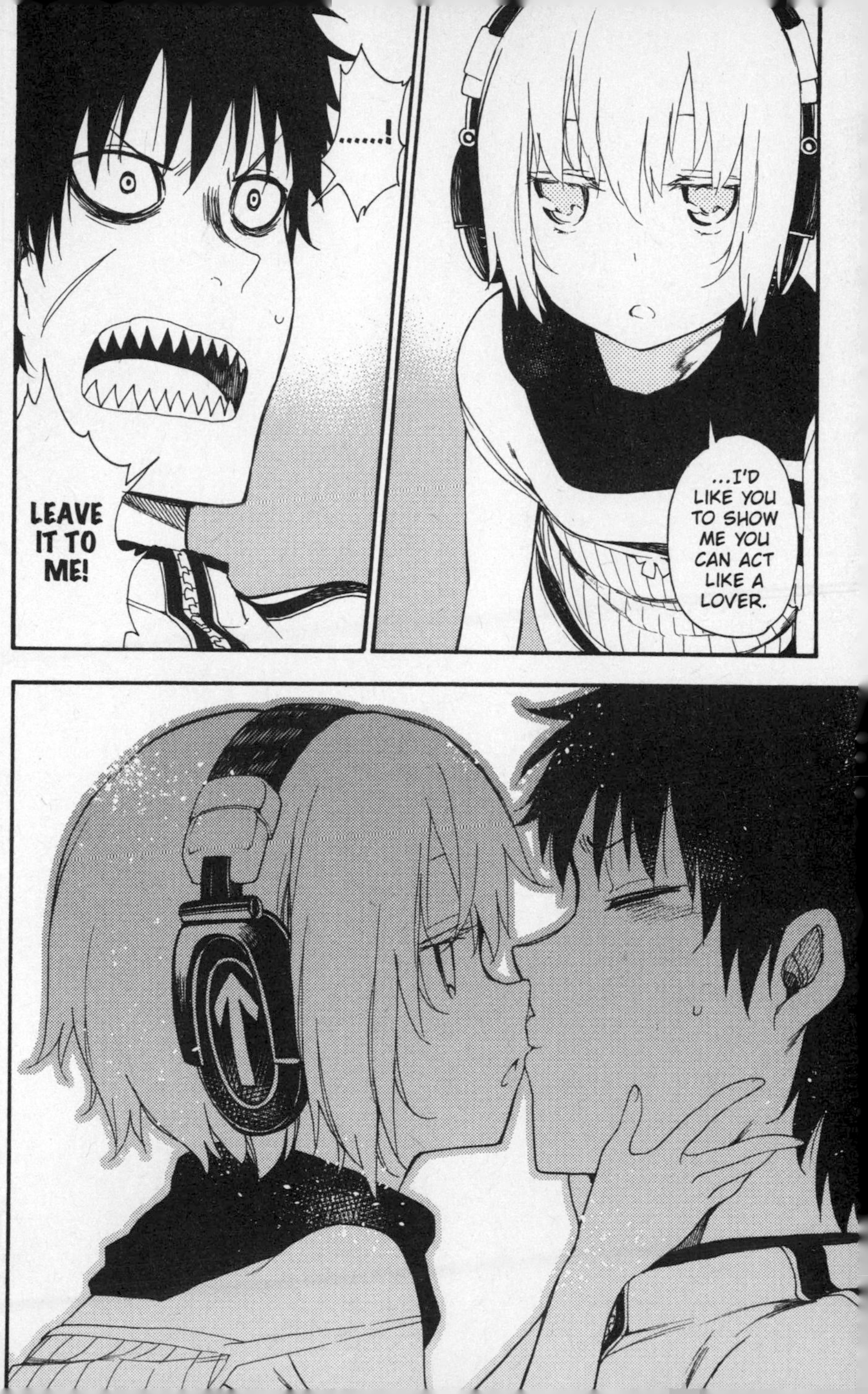
...I'D LIKE YOU TO SHOW ME YOU CAN ACT LIKE A LOVER.
......!
LEAVE IT TO ME!

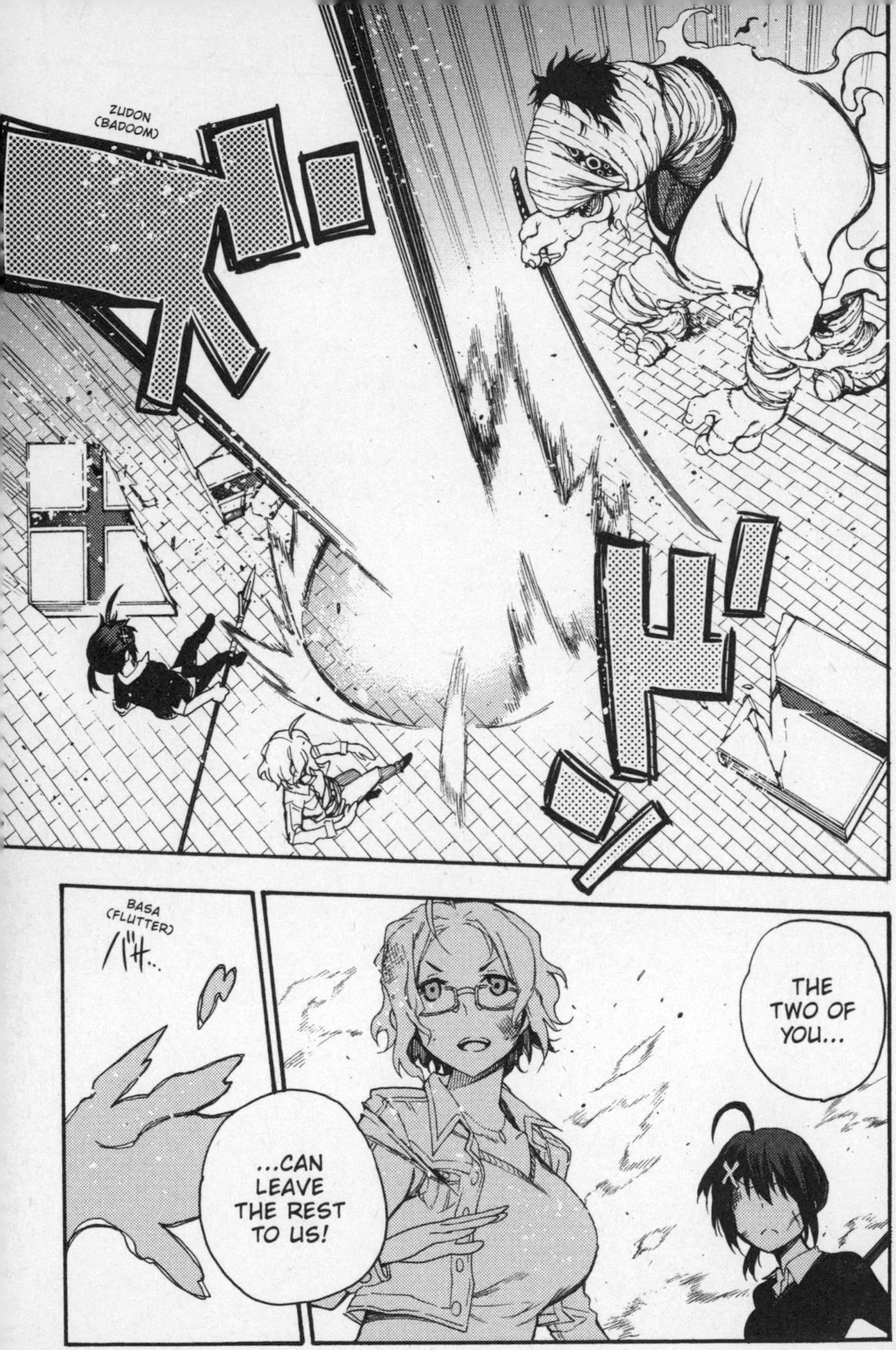
ZUDON
(BADOOM)
THE TWO OF YOU...
...CAN LEAVE THE REST TO US!
BASA
(FLUTTER)
バサ…

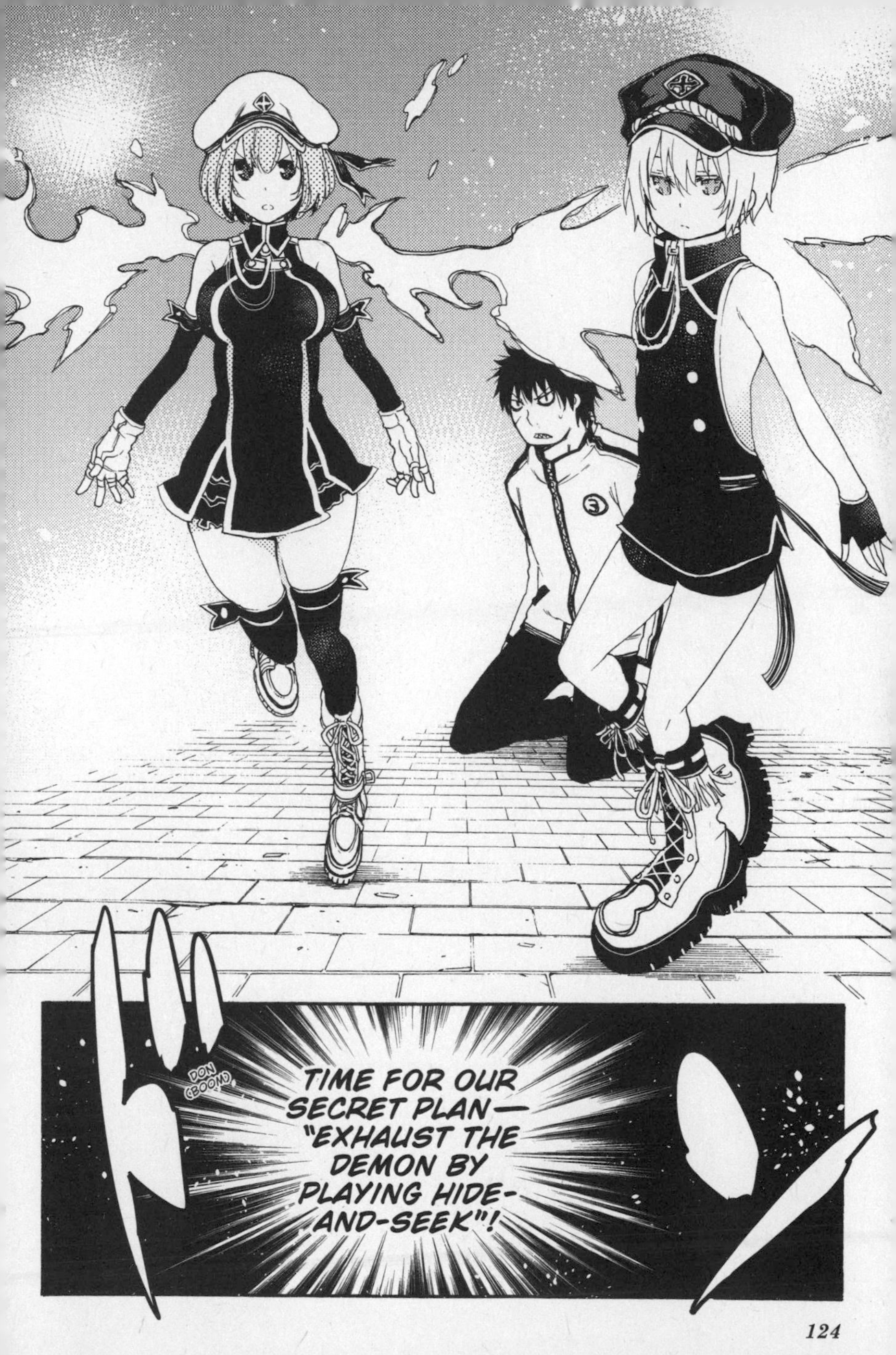
DON (BOOM)
TIME FOR OUR SECRET PLAN—"EXHAUST THE DEMON BY PLAYING HIDE-AND-SEEK"!

Val × Love

FULFILLED HIS QUOTA

PHEW.

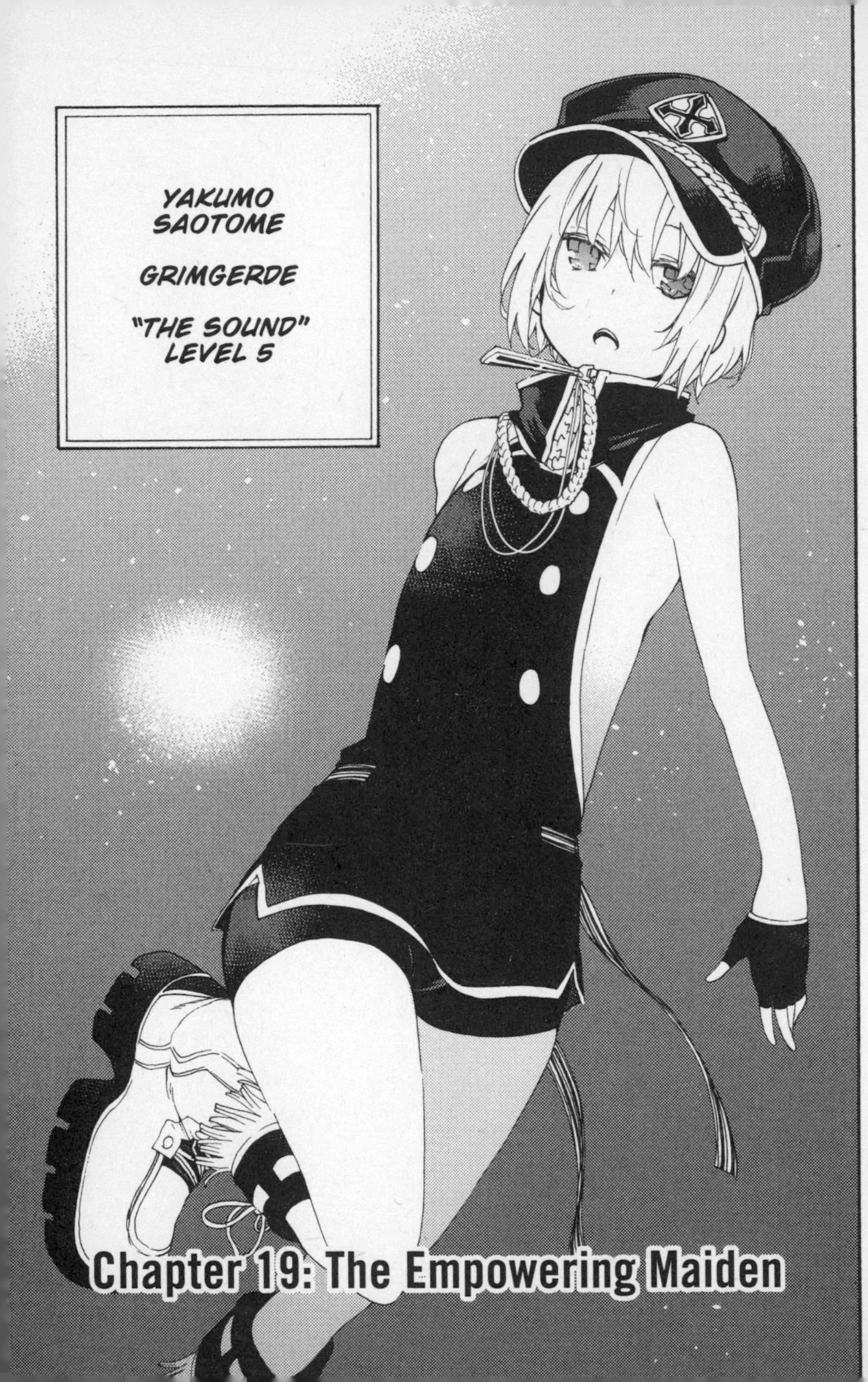
YAKUMO SAOTOME
GRIMGERDE
"THE SOUND" LEVEL 5

Chapter 19: The Empowering Maiden

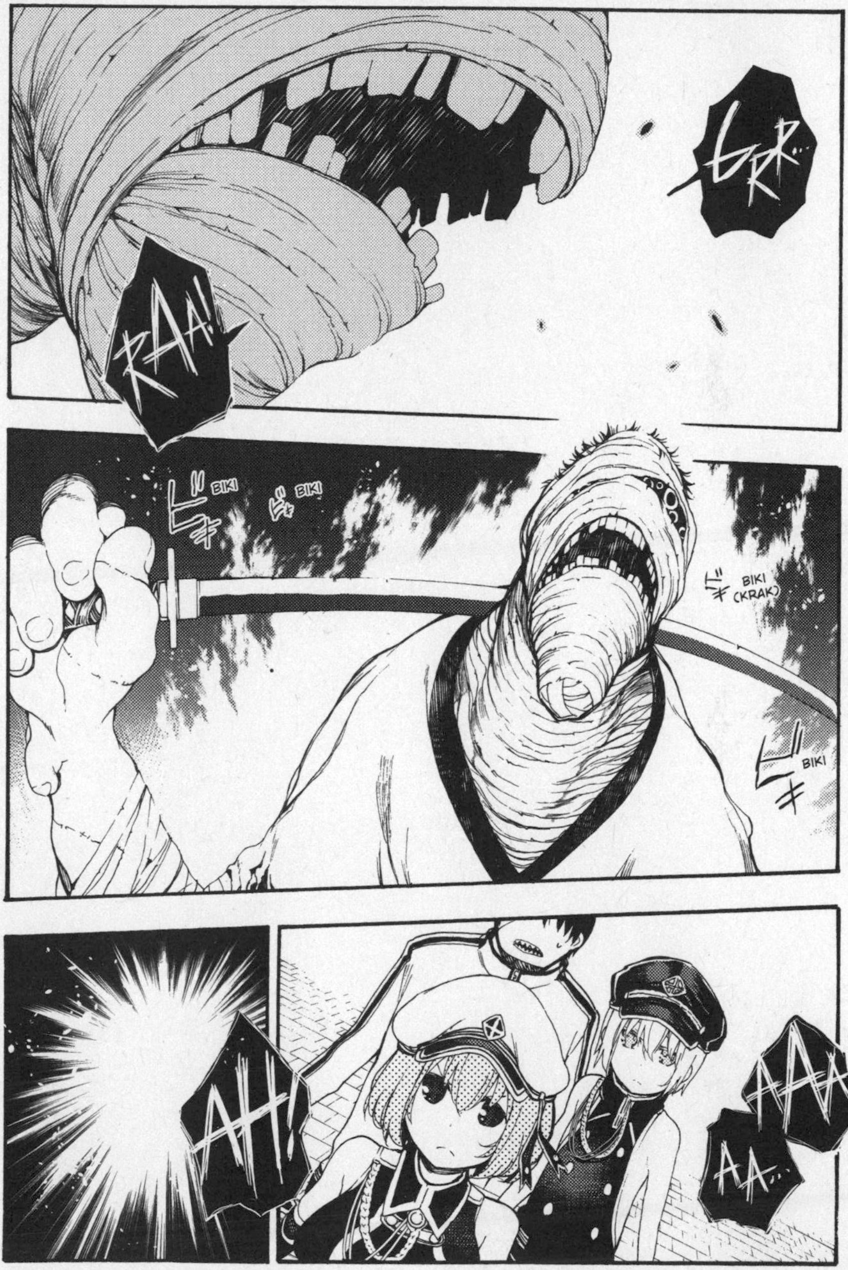
GRR...
RAA!
BIKI (KRAK)
BIKI
BIKI
BIKI
AAA
AA...
AH!

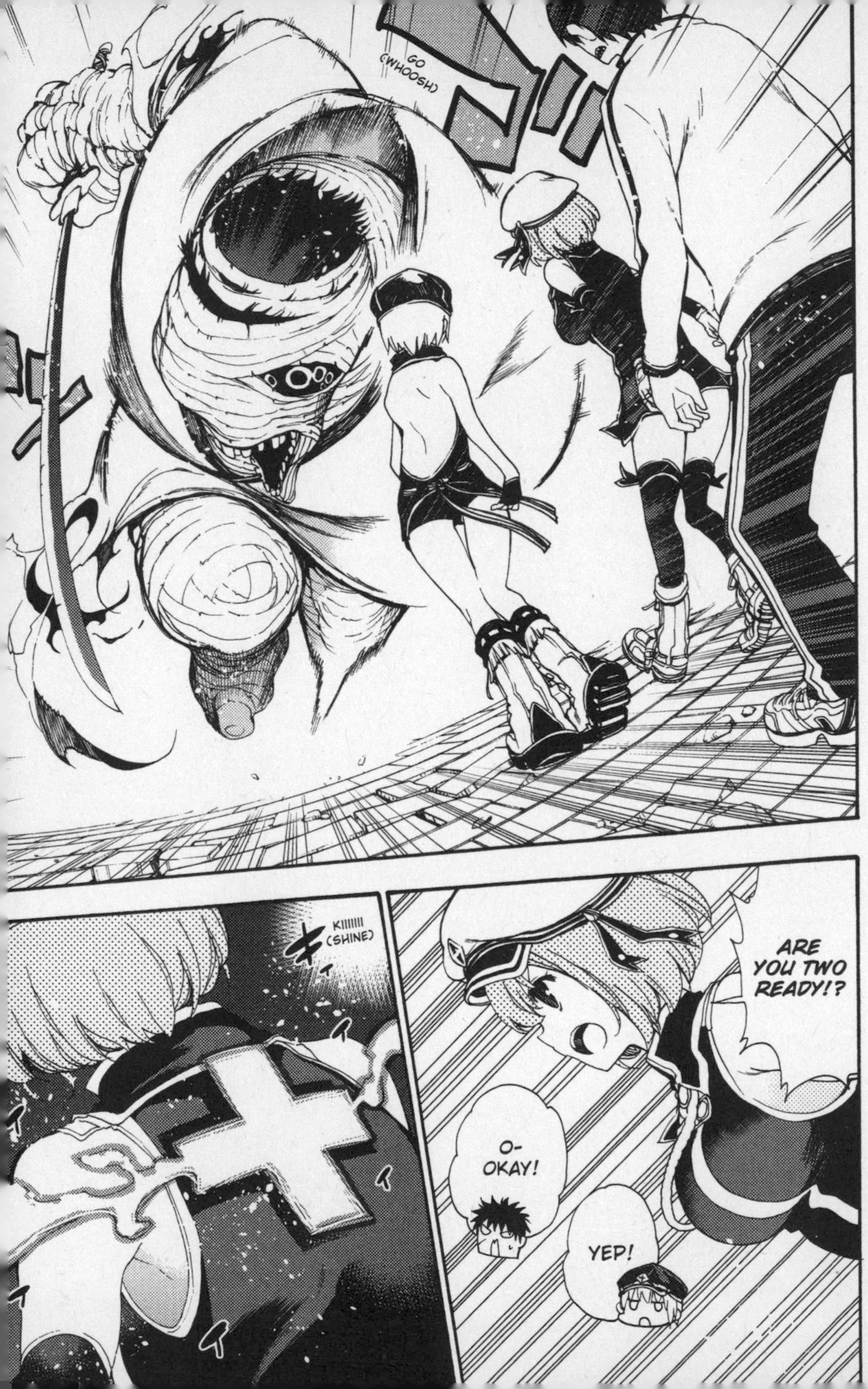
GO
(WHOOSH)
ARE YOU TWO READY!?
O-OKAY!
YEP!
KIIIIIII
(SHINE)

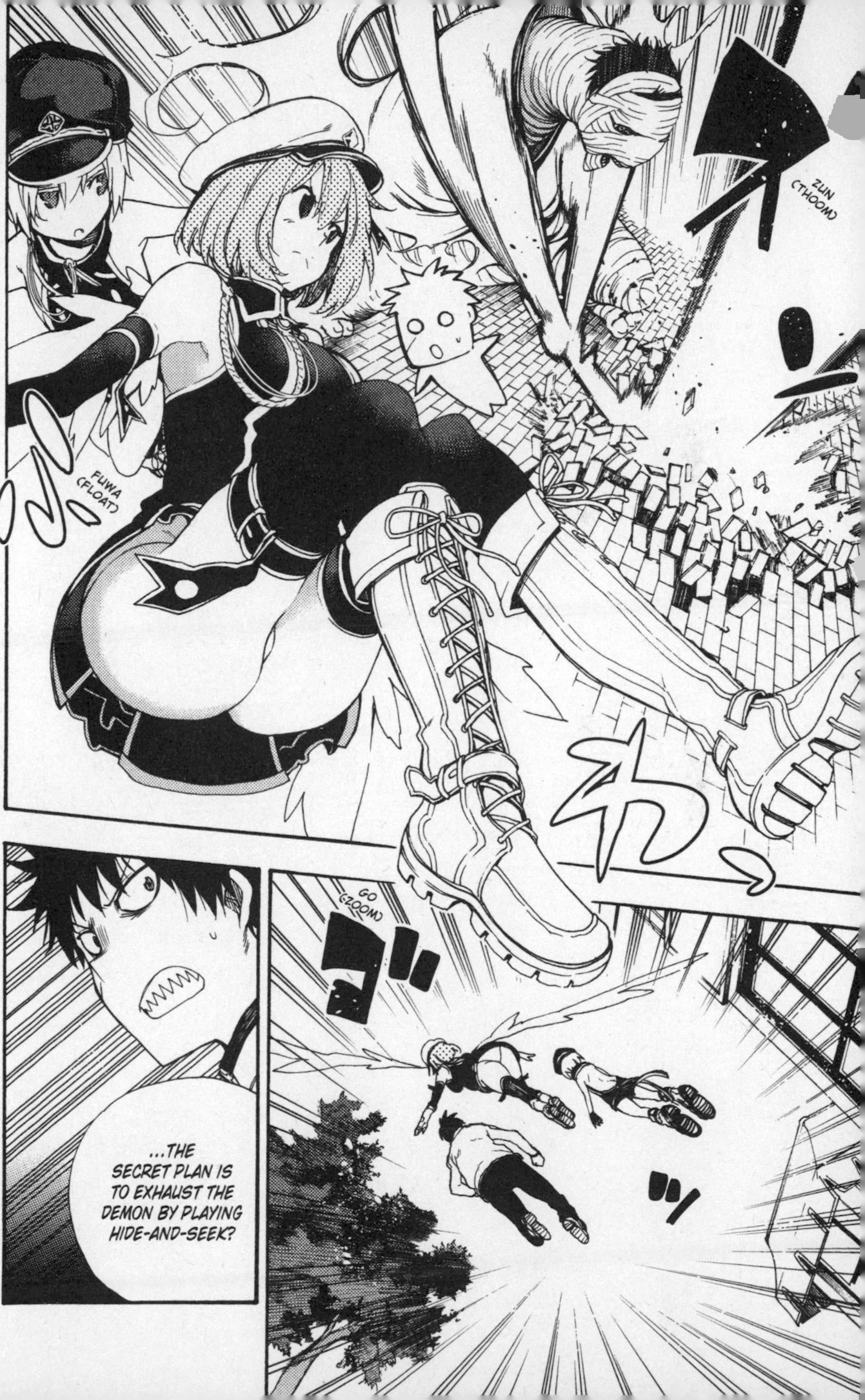
ZUN
(THOOM)
FUWA
(FLOAT)
GO
(ZOOM)
...THE SECRET PLAN IS TO EXHAUST THE DEMON BY PLAYING HIDE-AND-SEEK?

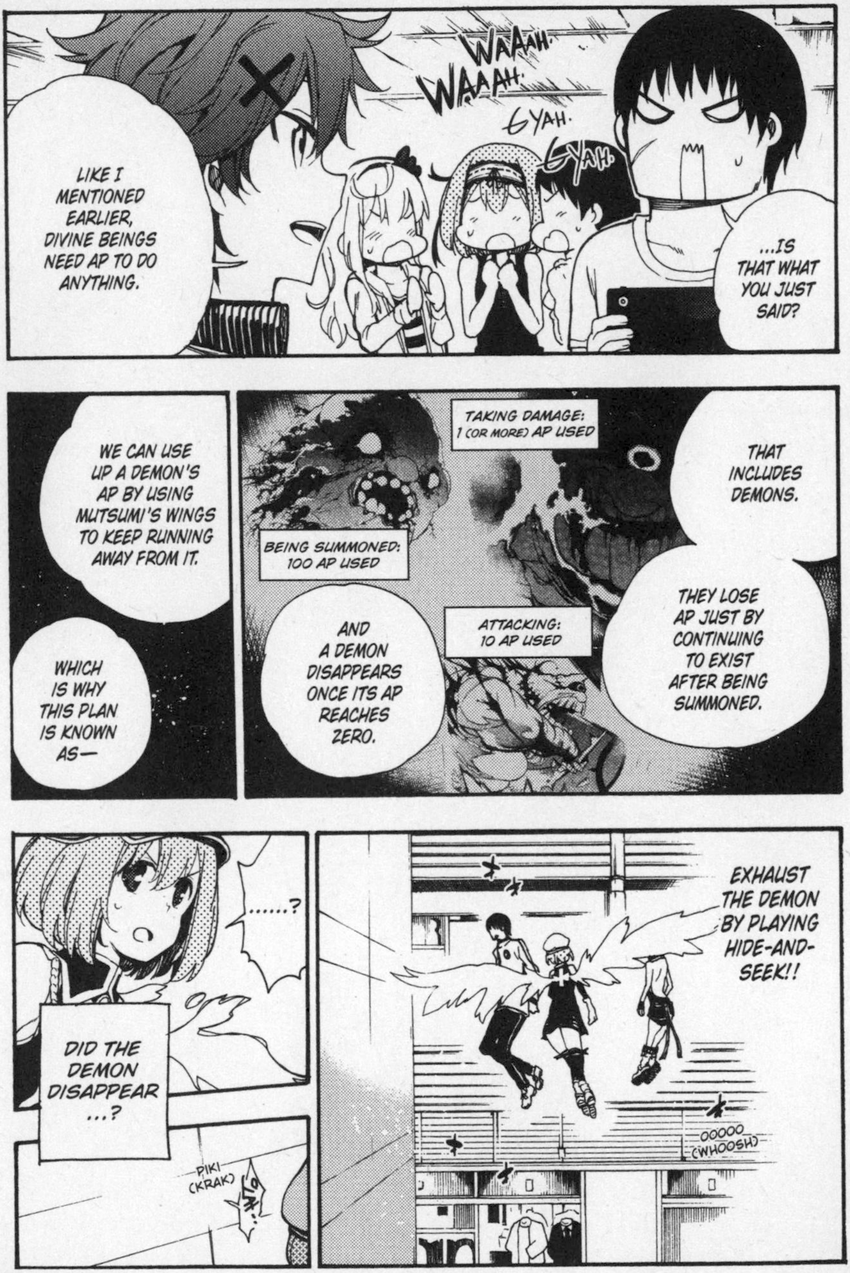
WAAAH.
WAAAH.
GYAH.
GYAH.
LIKE I MENTIONED EARLIER, DIVINE BEINGS NEED AP TO DO ANYTHING.
...IS THAT WHAT YOU JUST SAID?
THAT INCLUDES DEMONS.
THEY LOSE AP JUST BY CONTINUING TO EXIST AFTER BEING SUMMONED.
TAKING DAMAGE: 1 (OR MORE) AP USED
BEING SUMMONED: 100 AP USED
ATTACKING: 10 AP USED
AND A DEMON DISAPPEARS ONCE ITS AP REACHES ZERO.
WE CAN USE UP A DEMON'S AP BY USING MUTSUMI'S WINGS TO KEEP RUNNING AWAY FROM IT.
WHICH IS WHY THIS PLAN IS KNOWN AS—
EXHAUST THE DEMON BY PLAYING HIDE-AND-SEEK!!
OOOOO (WHOOSH)
......?
DID THE DEMON DISAPPEAR ...?
PIKI (KRAK)

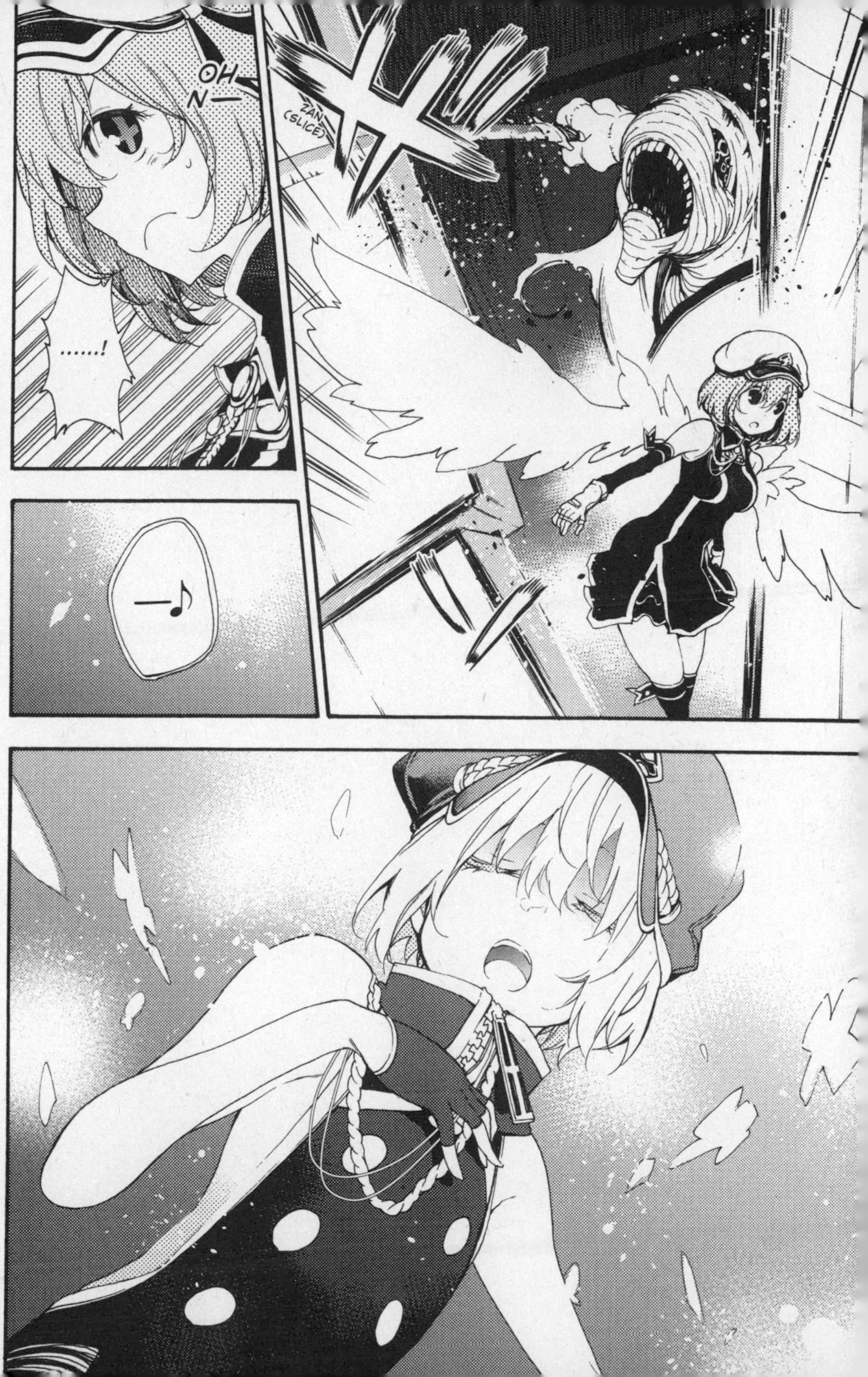
ZAN (SLICE)
OH N—
……!
—♪

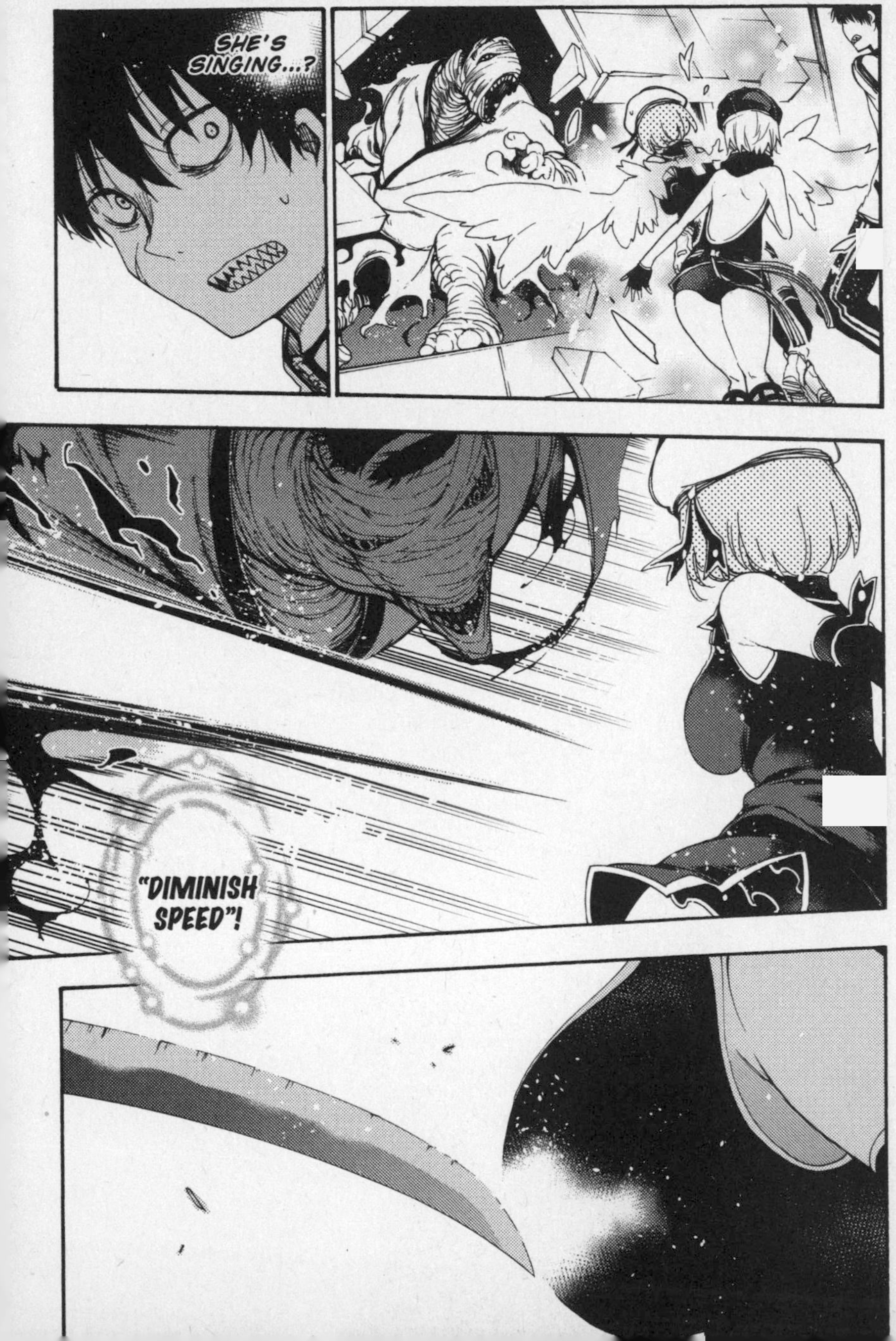
SHE'S SINGING...?
"DIMINISH SPEED"!

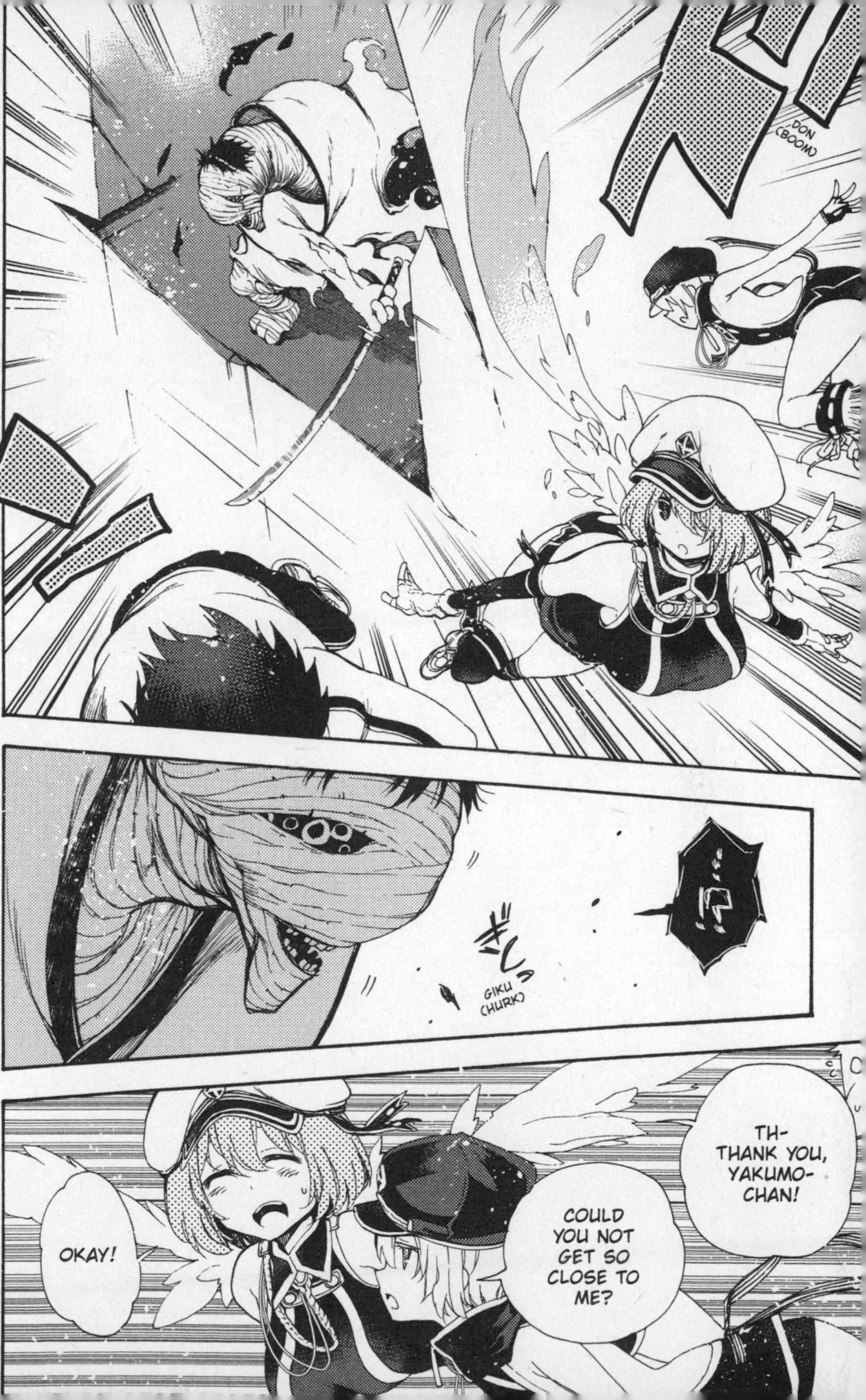
DON
(BOOM)
GIKU
(HURK)
TH-
THANK YOU,
YAKUMO-
CHAN!
COULD
YOU NOT
GET SO
CLOSE TO
ME?
OKAY!

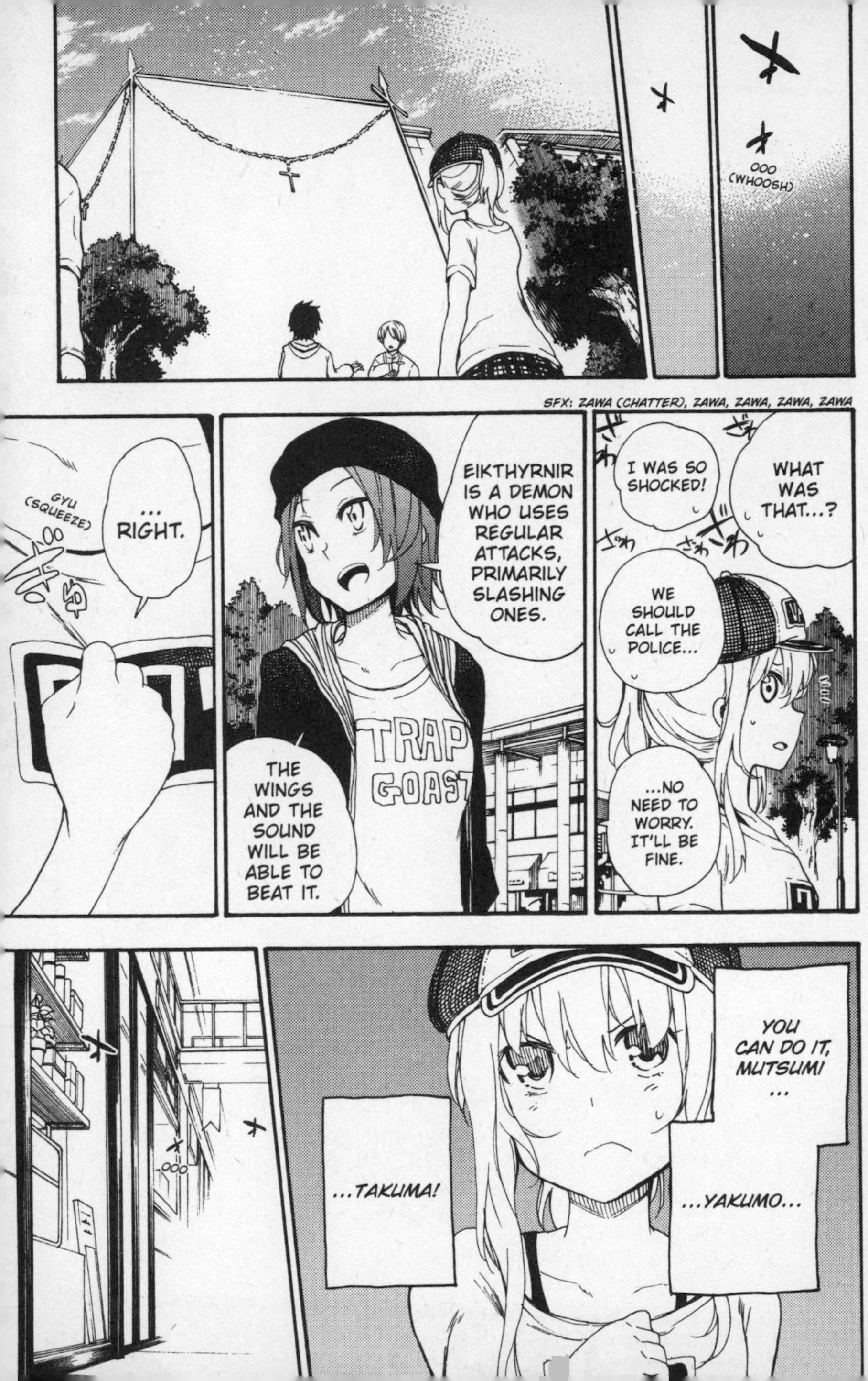
OOO (WHOOSH)
SFX: ZAWA (CHATTER), ZAWA, ZAWA, ZAWA, ZAWA
WHAT WAS THAT...?
I WAS SO SHOCKED!
WE SHOULD CALL THE POLICE...
...NO NEED TO WORRY. IT'LL BE FINE.
EIKTHYRNIR IS A DEMON WHO USES REGULAR ATTACKS, PRIMARILY SLASHING ONES.
TRAP GOAST
THE WINGS AND THE SOUND WILL BE ABLE TO BEAT IT.
GYU (SQUEEZE)
...RIGHT.
YOU CAN DO IT, MUTSUMI...
...YAKUMO...
...TAKUMA!
OOO

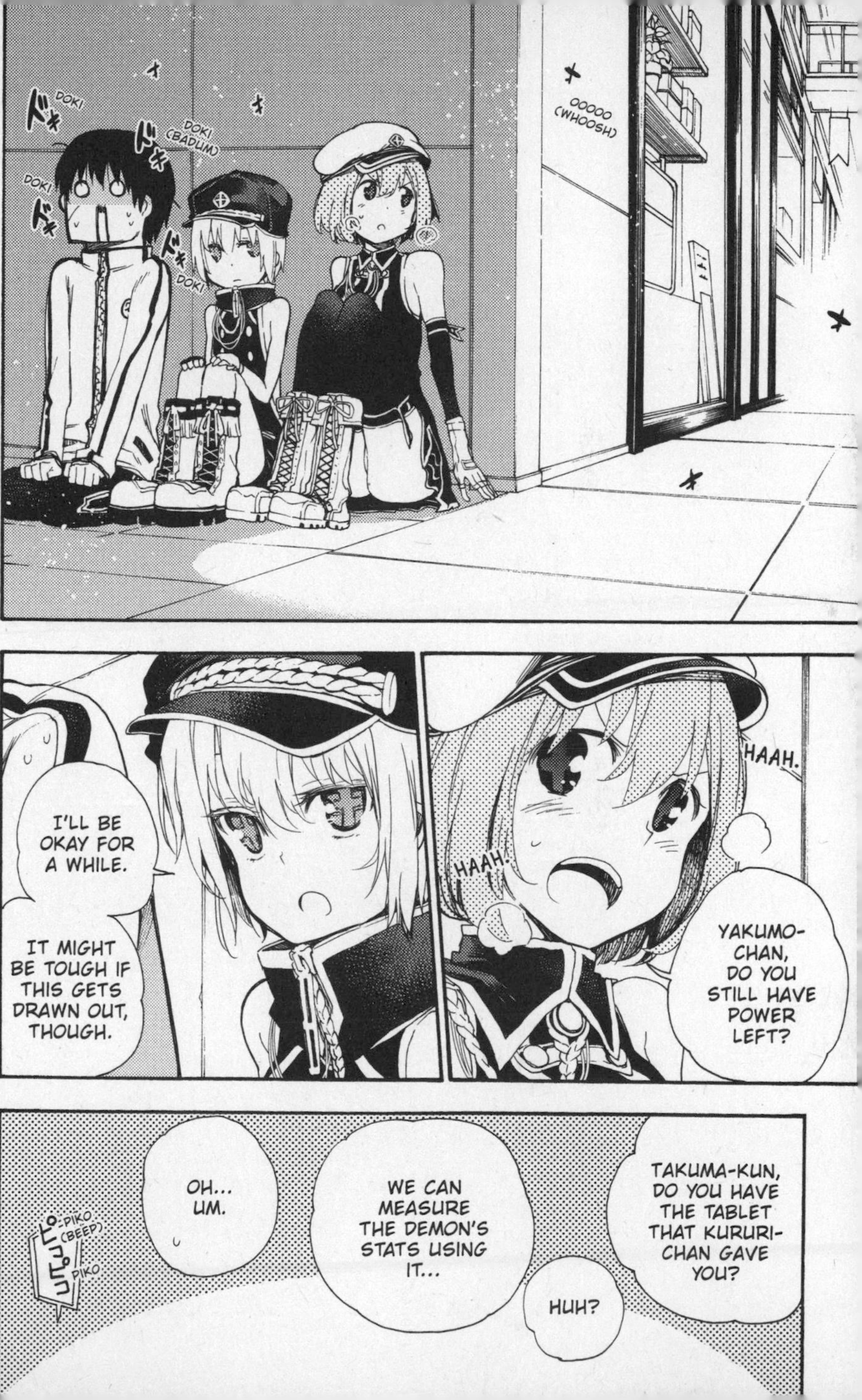
OOOOO (WHOOSH)
DOKI
DOKI (BADUM)
DOKI
DOKI
HAAH.
HAAH.
YAKUMO-CHAN, DO YOU STILL HAVE POWER LEFT?
I'LL BE OKAY FOR A WHILE.
IT MIGHT BE TOUGH IF THIS GETS DRAWN OUT, THOUGH.
TAKUMA-KUN, DO YOU HAVE THE TABLET THAT KURURI-CHAN GAVE YOU?
HUH?
WE CAN MEASURE THE DEMON'S STATS USING IT...
OH... UM.
PIKO (BEEP) PIKO

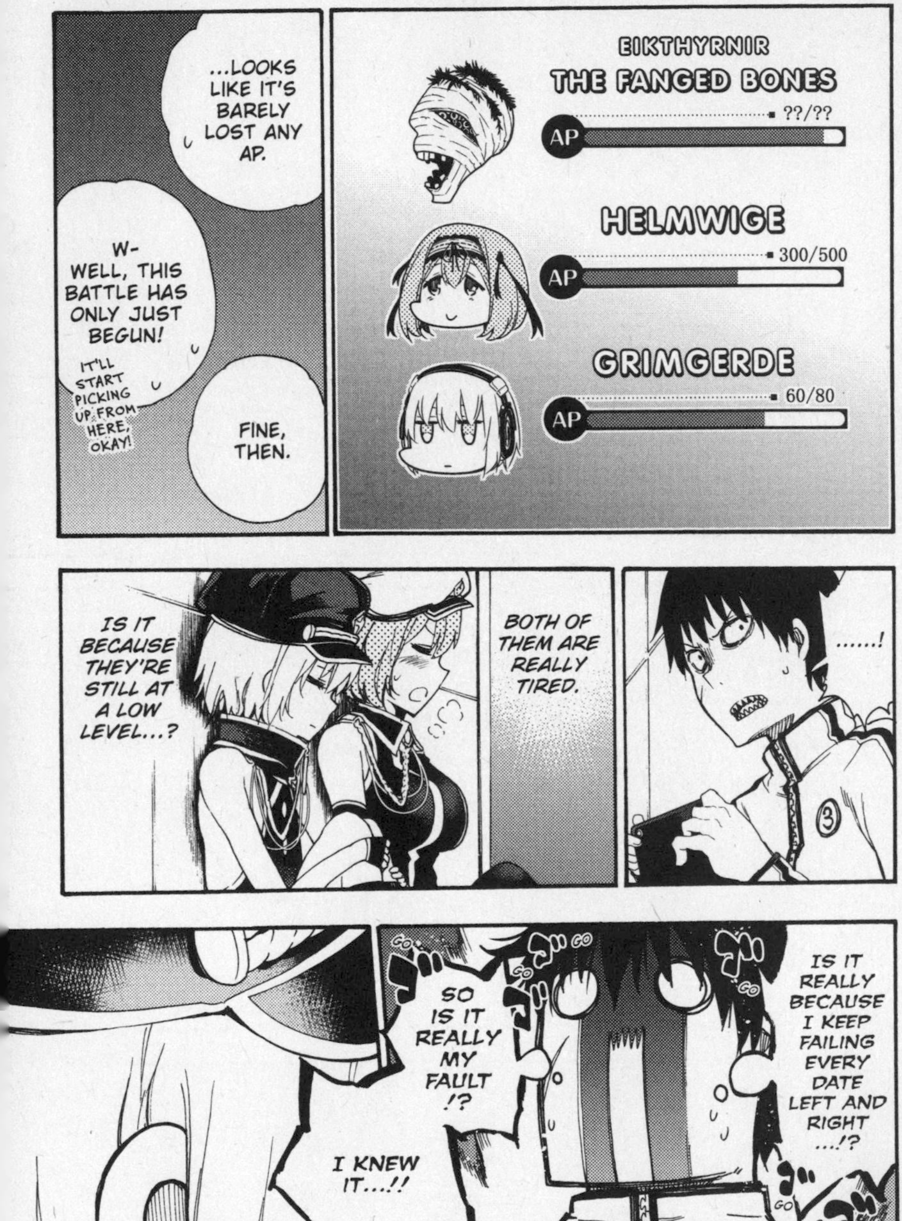
EIKTHYRNIR
THE FANGED BONES
AP ??/??
HELMWIGE
AP 300/500
GRIMGERDE
AP 60/80
...LOOKS LIKE IT'S BARELY LOST ANY AP.
W- WELL, THIS BATTLE HAS ONLY JUST BEGUN!
IT'LL START PICKING UP FROM HERE, OKAY!
FINE, THEN.
......!
BOTH OF THEM ARE REALLY TIRED.
IS IT BECAUSE THEY'RE STILL AT A LOW LEVEL...?
GO GO GO GO
IS IT REALLY BECAUSE I KEEP FAILING EVERY DATE LEFT AND RIGHT...!?
SO IS IT REALLY MY FAULT!?
I KNEW IT...!!
GO GO (RUMBLE)

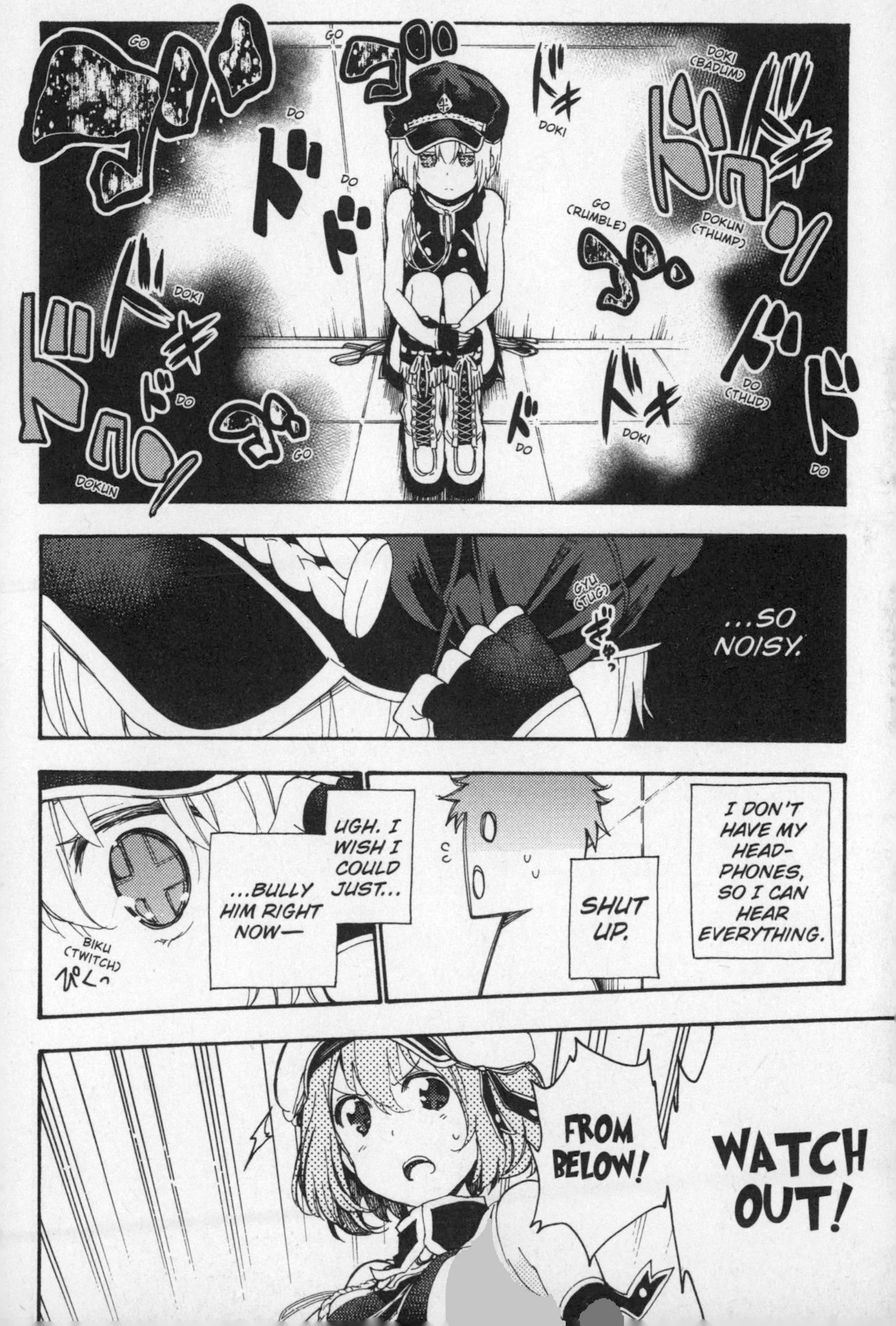
DOKI (BADUMP)
DOKUN (THUMP)
DO (THUD)
DO
DOKI
GO (RUMBLE)
DOKI
DO
GO
DO
DO
GO
DOKI
DO
GO
DOKUN
...SO NOISY.
GYU (TUG)
I DON'T HAVE MY HEAD-PHONES, SO I CAN HEAR EVERYTHING.
SHUT UP.
UGH. I WISH I COULD JUST...
...BULLY HIM RIGHT NOW—
BIKU (TWITCH)
WATCH OUT!
FROM BELOW!

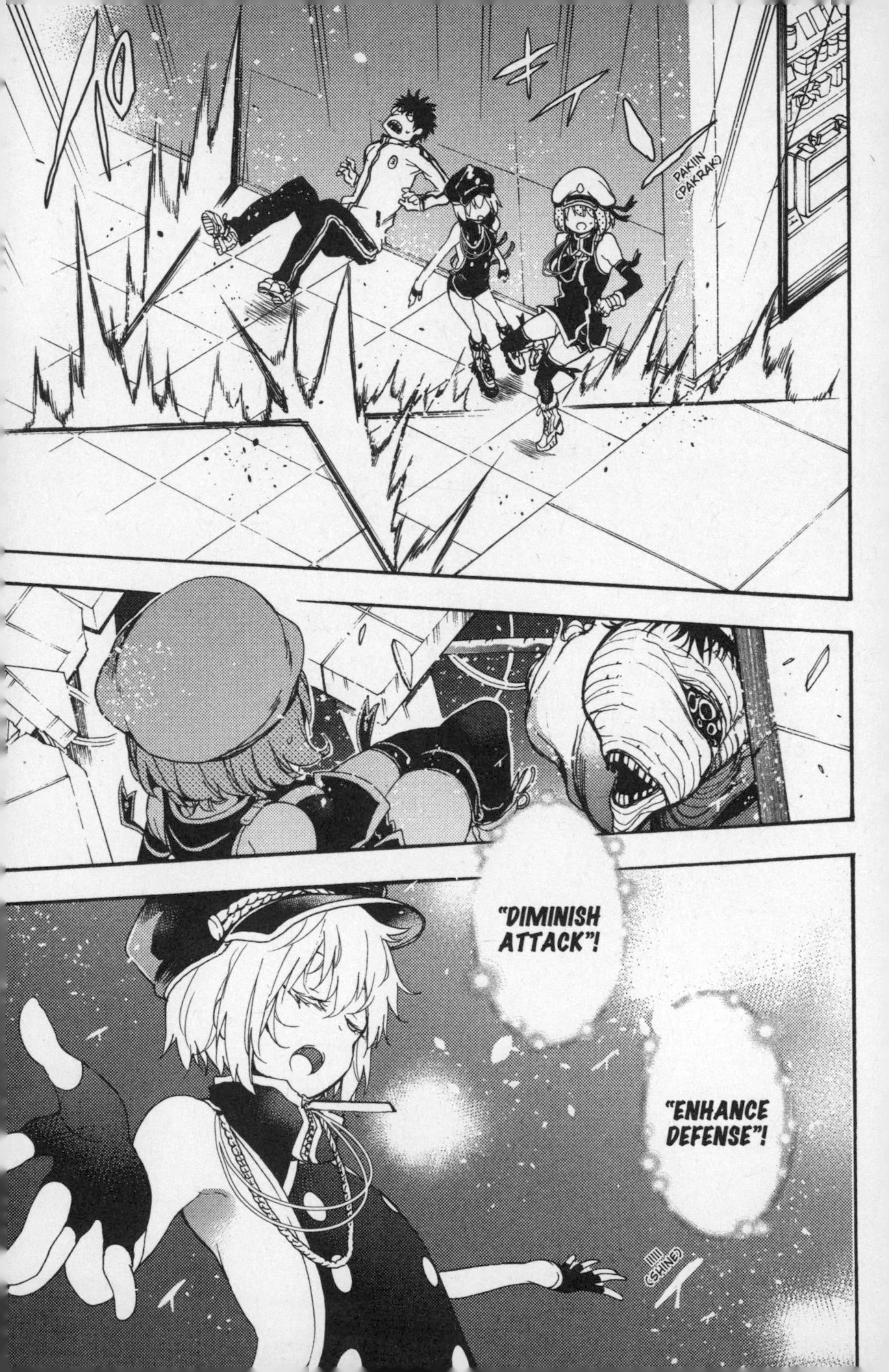
PAKIIN (PAKRAK)
"DIMINISH ATTACK"!
"ENHANCE DEFENSE"!
(SHINE)

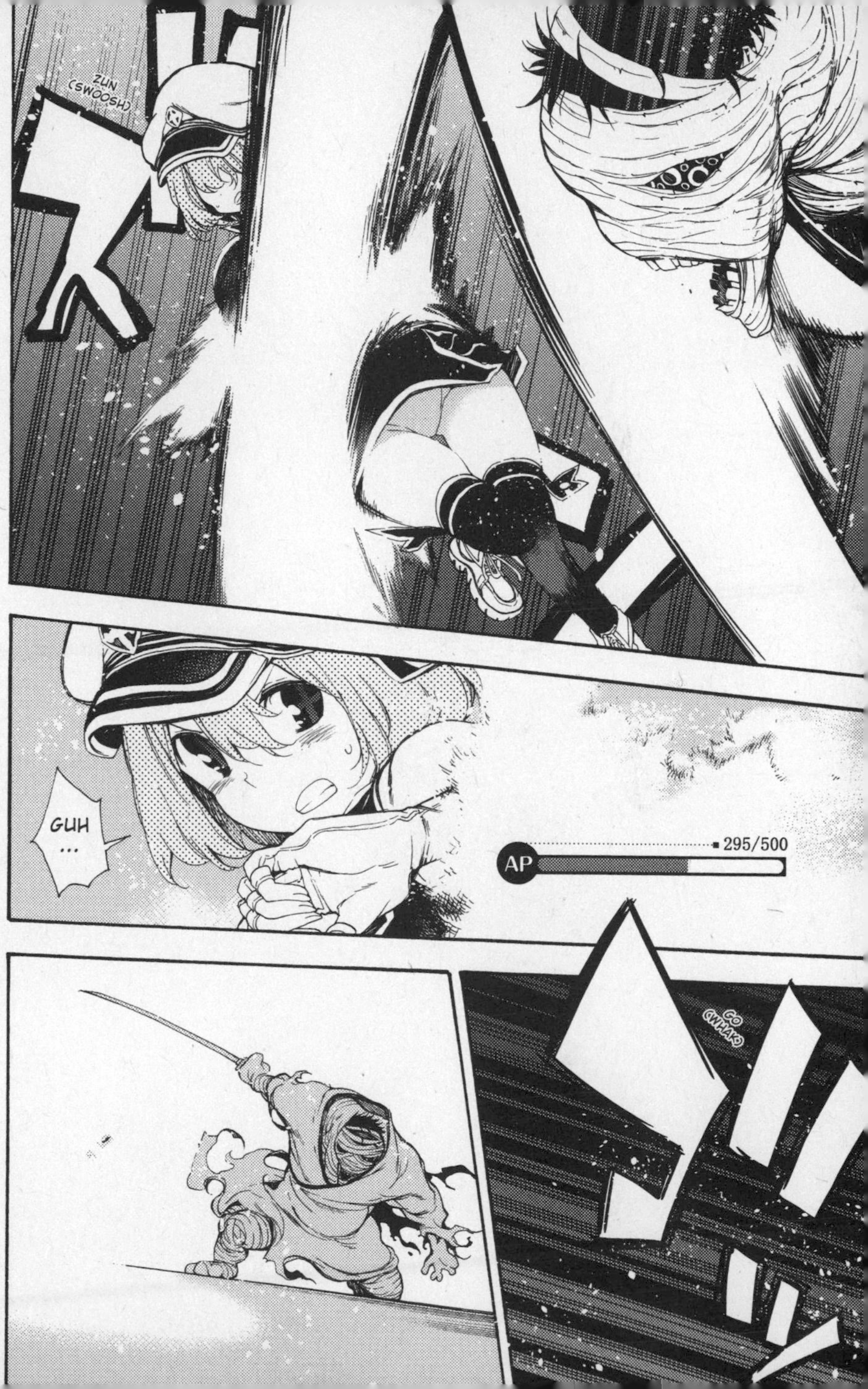
ZUN (SWOOSH)
GUH ...
AP 295/500
GO (WHAK)

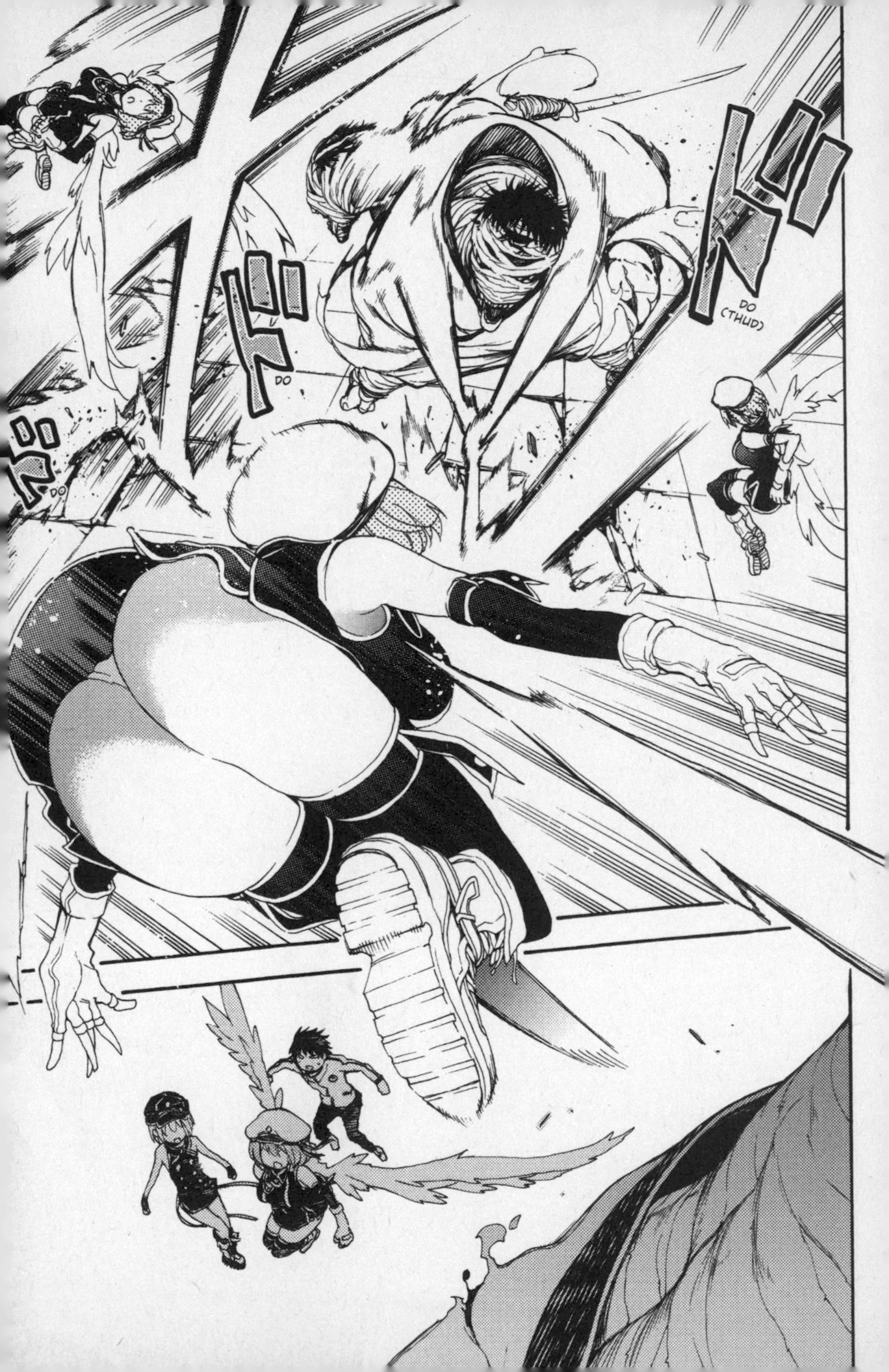
DO
(THUD)
DO
DO

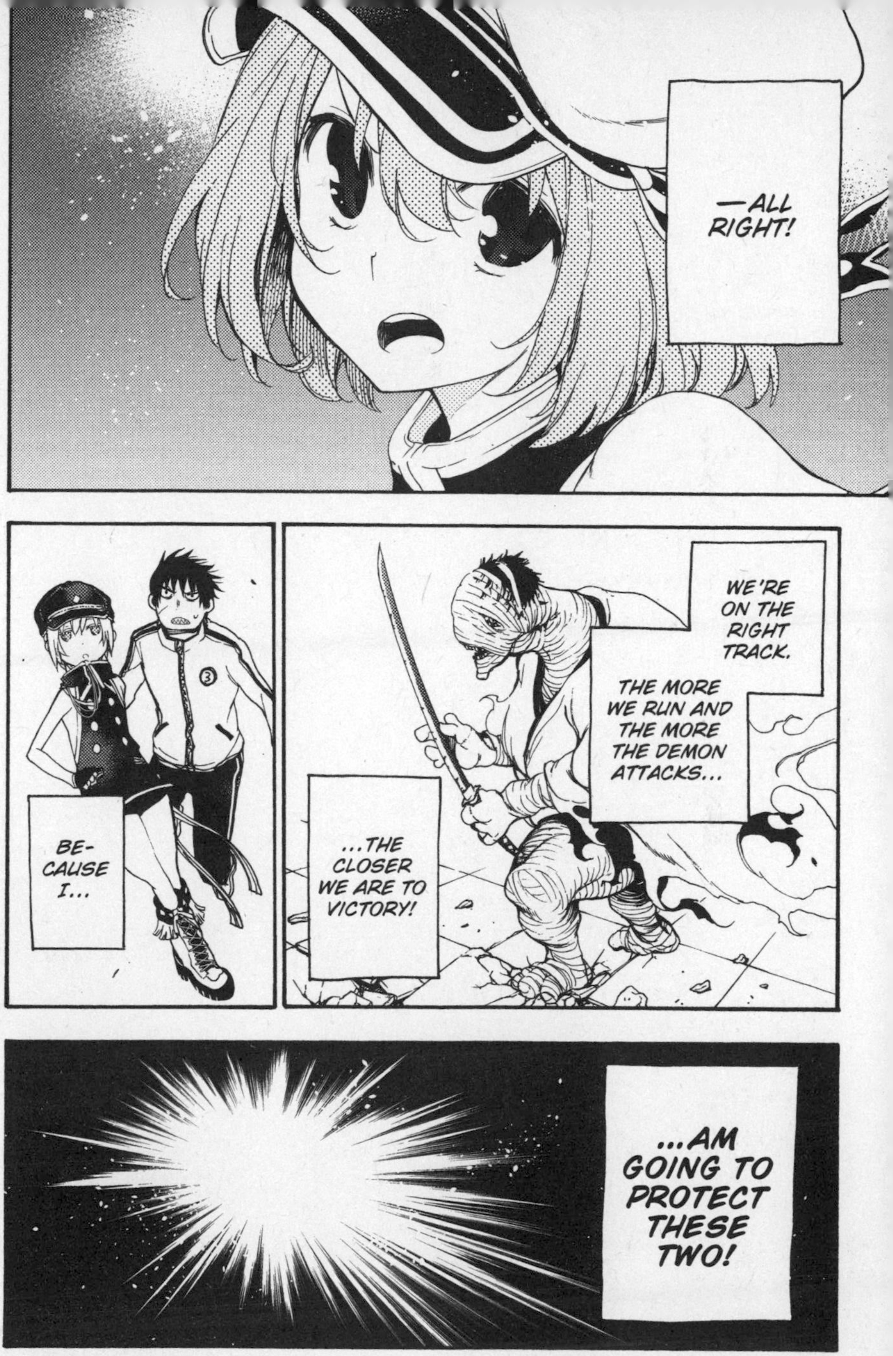
—ALL RIGHT!
WE'RE ON THE RIGHT TRACK.
THE MORE WE RUN AND THE MORE THE DEMON ATTACKS...
...THE CLOSER WE ARE TO VICTORY!
BE-CAUSE I...
...AM GOING TO PROTECT THESE TWO!

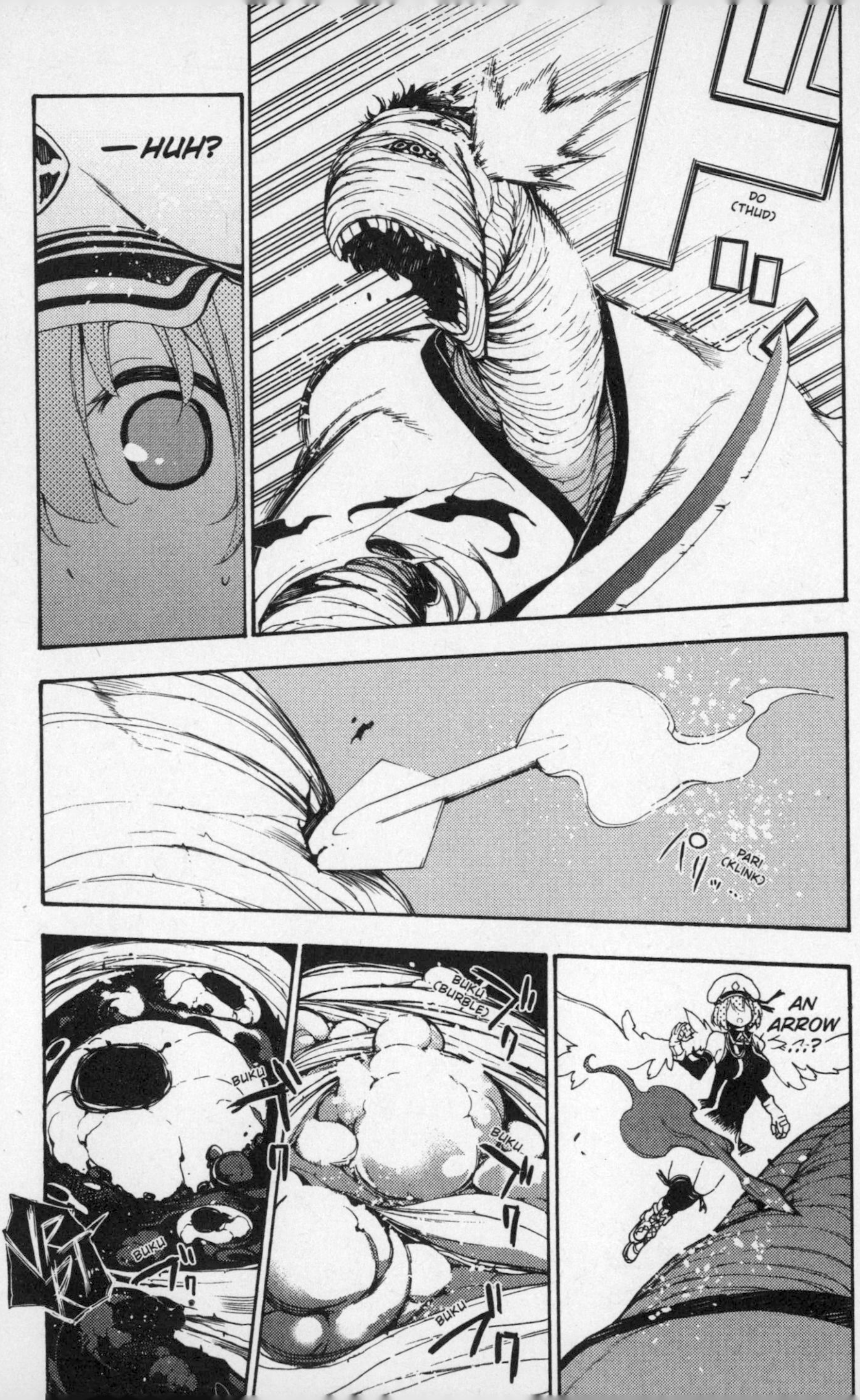
DO
(THUD)
—HUH?
PARI
(KLINK)
AN ARROW...?
BUKU
(BURBLE)
BUKU
BUKU
BUKU
BUKU

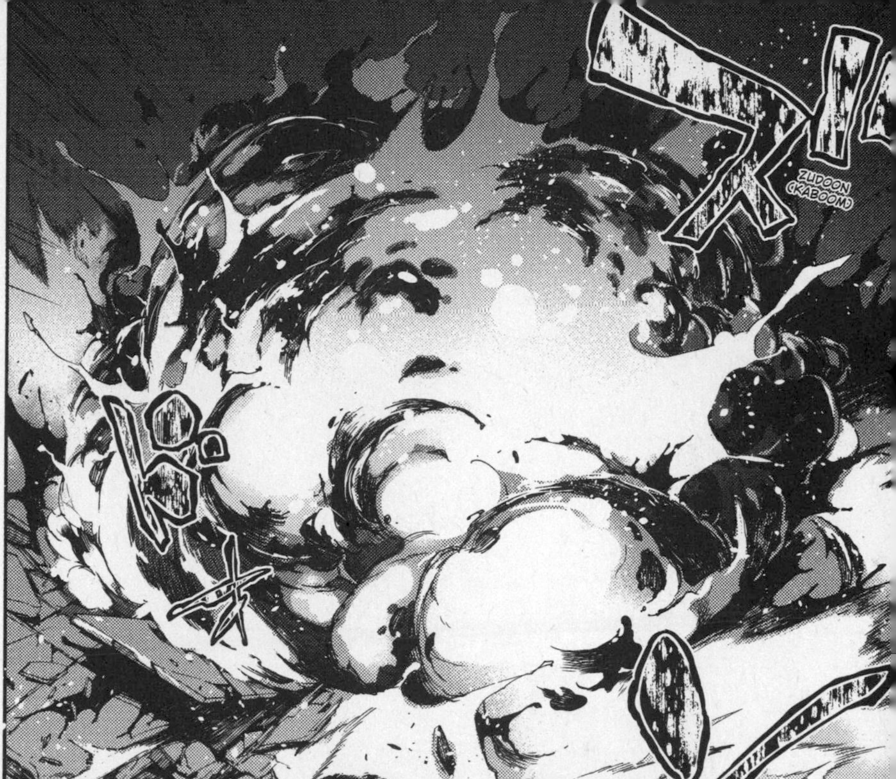
ZUDOON (KABOOM)

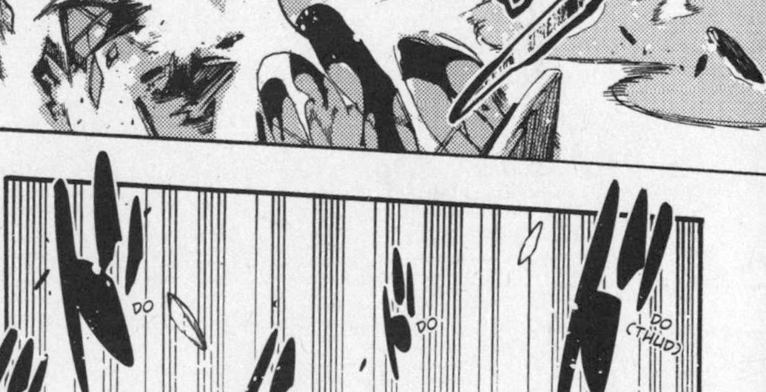
DO (THUD)
DO
DO
DO
DO
DO

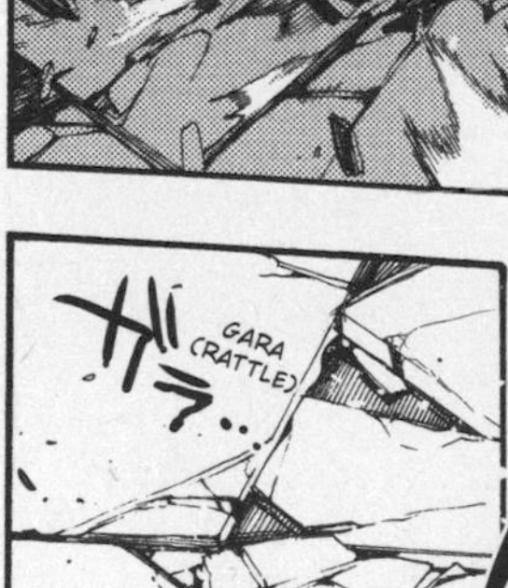
GARA (RATTLE)
DO

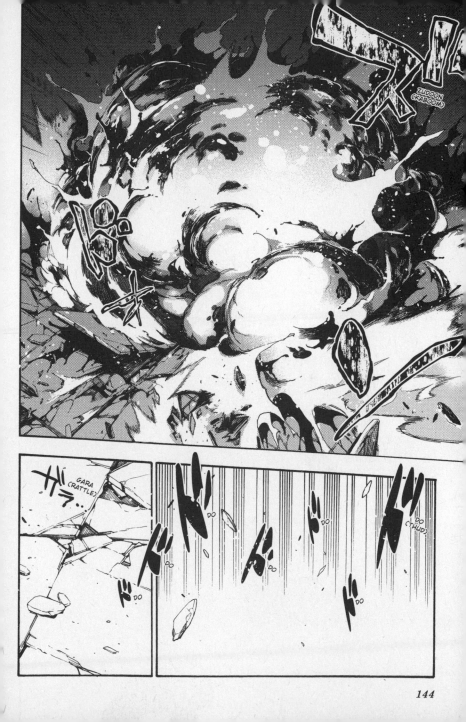

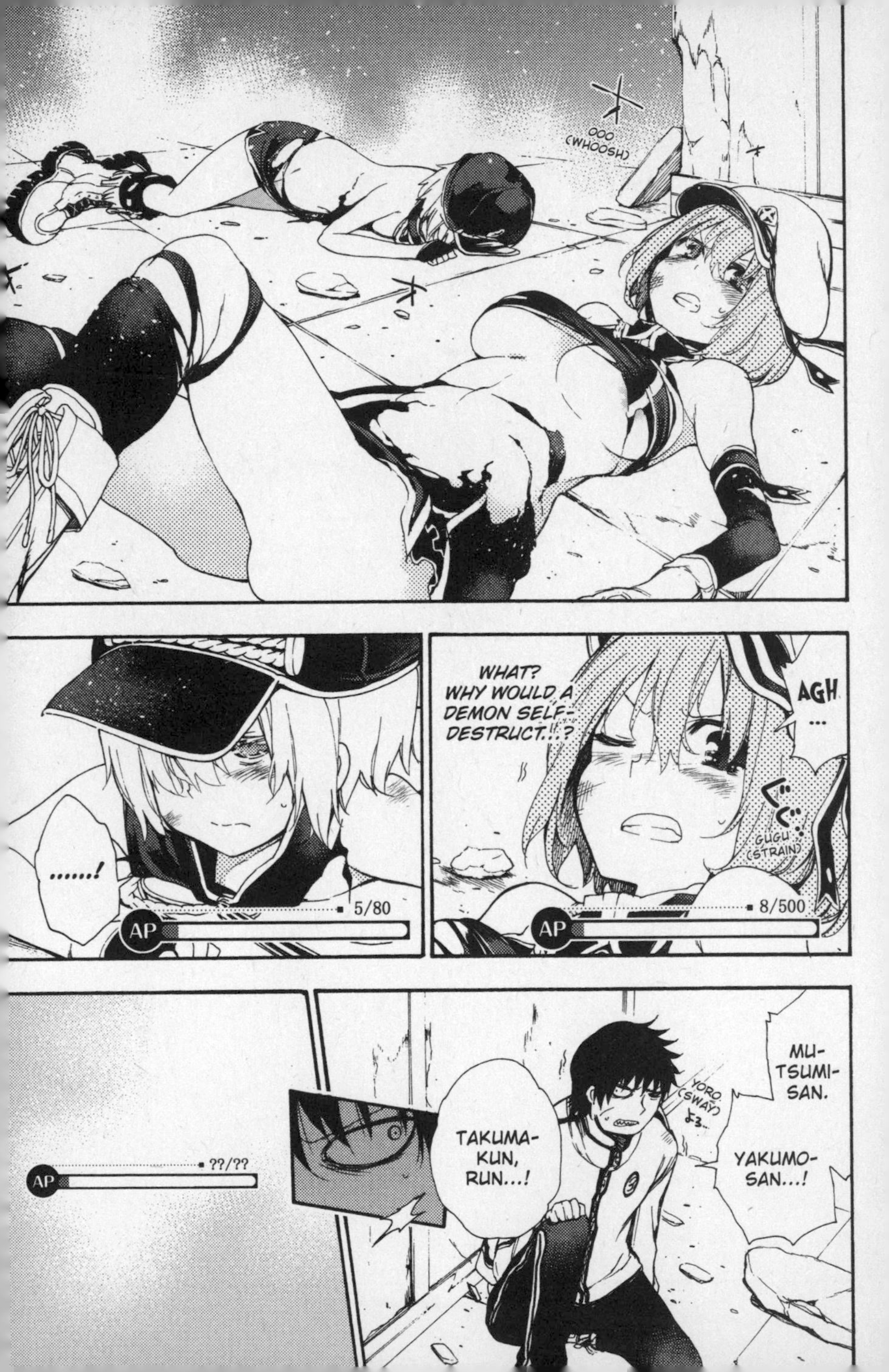
OOO (WHOOSH)
AGH ...
ぐぐ… GUGU (STRAIN)
WHAT? WHY WOULD A DEMON SELF-DESTRUCT...!?
8/500
AP
......!
5/80
AP
MU-TSUMI-SAN.
YAKUMO-SAN...!
よろ… YORO (SWAY)
TAKUMA-KUN, RUN...!
??/??
AP

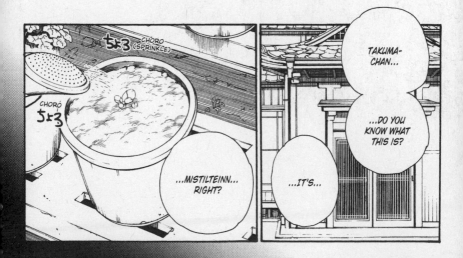

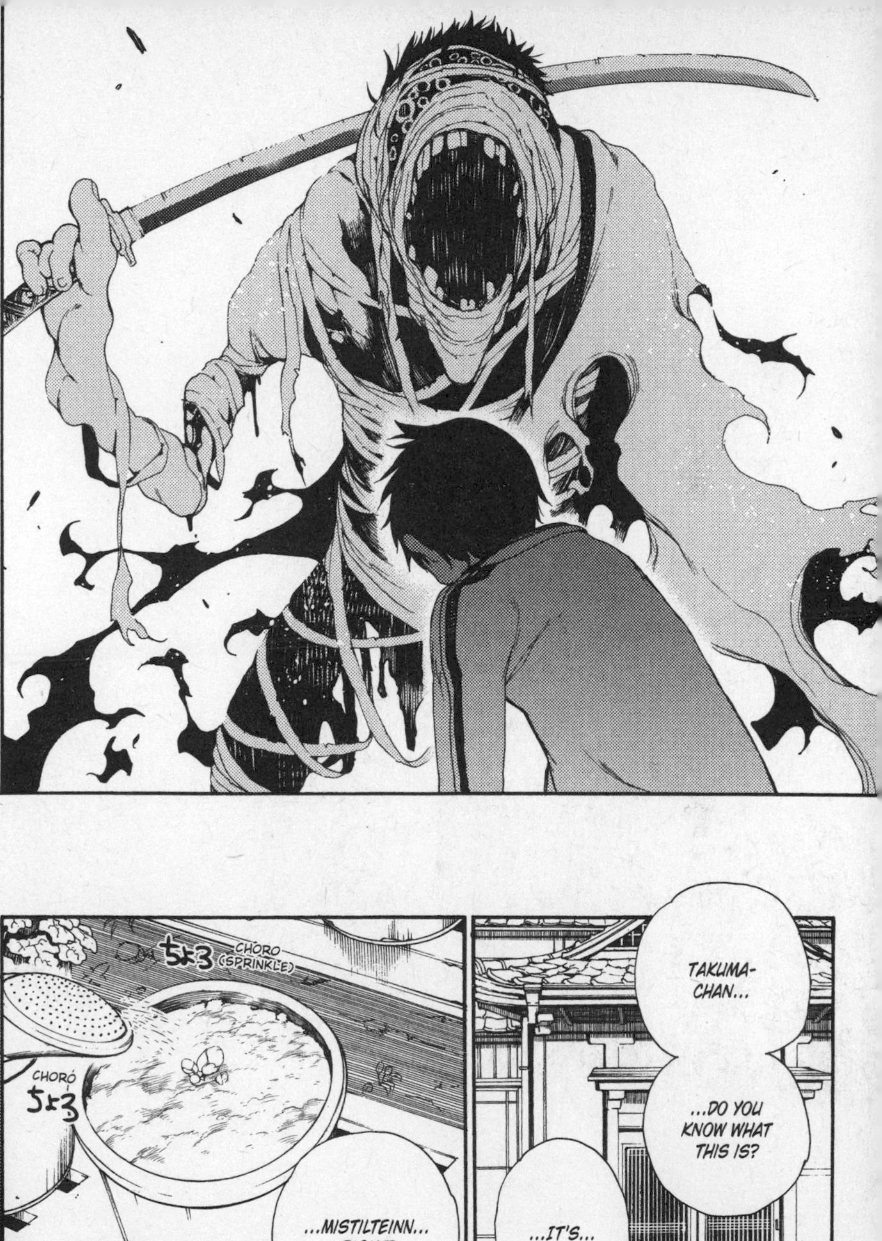
TAKUMA-CHAN...
...DO YOU KNOW WHAT THIS IS?
...IT'S...
ちょろ CHORO (SPRINKLE)
CHORO ちょろ
...MISTILTEINN... RIGHT?

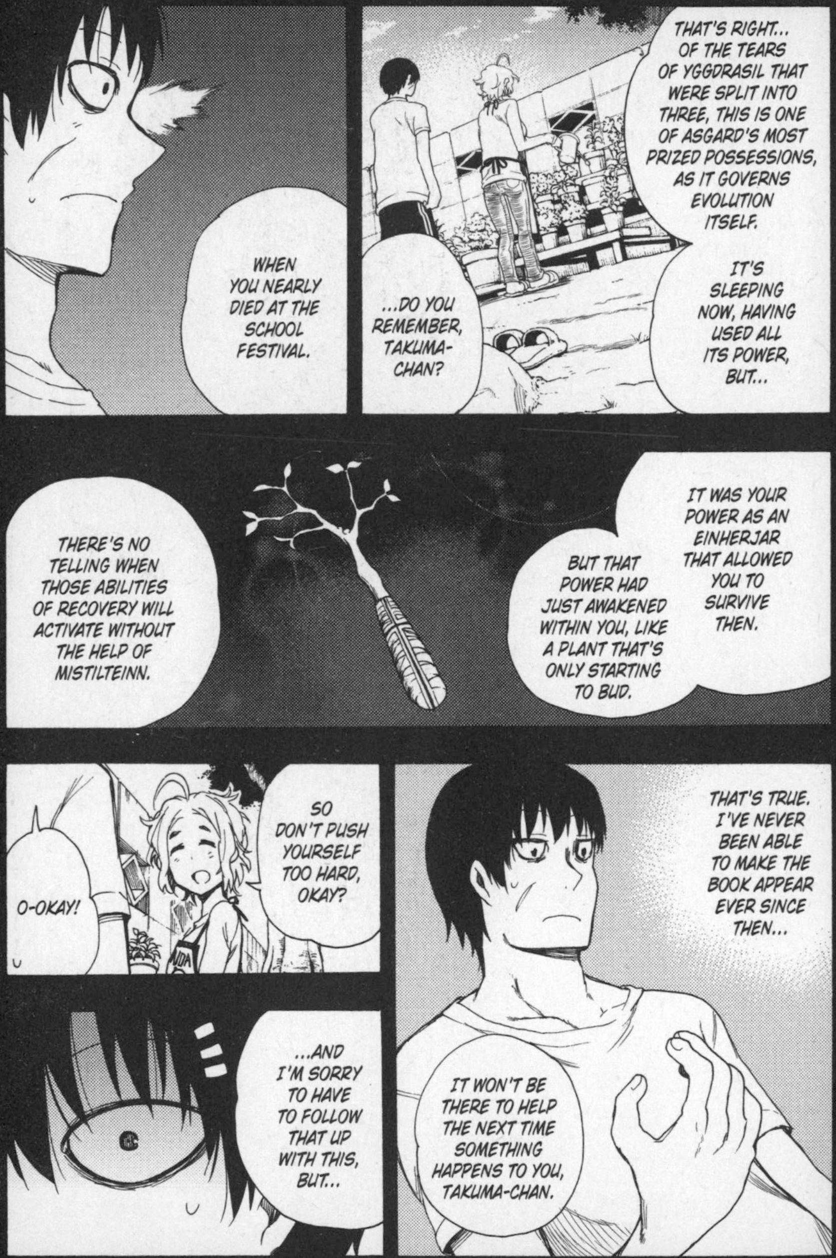
THAT'S RIGHT... OF THE TEARS OF YGGDRASIL THAT WERE SPLIT INTO THREE, THIS IS ONE OF ASGARD'S MOST PRIZED POSSESSIONS, AS IT GOVERNS EVOLUTION ITSELF.
IT'S SLEEPING NOW, HAVING USED ALL ITS POWER, BUT...
...DO YOU REMEMBER, TAKUMA-CHAN?
WHEN YOU NEARLY DIED AT THE SCHOOL FESTIVAL.
IT WAS YOUR POWER AS AN EINHERJAR THAT ALLOWED YOU TO SURVIVE THEN.
BUT THAT POWER HAD JUST AWAKENED WITHIN YOU, LIKE A PLANT THAT'S ONLY STARTING TO BUD.
THERE'S NO TELLING WHEN THOSE ABILITIES OF RECOVERY WILL ACTIVATE WITHOUT THE HELP OF MISTILTEINN.
THAT'S TRUE. I'VE NEVER BEEN ABLE TO MAKE THE BOOK APPEAR EVER SINCE THEN...
IT WON'T BE THERE TO HELP THE NEXT TIME SOMETHING HAPPENS TO YOU, TAKUMA-CHAN.
SO DON'T PUSH YOURSELF TOO HARD, OKAY?
O-OKAY!
...AND I'M SORRY TO HAVE TO FOLLOW THAT UP WITH THIS, BUT...

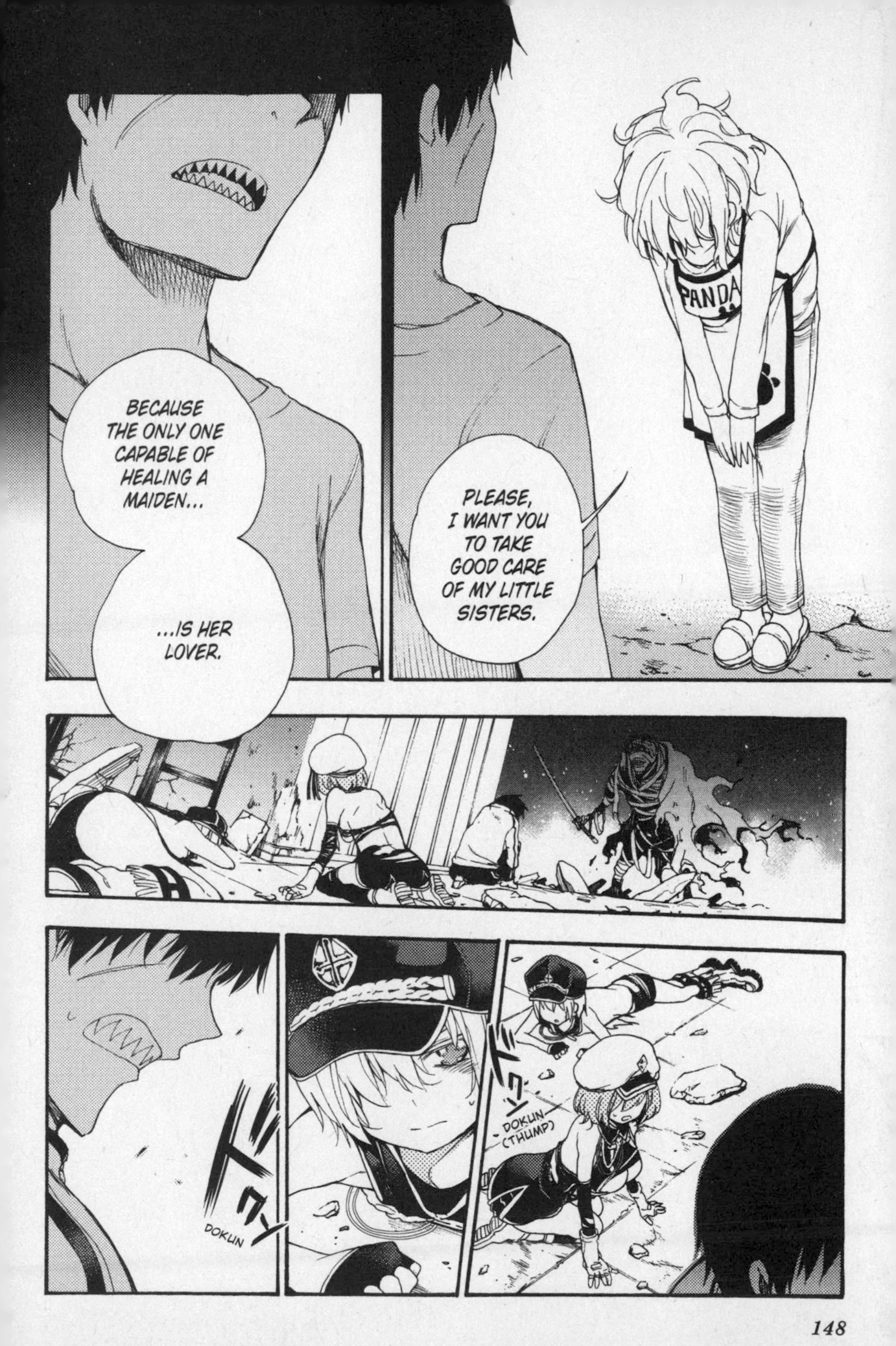
PLEASE, I WANT YOU TO TAKE GOOD CARE OF MY LITTLE SISTERS.
BECAUSE THE ONLY ONE CAPABLE OF HEALING A MAIDEN...
...IS HER LOVER.
DOKUN (THUMP)
DOKUN

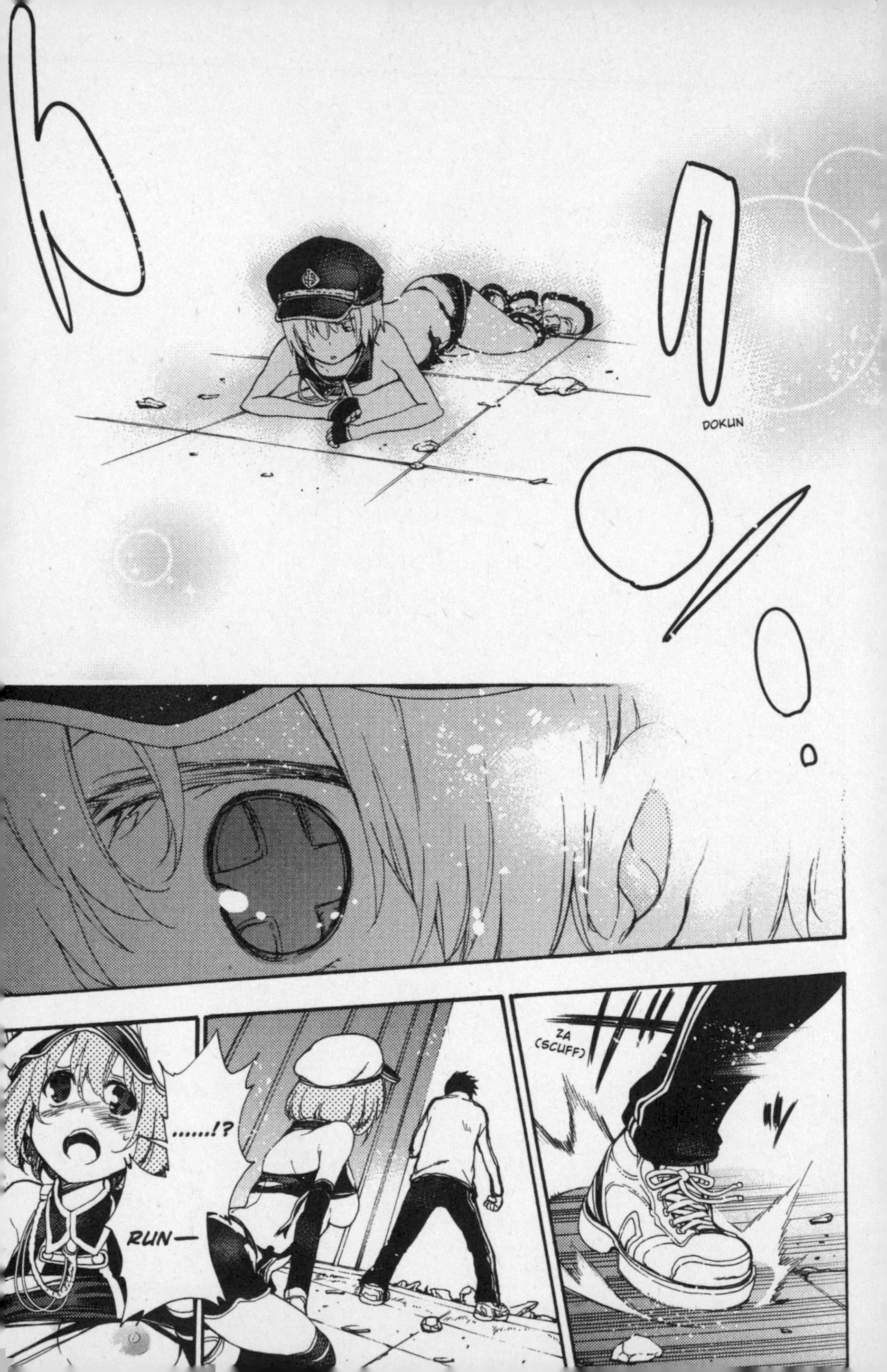
DOKUN
ZA
(SCUFF)
......!?
RUN—

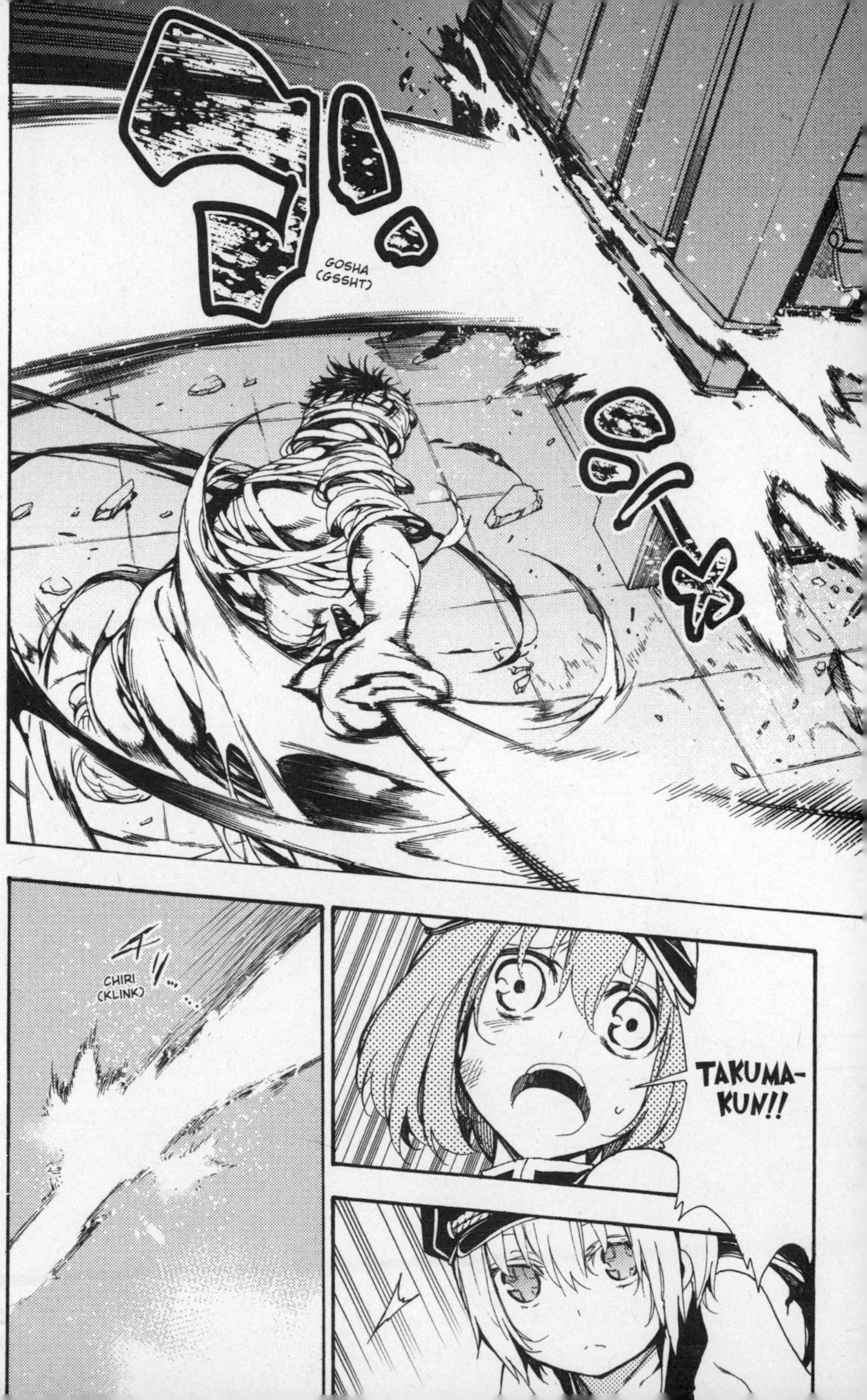
GOSHA
(GSSHT)
TAKUMA-KUN!!
CHIRI
(KLINK)

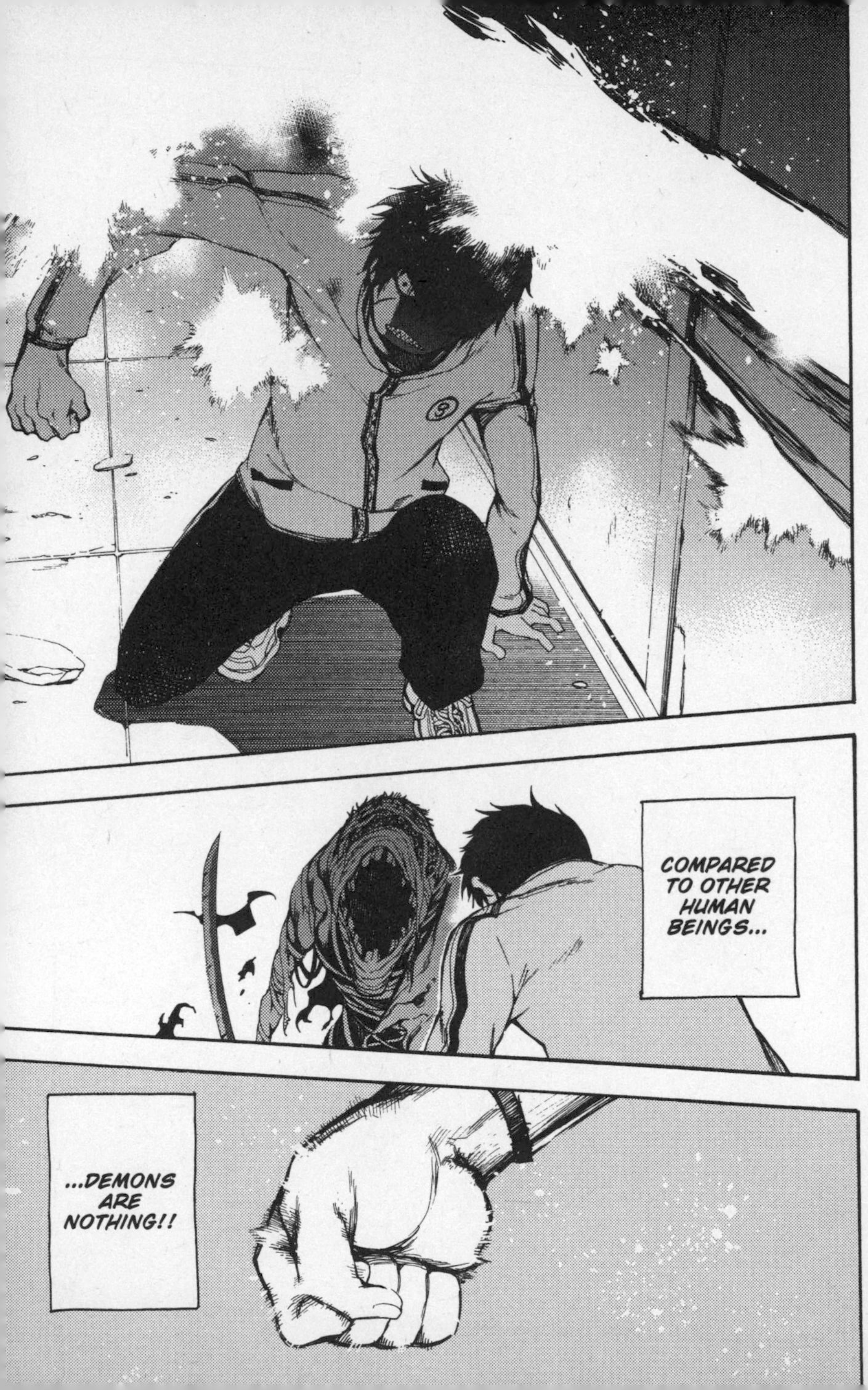
COMPARED TO OTHER HUMAN BEINGS...
...DEMONS ARE NOTHING!!

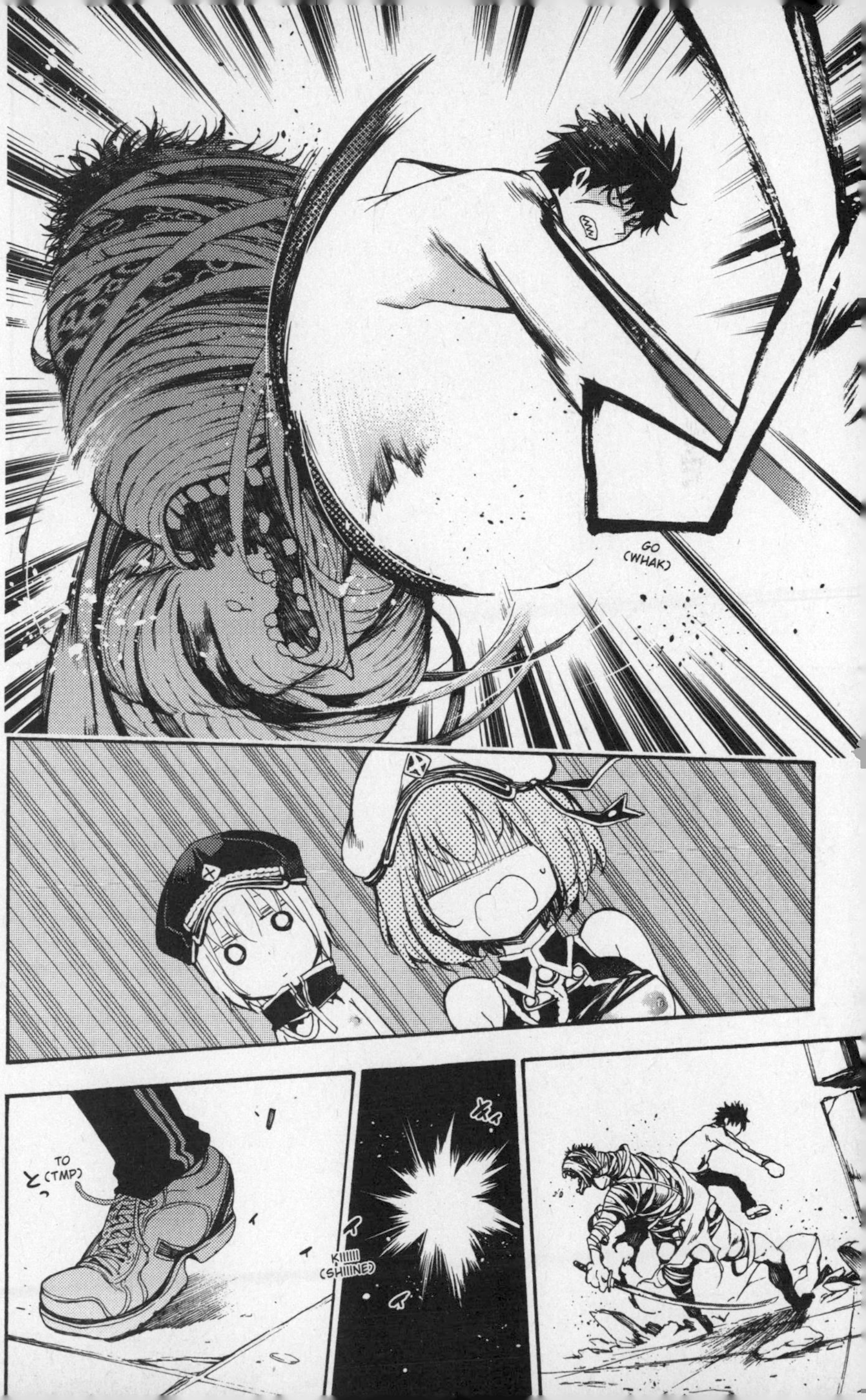
GO
(WHAK)
KIIIII
(SHIIINE)
TO
(TMP)

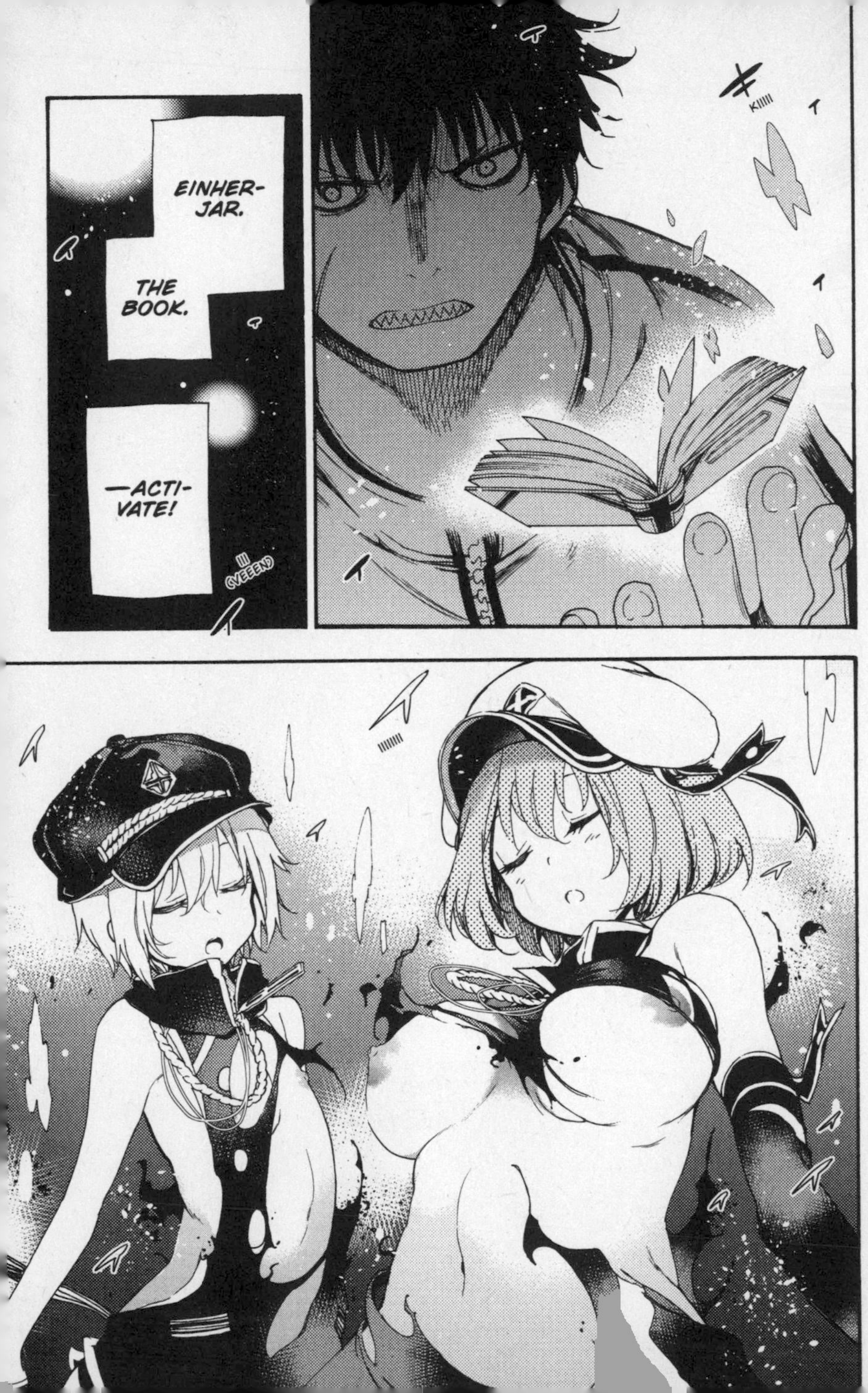
KIIII
EINHER-JAR.
THE BOOK.
—ACTI-VATE!
(VEEEN)

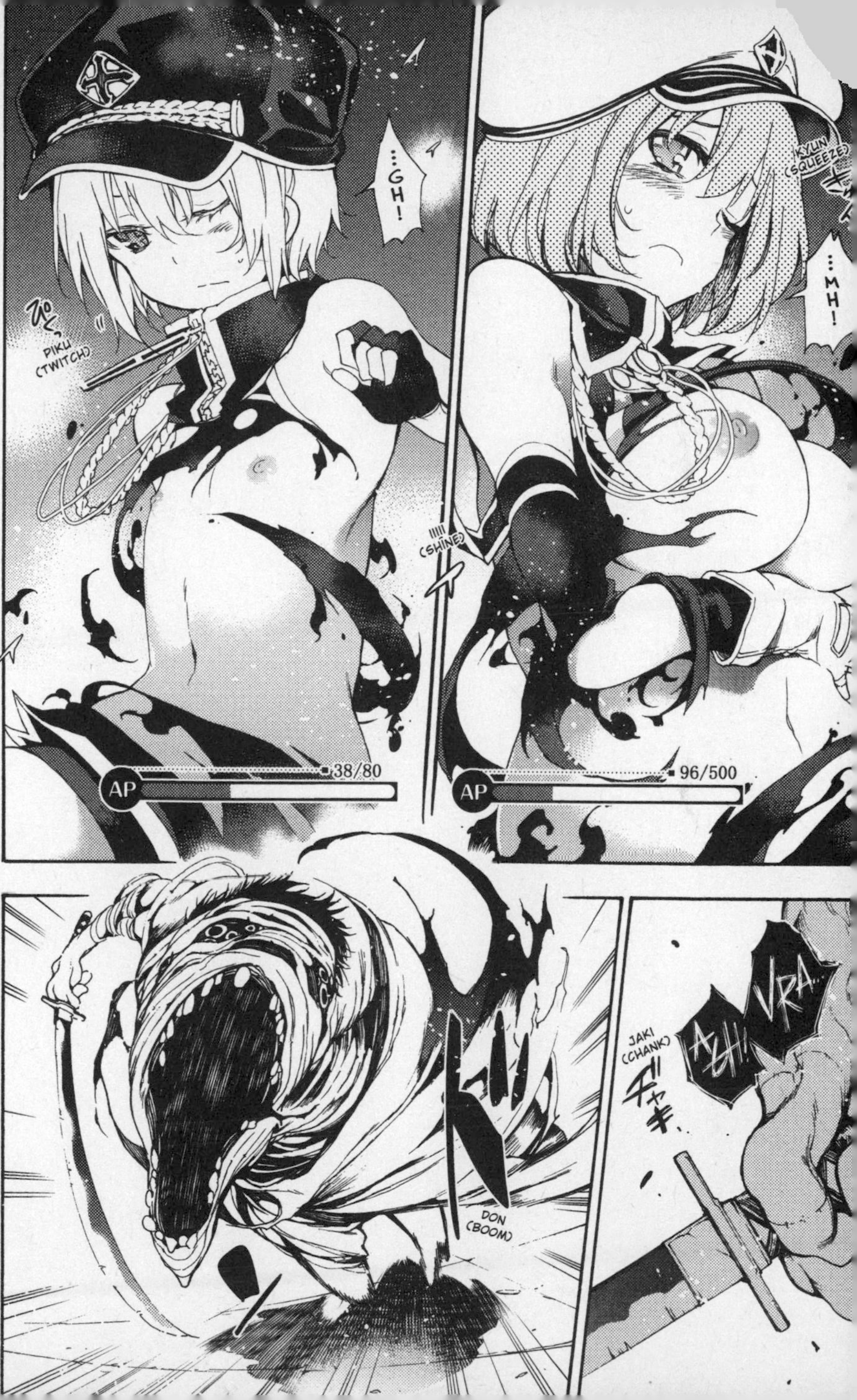
KYUN (SQUEEZE)
...MH!
(SHINE)
AP 96/500
...GH!
PIKU (TWITCH)
AP 38/80
VRA
AGH!
JAKI (CHANK)
DON (BOOM)

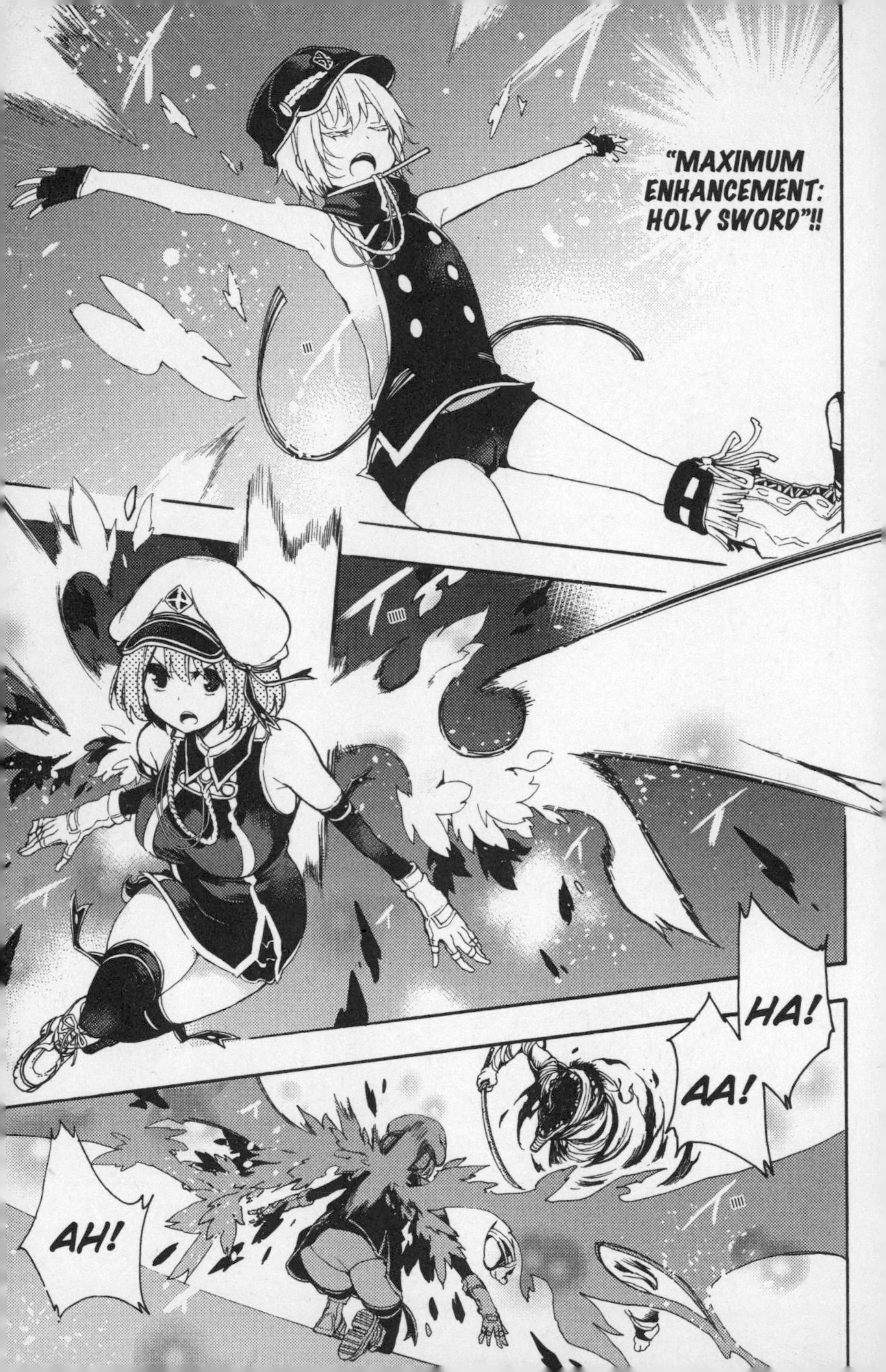
"MAXIMUM ENHANCEMENT: HOLY SWORD"!!
HA!
AA!
AH!

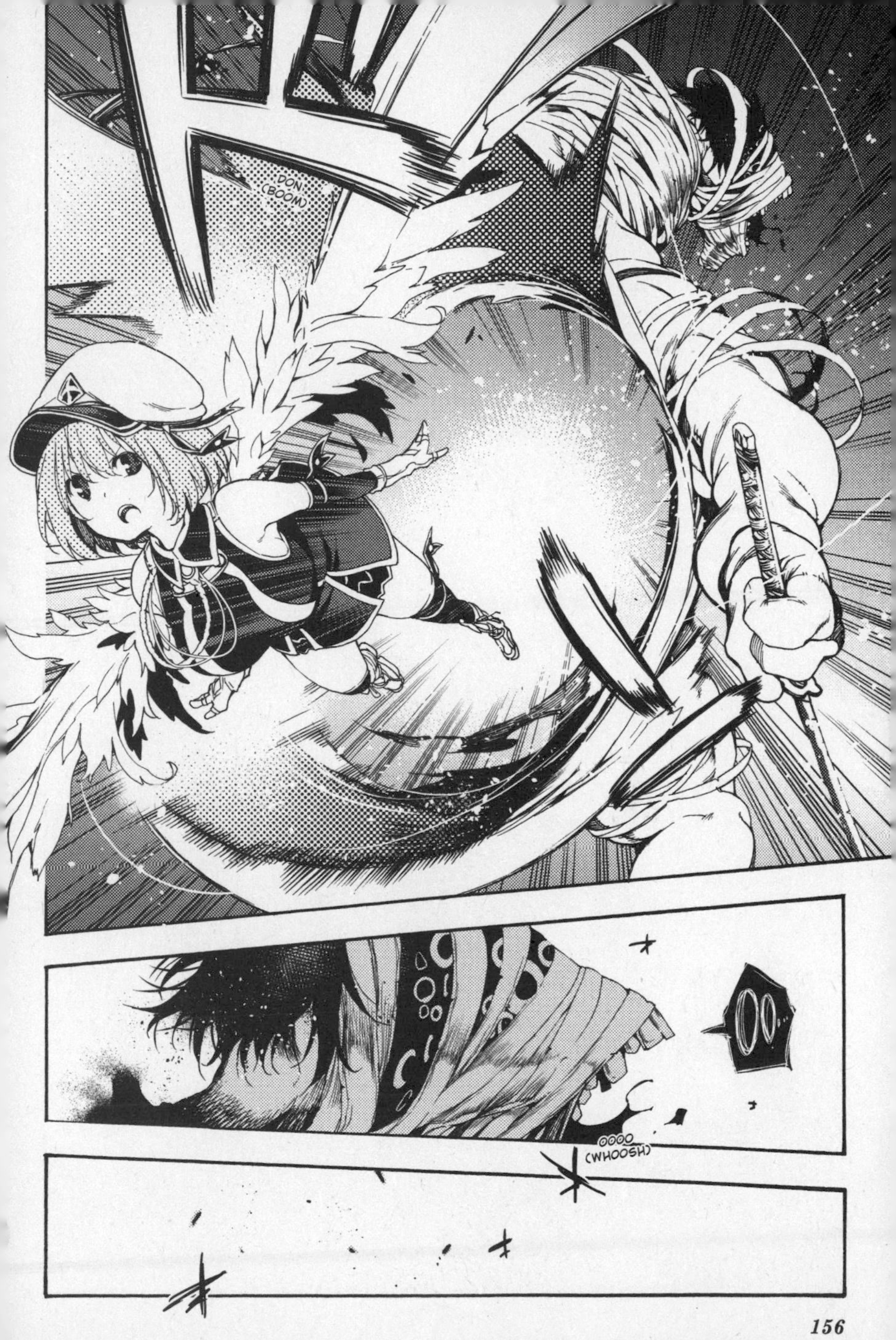
DON
(BOOM)
OOOO
(WHOOSH)

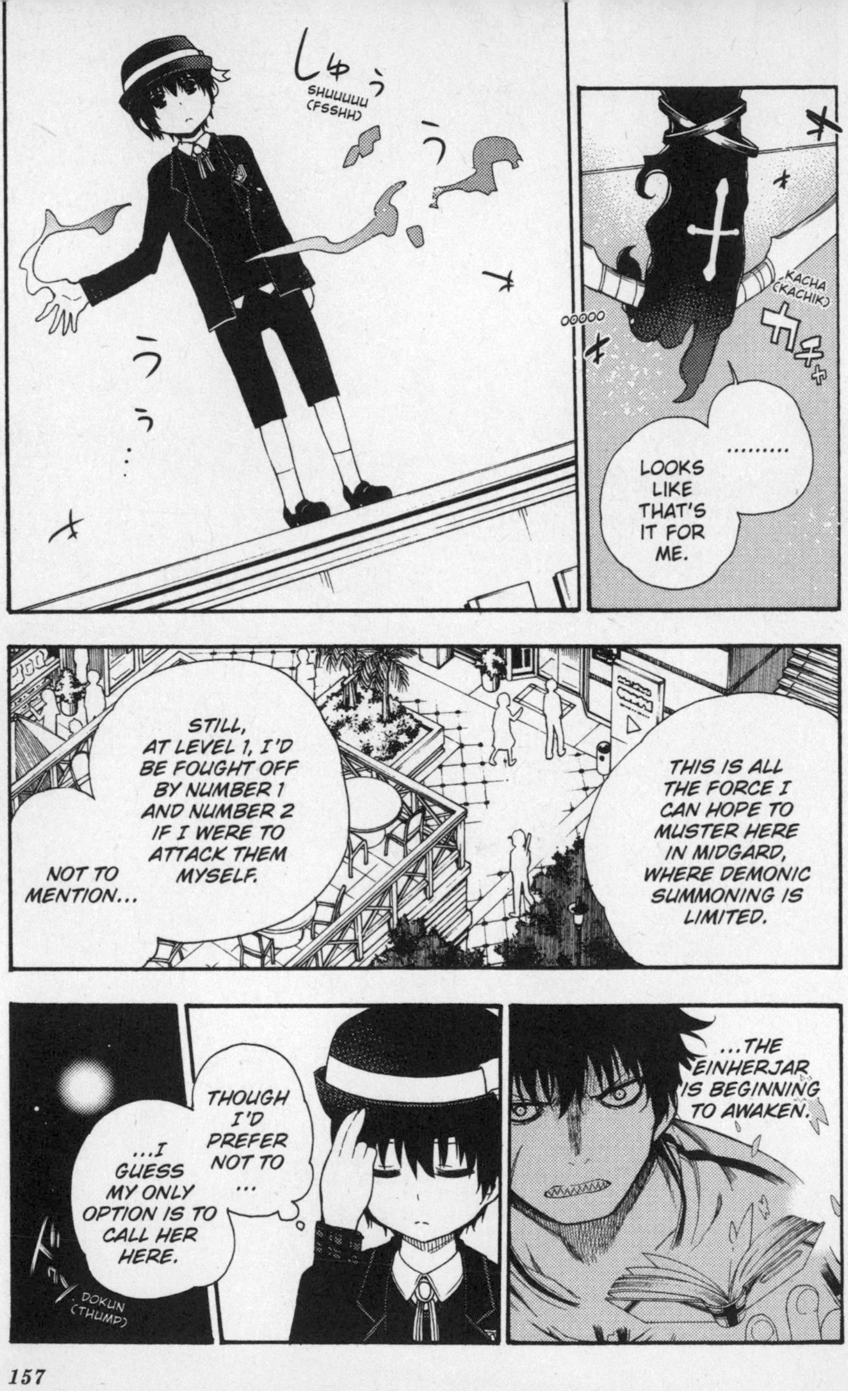
KACHA (KACHIK)
OOOOO
....
LOOKS LIKE THAT'S IT FOR ME.
SHUUUUU (FSSHH)
THIS IS ALL THE FORCE I CAN HOPE TO MUSTER HERE IN MIDGARD, WHERE DEMONIC SUMMONING IS LIMITED.
STILL, AT LEVEL 1, I'D BE FOUGHT OFF BY NUMBER 1 AND NUMBER 2 IF I WERE TO ATTACK THEM MYSELF.
NOT TO MENTION...
...THE EINHERJAR IS BEGINNING TO AWAKEN.
THOUGH I'D PREFER NOT TO ...
...I GUESS MY ONLY OPTION IS TO CALL HER HERE.
DOKUN (THUMP)

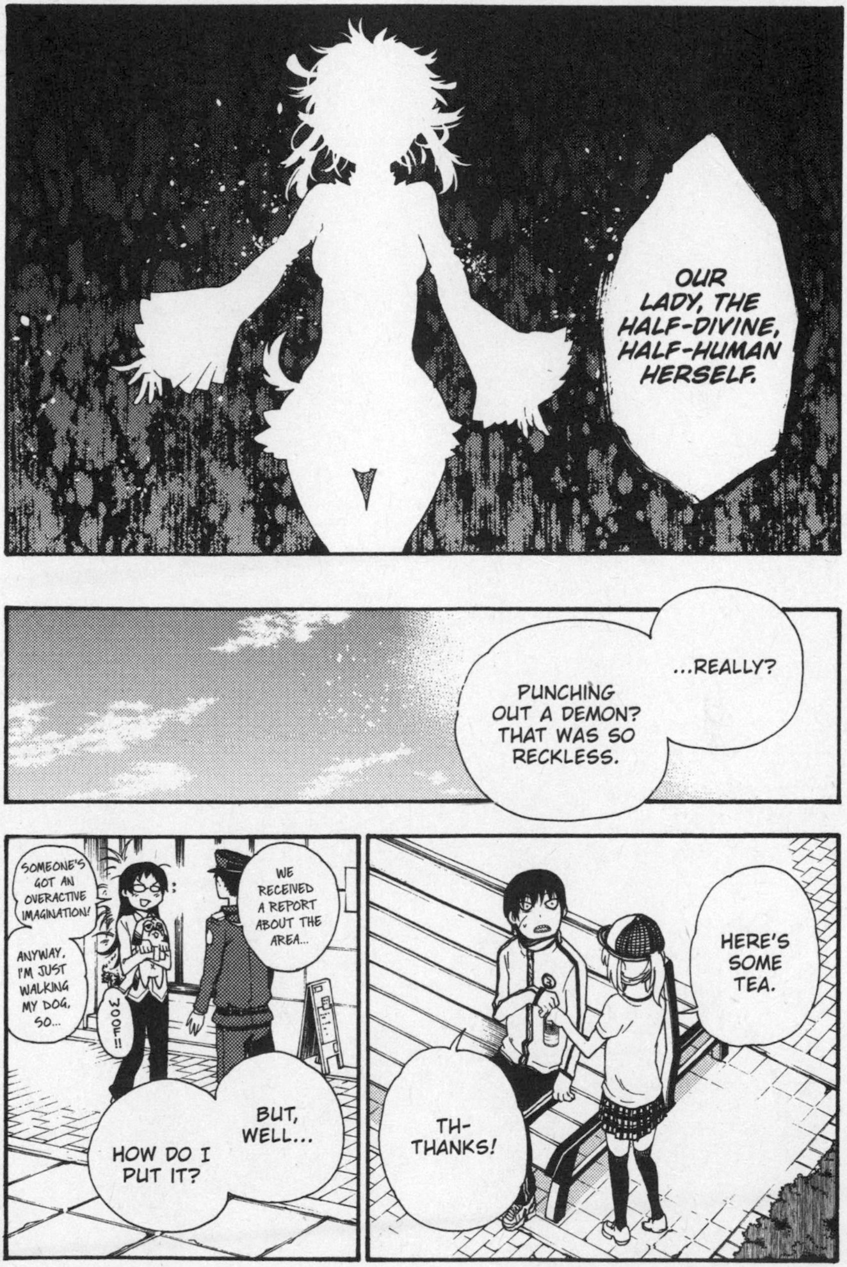
OUR LADY, THE HALF-DIVINE, HALF-HUMAN HERSELF.
...REALLY?
PUNCHING OUT A DEMON? THAT WAS SO RECKLESS.
HERE'S SOME TEA.
TH- THANKS!
WE RECEIVED A REPORT ABOUT THE AREA...
SOMEONE'S GOT AN OVERACTIVE IMAGINATION!
ANYWAY, I'M JUST WALKING MY DOG, SO...
WOOF!!
BUT, WELL...
HOW DO I PUT IT?

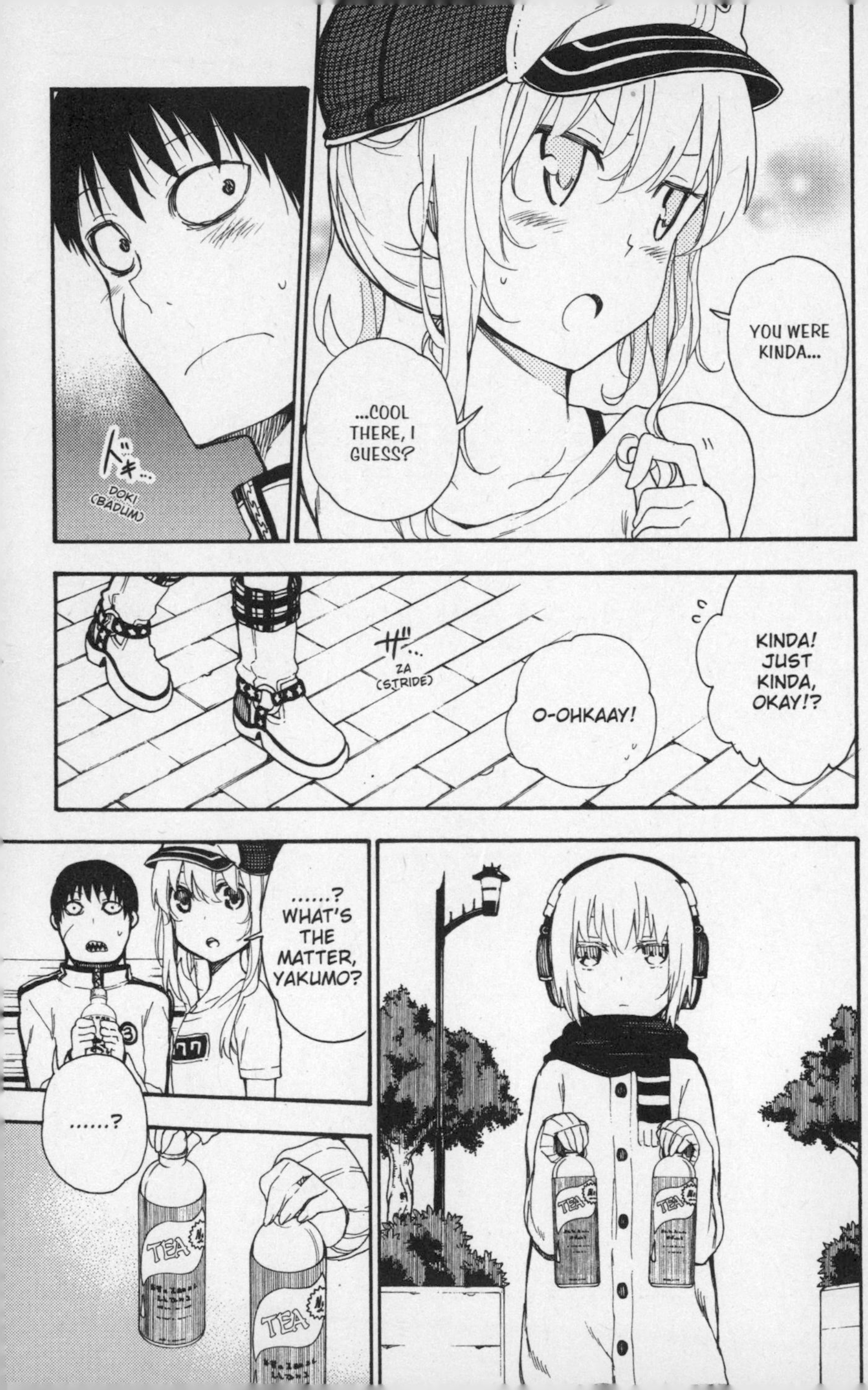
YOU WERE KINDA...
...COOL THERE, I GUESS?
ドキ...
DOKI (BADUM)
KINDA! JUST KINDA, OKAY!?
O-OHKAAY!
ザ...
ZA (STRIDE)
......? WHAT'S THE MATTER, YAKUMO?
......?

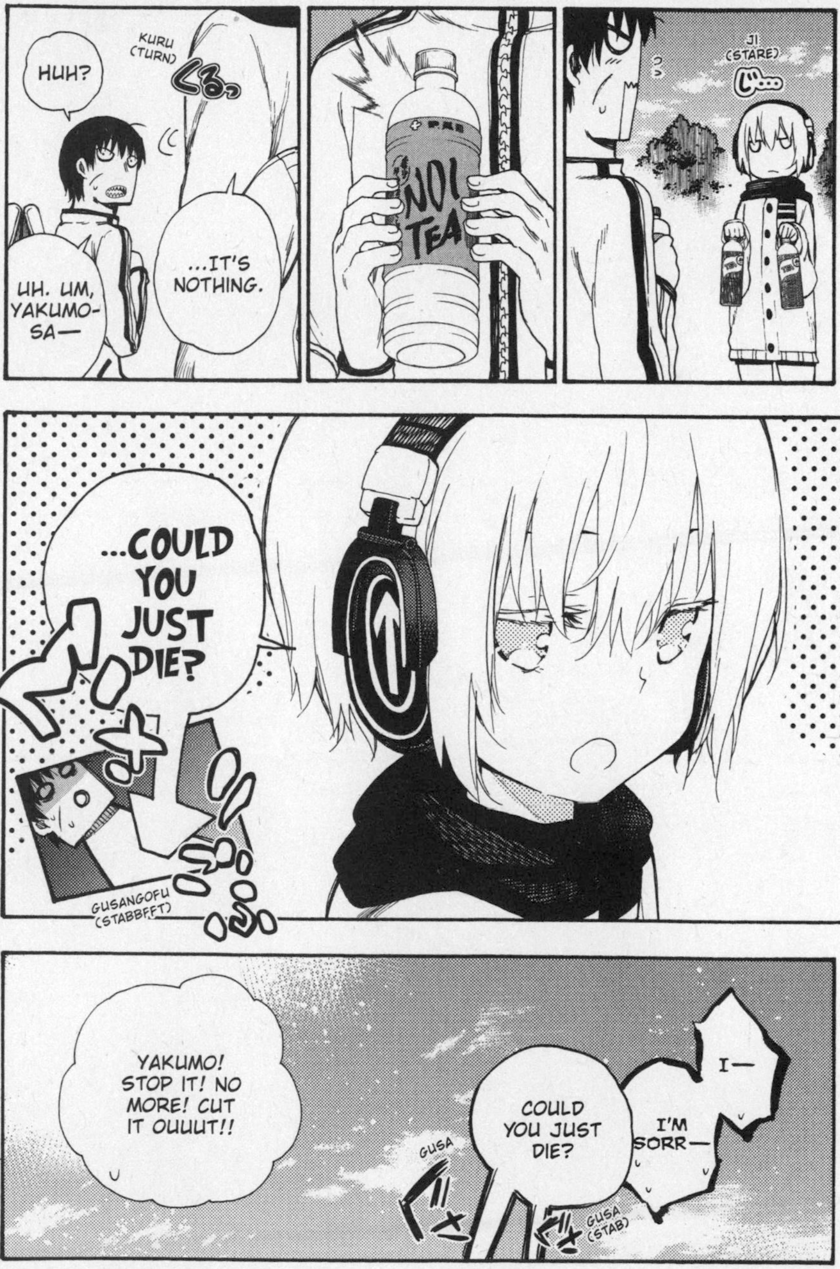
JI (STARE)
KURU (TURN)
HUH?
...IT'S NOTHING.
UH. UM, YAKUMO-SA—
...COULD YOU JUST DIE?
GUSANGOFU (STABBFFT)
I—
I'M SORR—
COULD YOU JUST DIE?
GUSA (STAB)
GUSA
YAKUMO! STOP IT! NO MORE! CUT IT OUUUT!!

Val × Love

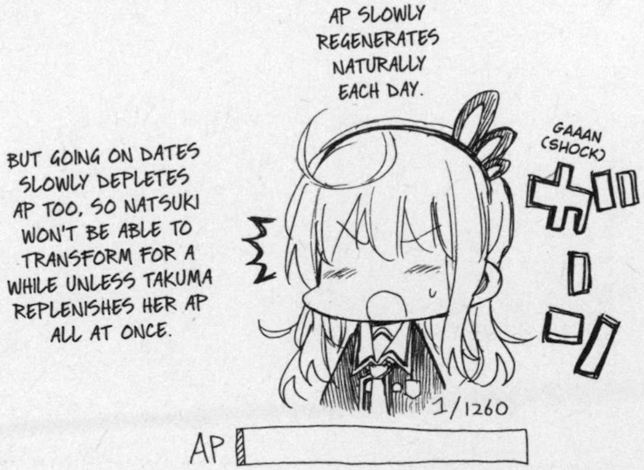
AP SLOWLY REGENERATES NATURALLY EACH DAY.
GAAAN (SHOCK)
BUT GOING ON DATES SLOWLY DEPLETES AP TOO, SO NATSUKI WON'T BE ABLE TO TRANSFORM FOR A WHILE UNLESS TAKUMA REPLENISHES HER AP ALL AT ONCE.
1/1260
AP

Chapter 20

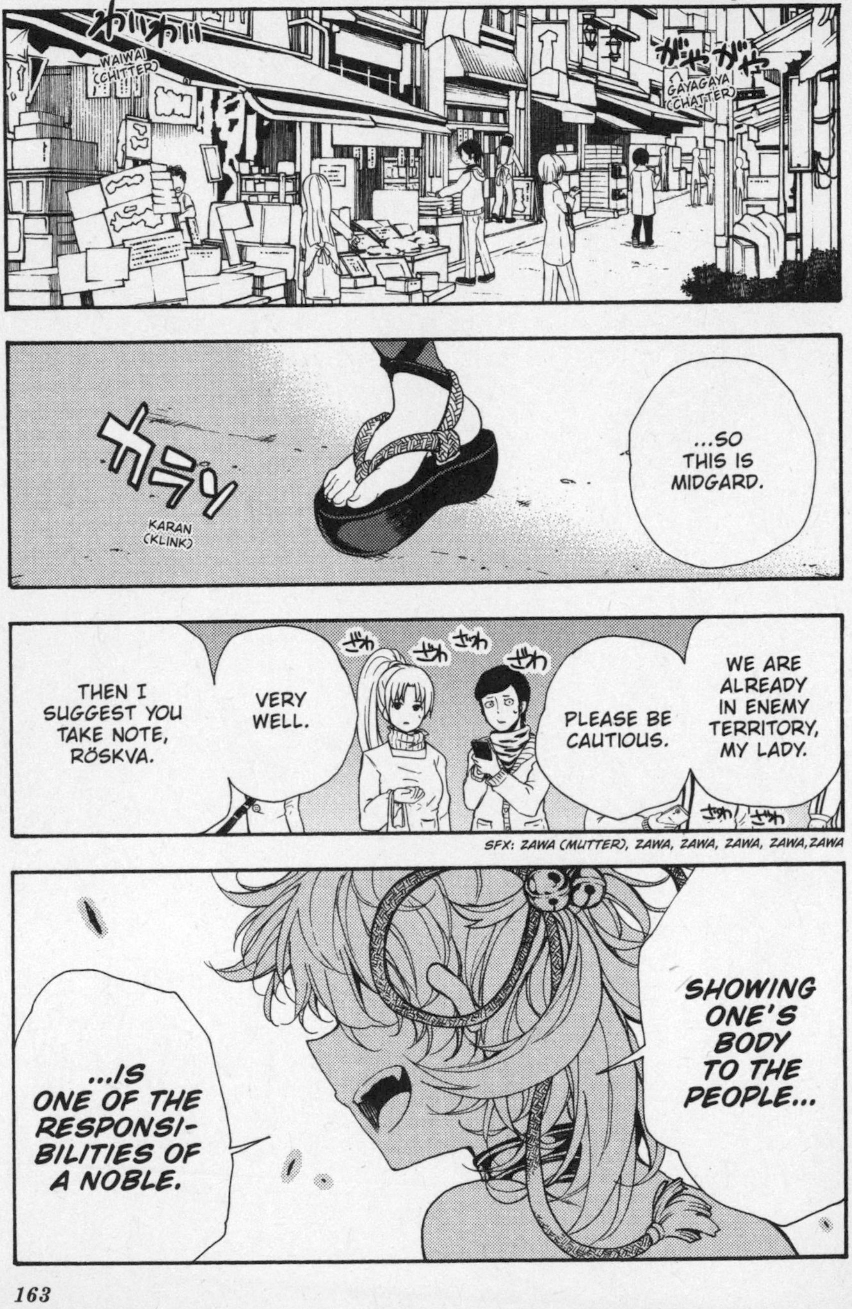
GAYAGAYA (CHATTER)
WAIWAI (CHITTER)
...SO THIS IS MIDGARD.
KARAN (KLINK)
WE ARE ALREADY IN ENEMY TERRITORY, MY LADY.
PLEASE BE CAUTIOUS.
VERY WELL.
THEN I SUGGEST YOU TAKE NOTE, RÖSKVA.
SFX: ZAWA (MUTTER), ZAWA, ZAWA, ZAWA, ZAWA,ZAWA
SHOWING ONE'S BODY TO THE PEOPLE...
...IS ONE OF THE RESPONSI-BILITIES OF A NOBLE.

Chapter 20: The Touching Maiden and the Touched Maiden

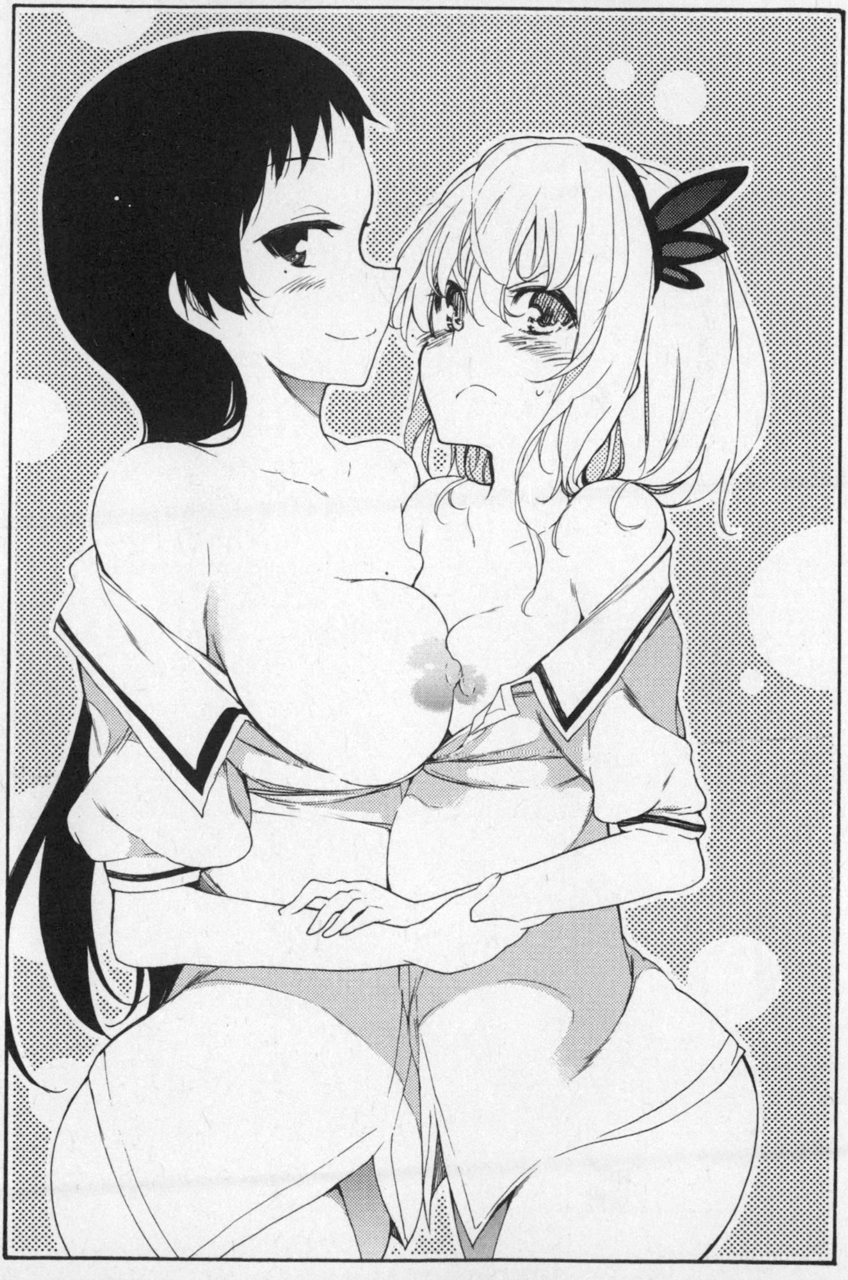

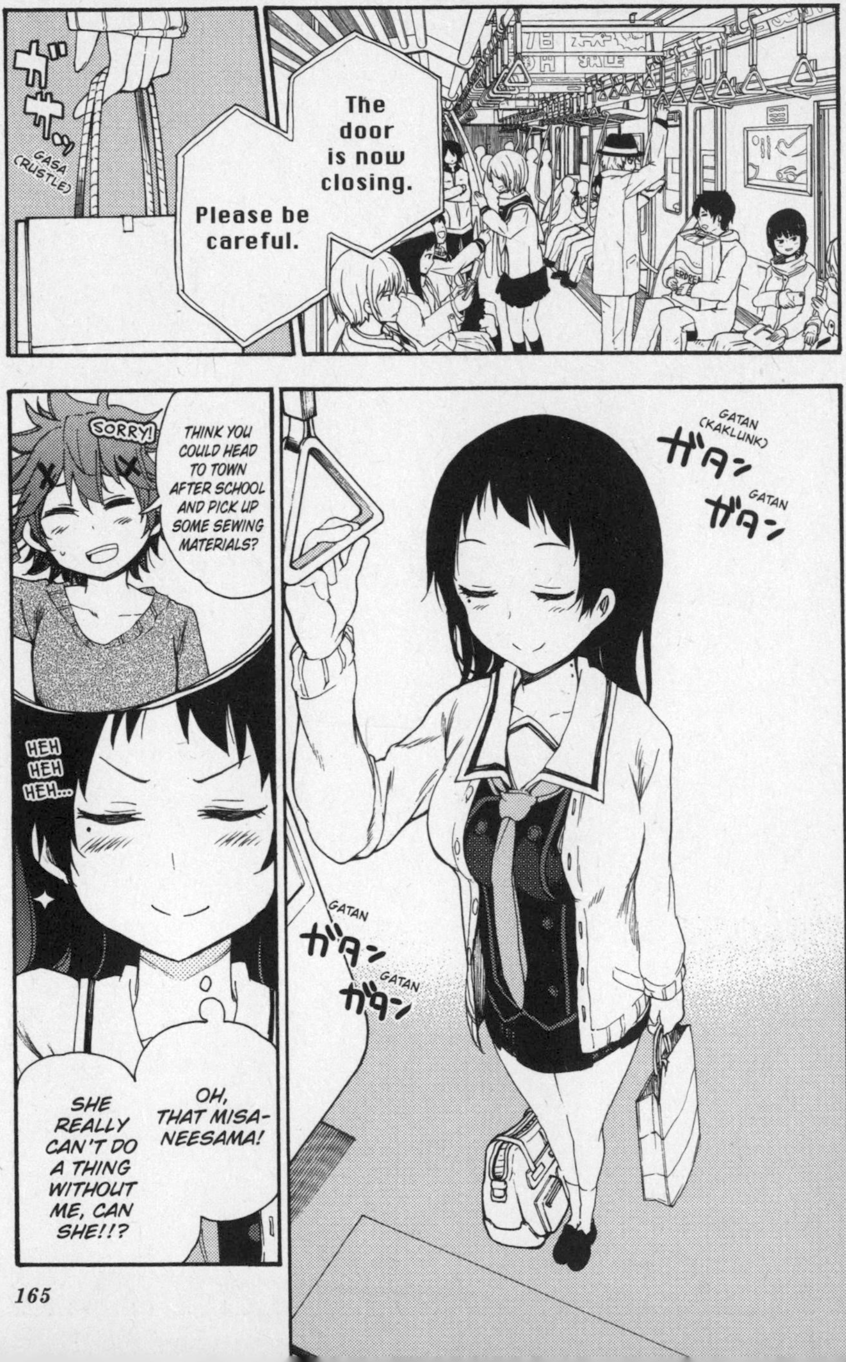
The door is now closing.
Please be careful.
ガサッ GASA (RUSTLE)
ガタン GATAN (KAKLUNK)
ガタン GATAN
ガタン GATAN
ガタン GATAN
SORRY!
THINK YOU COULD HEAD TO TOWN AFTER SCHOOL AND PICK UP SOME SEWING MATERIALS?
HEH HEH HEH...
OH, THAT MISA-NEESAMA!
SHE REALLY CAN'T DO A THING WITHOUT ME, CAN SHE!!?

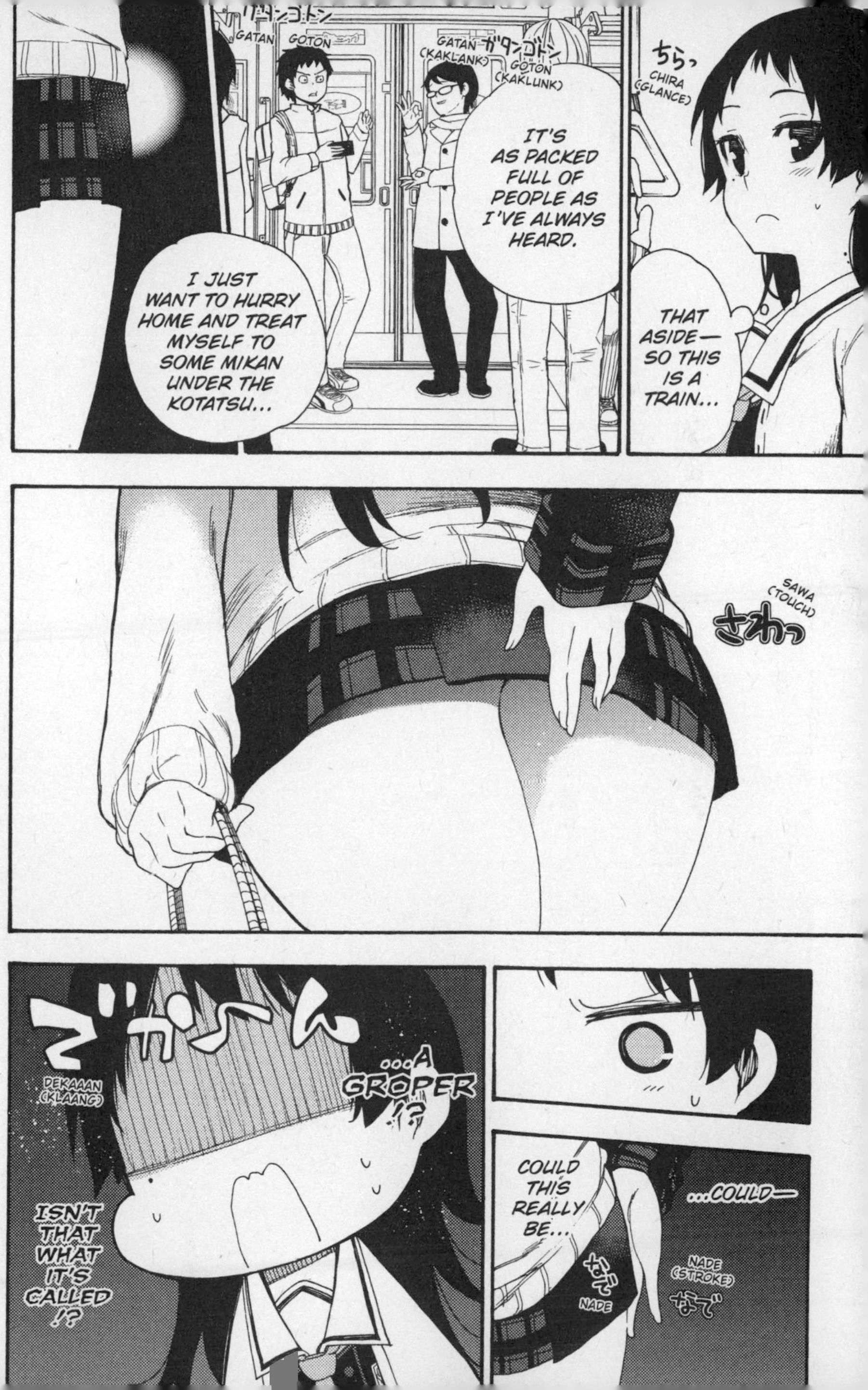
ちらっ
CHIRA (GLANCE)
THAT ASIDE— SO THIS IS A TRAIN...
ガタンゴトン
GATAN GOTON
GATAN ガタンゴトン (KAKLANK)
GOTON (KAKLUNK)
IT'S AS PACKED FULL OF PEOPLE AS I'VE ALWAYS HEARD.
I JUST WANT TO HURRY HOME AND TREAT MYSELF TO SOME MIKAN UNDER THE KOTATSU...
SAWA (TOUCH)
さわっ
...COULD—
NADE (STROKE)
なで
COULD THIS REALLY BE...
なで
NADE
でかーん
DEKAAAN (KLAANG)
...A GROPER !?
ISN'T THAT WHAT IT'S CALLED !?

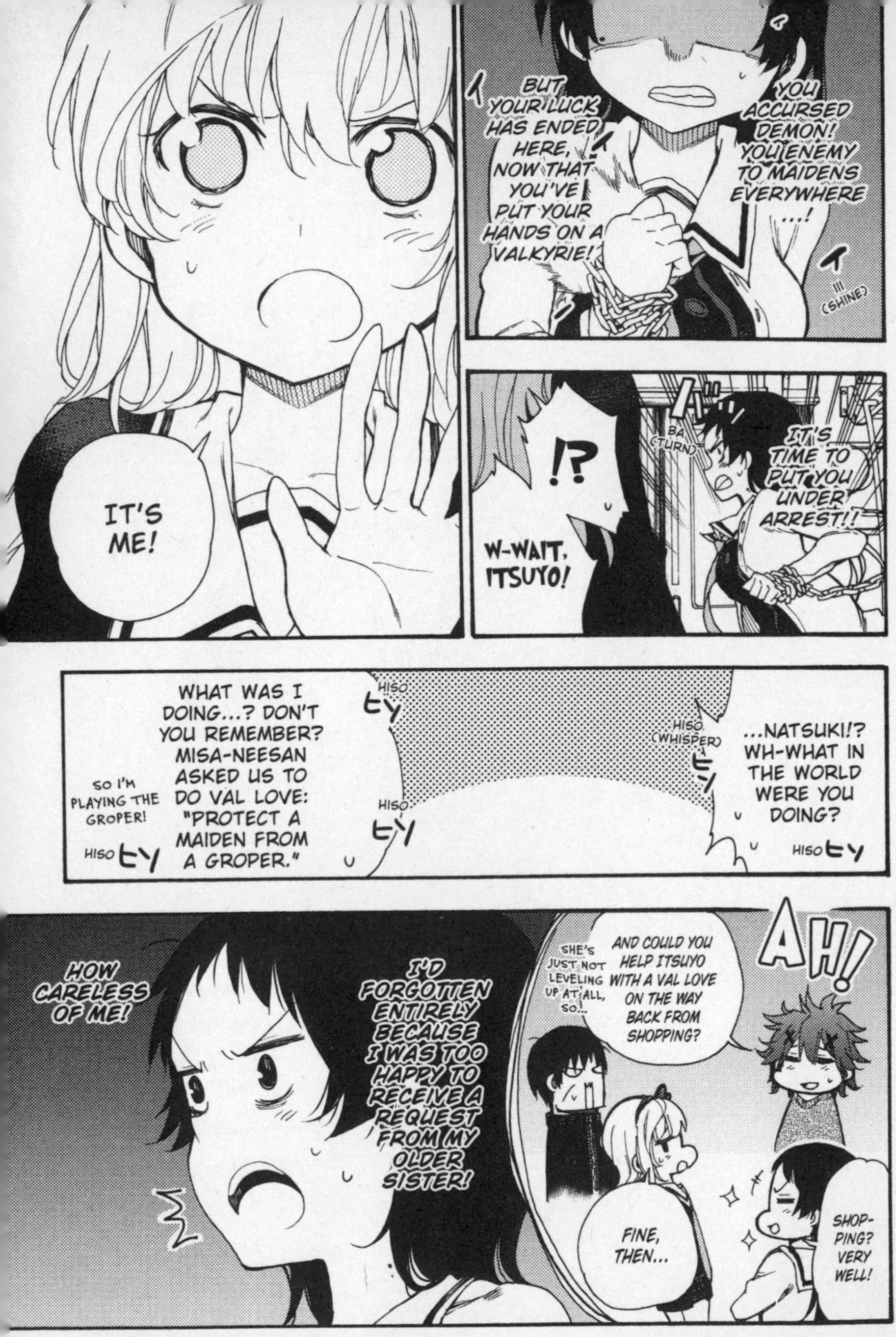
YOU ACCURSED DEMON! YOU ENEMY TO MAIDENS EVERYWHERE...!
BUT YOUR LUCK HAS ENDED HERE, NOW THAT YOU'VE PUT YOUR HANDS ON A VALKYRIE!
(SHINE)
BA (TURN)
IT'S TIME TO PUT YOU UNDER ARREST!!
!?
W-WAIT, ITSUYO!
IT'S ME!
...NATSUKI!? WH-WHAT IN THE WORLD WERE YOU DOING?
HISO
HISO (WHISPER)
WHAT WAS I DOING...? DON'T YOU REMEMBER? MISA-NEESAN ASKED US TO DO VAL LOVE: "PROTECT A MAIDEN FROM A GROPER."
HISO
SO I'M PLAYING THE GROPER!
HISO
AH!
AND COULD YOU HELP ITSUYO WITH A VAL LOVE ON THE WAY BACK FROM SHOPPING?
SHE'S JUST NOT LEVELING UP AT ALL, SO...
SHOP-PING? VERY WELL!
FINE, THEN...
I'D FORGOTTEN ENTIRELY BECAUSE I WAS TOO HAPPY TO RECEIVE A REQUEST FROM MY OLDER SISTER!
HOW CARELESS OF ME!

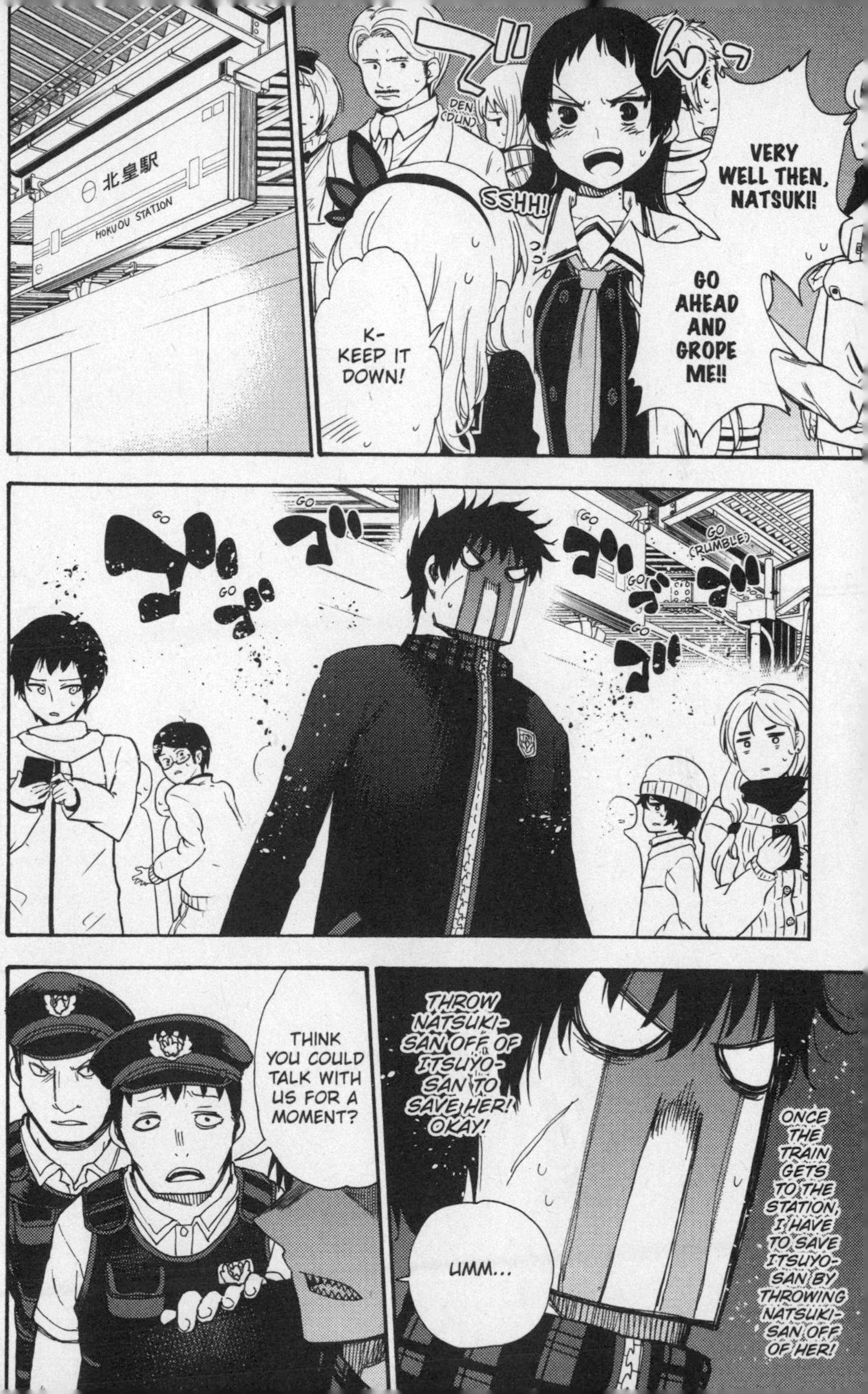

VERY WELL THEN, NATSUKI!
GO AHEAD AND GROPE ME!!
DEN (DUN)
SSHH!
K-KEEP IT DOWN!
北皇駅
HOKUOU STATION
GO (RUMBLE)
GO
GO
GO
GO
GO
GO
ONCE THE TRAIN GETS TO THE STATION, I HAVE TO SAVE ITSUYO-SAN BY THROWING NATSUKI-SAN OFF OF HER!
THROW NATSUKI-SAN OFF OF ITSUYO-SAN TO SAVE HER! OKAY!
UMM...
THINK YOU COULD TALK WITH US FOR A MOMENT?

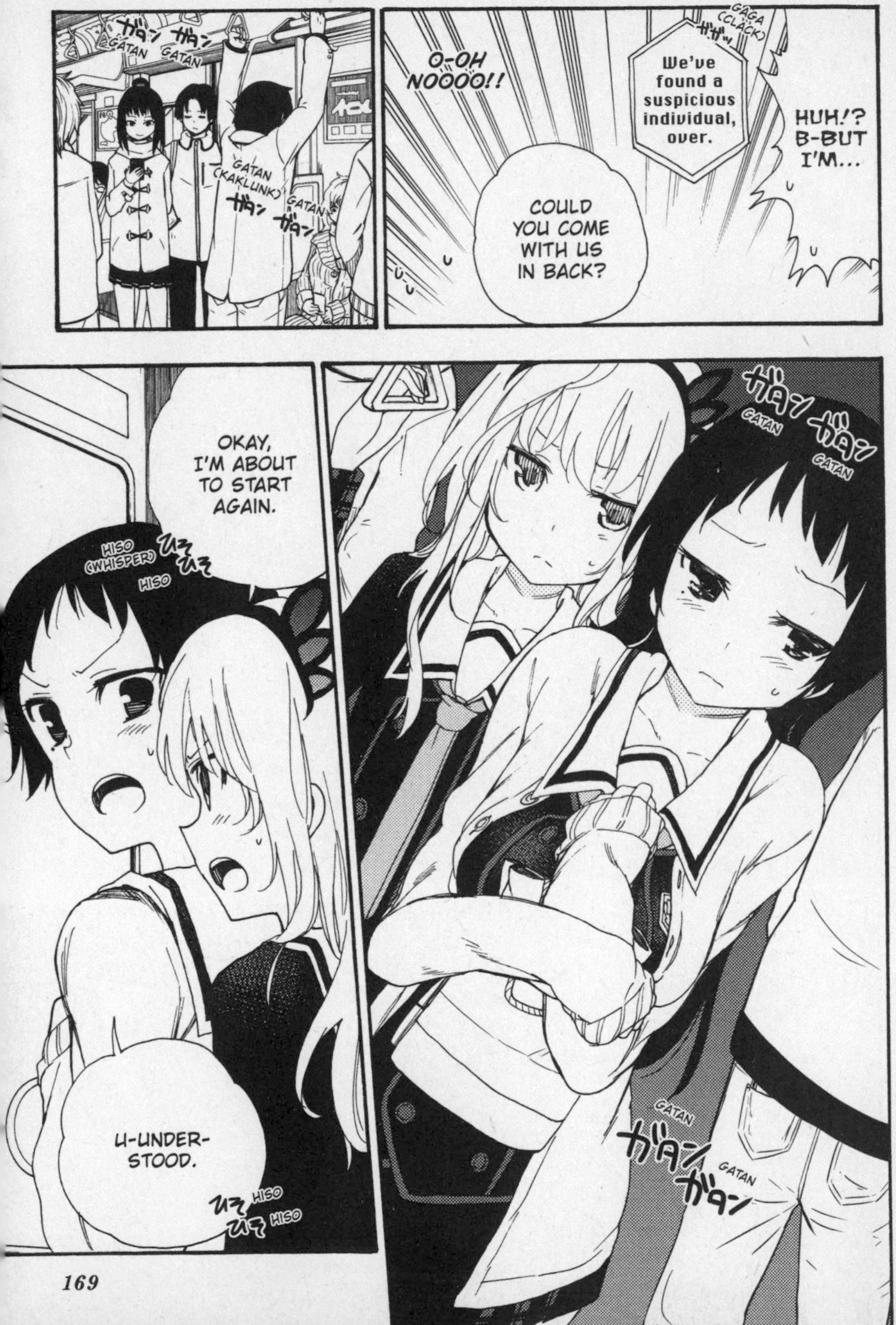

GAGA (CLACK)
We've found a suspicious individual, over.
HUH!? B-BUT I'M...
O-OH NOOOO!!
COULD YOU COME WITH US IN BACK?
GATAN GATAN
GATAN (KAKLUNK)
GATAN
GATAN GATAN
GATAN GATAN
OKAY, I'M ABOUT TO START AGAIN.
HISO (WHISPER) HISO
U-UNDER-STOOD.
HISO HISO

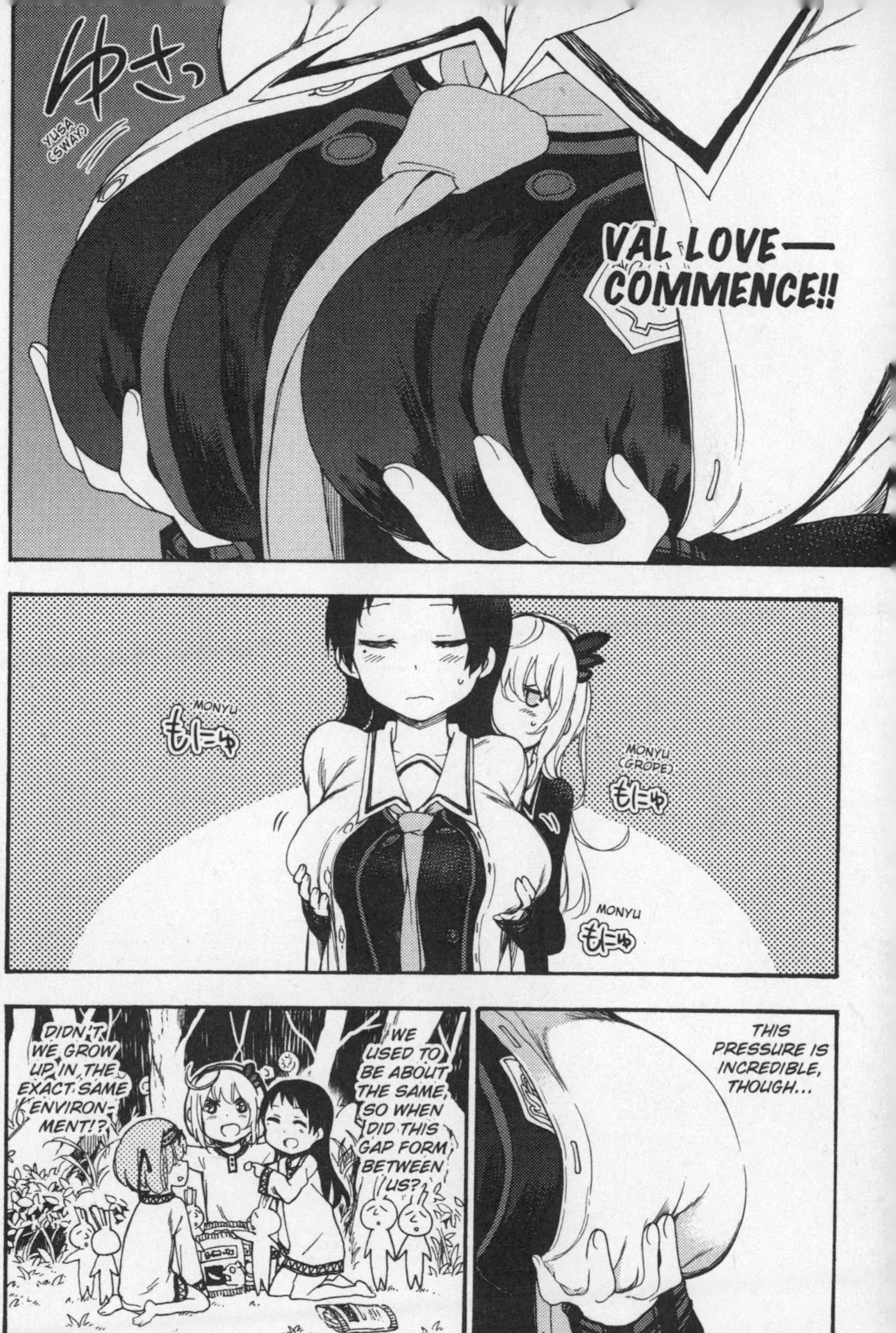
ゆさっ
YUSA (SWAY)
VAL LOVE—COMMENCE!!
MONYU (GROPE)
もにゅ
MONYU
もにゅ
MONYU
もにゅ
THIS PRESSURE IS INCREDIBLE, THOUGH...
WE USED TO BE ABOUT THE SAME, SO WHEN DID THIS GAP FORM BETWEEN US?
DIDN'T WE GROW UP IN THE EXACT SAME ENVIRON-MENT!?

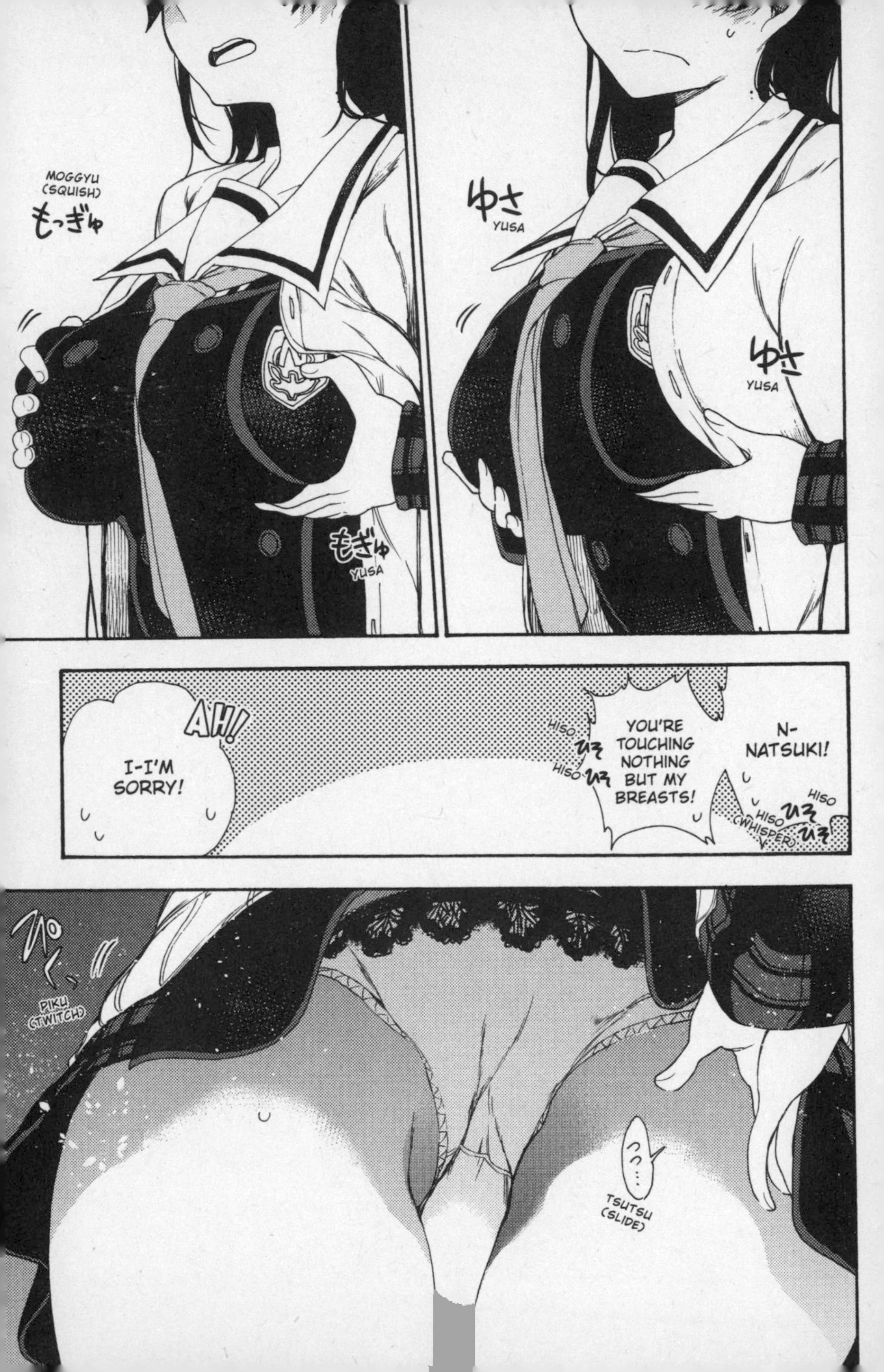
ゆさ
YUSA
ゆさ
YUSA
MOGGYU (SQUISH)
もっぎゅ
もぎゅ
YUSA
N-NATSUKI!
HISO
ひそ
HISO (WHISPER)
ひそ
YOU'RE TOUCHING NOTHING BUT MY BREASTS!
HISO
ひそ
HISO
ひそ
AH!
I-I'M SORRY!
っ…
TSUTSU (SLIDE)
ぴくっ
PIKU (TWITCH)

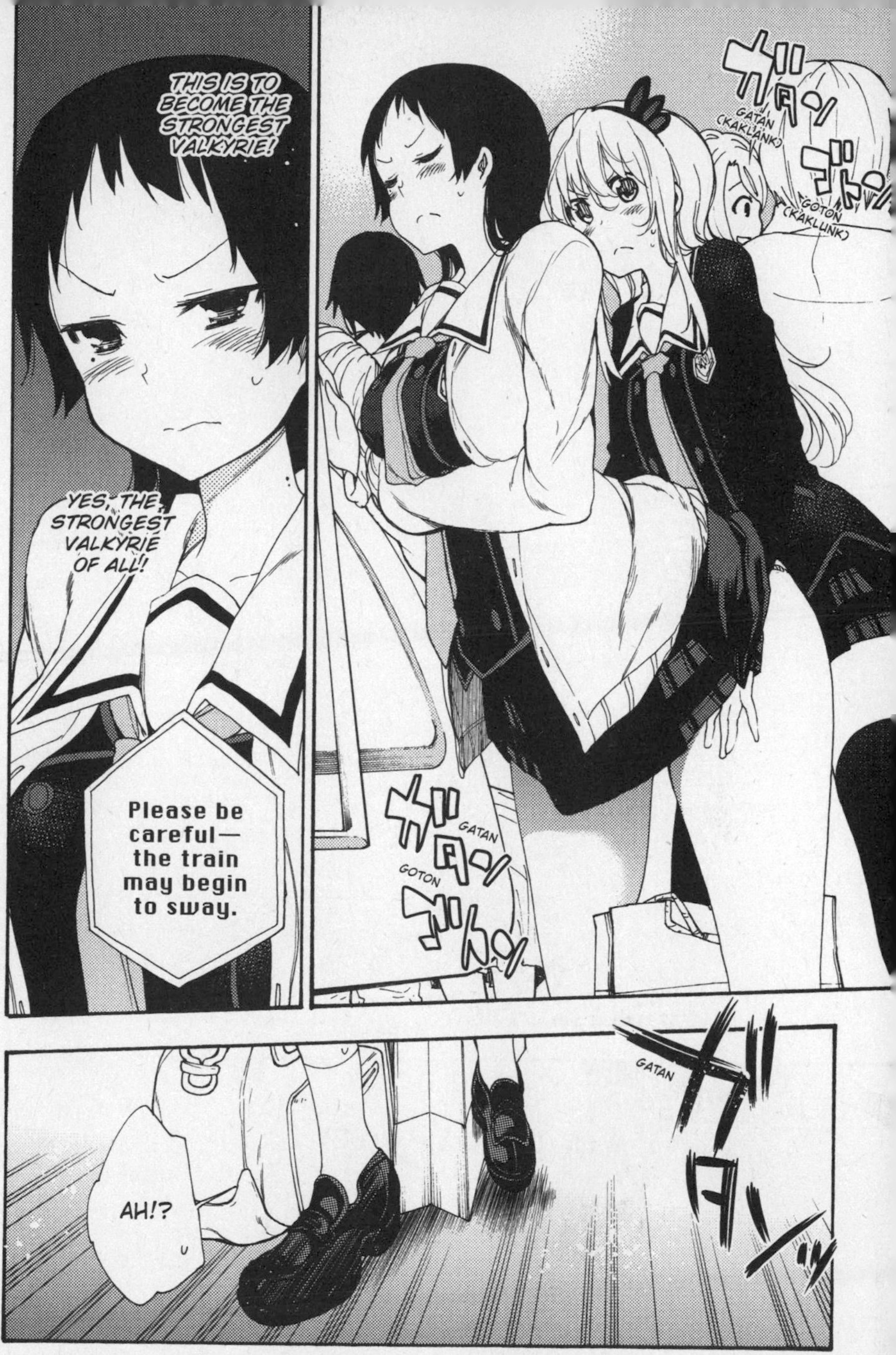
GATAN (KAKLANK)
GOTON (KAKLUNK)
GATAN
GOTON
THIS IS TO BECOME THE STRONGEST VALKYRIE!
YES, THE STRONGEST VALKYRIE OF ALL!
Please be careful—the train may begin to sway.
GATAN
AH!?

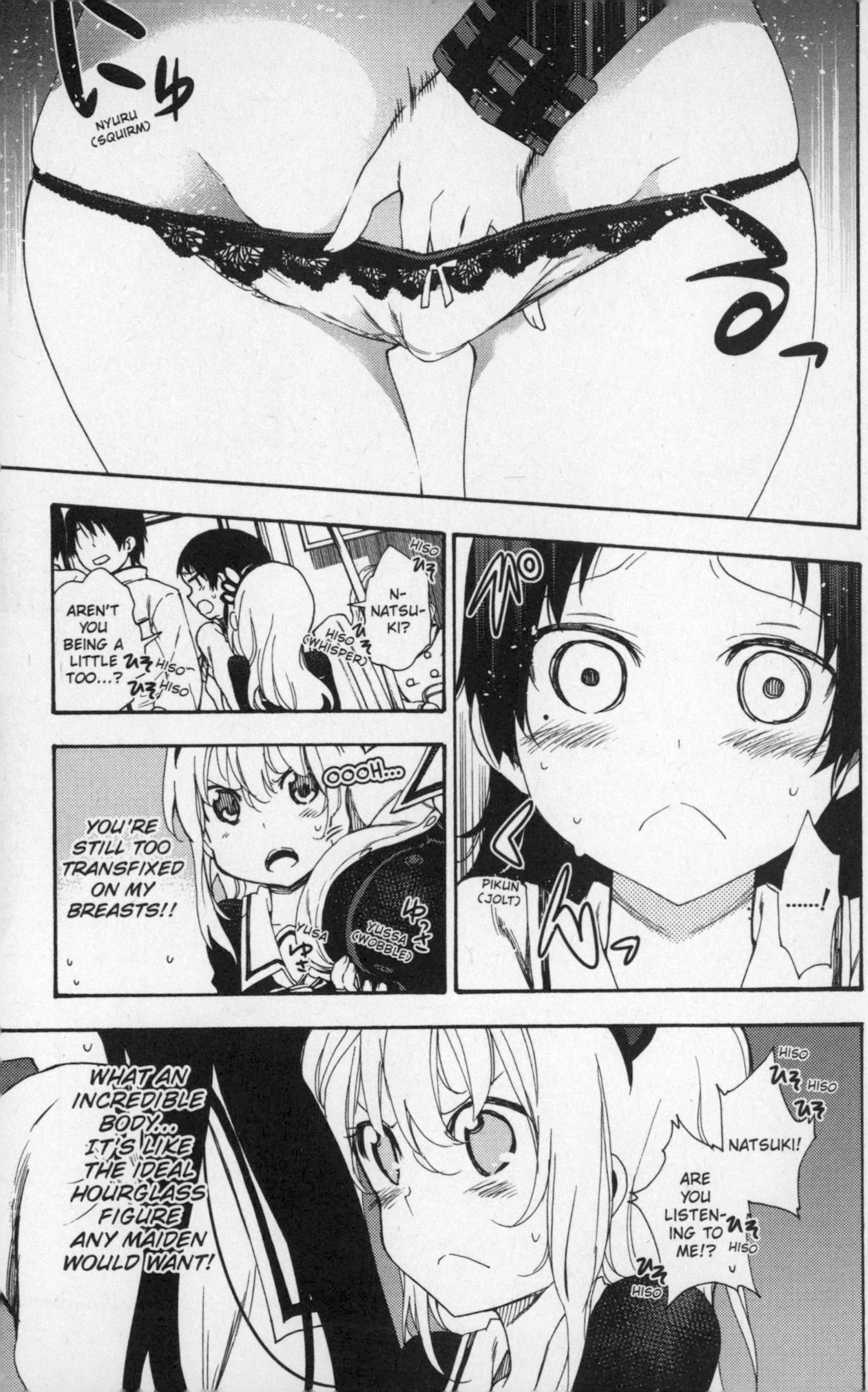
NYURU (SQUIRM)
PIKUN (JOLT)
......!
HISO
N-NATSUKI?
HISO (WHISPER)
AREN'T YOU BEING A LITTLE TOO...?
HISO
HISO
OOOH...
YOU'RE STILL TOO TRANSFIXED ON MY BREASTS!!
YUSSA (WOBBLE)
YUSA
HISO
HISO
NATSUKI!
ARE YOU LISTENING TO ME!?
HISO
HISO
WHAT AN INCREDIBLE BODY... IT'S LIKE THE IDEAL HOURGLASS FIGURE ANY MAIDEN WOULD WANT!

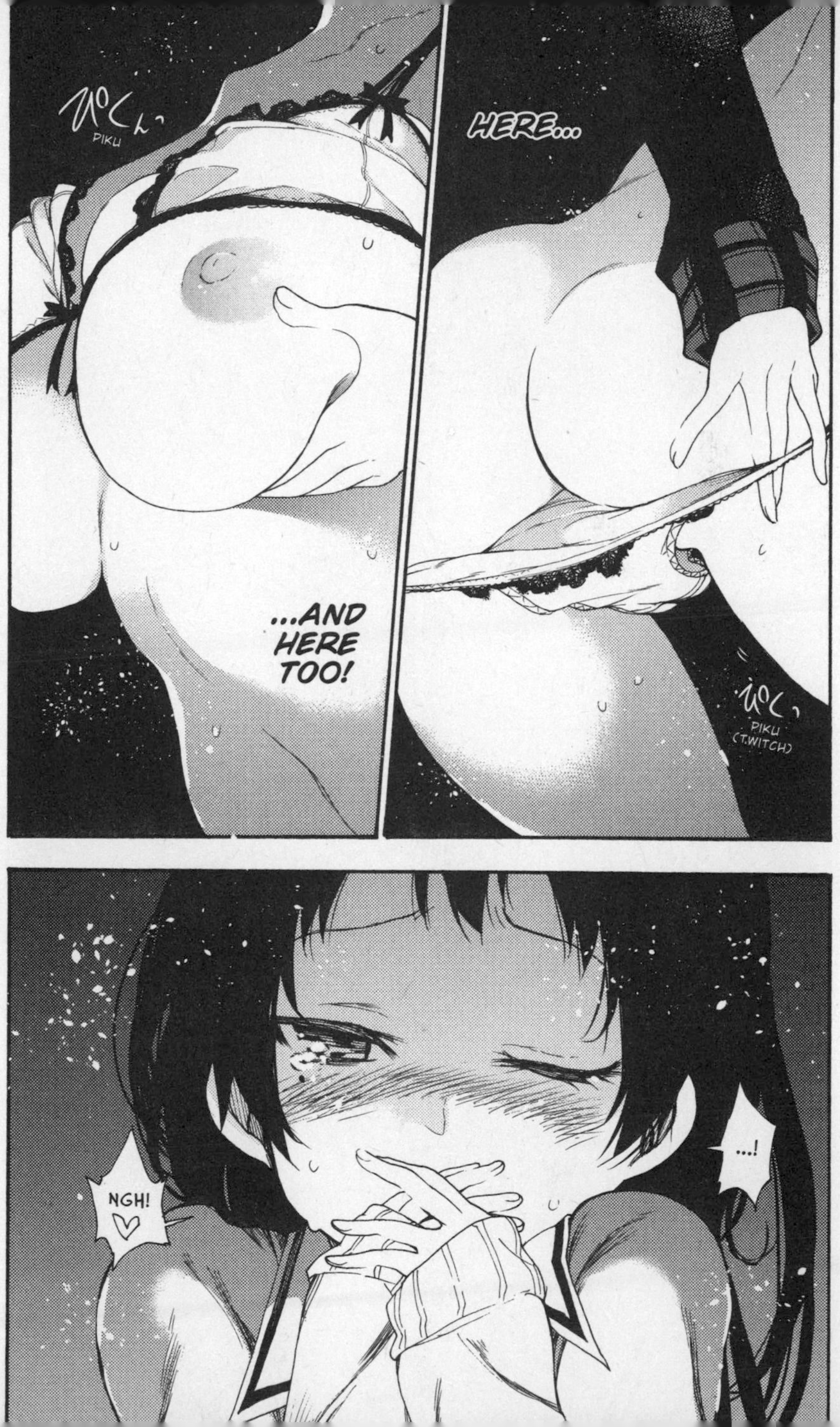
HERE...
ぴくっ
PIKU (TWITCH)
ぴくんっ
PIKU
...AND HERE TOO!
...!
NGH! ♡

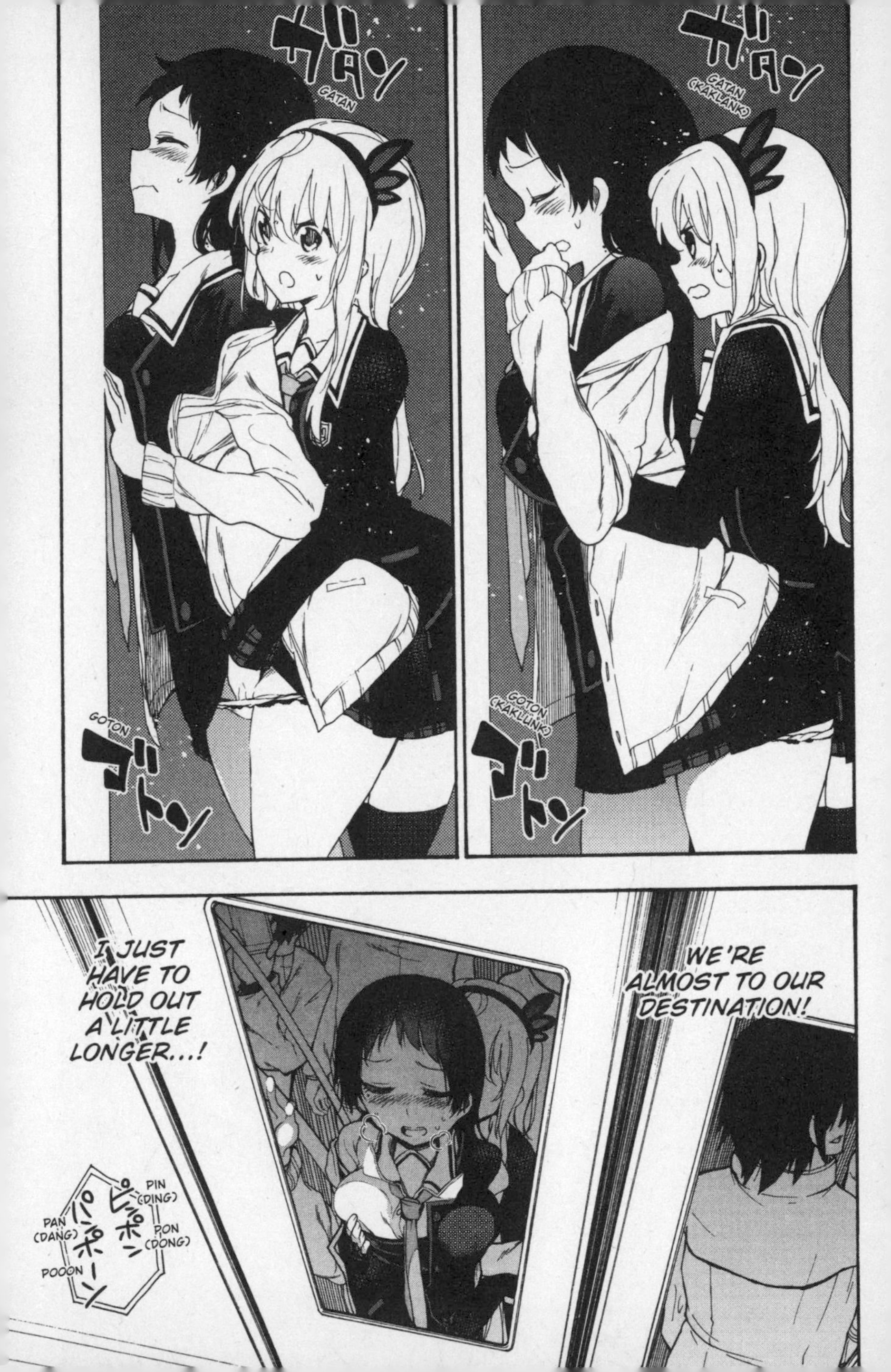

GATAN (KAKLANK)
GOTON (KAKLUNK)
GATAN
GOTON
WE'RE ALMOST TO OUR DESTINATION!
I JUST HAVE TO HOLD OUT A LITTLE LONGER...!
PIN (DING)
PON (DONG)
PAN (DANG)
POOON

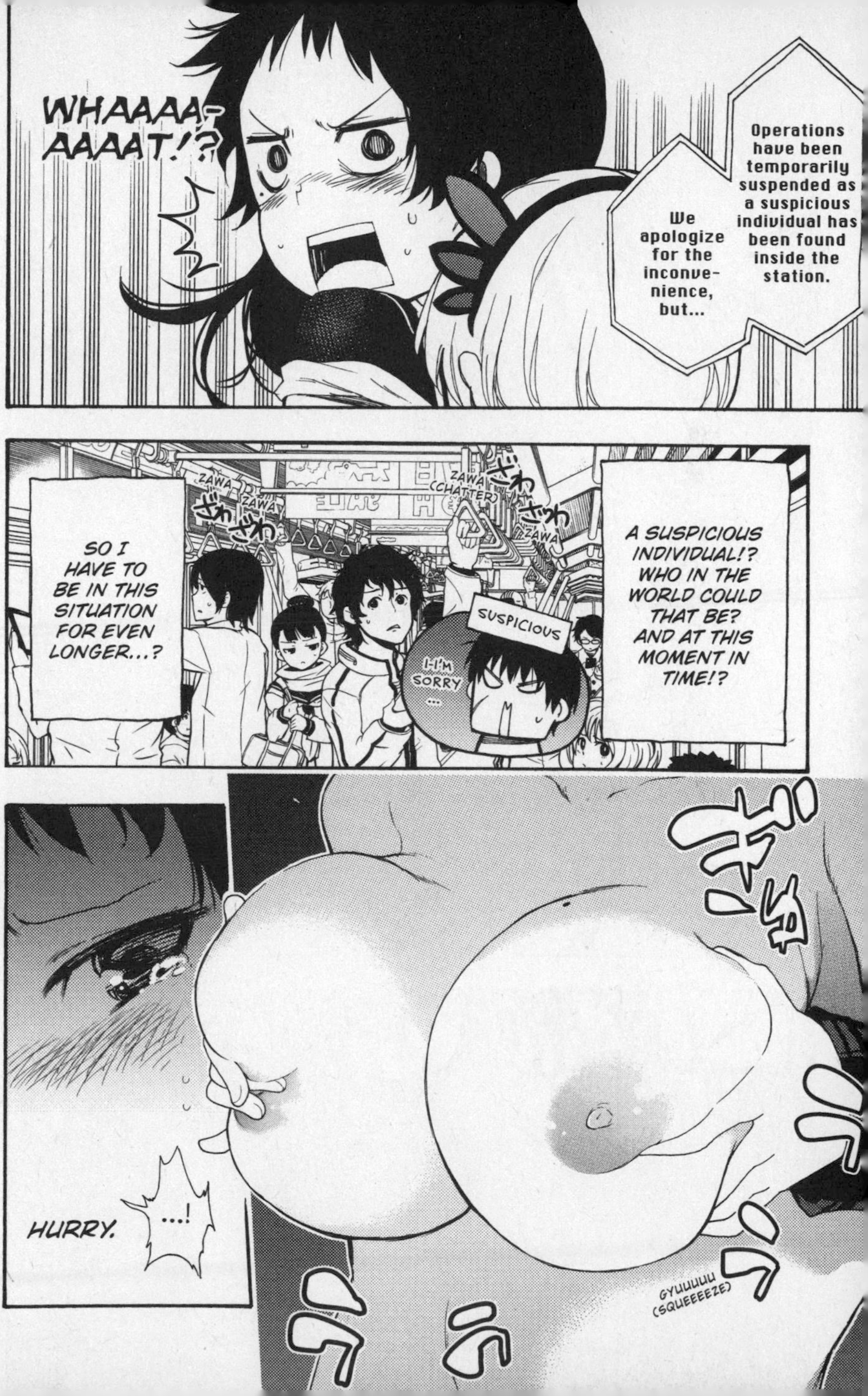
Operations have been temporarily suspended as a suspicious individual has been found inside the station.
We apologize for the inconvenience, but...
WHAAAA-AAAAT!?
A SUSPICIOUS INDIVIDUAL!? WHO IN THE WORLD COULD THAT BE? AND AT THIS MOMENT IN TIME!?
ZAWA (CHATTER)
ZAWA
ZAWA
ZAWA
SUSPICIOUS
I-I'M SORRY...
SO I HAVE TO BE IN THIS SITUATION FOR EVEN LONGER...?
GYUUUUU (SQUEEEEZE)
...!
HURRY.

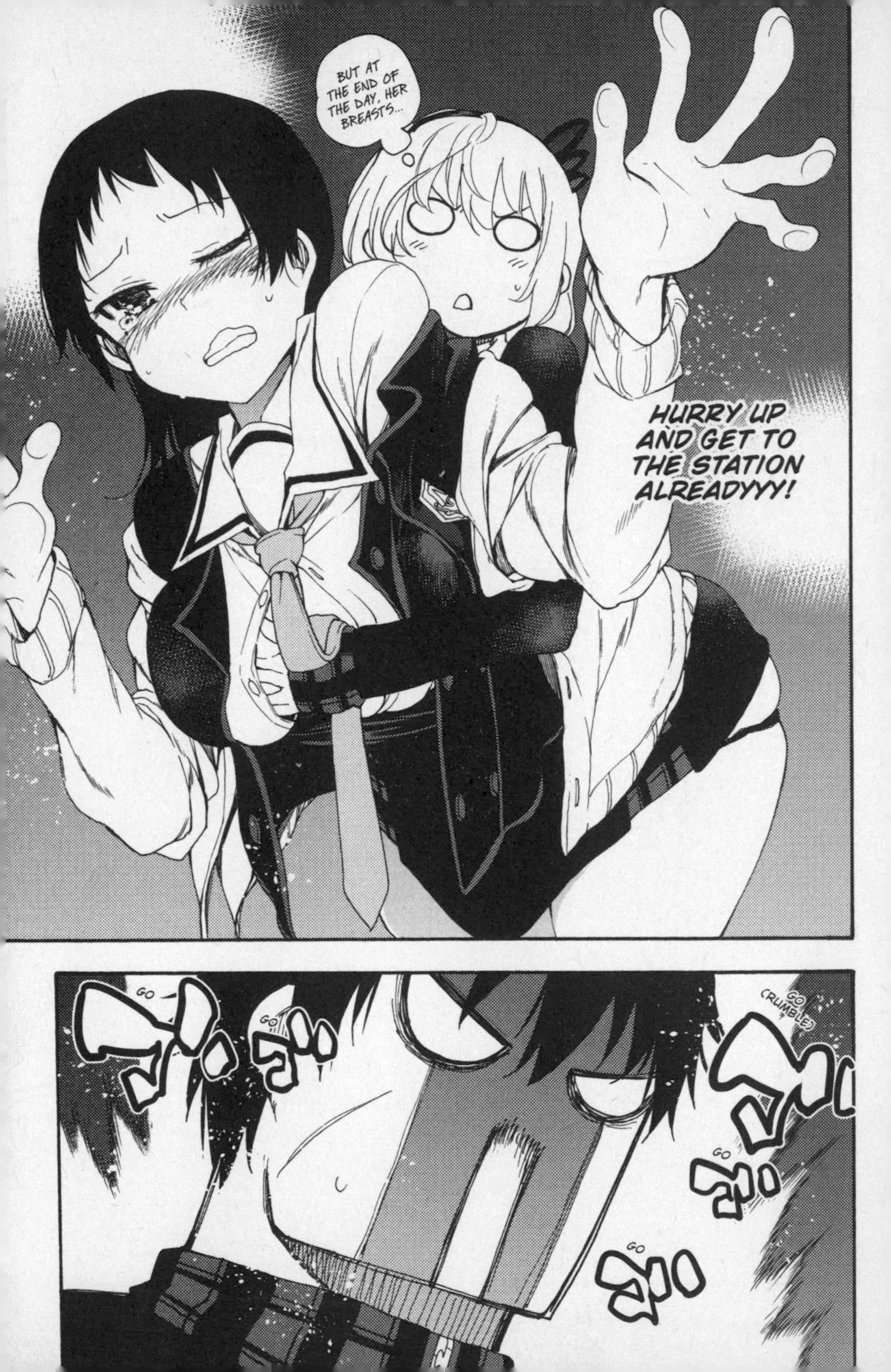

BUT AT THE END OF THE DAY, HER BREASTS...
HURRY UP AND GET TO THE STATION ALREADYYY!
GO (RUMBLE)
GO
GO
GO
GO

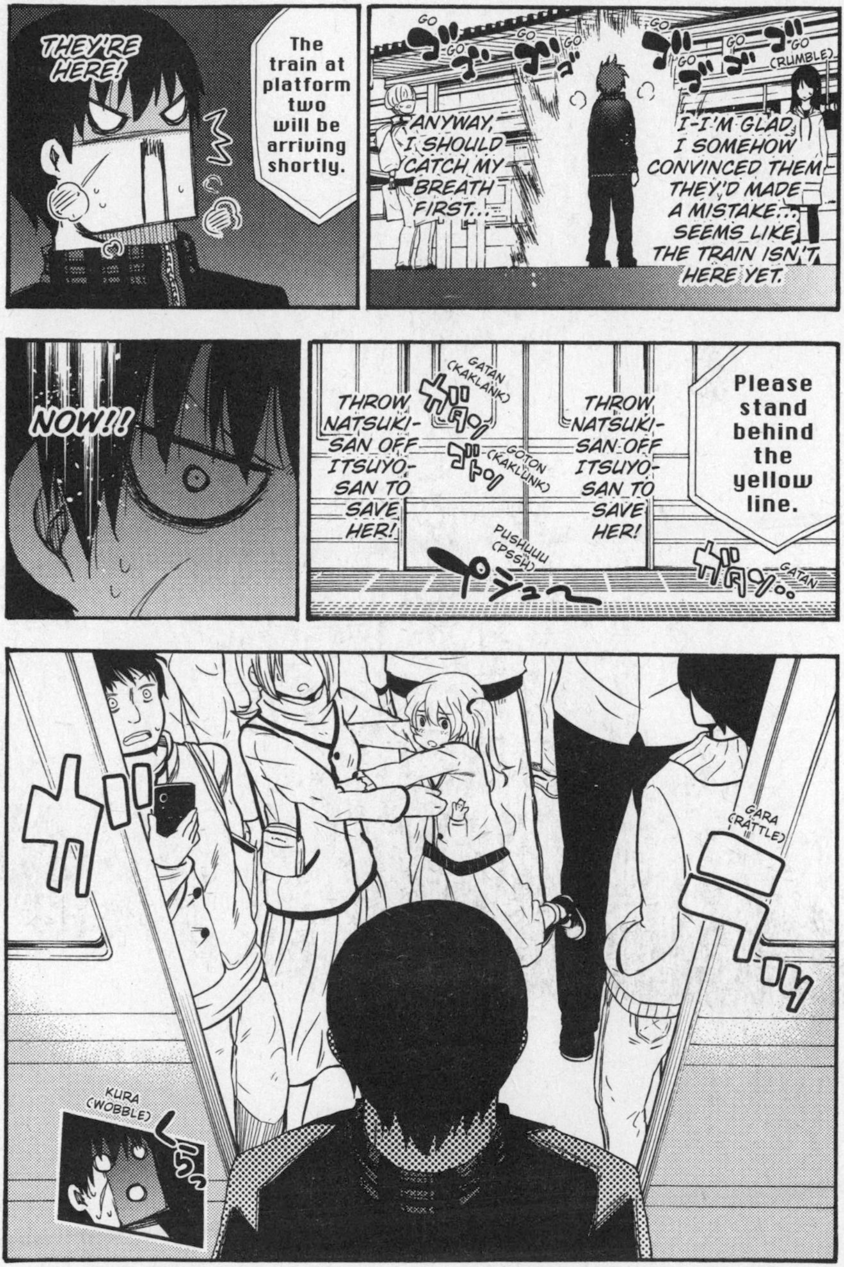
GO GO GO GO GO GO GO GO GO (RUMBLE)
I-I'M GLAD I SOMEHOW CONVINCED THEM THEY'D MADE A MISTAKE... SEEMS LIKE THE TRAIN ISN'T HERE YET.
ANYWAY, I SHOULD CATCH MY BREATH FIRST...
The train at platform two will be arriving shortly.
THEY'RE HERE!
Please stand behind the yellow line.
GATAN
THROW NATSUKI-SAN OFF ITSUYO-SAN TO SAVE HER!
GATAN (KAKLANK)
GOTON (KAKLUNK)
PUSHUUU (PSSH)
THROW NATSUKI-SAN OFF ITSUYO-SAN TO SAVE HER!
NOW!!
GARA (RATTLE)
KURA (WOBBLE)

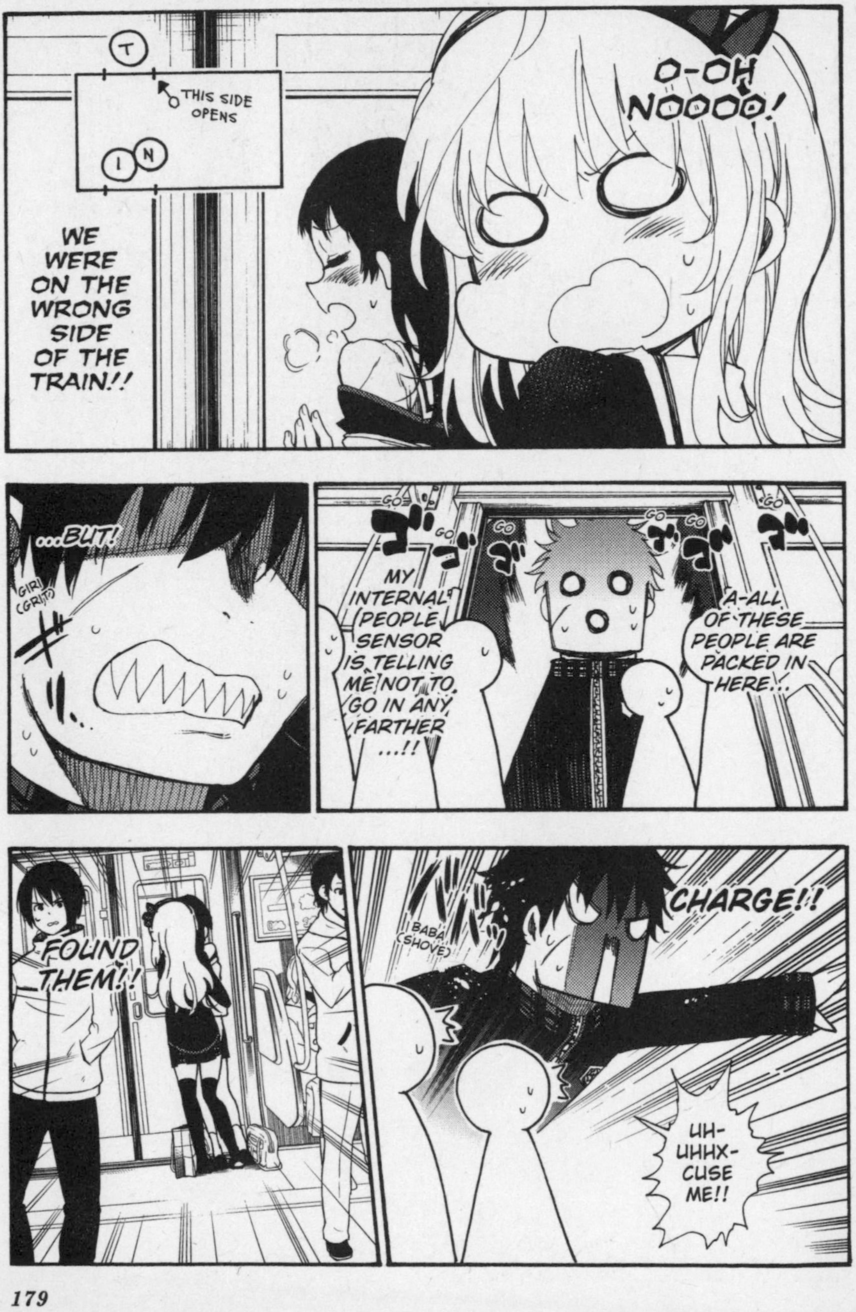
O-OH NOOOO!
THIS SIDE OPENS
WE WERE ON THE WRONG SIDE OF THE TRAIN!!
GO GO GO GO GO GO
A-ALL OF THESE PEOPLE ARE PACKED IN HERE...
MY INTERNAL PEOPLE SENSOR IS TELLING ME NOT TO GO IN ANY FARTHER...!!
...BUT!
GIRI (GRIT)
CHARGE!!
BABA (SHOVE)
UH-UHHX-CUSE ME!!
FOUND THEM!!

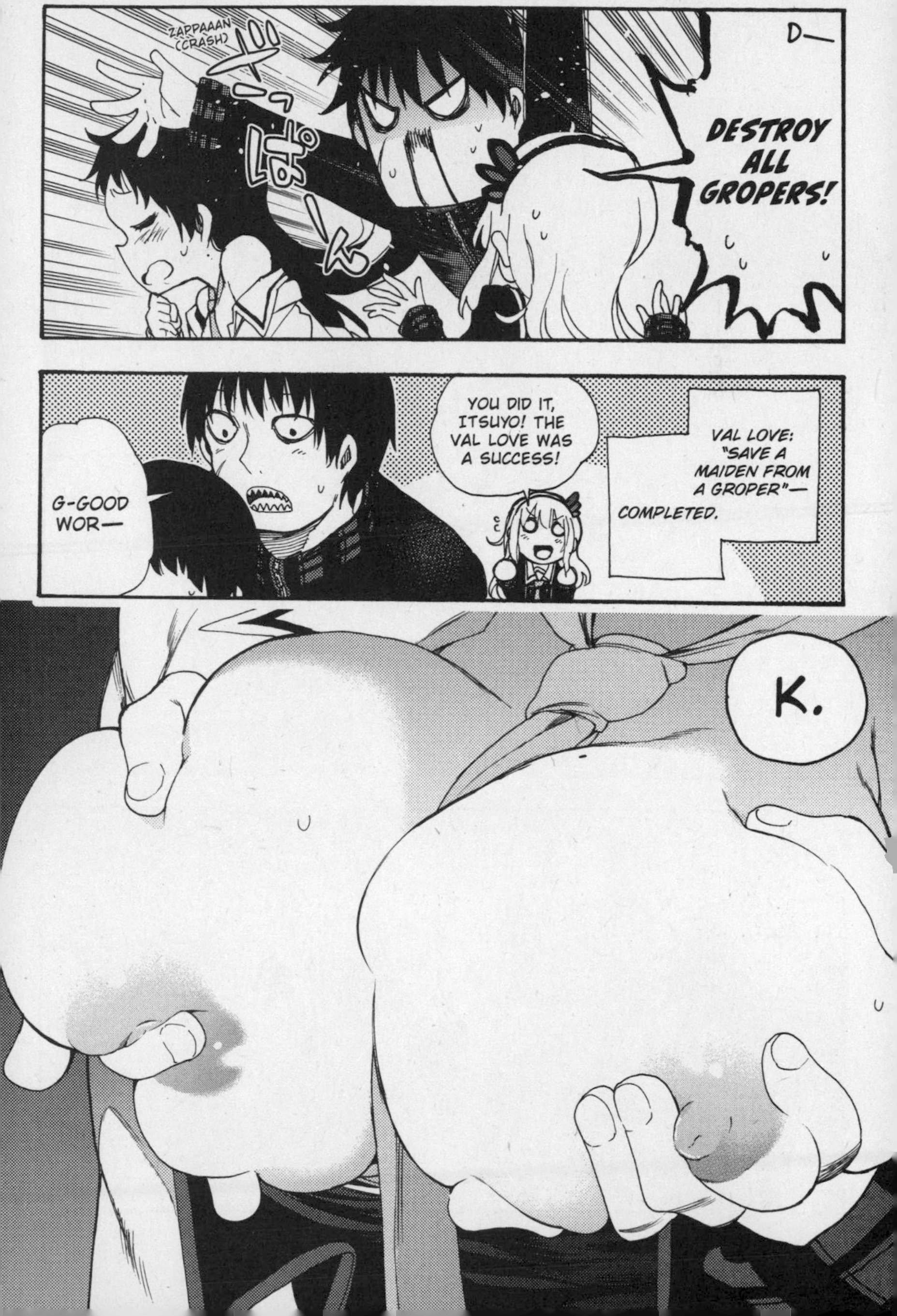
D—
DESTROY ALL GROPERS!
ZAPPAAAN (CRASH)
VAL LOVE: "SAVE A MAIDEN FROM A GROPER"—
COMPLETED.
YOU DID IT, ITSUYO! THE VAL LOVE WAS A SUCCESS!
G-GOOD WOR—
K.

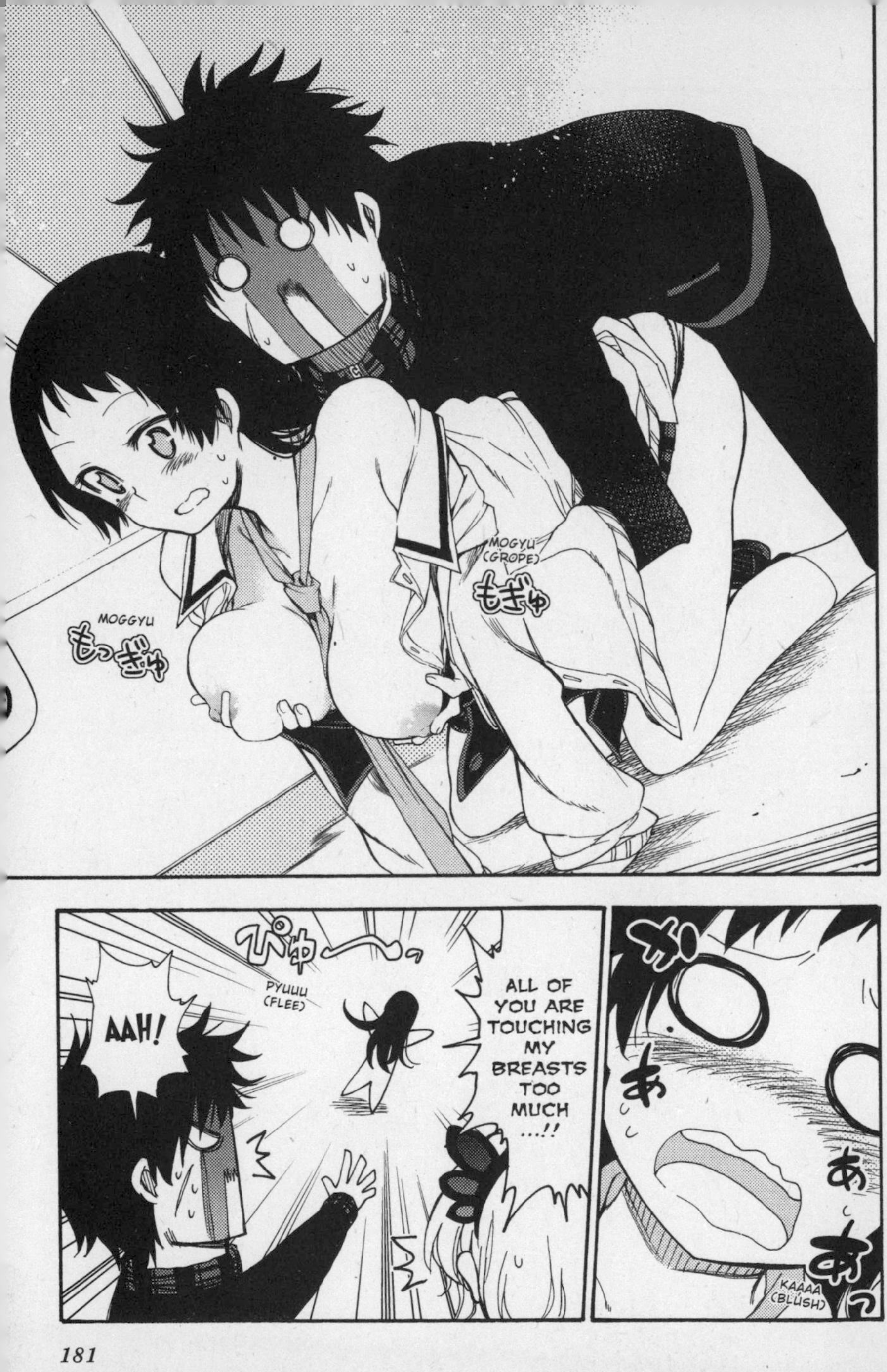
MOGYU (GROPE)
もぎゅ
MOGGYU
もっぎゅ
あ
あ
あっ
KAAAA (BLUSH)
ALL OF YOU ARE TOUCHING MY BREASTS TOO MUCH ...!!
ぴゅ～～っ
PYUUU (FLEE)
AAH!

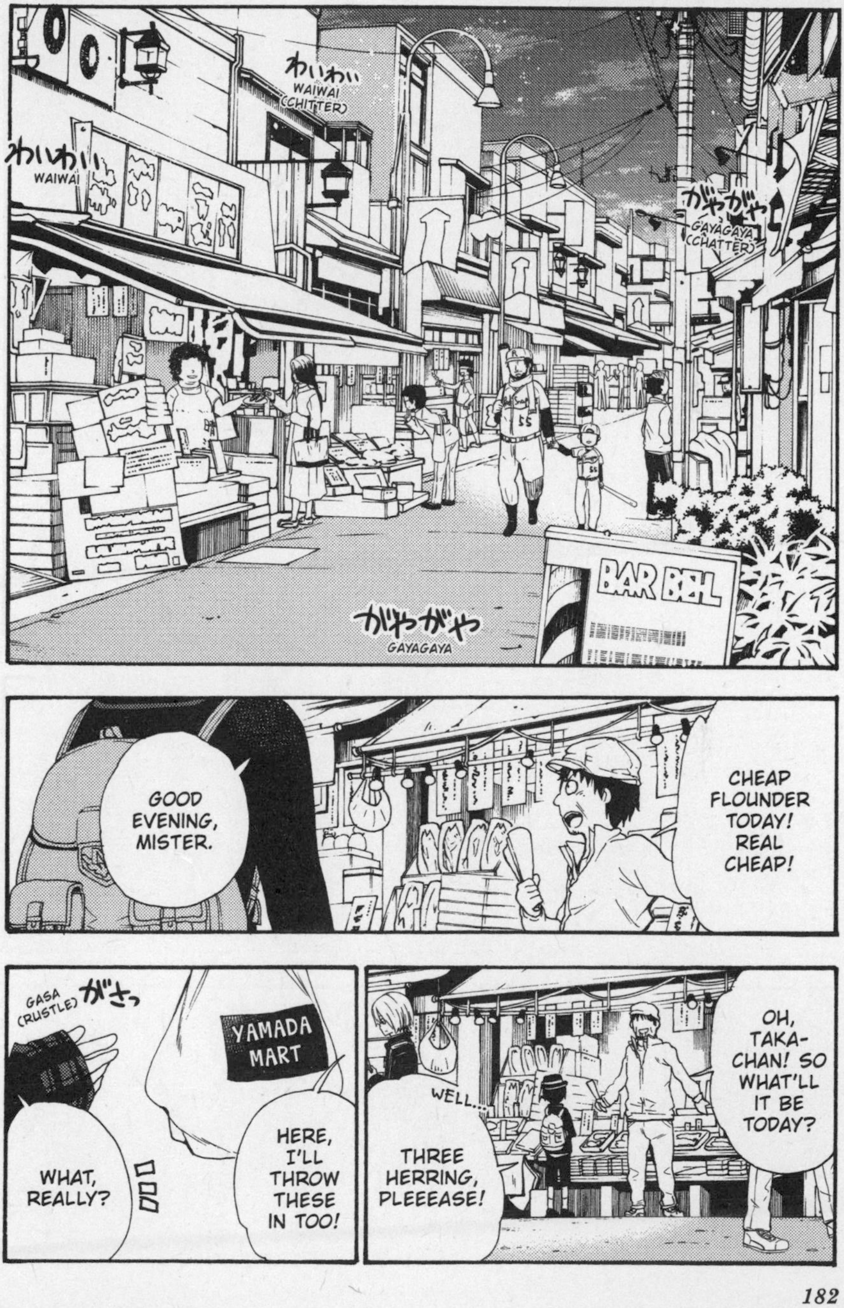

がやがや
GAYAGAYA
(CHATTER)
わいわい
WAIWAI
(CHITTER)
わいわい
WAIWAI
BAR B&L
がやがや
GAYAGAYA
CHEAP FLOUNDER TODAY! REAL CHEAP!
GOOD EVENING, MISTER.
OH, TAKA-CHAN! SO WHAT'LL IT BE TODAY?
WELL...
THREE HERRING, PLEEEASE!
YAMADA MART
GASA (RUSTLE) がさっ
HERE, I'LL THROW THESE IN TOO!
□□□
WHAT, REALLY?

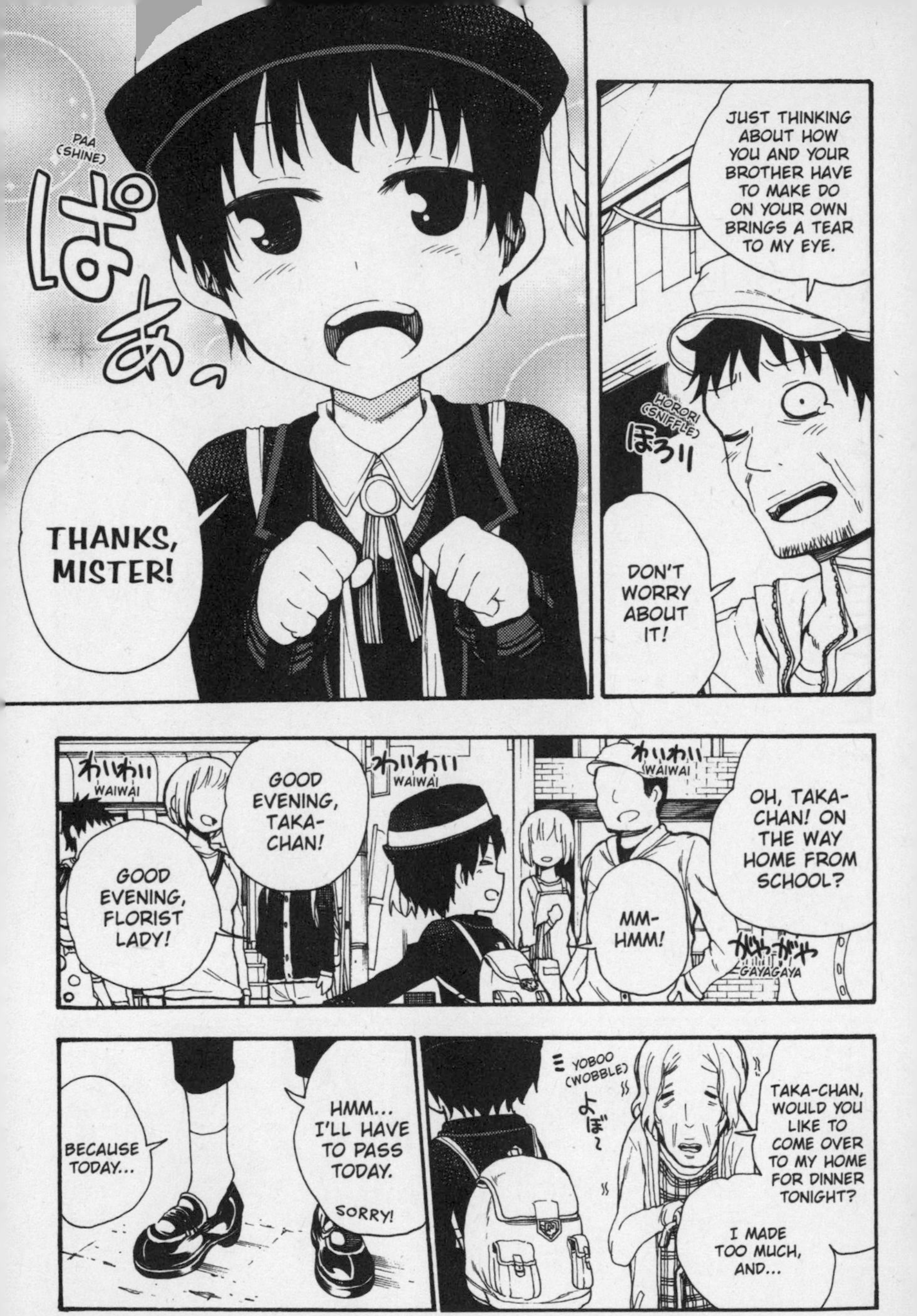
JUST THINKING ABOUT HOW YOU AND YOUR BROTHER HAVE TO MAKE DO ON YOUR OWN BRINGS A TEAR TO MY EYE.
HORORI (SNIFFLE)
ほろリ
DON'T WORRY ABOUT IT!
PAA (SHINE)
ぱあっ
THANKS, MISTER!
OH, TAKA-CHAN! ON THE WAY HOME FROM SCHOOL?
わいわい
WAIWAI
MM-HMM!
がやがや
GAYAGAYA
GOOD EVENING, TAKA-CHAN!
わいわい
WAIWAI
GOOD EVENING, FLORIST LADY!
わいわい
WAIWAI
TAKA-CHAN, WOULD YOU LIKE TO COME OVER TO MY HOME FOR DINNER TONIGHT?
I MADE TOO MUCH, AND...
YOBOO (WOBBLE)
よぼ~
HMM... I'LL HAVE TO PASS TODAY.
SORRY!
BECAUSE TODAY...

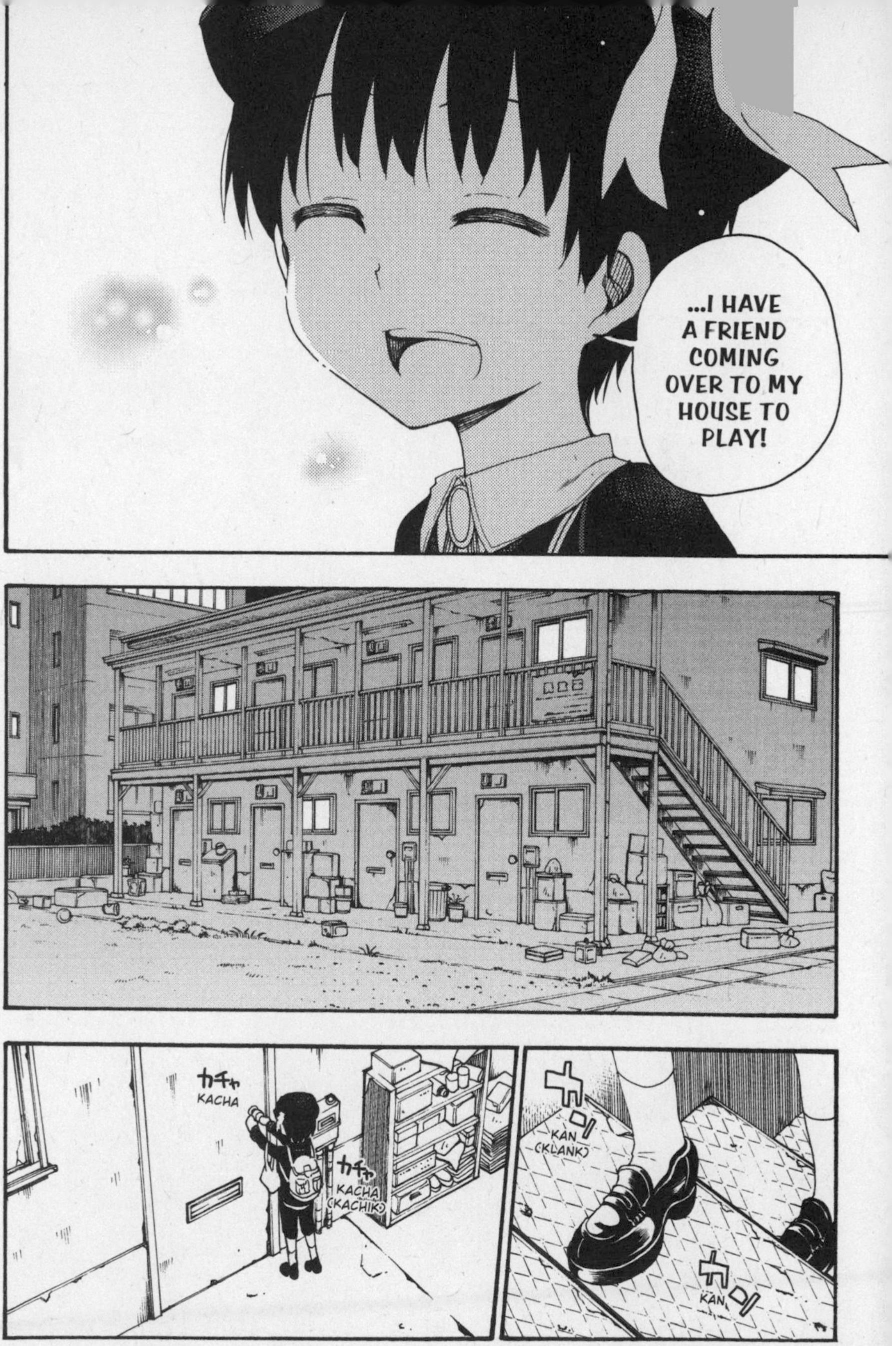
...I HAVE A FRIEND COMING OVER TO MY HOUSE TO PLAY!
カン
KAN (KLANK)
カン
KAN
カチャ
KACHA
カチャ
KACHA (KACHIK)

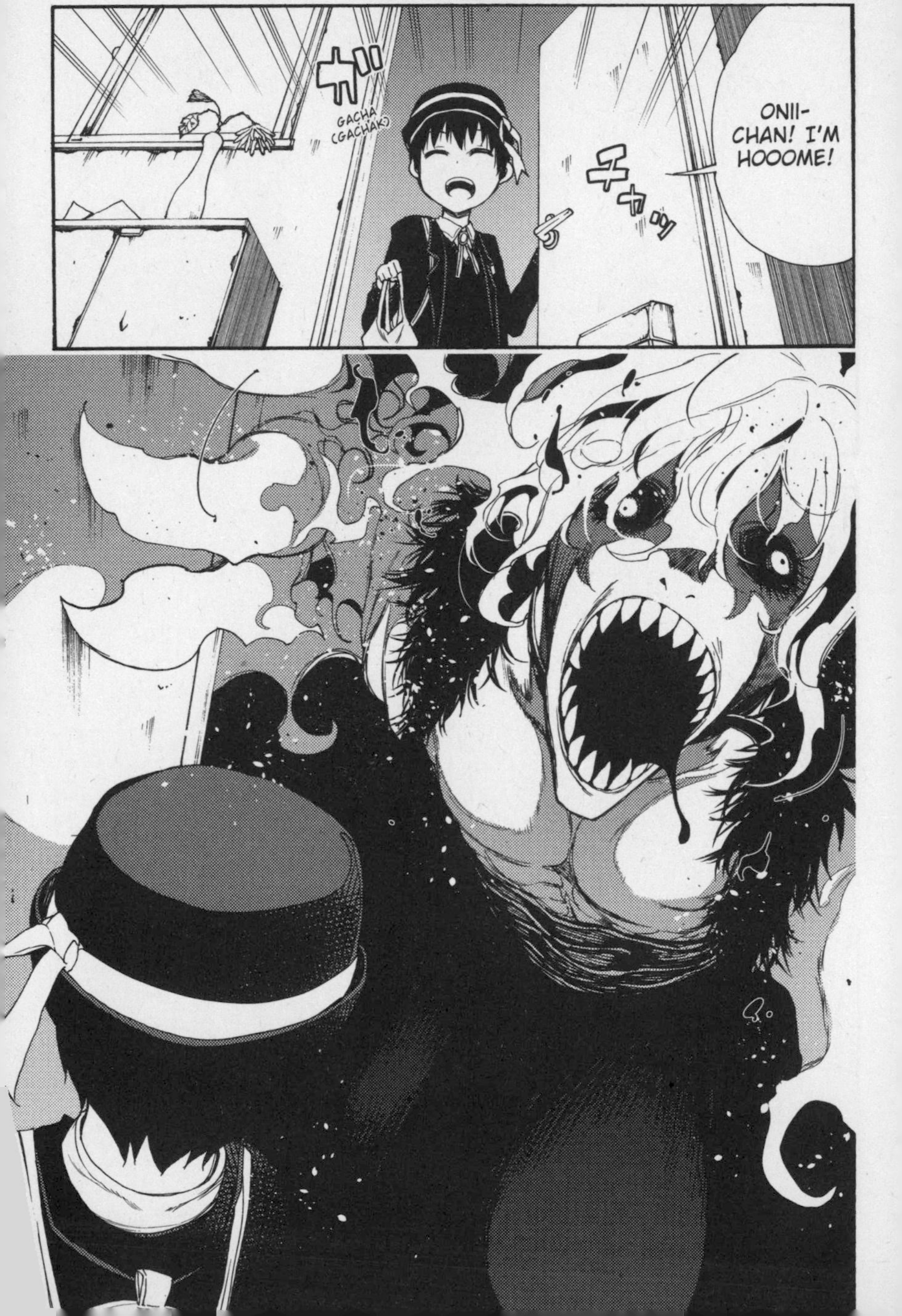

ONII-CHAN! I'M HOOOME!
GACHA (GACHAK)

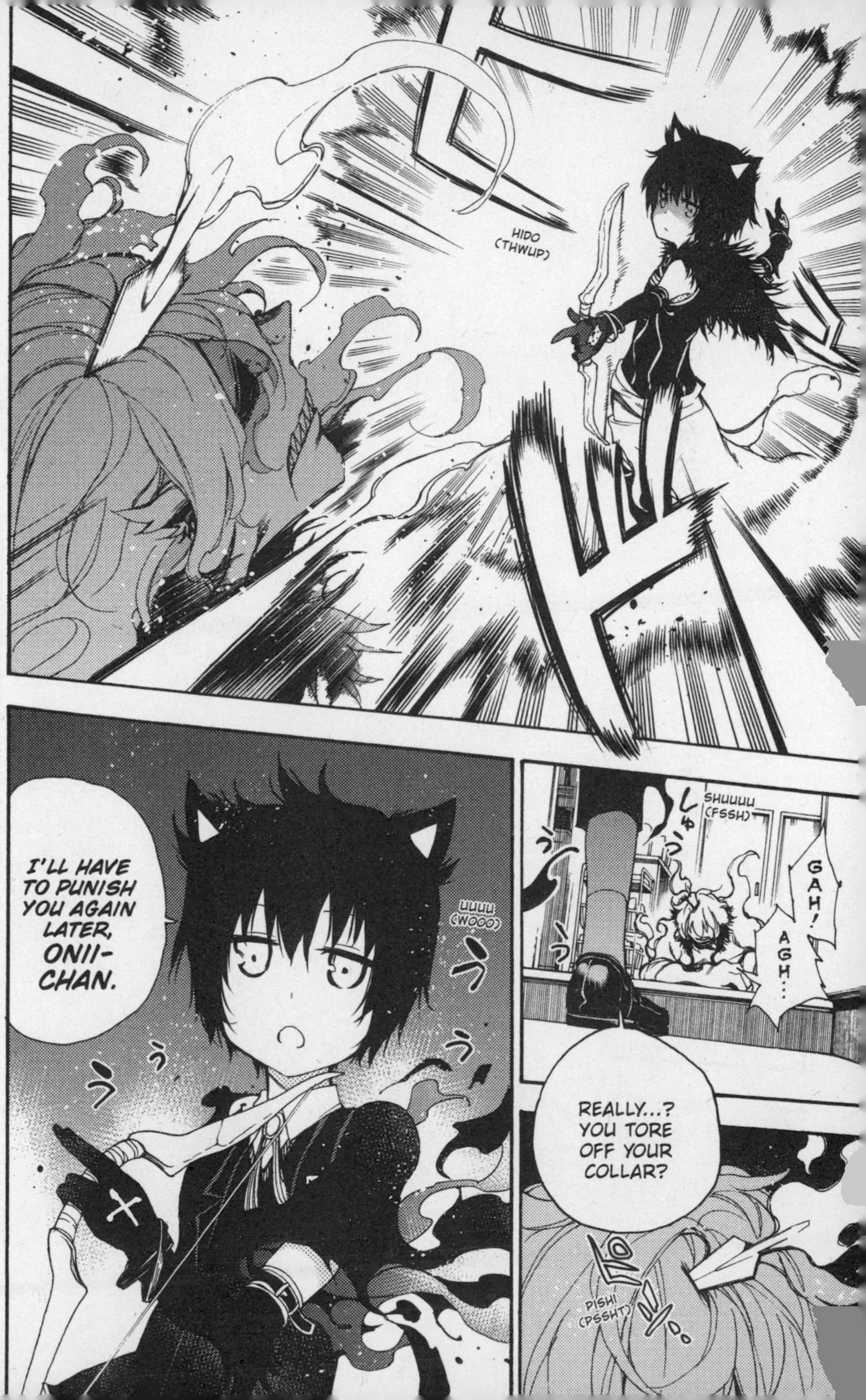
HIDO
(THWUP)
GAH! AGH...
SHUUUU
(FSSH)
REALLY...? YOU TORE OFF YOUR COLLAR?
PISHI
(PSSHT)
I'LL HAVE TO PUNISH YOU AGAIN LATER, ONII-CHAN.
UUUU
(WOOO)

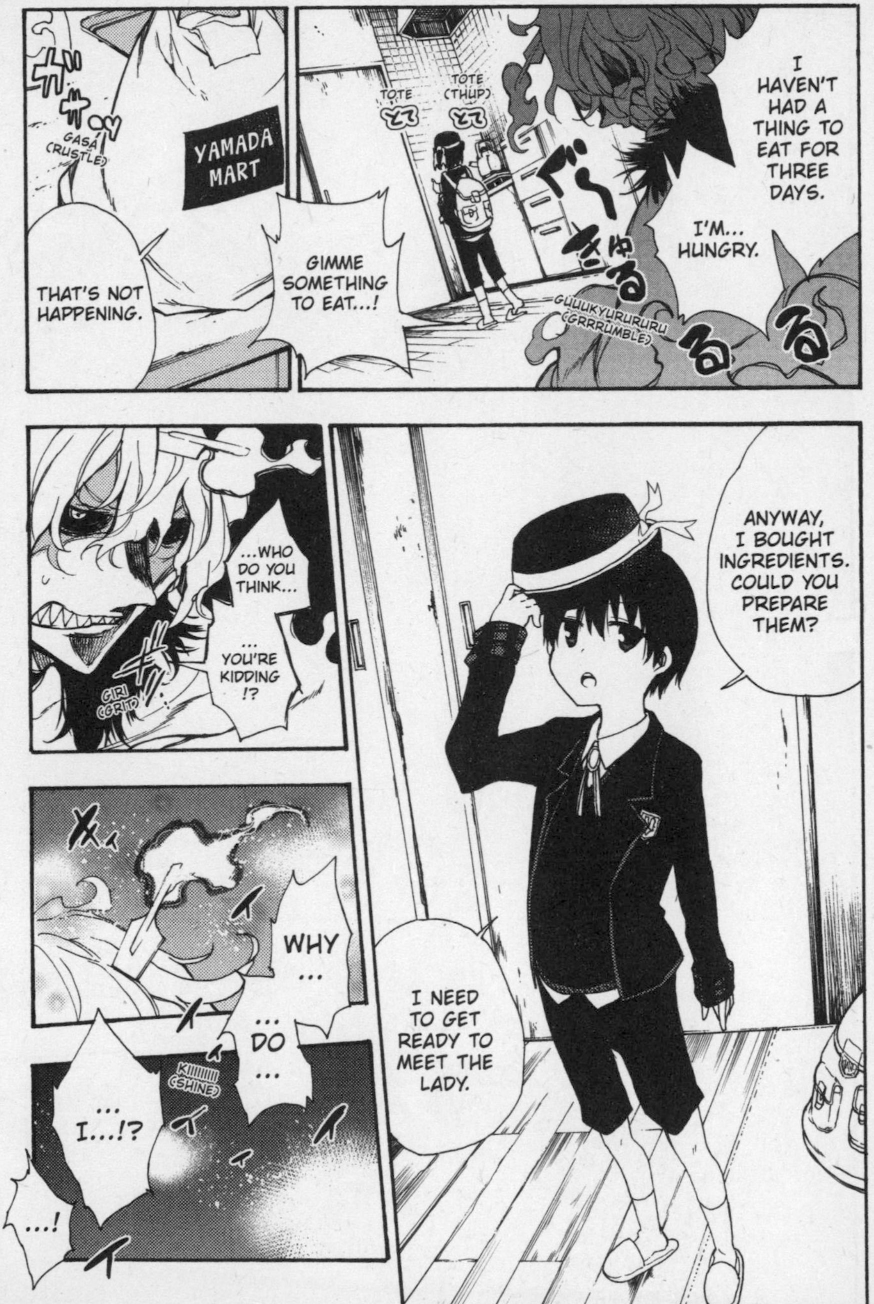
I HAVEN'T HAD A THING TO EAT FOR THREE DAYS.
I'M... HUNGRY.
GUUUKYURURURU (GRRRUMBLE)
TOTE (THUP)
TOTE
とて とて
GIMME SOMETHING TO EAT...!
GASA (RUSTLE)
YAMADA MART
THAT'S NOT HAPPENING.
ANYWAY, I BOUGHT INGREDIENTS. COULD YOU PREPARE THEM?
I NEED TO GET READY TO MEET THE LADY.
...WHO DO YOU THINK...
...YOU'RE KIDDING!?
GIRI (GRIT)
WHY...
...DO...
...I...!?
KIIIIIII (SHINE)
...!

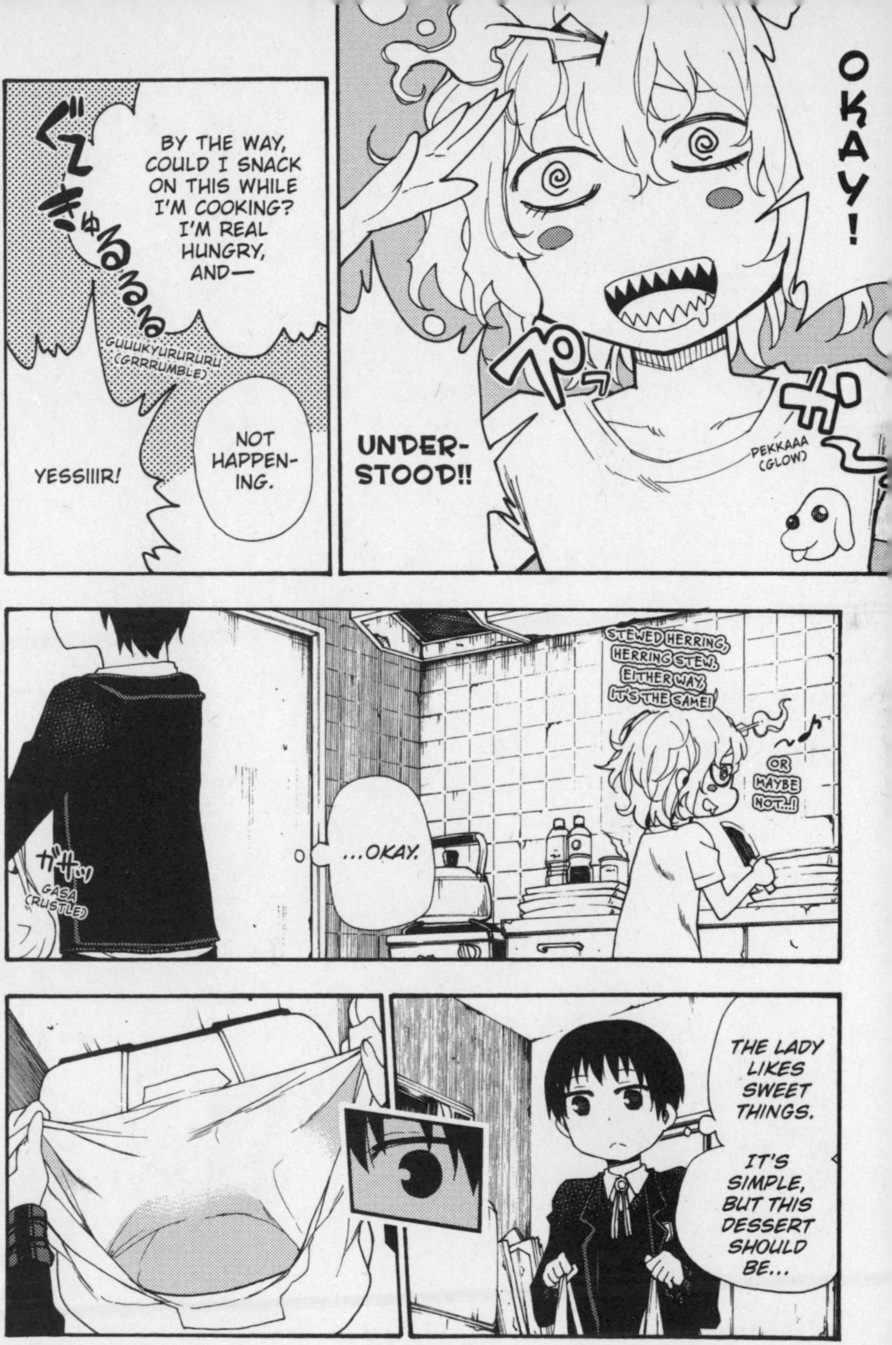

OKAY!
PEKKAAA (GLOW)
UNDER-STOOD!!
BY THE WAY, COULD I SNACK ON THIS WHILE I'M COOKING? I'M REAL HUNGRY, AND—
GUUUKYURURURU (GRRRUMBLE)
NOT HAPPEN-ING.
YESSIIIR!
STEWED HERRING, HERRING STEW. EITHER WAY, IT'S THE SAME!
OR MAYBE NOT...!
...OKAY.
GASA (RUSTLED)
THE LADY LIKES SWEET THINGS.
IT'S SIMPLE, BUT THIS DESSERT SHOULD BE...

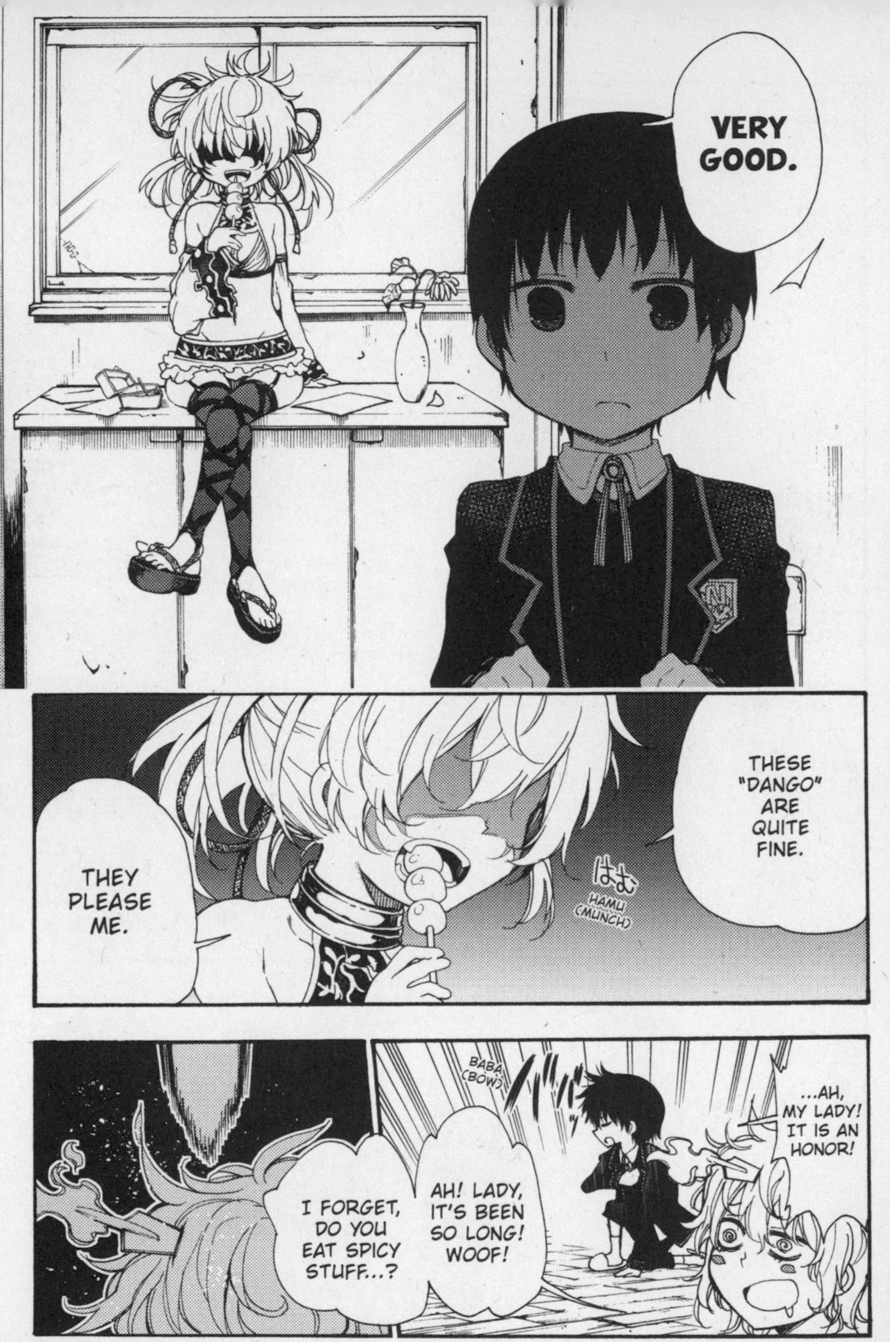
VERY GOOD.
THESE "DANGO" ARE QUITE FINE.
はむ
HAMU (MUNCH)
THEY PLEASE ME.
...AH, MY LADY! IT IS AN HONOR!
BABA (BOW)
AH! LADY, IT'S BEEN SO LONG! WOOF!
I FORGET, DO YOU EAT SPICY STUFF...?

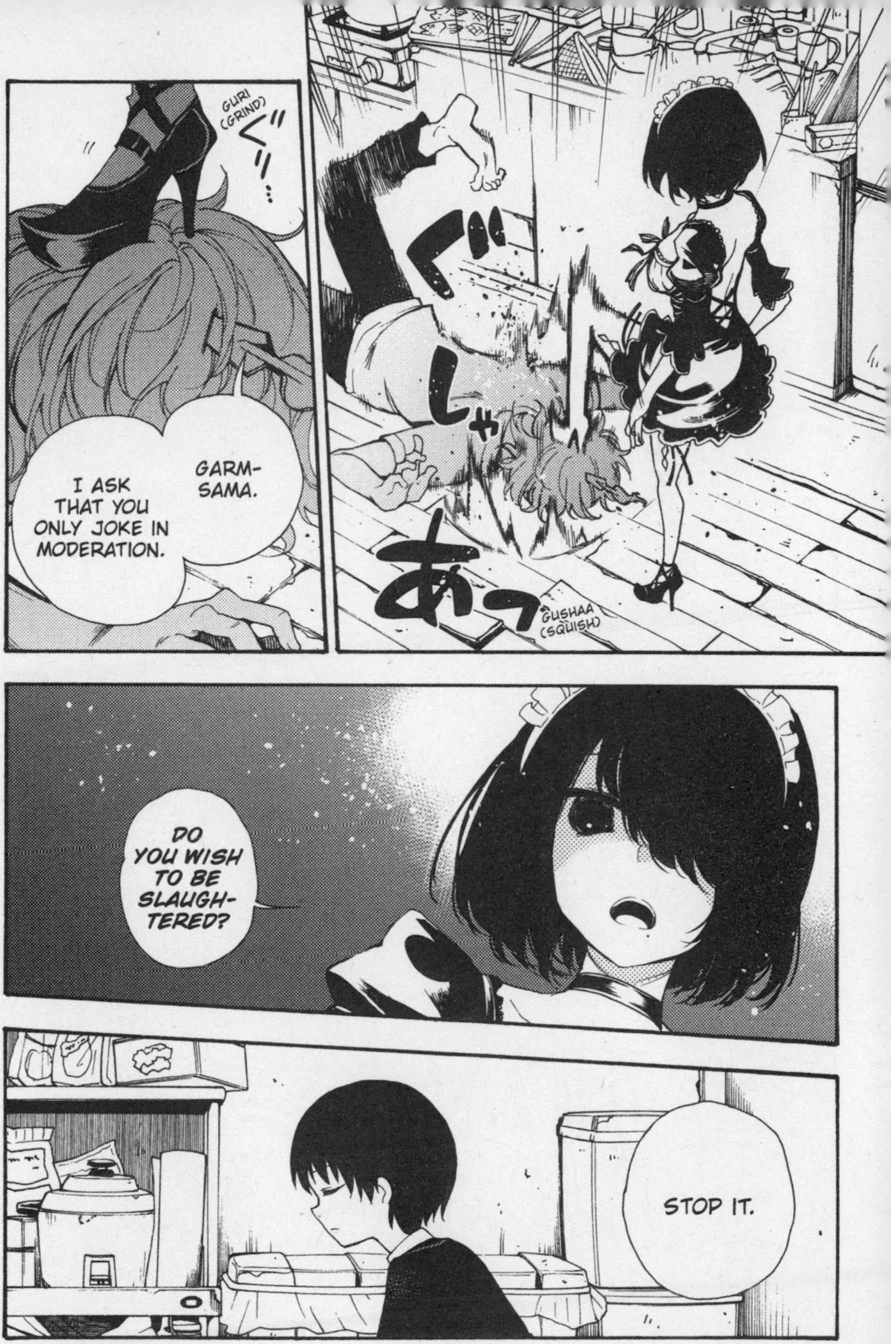
ぐしゃあっ
GUSHAA (SQUISH)
GURI (GRIND)
GARM-SAMA.
I ASK THAT YOU ONLY JOKE IN MODERATION.
DO YOU WISH TO BE SLAUGHTERED?
STOP IT.

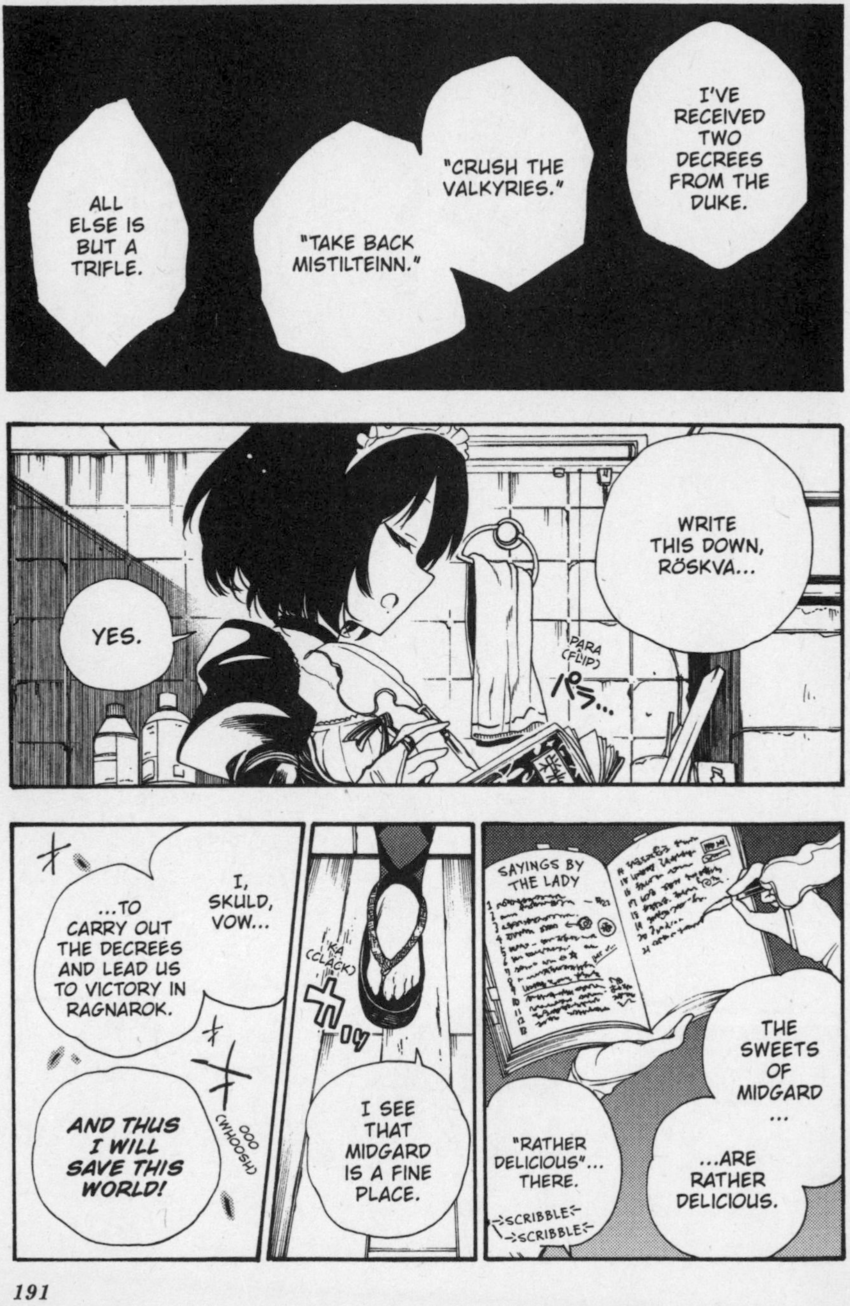
I'VE RECEIVED TWO DECREES FROM THE DUKE.
"CRUSH THE VALKYRIES."
"TAKE BACK MISTILTEINN."
ALL ELSE IS BUT A TRIFLE.
WRITE THIS DOWN, RÖSKVA...
PARA (FLIP)
パラ…
YES.
SAYINGS BY THE LADY
THE SWEETS OF MIDGARD...
...ARE RATHER DELICIOUS.
"RATHER DELICIOUS"... THERE.
SCRIBBLE
SCRIBBLE
KA (CLACK)
カッ
I SEE THAT MIDGARD IS A FINE PLACE.
I, SKULD, VOW...
...TO CARRY OUT THE DECREES AND LEAD US TO VICTORY IN RAGNAROK.
AND THUS I WILL SAVE THIS WORLD!
OOO (WHOOSH)

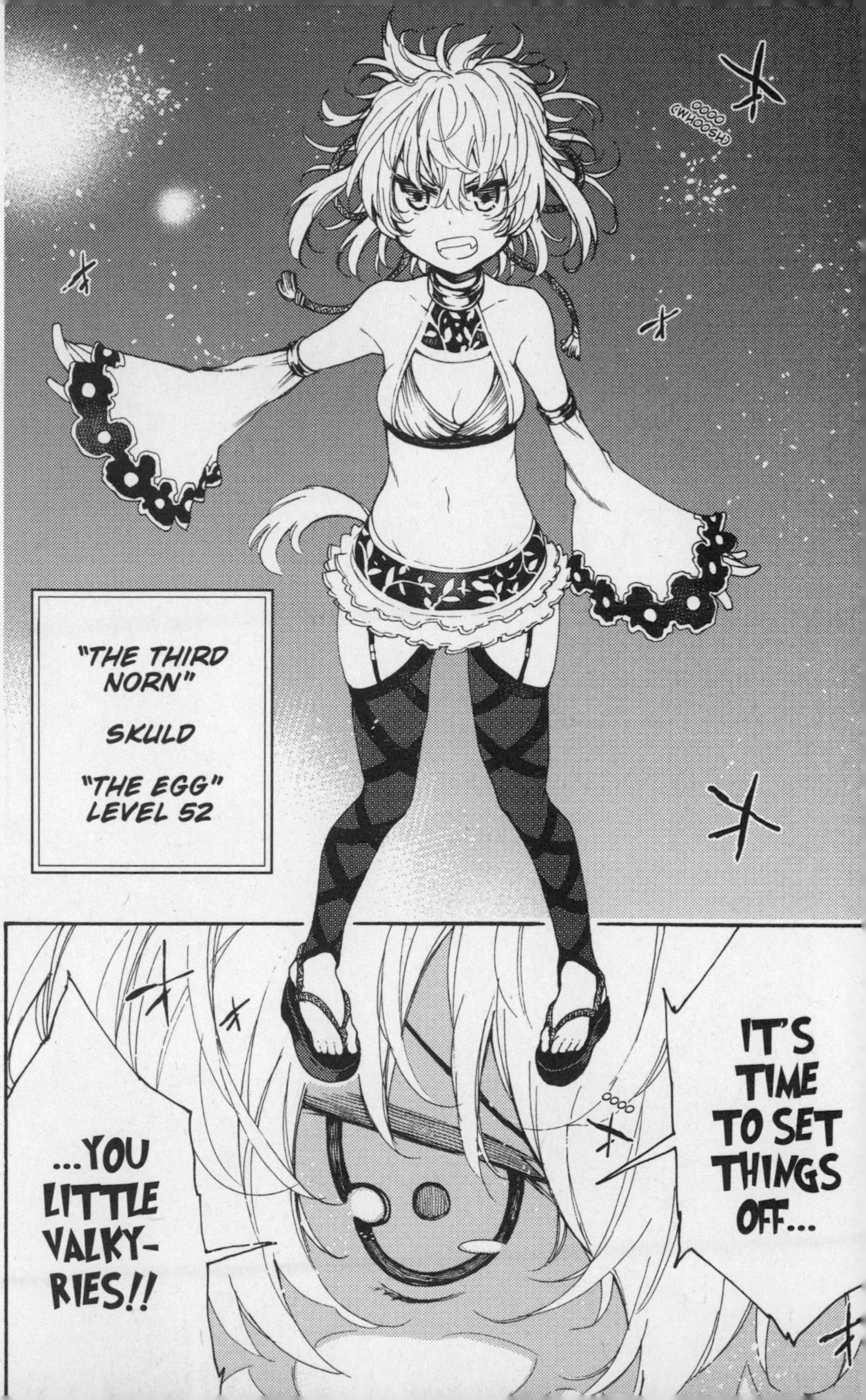

(WHOOSH)
OOOO
"THE THIRD NORN"
SKULD
"THE EGG" LEVEL 52
IT'S TIME TO SET THINGS OFF...
...YOU LITTLE VALKY-RIES!!

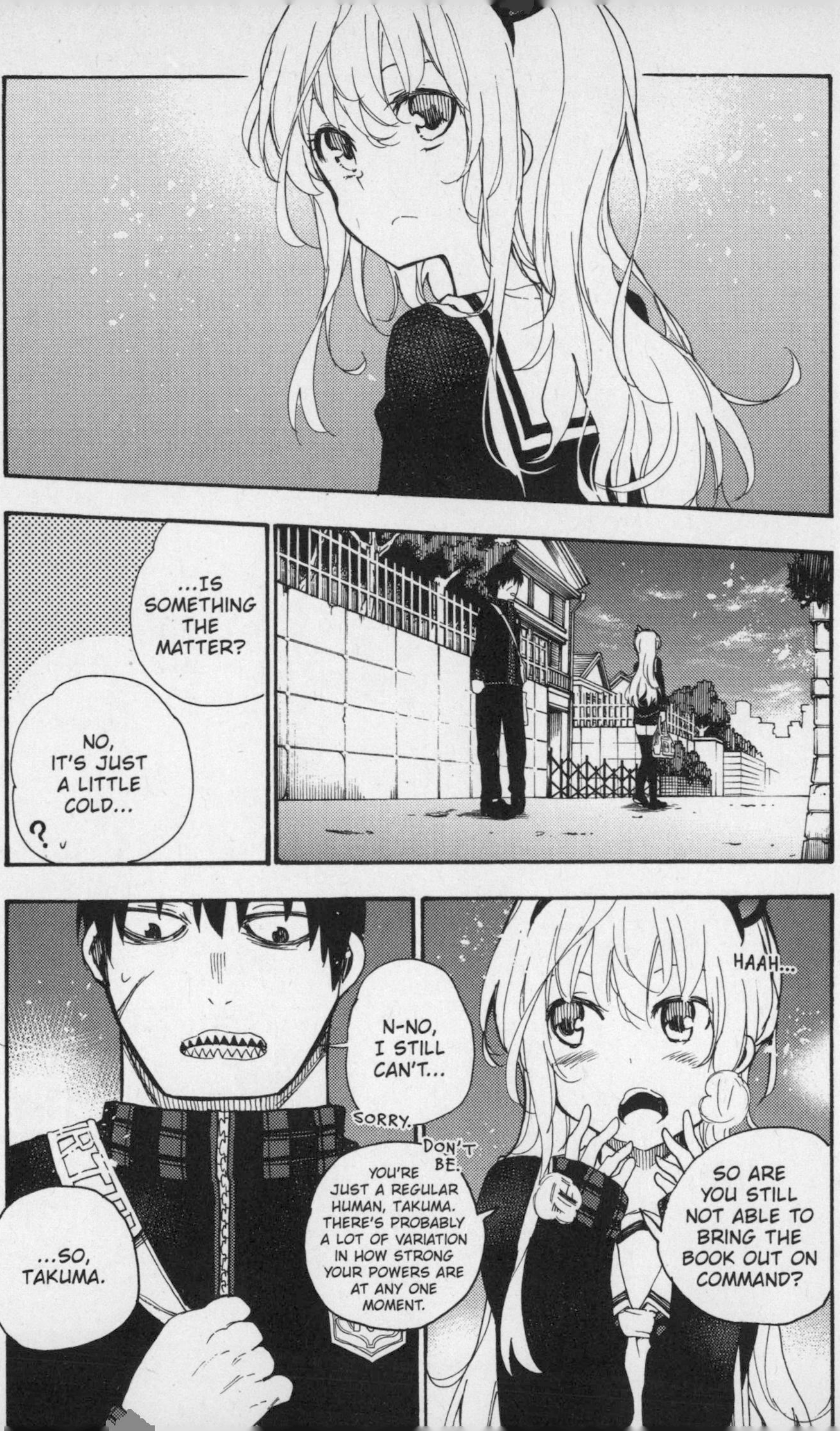
...IS SOMETHING THE MATTER?
NO, IT'S JUST A LITTLE COLD...
?
HAAH...
SO ARE YOU STILL NOT ABLE TO BRING THE BOOK OUT ON COMMAND?
N-NO, I STILL CAN'T...
SORRY.
DON'T BE.
YOU'RE JUST A REGULAR HUMAN, TAKUMA. THERE'S PROBABLY A LOT OF VARIATION IN HOW STRONG YOUR POWERS ARE AT ANY ONE MOMENT.
...SO, TAKUMA.

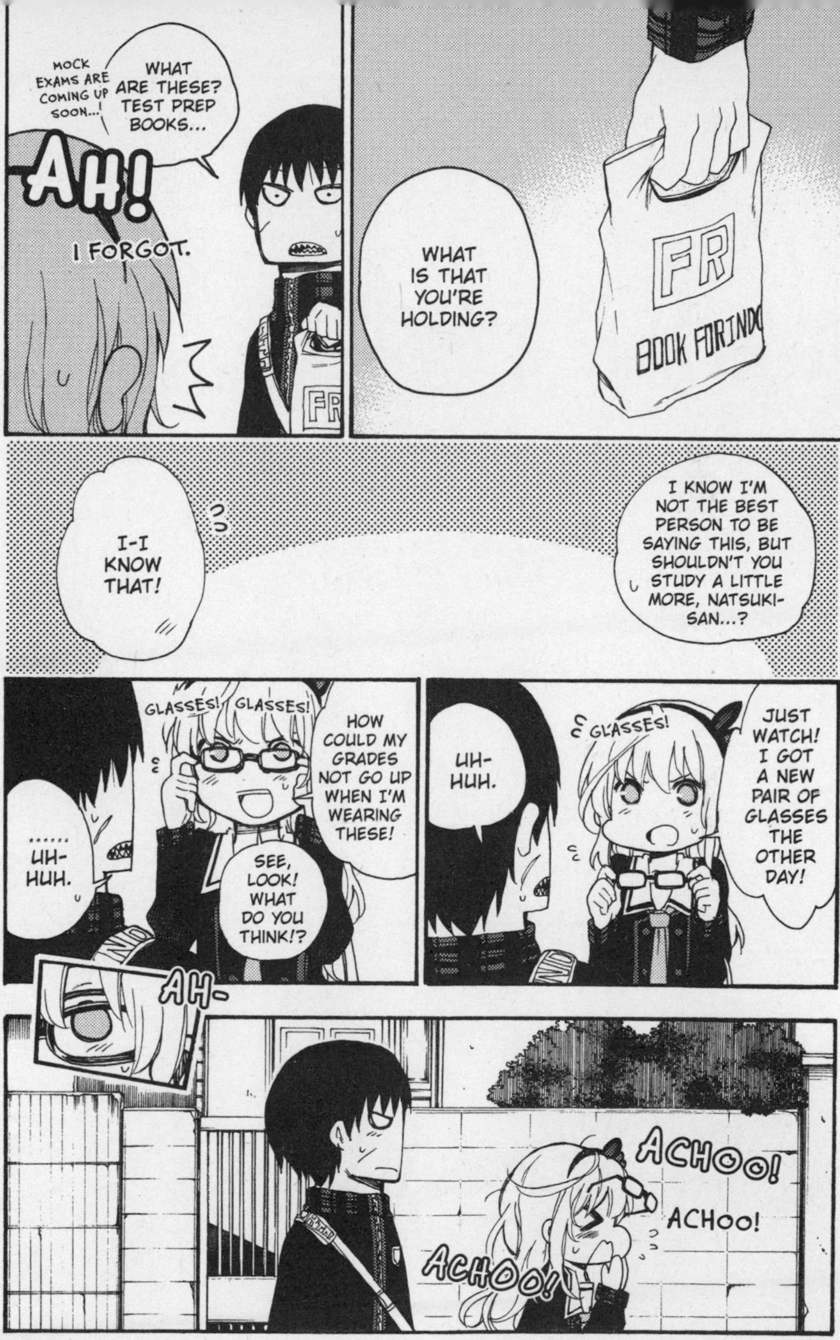
WHAT IS THAT YOU'RE HOLDING?
FR
BOOK FORINDO
WHAT ARE THESE? TEST PREP BOOKS...
MOCK EXAMS ARE COMING UP SOON...!
AH!
I FORGOT.
FR
I KNOW I'M NOT THE BEST PERSON TO BE SAYING THIS, BUT SHOULDN'T YOU STUDY A LITTLE MORE, NATSUKI-SAN...?
I-I KNOW THAT!
GLASSES!
JUST WATCH! I GOT A NEW PAIR OF GLASSES THE OTHER DAY!
UH-HUH.
GLASSES! GLASSES!
HOW COULD MY GRADES NOT GO UP WHEN I'M WEARING THESE!
SEE, LOOK! WHAT DO YOU THINK!?
...... UH-HUH.
AH-
ACHOO!
ACHOO!
ACHOO!

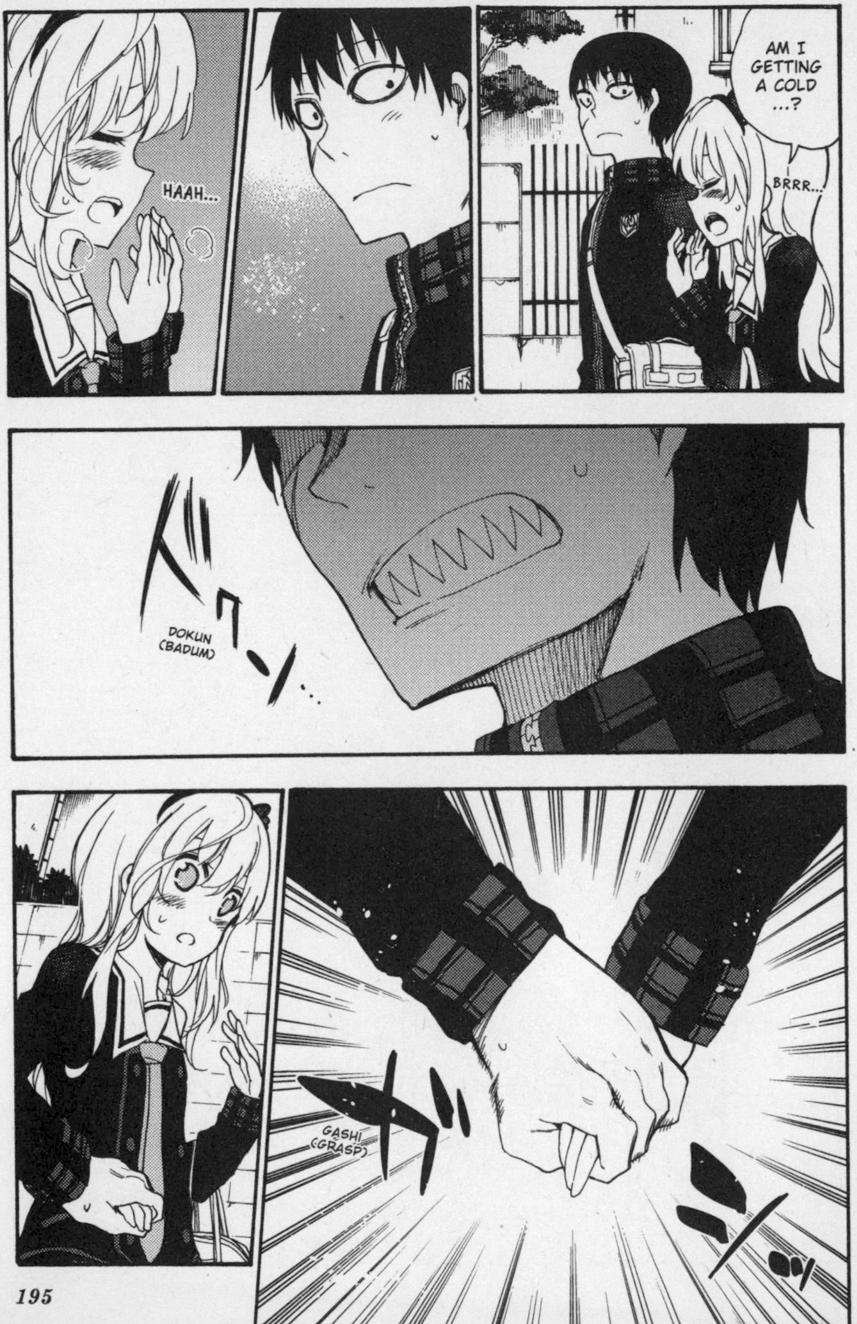
AM I GETTING A COLD ...?
BRRR...
HAAH...
DOKUN (BADUM)
GASHI (GRASP)

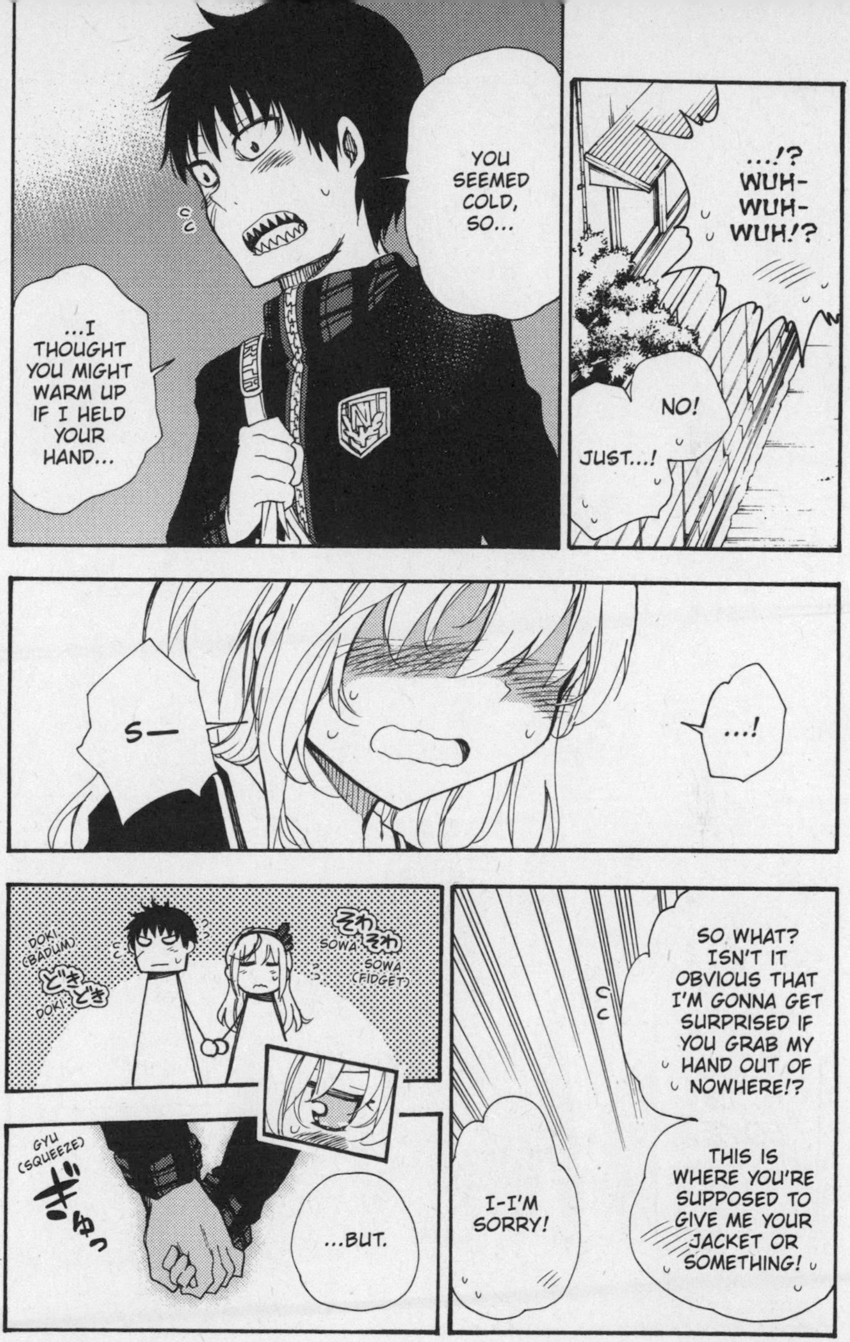

...!? WUH-WUH-WUH!?
NO!
JUST...!
YOU SEEMED COLD, SO...
...I THOUGHT YOU MIGHT WARM UP IF I HELD YOUR HAND...
...!
S—
SO WHAT? ISN'T IT OBVIOUS THAT I'M GONNA GET SURPRISED IF YOU GRAB MY HAND OUT OF NOWHERE!?
THIS IS WHERE YOU'RE SUPPOSED TO GIVE ME YOUR JACKET OR SOMETHING!
I-I'M SORRY!
そわそわ
SOWA SOWA (FIDGET)
どきどき
DOKI DOKI (BADUM)
ぎゅっ
GYU (SQUEEZE)
...BUT.

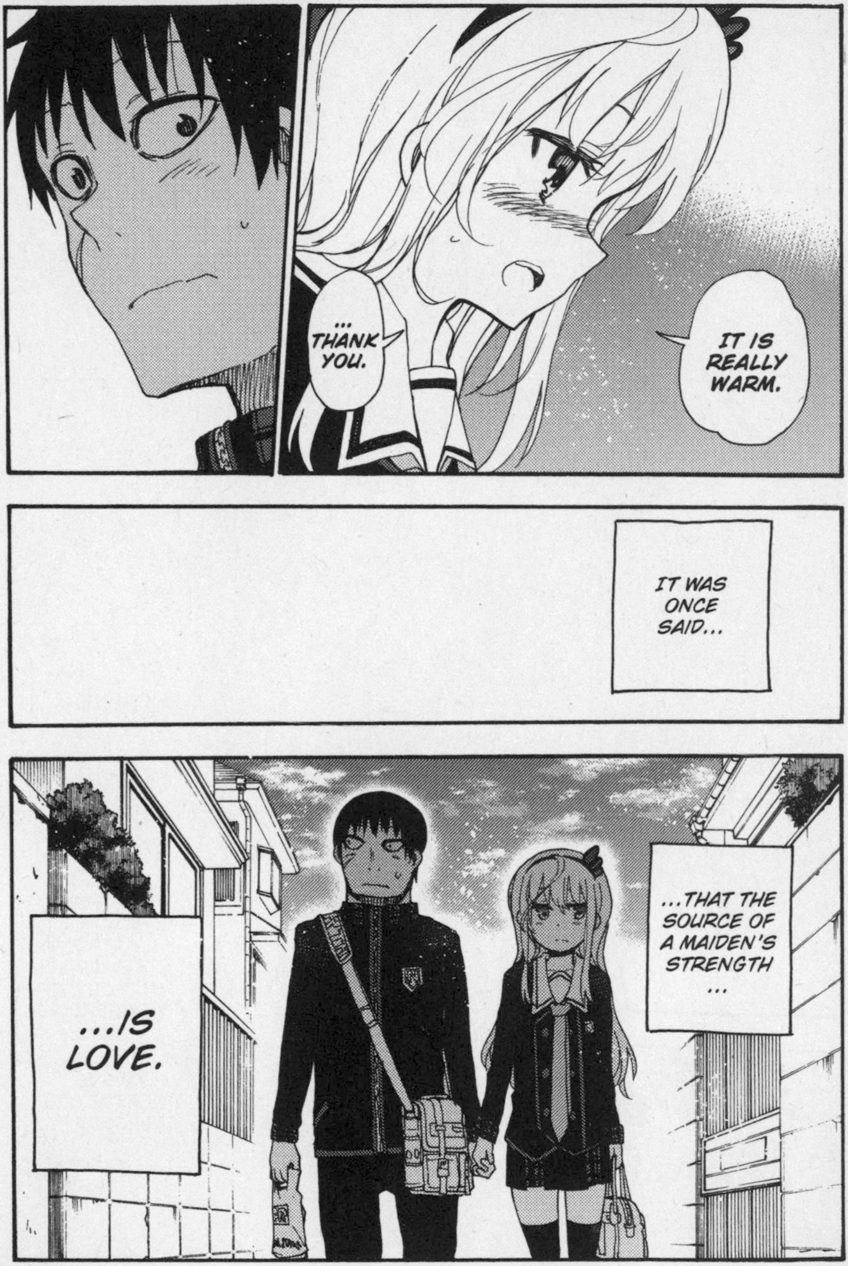
IT IS REALLY WARM.
...THANK YOU.
IT WAS ONCE SAID...
...THAT THE SOURCE OF A MAIDEN'S STRENGTH ...
...IS LOVE.

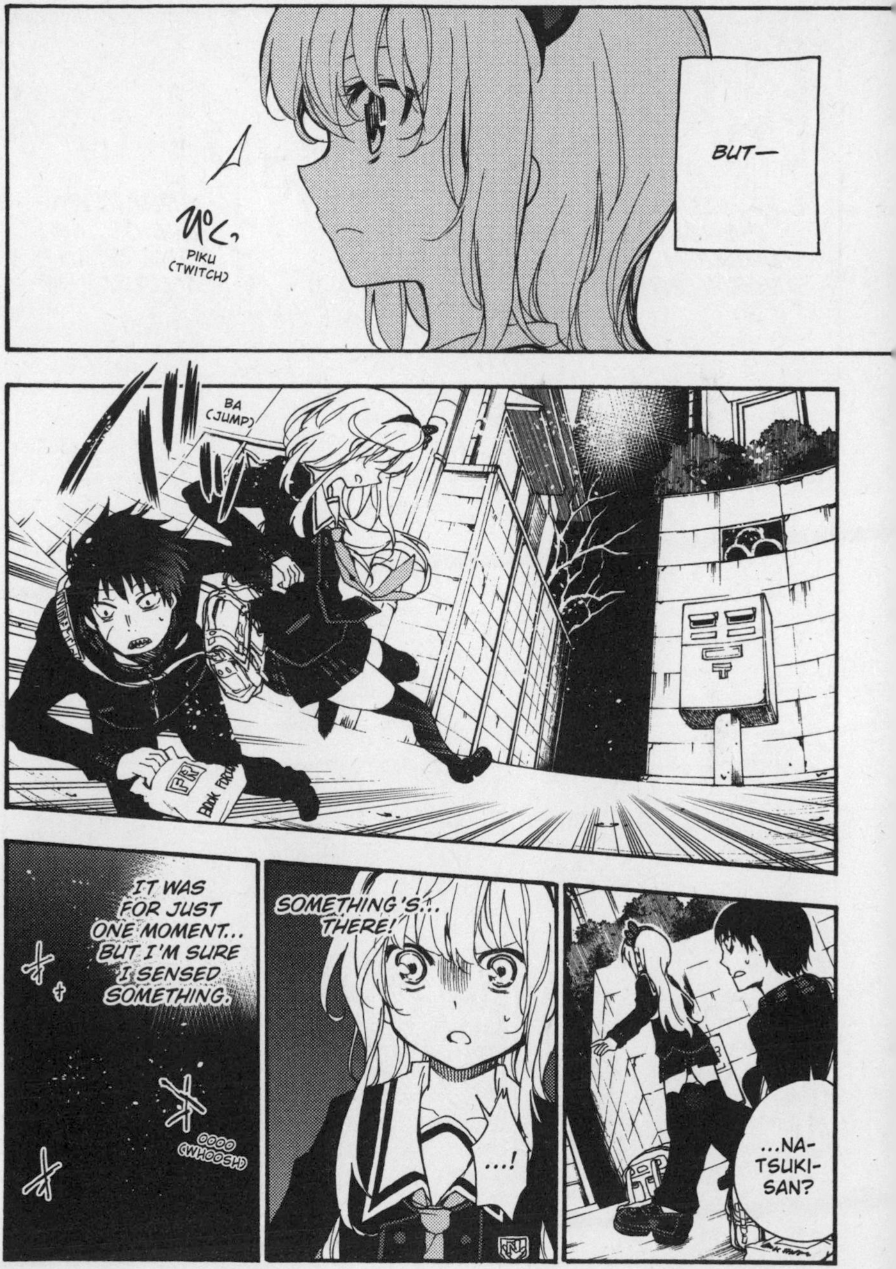
BUT—
ぴくっ
PIKU (TWITCH)
BA (JUMP)
...NA-TSUKI-SAN?
SOMETHING'S... THERE!
...!
IT WAS FOR JUST ONE MOMENT... BUT I'M SURE I SENSED SOMETHING.
OOOO (WHOOSH)

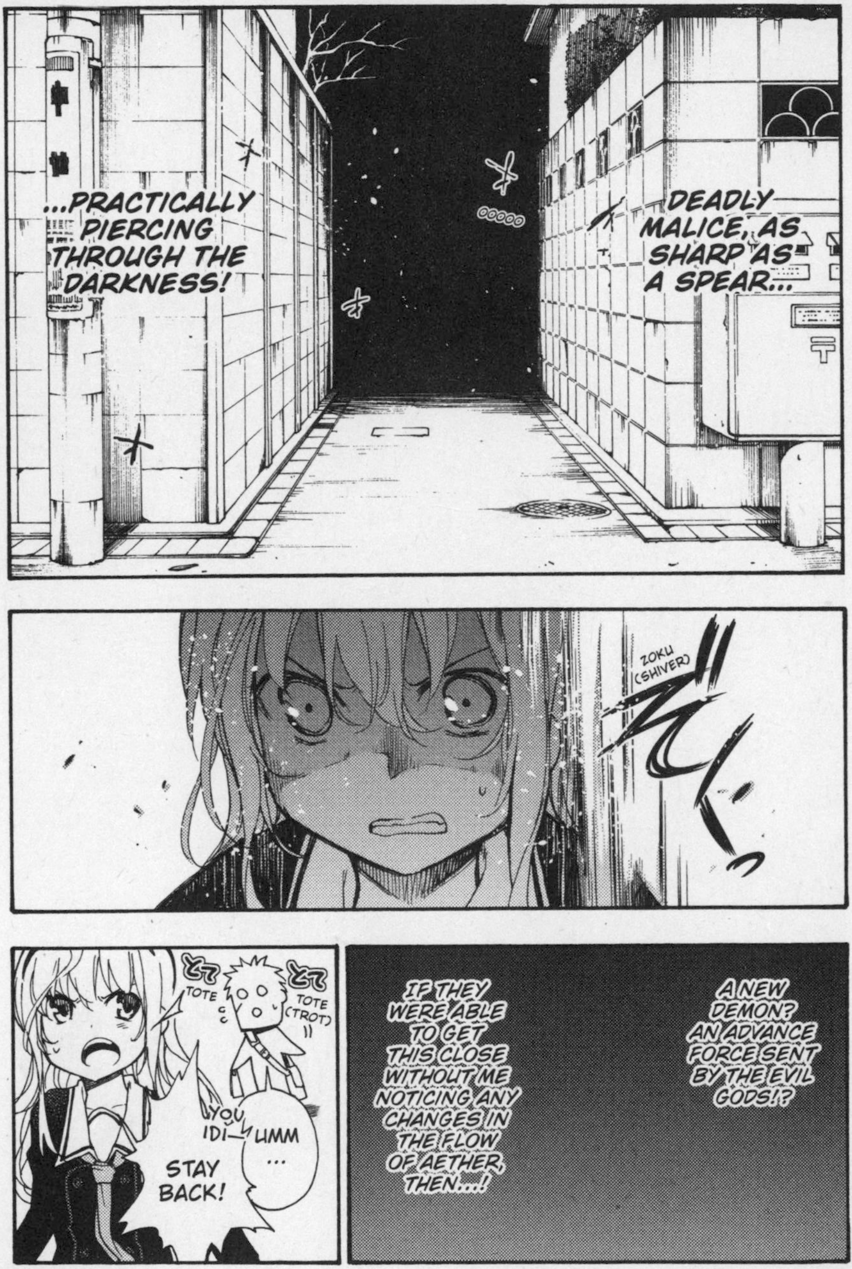
DEADLY MALICE, AS SHARP AS A SPEAR...
...PRACTICALLY PIERCING THROUGH THE DARKNESS!
ZOKU (SHIVER)
A NEW DEMON? AN ADVANCE FORCE SENT BY THE EVIL GODS!?
IF THEY WERE ABLE TO GET THIS CLOSE WITHOUT ME NOTICING ANY CHANGES IN THE FLOW OF AETHER, THEN...!
とて TOTE (TROT)
とて TOTE
YOU IDI— UMM ...
STAY BACK!

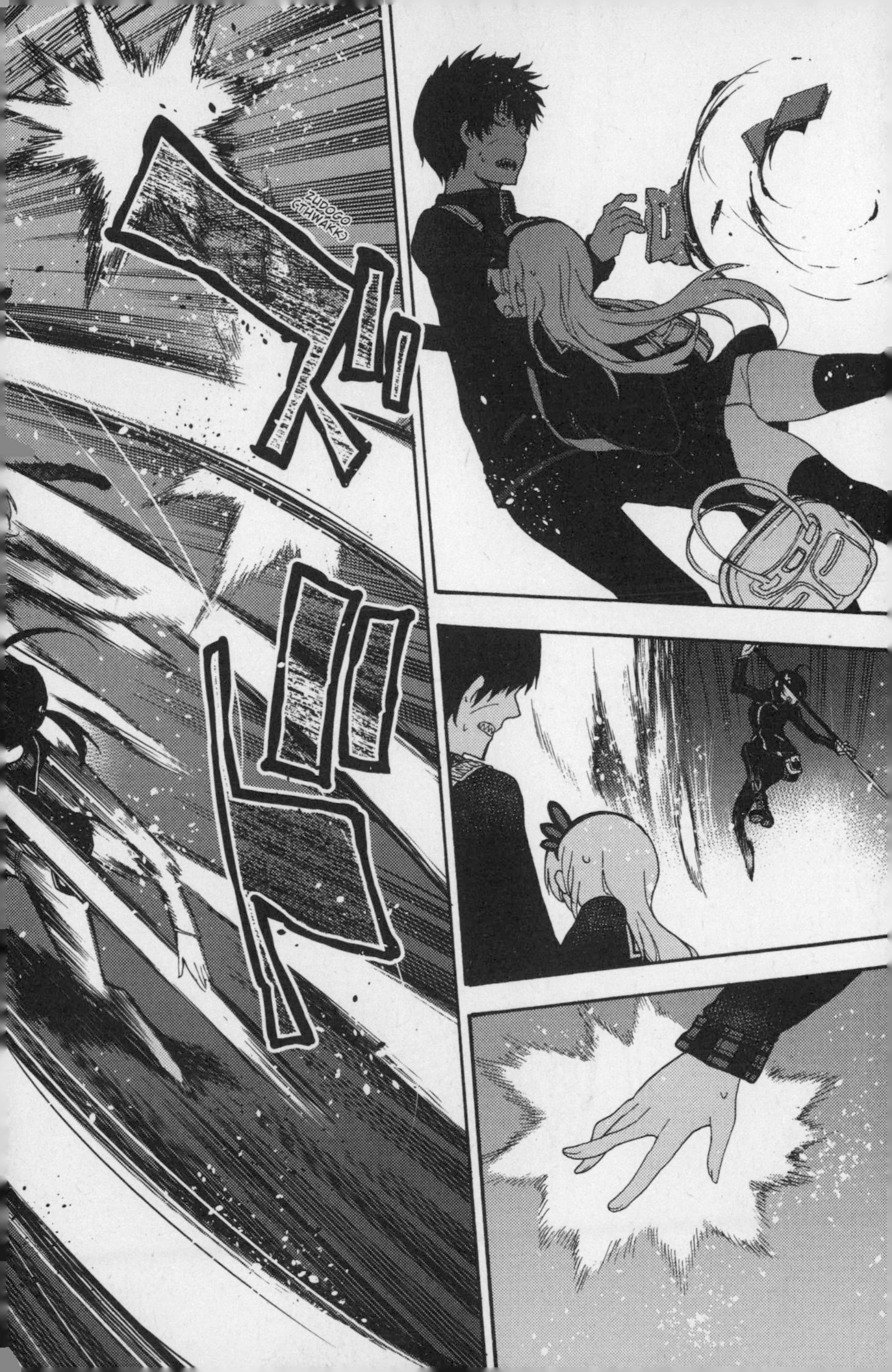
ZUDOGO
(THWAKK)

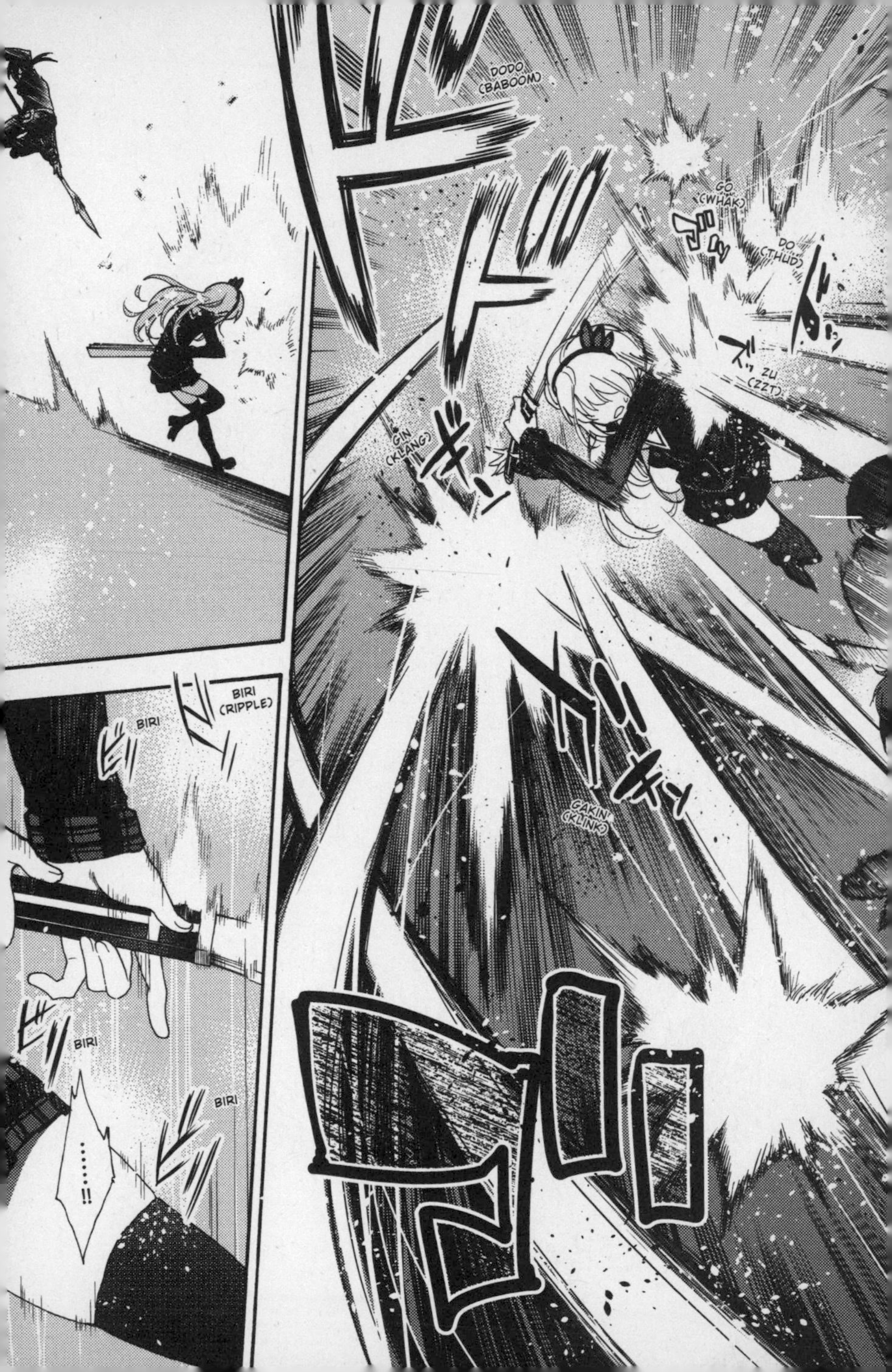
DODO (BABOOM)
DO (THUD)
GO (WHAK)
ZU (ZZT)
GIN (KLANG)
GAKIN (KLINK)
BIRI (RIPPLE)
BIRI
BIRI
BIRI
......!!

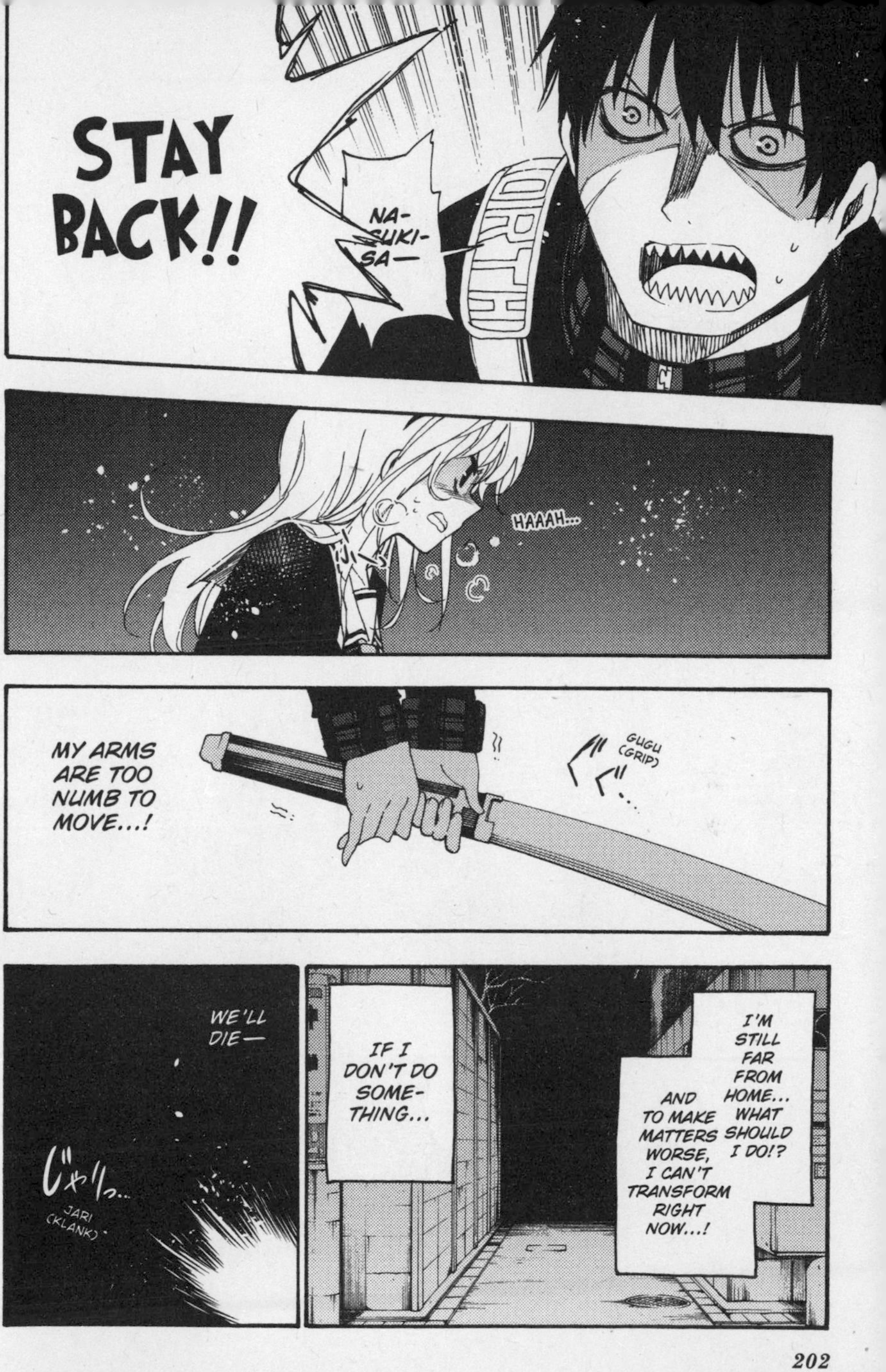
STAY BACK!!
NA-SUKI-SA—
HAAAH...
GUGU (GRIP)
MY ARMS ARE TOO NUMB TO MOVE...!
I'M STILL FAR FROM HOME... WHAT SHOULD I DO!?
AND TO MAKE MATTERS WORSE, I CAN'T TRANSFORM RIGHT NOW...!
IF I DON'T DO SOME-THING...
WE'LL DIE—
じゃりっ...
JARI (KLANK)

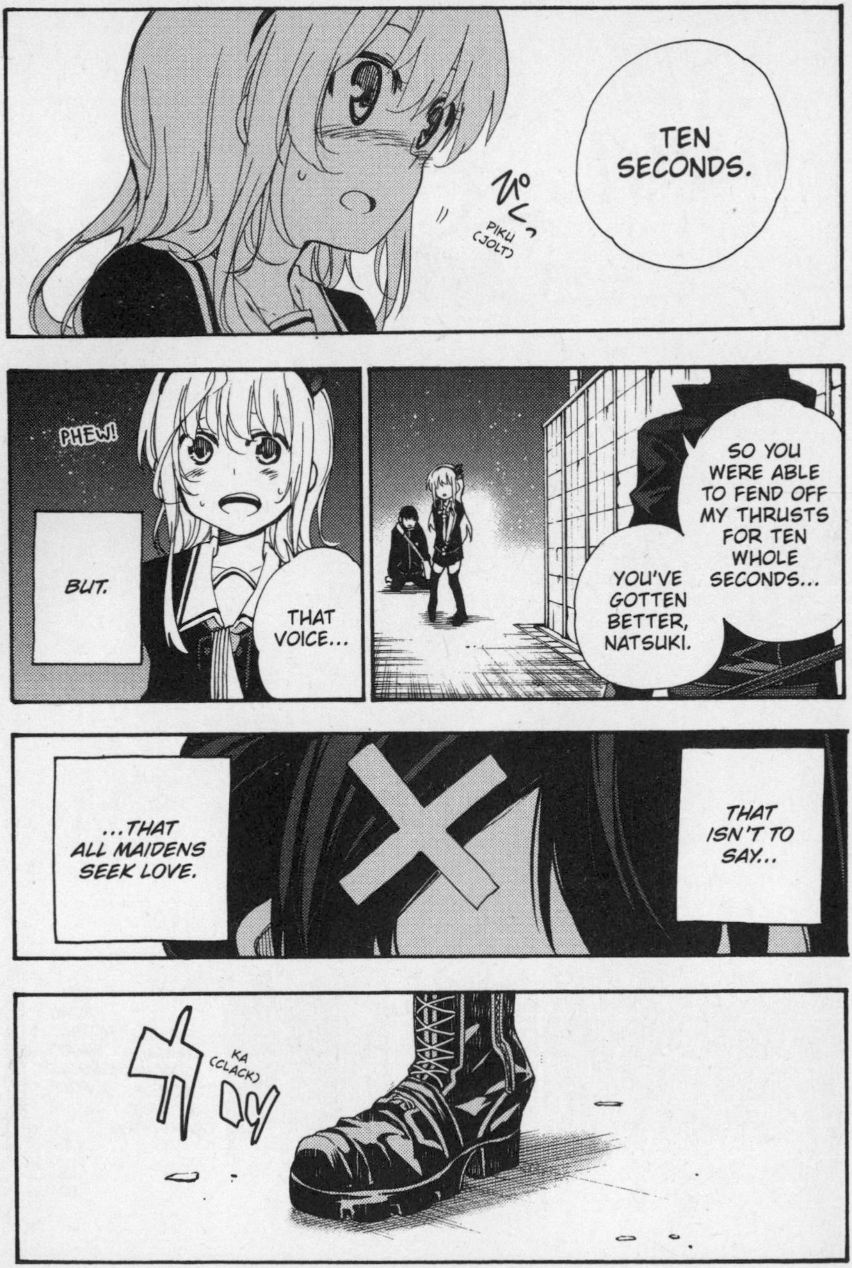

TEN SECONDS.
PIKU (JOLT)
SO YOU WERE ABLE TO FEND OFF MY THRUSTS FOR TEN WHOLE SECONDS...
YOU'VE GOTTEN BETTER, NATSUKI.
...
PHEW!
THAT VOICE...
BUT.
THAT ISN'T TO SAY...
...THAT ALL MAIDENS SEEK LOVE.
KA (CLACK)

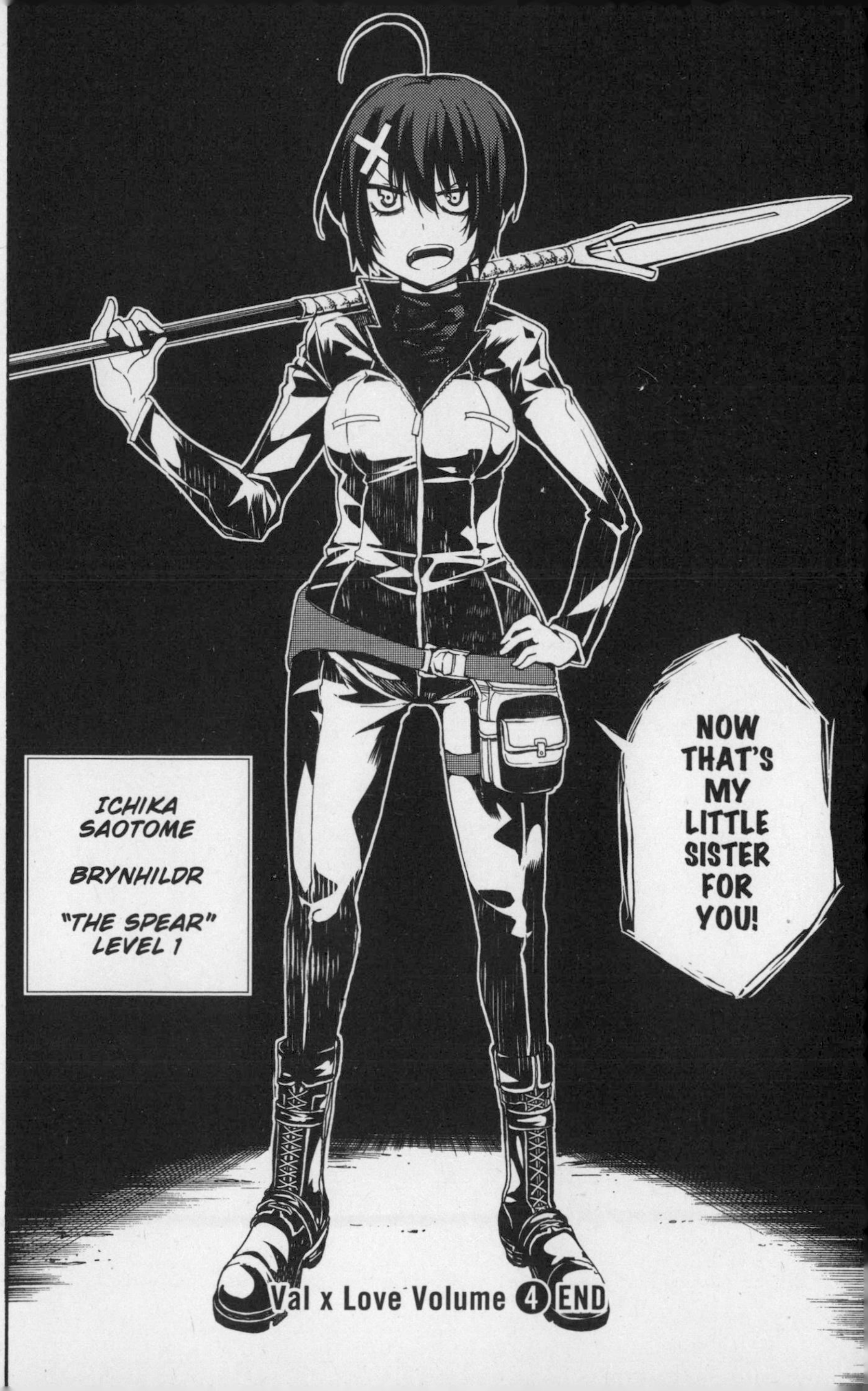
NOW THAT'S MY LITTLE SISTER FOR YOU!
ICHIKA SAOTOME
BRYNHILDR
"THE SPEAR" LEVEL 1
Val x Love Volume 4 END

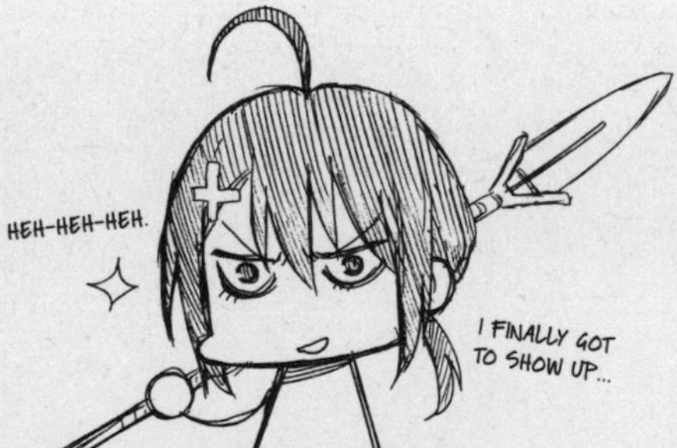
HEH-HEH-HEH.
I FINALLY GOT TO SHOW UP...

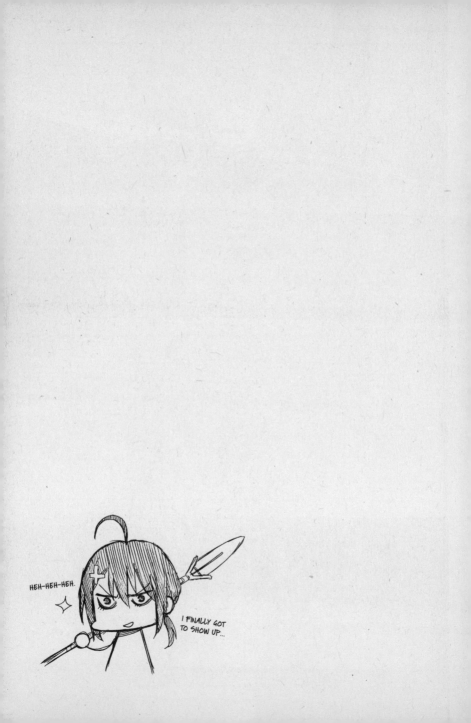

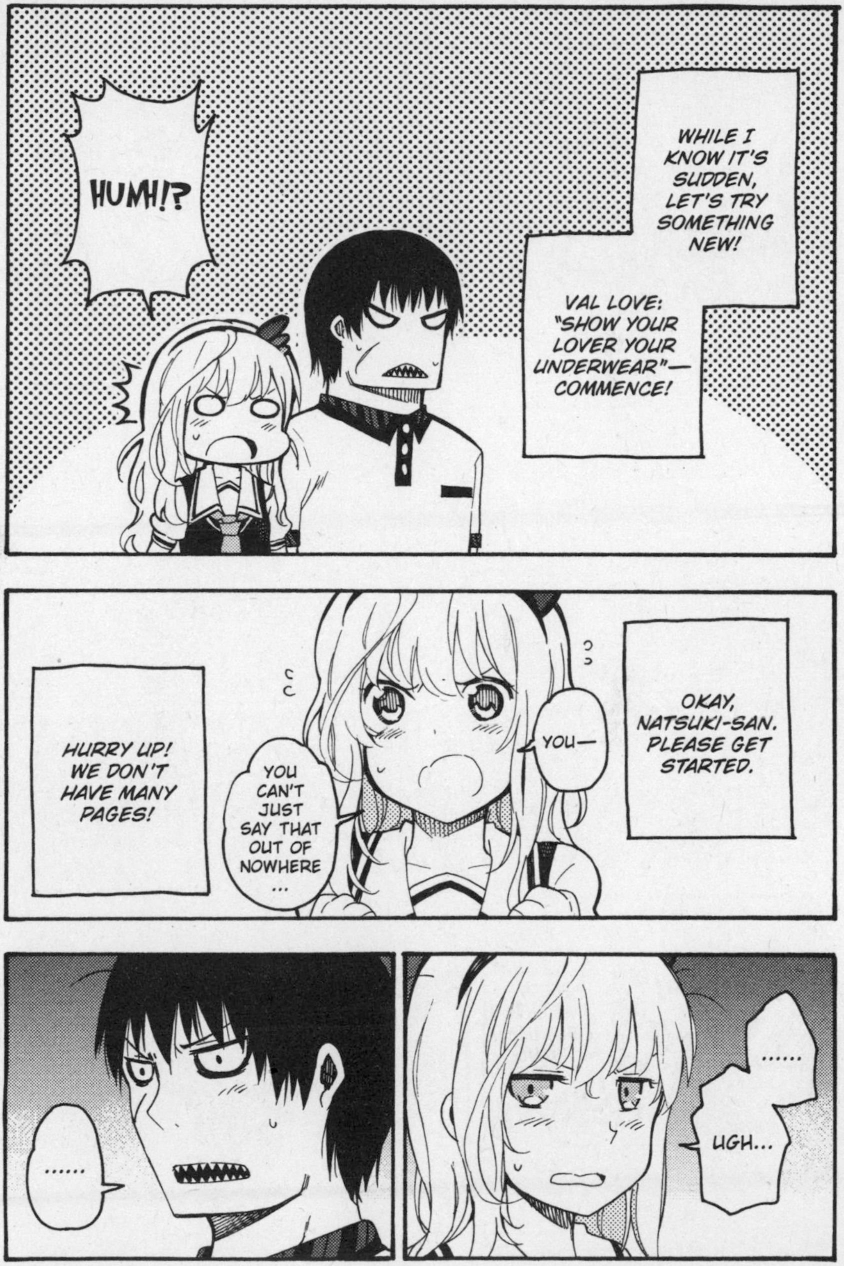
WHILE I KNOW IT'S SUDDEN, LET'S TRY SOMETHING NEW!
VAL LOVE: "SHOW YOUR LOVER YOUR UNDERWEAR"—COMMENCE!
HUMH!?
OKAY, NATSUKI-SAN. PLEASE GET STARTED.
YOU—
YOU CAN'T JUST SAY THAT OUT OF NOWHERE...
HURRY UP! WE DON'T HAVE MANY PAGES!
......
UGH...
......

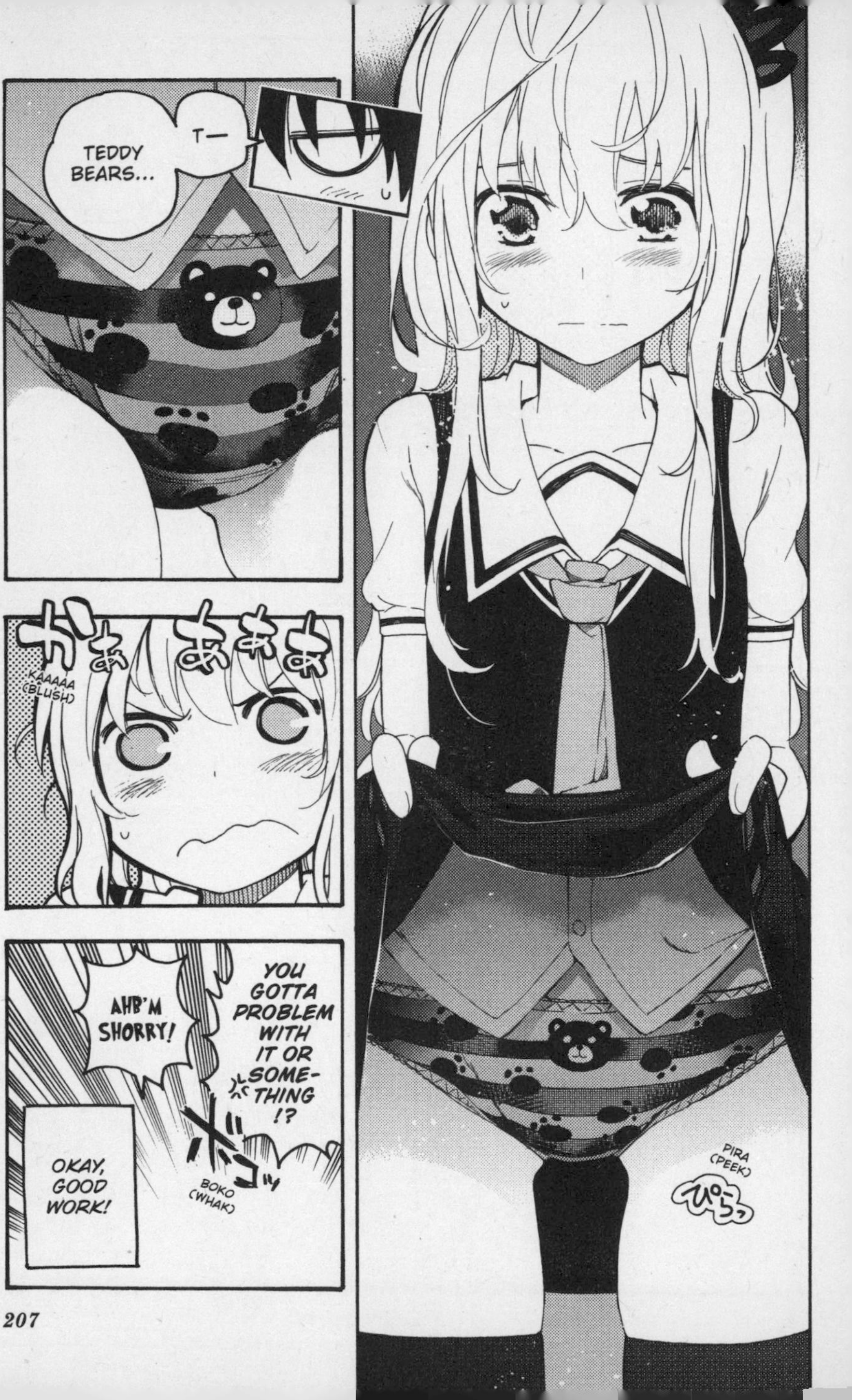
PIRA (PEEK)
ぴらっ
T—
TEDDY BEARS...
かぁぁぁぁ
KAAAAA (BLUSH)
YOU GOTTA PROBLEM WITH IT OR SOME-THING !?
AHB'M SHORRY!
ボコッ
BOKO (WHAK)
OKAY, GOOD WORK!

NEXT VOLUME PREVIEW

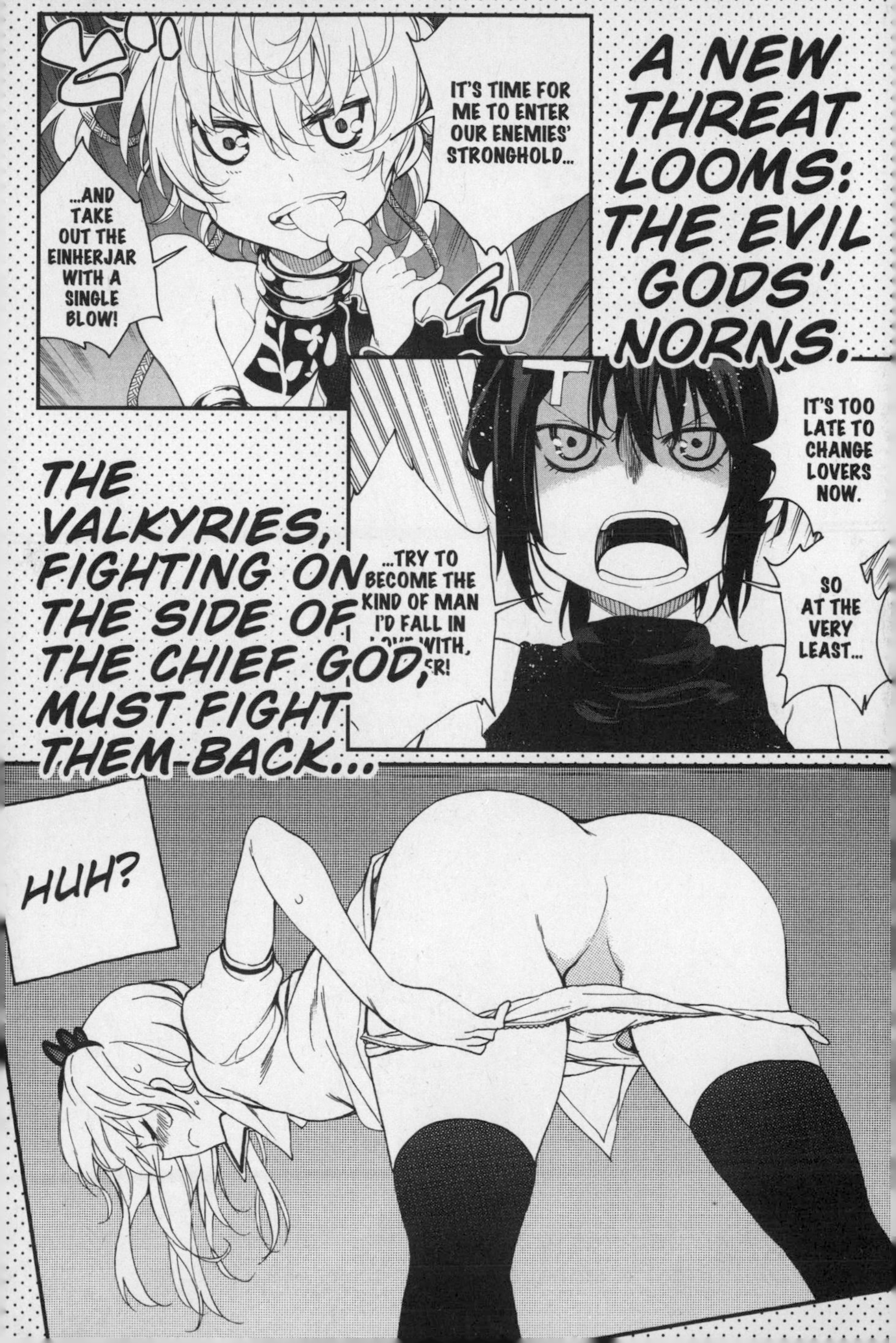
A NEW THREAT LOOMS: THE EVIL GODS' NORNS.
IT'S TIME FOR ME TO ENTER OUR ENEMIES' STRONGHOLD...
...AND TAKE OUT THE EINHERJAR WITH A SINGLE BLOW!
IT'S TOO LATE TO CHANGE LOVERS NOW.
SO AT THE VERY LEAST...
...TRY TO BECOME THE KIND OF MAN I'D FALL IN
THE VALKYRIES, FIGHTING ON THE SIDE OF THE CHIEF GOD, MUST FIGHT THEM BACK...
HUH?

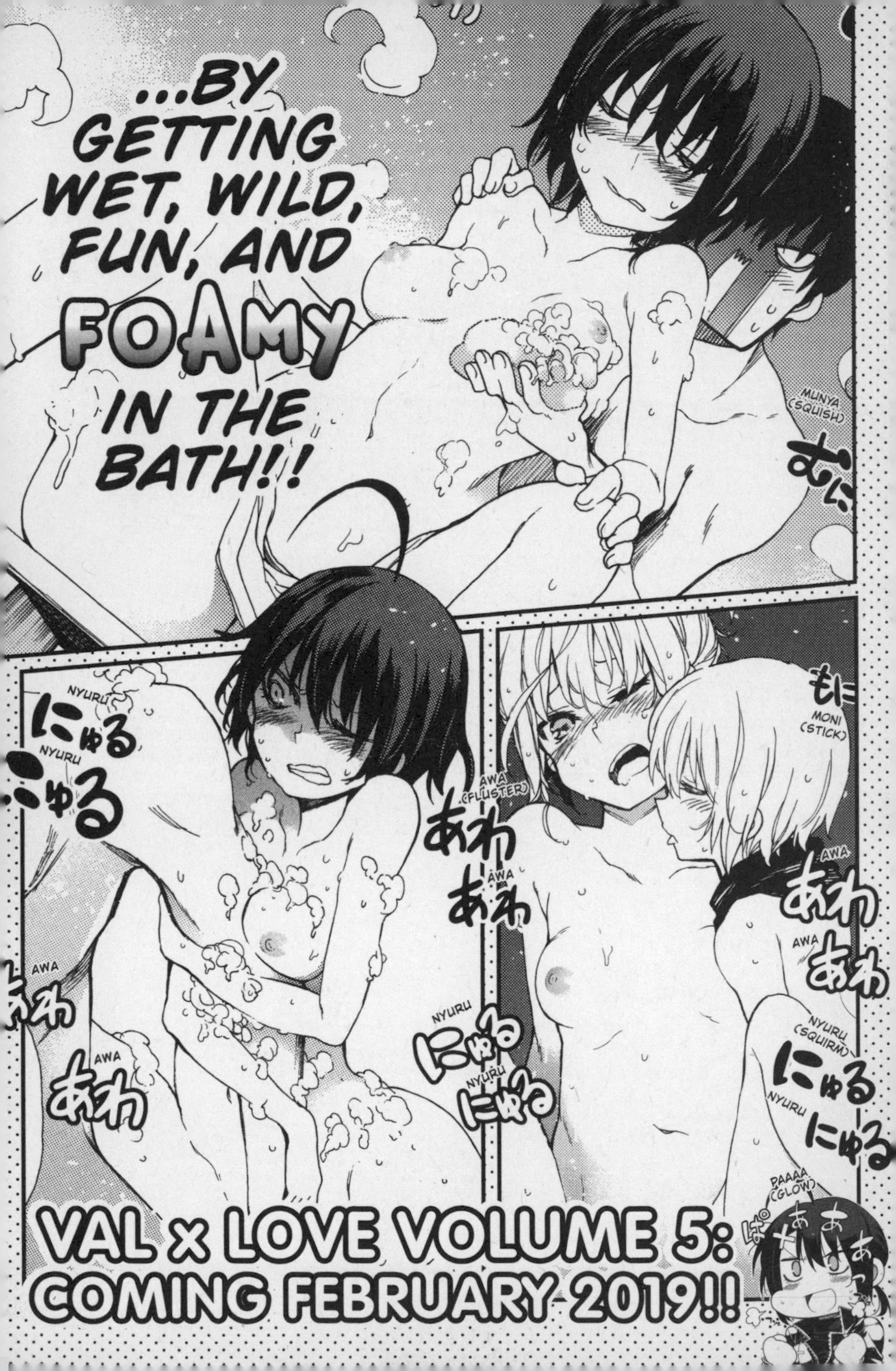

...BY GETTING WET, WILD, FUN, AND FOAMY IN THE BATH!!
MUNYA (SQUISH)
むに
もに
MONI (STICK)
AWA
あわ
AWA
あわ
NYURU (SQUIRM)
にゅる
NYURU
にゅる
PAAAA (GLOW)
ぱあああ
NYURU
にゅる
NYURU
にゅる
AWA (FLUSTER)
あわ
AWA
あわ
AWA
あわ
AWA
あわ
NYURU
にゅる
NYURU
にゅる
VAL x LOVE VOLUME 5: COMING FEBRUARY 2019!!

RYOSUKE ASAKURA

TRANSLATION: KO RANSOM
LETTERING: ROCHELLE GANCIO

VAL LOVE vol. 4
© 2017 Ryosuke Asakura / SQUARE ENIX CO., LTD.
First published in Japan in 2017 by SQUARE ENIX CO., LTD. English translation rights arranged with SQUARE ENIX CO., LTD. and Yen Press, LLC through Tuttle-Mori Agency, Inc.

English translation © 2018 by SQUARE ENIX CO., LTD.

Yen Press
1290 Avenue of the Americas
New York, NY 10104

Visit us at yenpress.com
facebook.com/yenpress
twitter.com/yenpress
yenpress.tumblr.com
instagram.com/yenpress

First Yen Press Edition: October 2018

Yen Press is an imprint of Yen Press, LLC.
The Yen Press name and logo are trademarks of Yen Press, LLC.

The publisher is not responsible for websites (or their content) that are not owned by the publisher.

Library of Congress Control Number: 2017954705

ISBNs: 978-1-9753-5430-5 (paperback)
       978-1-9753-5431-2 (ebook)

10 9 8 7 6 5 4 3 2 1

WOR

Printed in the United States of America